Top 60
Canoe Routes
of Ontario

KEVIN CALLAN

FIREFLY BOOKS

A FIREFLY BOOK

Published by Firefly Books Ltd. 2018
Copyright © 2018 Firefly Books Ltd.
Text copyright © 2018 Kevin Callan
Photographs © Kevin Callan, except as listed below

FIRST PRINTING

Library of Congress Control Number: 2017959837

Library and Archives Canada Cataloguing in Publication
Callan, Kevin
[Top 50 canoe routes of Ontario]
    Top 60 canoe routes of Ontario / Kevin Callan.

Previously published under title: Top 50 canoe routes of Ontario.
Includes bibliographical references and index.
ISBN 978-0-228-10024-9 (softcover)

    1. Canoes and canoeing—Ontario—Guidebooks.
2. Ontario—Guidebooks. 3. Guidebooks.
I. Title. II. Title: Top sixty canoe routes of Ontario.
III. Title: Top 50 canoe routes of Ontario.

GV776.15.O5C346 2018   797.12209713   C2017-907242-0

Published in the United States by
Firefly Books (U.S.) Inc.
P.O. Box 1338, Ellicott Station
Buffalo, New York 14205

Published in Canada by
Firefly Books Ltd.
50 Staples Avenue, Unit 1
Richmond Hill, Ontario L4B 0A7

Cover and interior design: Gareth Lind, Lind Design

Printed in China

Canadä

We acknowledge the financial support of the Government of Canada.

Additional photo credits:
Front cover © Gary and Joanie McGuffin
Page 86 © Jim Cumming/Shutterstock

Acknowledgments

RESEARCHING AND WRITING about paddling routes—wow! What a blessing. I can't imagine how many nights I've slept in the wilderness or how many paddle strokes it took me to gather all the material for this book (as well as my previous paddling guides). Not only that, I've also made countless friends along the way who've helped me with my writing projects. First off, my daughter, Kyla. She was six weeks old the first time she went canoeing. Now we spend weeks out there paddling around. And second, all the other paddlers who've shared countless misadventures in the wilderness with me, especially my good friends Ashley McBride, Scott Adams, Bill and Anne Ostrom and Andy Baxter.

Thanks also goes to friends I've made along the way who have let me test out a bunch of their gear on my trips (and a few who even joined me on trips themselves). Thanks to Jim Stevens at Eureka Tents, Tim Foley at Canadian Outdoor Equipment, the gang at Nova Craft Canoe, Outdoor Research, Badger Paddles, Ben's, Adventure Medical Kit, SOL, Wool Power and Kelly Kettle.

A big thanks also goes to the staff at Firefly Books and Gareth Lind and George Walker who both created the maps for this book—a daunting task to say the least.

Contents

Key Map of Ontario Canoe Routes

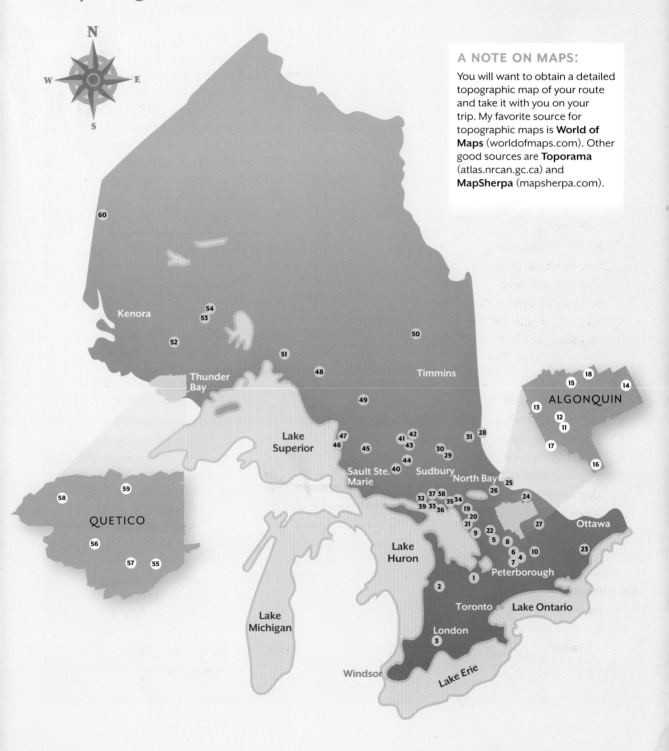

N
W · E
S

A NOTE ON MAPS:

You will want to obtain a detailed topographic map of your route and take it with you on your trip. My favorite source for topographic maps is **World of Maps** (worldofmaps.com). Other good sources are **Toporama** (atlas.nrcan.gc.ca) and **MapSherpa** (mapsherpa.com).

60

Kenora

54
53

52

51

50

Thunder
Bay

48

Timmins

49

15   18
13   ALGONQUIN   14
12
11
17
16

Lake
Superior

47
46   45   41   42
43   31   28
30
29
44   40   Sudbury   North Bay
Sault Ste.
Marie   32 37 38   26   25
35 34   24
39 33   36
19   27   Ottawa
20
59   21   22
58   9
5   8   23
QUETICO   6   10
7   4
56   1
Peterborough
57   55   Lake
Huron   2

Lake
Michigan   Toronto   Lake Ontario

London
3

Windsor   Lake Erie

Introduction

W HAT'S YOUR FAVORITE ROUTE? That's the one question I get from paddlers all the time. It's also the most difficult to answer. My first response is to list off familiar places like a chain of turquoise lakes in Killarney or some much-loved trout stream in Algonquin. Then I'll add a route closer to my home in the Kawartha Highlands or the Haliburton Highlands Water Trails. After that, it's a preferred river in Algoma, followed by a list of lakes in Quetico, then Temagami. You see, it's simply impossible to choose one particular route. We're just blessed with too many perfect paddling destinations in Ontario.

So, choosing Ontario's "best" routes for this book was quite an overwhelming task. It was like the Rolling Stones collecting songs for their *Forty Licks* album. Well, maybe not—but it seemed like it at the time. I ended up settling on these 60 routes by making a wish list of trips I'd instantly pack up and re-do, without question.

Truthfully, my favorite route is the next one I'm going on. Yes, there were some paddling routes in the past that were better than others, whether it was due to the scenery, a sense of solitude or just good group dynamics that happened along the way. But it's the next one I'm planning that's by far the best.

To me, that's what this book is really all about—to help you reminisce about past trips, remind you how many paddling possibilities Ontario has to offer and, most important, help you discover new routes and find your own new favorite place to paddle. I hope you enjoy it. I certainly had a great time writing it.

Before You Go

To help you organize your trip, I've created a checklist. It is more of a "have I forgotten anything?" list, and you should by no means consider it the ultimate inventory meant for everyone, but it is a good place to start.

ITEMS REQUIRED BY LAW TO HAVE IN CANOE
- two 30-m (90-ft) lengths of nylon rope stuffed in a throwbag
- flashlight
- whistle
- approved and properly fitted PFD (personal flotation device)
- bailer
- extra paddle

CLOTHES (for a two-to-four-day trip)
- two cotton or canvas shirts
- two T-shirts
- one wool sweater or fleece top
- two extra pairs of socks
- one extra pair of underwear
- two pairs of pants (no jeans)
- one pair of shorts (doubles as swimsuit if you're not into skinny dipping)
- hiking boots
- sneakers, moccasins or sport sandals for around camp
- bug hat (finer mesh for blackfly season)
- bandanna (useful for spraying bug dope on rather than directly onto your skin)
- hat
- rain gear (make sure to keep it handy, on the top of your pack)
- good sunglasses

TOILETRIES
- beach towel
- portable toothbrush and toothpaste (small travel sizes can usually be purchased at drugstore)
- toilet paper (store in resealable plastic bag)
- hairbrush
- biodegradable soap
- hairband
- razor
- contact lens solution
- extra pair of glasses
- prescription medications

KITCHEN SET
- one medium and one small cooking pot with lids, and non-stick frying pan
- plastic travel mug
- metal plate (plastic frisbee can also be used as a plate, bowl and toy for the beach)
- hard plastic spoon and metal fork
- metal or plastic spatula
- aluminum foil
- campstove with extra fuel container and funnel
- waterproof matches in waterproof container, plus a butane lighter
- scouring pad and sponge mixture
- tea towel
- pair of utility gloves for grabbing cooking pot off the fire
- lightweight saw
- water bottle(s)
- water purification gadget (water filter)
- spices, jam, peanut butter, coffee, sugar, maple syrup, honey, margarine, in plastic containers
- meals packed in separate containers and in one large food bag (with instructions and labels)

SLEEPING GEAR
- tent
- ground sheet that fits inside tent
- large rain tarp
- sleeping bag
- Therm-a-Rest or foam pad

PACKS
- external or internal frame pack
- various stuff sacks for clothes and other items
- separate pack/barrel for food
- daypack
- camera bag

INDIVIDUAL ITEMS
- maps
- waterproof map case
- compass
- bug dope
- hand lotion
- sunscreen
- camera, film and extra batteries
- playing cards, cribbage board, etc.
- fishing license
- camping permit
- first-aid kit
- repair kit
- roll of duct tape
- extra resealable bags
- a couple of strong garbage bags
- journal and pencil
- paperback novel
- hammock
- bird, tree, animal-track ID guides
- binoculars
- star chart
- fishing rod and compact tackle box
- pocketknife

Minesing Swamp

🕐 1 day (4 to 5 hours)   🛶 2 portages   ●----● 10 km   **Compass and map skills are required.**

OVER THE YEARS I've heard a number of canoeists raving about spring paddling on Minesing Swamp—a 15,000-acre wetland just west of Barrie. Personally, I had a difficult time seeing the thrill in paddling through a giant patch of stagnant water, especially during prime bug season, and one year I decided to head out and see what all the fuss was about. I partnered up with Brian MacFadzen, a co-worker from Sir Sandford Fleming College, and to avoid the bug problem, we chose one of those warm spring days in early April when the mosquitoes have yet to hatch and high water levels make the swamp totally accessible.

The usual plan for exploring Minesing Swamp is to follow the Nottawasaga River, which flows almost directly through the middle of the wetland. The best put-in is located just north of Angus, on the east side of the Highway 90 bridge. The designated take-out is at Edenvale Conservation Authority, on the west side of the Highway 26 bridge. But this route takes a full day to paddle, and since Brian and I didn't arrive until well after 10:00 a.m., we chose to begin at Edenvale Conservation Authority and simply paddle upstream on the Nottawasaga River as far as Willow Creek and return via the same route. In doing so, we were able to avoid the hassles of a car shuttle (we had only one vehicle with us, anyway) as well as the only two portages en route, located just above the confluence of the Nottawasaga River and Willow Creek.

There was a strong current before and after the highway bridge, and at first, Brian and I wondered if upstream travel was actually possible on the river. Eventually, however, the waterway expanded, flooding over the neighboring farm fields and through a massive stand of silver maple. The flow soon slowed to a crawl and the area seemed more like the Florida Everglades or Georgia's Okefenokee Swamp than some rural wetland in Southern Ontario. At times, Brian and I even found ourselves lost in the flooded-out forest and had to resort to our map and compass skills to find our way back to the Nottawasaga.

It took two and a half hours of paddling to reach where Willow Creek flows into the Nottawasaga River. Here, Brian and I took full advantage of finally having a dry place to get out and stretch our legs. We walked the two portages on the west side of the Nottawasaga,

Minesing Swamp

Legend

- **S** Start
- **F** Finish
- **A** Alternate start/finish
- ●━━● Portage
- **P975m** Portage length
- ⌒ Dam/Lift-over

Edenvale **26**

Fralick Rd. (11th Concession)

Glengarry Landing Rd. S.

F

Minesing **26**

28

43

Alternative access
for Willow Creek

A

P190m
Logjams
P50m

Willow
Creek

Cootes
Creek

FORT WILLOW
CONSERVATION AREA

George Johnston Rd.

Minesing
Swamp

Grenfel Rd.

Pinegrove Rd.

A

Baldwick Rd.

Sunnidale Rd.

CAUTION: road
washes out during
early spring

Nottawasaga
River

2nd Concession

Mad River

McKinnon Rd.

Don Ross Drive
(Essa Township Rd.)

Essa

90

S

Conservation
Authority Office

Angus

0   1   2
km

the first measuring 190 meters and the second only 50 meters. Both trails avoid extensive logjams that have clogged the river for so long that trees have taken root on top of the sun-bleached snags.

As we pushed our way upstream, with the creek itself disappearing and the entire area becoming one giant saturated forest, the swamp quickly became alive with various species of wildlife. Above us flew marsh hawks, ospreys, turkey vultures, a wide assortment of waterfowl and a large number of great blue herons (Minesing Swamp holds Southern Ontario's largest heron rockery). We even heard a gathering of sandhill cranes dancing away in a nearby fen and caught a glimpse of all three types of woodpeckers (downy, hairy and pileated). Down below, in the water, we spotted snapping turtles, huge carp and a few walleye, who, oddly enough, choose to spawn in the marsh rather than the gravel beds out on the river. Brian snapped a photo of a lone porcupine marooned up in the crook of a hackberry tree, patiently waiting for the water to recede.

This entire area, as well as the banks of the Nottawasaga River, quickly becomes impassable by mid-May, taken over by thick vegetation, low water levels and zillions of mosquitoes. This happens to be the saving grace for the area's wildlife, however. For most of the breeding season, the 206 species of birds, 23 species of mammals and more than 400 species of plants, ranging from Carolinian species to vegetation more commonly found in the Hudson Bay Lowlands, exist in a remote setting that is considered internationally important and is now protected under the Ramsar Convention.

LONGEST PORTAGE 190 meters

FEE A user fee permit is now required to help ongoing maintenance, protection and restoration of the Minesing Swamp. Permits can be obtained from the Nottawasaga Valley Conservation Area office, from selected retailers or by making use of a self-serve pay station at each of the access points.

ALTERNATIVE ACCESS McKinnon Road, off Highway 90, can be used to shorten the trip, but the road is usually flooded over in the spring and impossible to travel.

ALTERNATIVE ROUTE The entire Willow Creek section can be paddled by putting in at Minesing Swamp Conservation Area parking lot, 1 kilometer south of the village of Minesing and ending at Edenvale Conservation Area on Highway 26.

OUTFITTERS Canoe rentals and car shuttle at gas station in Edenvale (705-728-1676).

FOR MORE INFORMATION
Nottawasaga Valley
Conservation Authority
8195 Concession Line 8
Utopia, ON, L0M 1T0
705-424-1479
www.nvca.on.ca

TOPOGRAPHIC MAPS 31 D/5

GPS COORDINATES
44.334741, -79.871069

Saugeen River

 2 to 3 days

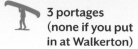 3 portages
(none if you put
in at Walkerton)

 104 km

A couple of challenging
Class I rapids, but
everything can be safely
run by novice paddlers.

THE SAUGEEN RIVER is different, I'll give it that. Threading its way through the farms of Bruce County, it can hardly be thought of as a remote river. But it has a kind of Huck Finn flavor all its own. The nearby hills support cows, corn and old tractor parts. The valley itself, under the watchful eye of the Saugeen Conservation Authority, is home to hundreds of birds and other wild creatures.

Paddling the 105-kilometer stretch of the Saugeen between Hanover and Southhampton was a last-minute decision for my wife and I. We had just become first-time dog owners, and Alana and I thought a short, easy trip would be best to get the dog (a springer spaniel named Bailey) used to canoe tripping. Originally we had planned to paddle a small river in Quebec (Papineau-Labelle's du Sourd River). When we called the park that morning to get directions, however, we were also informed that there was a $3,000 fine for having dogs in the forest reserve. All morning we flipped through maps and guidebooks, and it wasn't until noon that we decided on Ontario's Saugeen River.

The first 22-kilometer stretch of river,

between Hanover and Walkerton, has the only portages on the Saugeen, making Walkerton seem the better place to put in. Historically, however, the town of Hanover (known back in 1848 as Buck's Crossing) was the original starting point for settlers heading westward. Here they built scows and makeshift rafts and then dismantled them down the river to build the first shanties in the unknown territory called the Queen's Bush. Equipped with a plastic canoe and nylon tent, Alana and I weren't exactly purists when it came to reenacting the past, but we thought it would be neat to at least travel the same route as the pioneers and pushed off from Hanover rather than Walkerton.

First, however, we had to arrange a shuttle. The normal arrangement made through Thorncrest Outfitters is to drive down to their Southhampton store on High Street (east off Highway 21) and then continue to the T-intersection and turn left on Carlisle Street, heading to the take-out at Denny's Dam. From there, the outfitter would drive you back up to access the river at Hanover Park. With our late arrival we opted to do the reverse. To reach the put-in from the outfitter's Hanover store,

we drove west on the main street (Highway 4) and then turned right on 7th Avenue. The municipal park is on the left, and we stored our vehicle in the campground parking lot.

The first portage is not far past the Highway 4 bridge. It avoids a concrete dam about 3 meters past a second bridge. The 100-meter trail begins to the left of the bridge, crosses the highway to a dirt road and then follows a path back down to the river.

From the dam the current begins to quicken its pace, with four gravel swifts before Hoffy's Private Campground and several more, including a long Class I rapid, before the first of the two Walkerton dams. There is a 30-meter portage to the left of the dam. Alana and I, however, squeezed to the right of a chute and avoided having to get out of the canoe, but I wouldn't suggest this route in high water.

The current continues its fast pace right up until the next Walkerton dam, 2 kilometers downstream. Two trails can be used, one to the right (30 m) and the other the left (20 m). At first, Alana and I headed for the take-out to the right. Then suddenly a gun went off in the nearby woods, and we quickly ferried ourselves over to use the 20-meter trail to the left. It was odd to hear a gun blast so close to town, but as I watched a couple of towns-people walk by and take little notice of the gunfire, I figured it was best to just move on.

After the dam, Alana and I took on some more swifts, passing quickly by a group of fly-fishermen trying their luck for brown trout below the first town bridge and then a group of teenagers under the second.

Just past the second town bridge is a municipal park. We hauled our gear up on the right bank, set it beside a fire grate and a picnic

Saugeen River

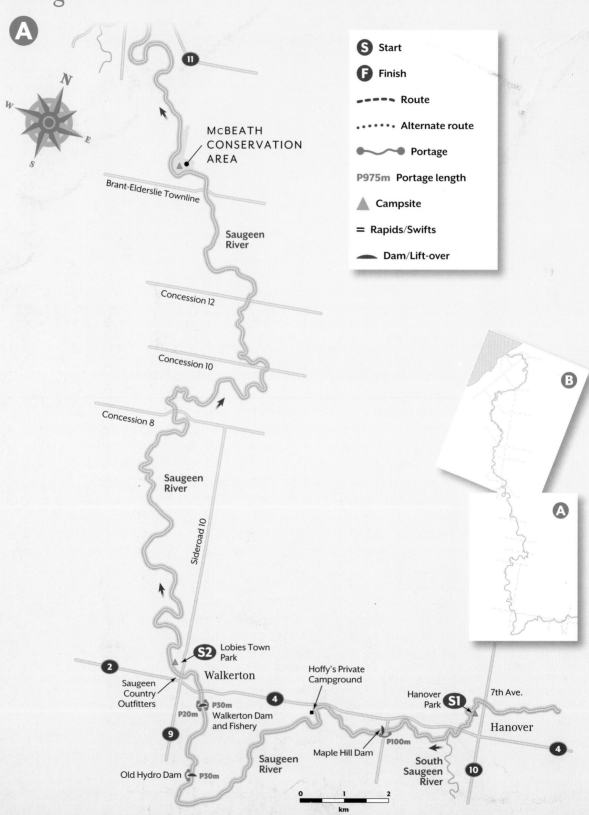

A

S Start
F Finish
- - - - Route
· · · · · Alternate route
●━━● Portage
P975m Portage length
▲ Campsite
= Rapids/Swifts
━━ Dam/Lift-over

B

A

McBEATH
CONSERVATION
AREA

Brant-Elderslie Townline

Saugeen
River

Concession 12

Concession 10

Concession 8

Saugeen
River

Sideroad 10

Lobies Town
Park

S2

2

Walkerton

Saugeen
Country
Outfitters

P30m

P20m

Walkerton Dam
and Fishery

9

4

Hoffy's Private
Campground

Maple Hill Dam

P100m

Hanover
Park

S1

7th Ave.

Hanover

4

South
Saugeen
River

10

Saugeen
River

Old Hydro Dam   **P30m**

N
W   **E**
S

0   1   2
km

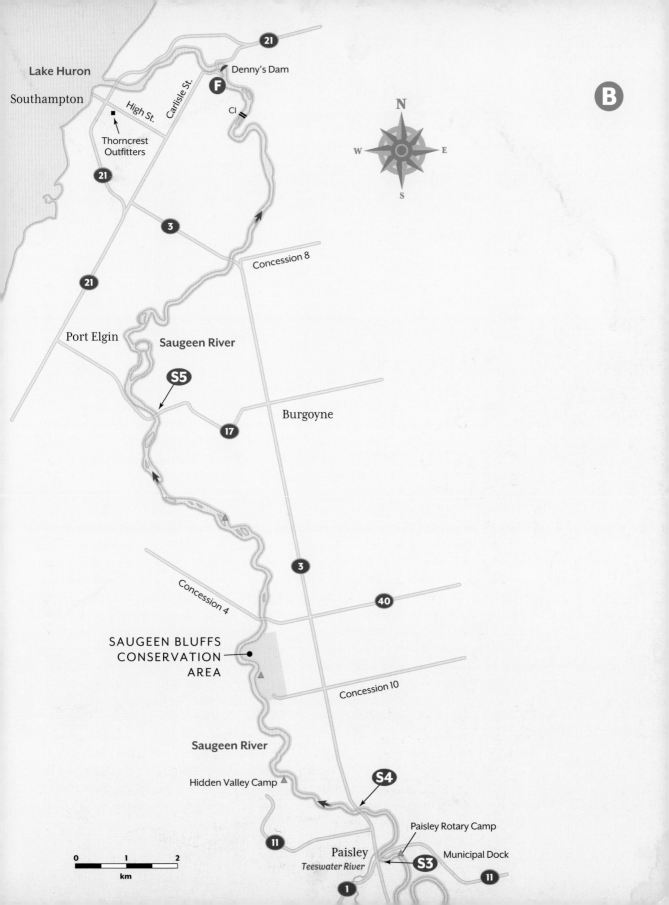

Lake Huron

Southampton

Denny's Dam

F

High St.

Carlisle St.

Cl

Thorncrest
Outfitters

21

21

3

Concession 8

Port Elgin

Saugeen River

21

S5

17

Burgoyne

3

40

Concession 4

SAUGEEN BLUFFS
CONSERVATION
AREA

Concession 10

Saugeen River

Hidden Valley Camp

S4

Paisley Rotary Camp

11

Paisley
Teeswater River

S3

Municipal Dock

11

1

B

N

W   E

S

0   1   2

km

table chained to a tree and then looked around for a place to pay. All 20 sites were empty, and the only people around to ask for information were the teenagers under the bridge. They told us to walk across the bridge to Saugeen Country Outfitters and Convenience Store to pick up our camp permit.

We paid the $12 for our night's stay in the park, loaded up with chips and pop and then headed back to the campground, where now the place was lit up by floodlights from a baseball diamond across the river, and two firetrucks and a police cruiser were parked right across from our campsite. Turned out the Walkerton's volunteer fire department was using the park's large field to test their hoses.

It was like being stuck in the Twilight Zone. We went to bed that night to the sounds of spraying fire hoses (they didn't leave until just before 11:00 p.m.), a junior ball tournament and the yelps of the Walkerton youth. The experience did have its positive side, however. After surviving a night in this modern version of Mayberry, Alana and I figured dealing with all the difficulties of wilderness camping would be a piece of cake.

The Saugeen was alive with birdsong the next morning. The farther we paddled away from Walkerton, the wilder the river became. The best set of rapids also happens to be only an hour's paddle downstream from the town. It's here that the Saugeen cuts into the side of the immense Walkerton moraine, exposing a 100-foot-high bank of sand and till that has become home to hundreds of bank and rough-winged swallows.

Our dog, Bailey, loved the rapids. Leaning over the bow the entire time, her ears cocked, she lifted her nose to sniff the dampness in the air. It was a perfect place to test her in the

canoe. Each channel was well defined, and the only real danger was that we might take the wrong route and find ourselves marooned on some gravel bar.

Dealing with the cattle grazing downriver was a different story, however. Bailey went nuts, barking and whining at the timid creatures until they finally had enough of her and retreated back to the barn. It was embarrassing, to say the least, having our dog scare off the local cow population. Surprisingly, however, when it came to sighting any feathered creatures, our bird dog kept completely silent, and we managed to build quite a list: a number of turkey vultures perched halfway up a dead elm, a kingfisher around almost every bend, a flock of mergansers that persisted on flying just ahead of us for almost an hour, scads of bobolinks and goldfinches brought in by the nearby fields, three great blue herons and a rare sighting of a green heron.

In 1879 it took the *Waterwitch* (a flat-bottomed steamer built by David Hanna) only four hours to travel the 39 kilometers between Walkerton and Paisley. It took us eight hours. After traveling through the almost desert-like scenery of overgrazed pastures past McBeath Conservation Area (a campground accessible only by water), Alana and I didn't mind our reconnection with civilization at all when we tied up at the municipal dock directly below Paisley's historic fire tower.

There was so much to see and do in this quaint hamlet—browse through shops, visit the local outfitters and swallow down a pint or two at Libby's Restaurant—that it was well into the afternoon when Alana and I walked back to our canoe and set off downriver to make camp at Saugeen Bluffs Conservation Area.

Shallow swifts sped us along most of the way, especially after Hidden Valley Camp, and by now we had become so proficient at reading the rapids ahead, knowing which channel held the most water and which would scrape the paint off the bottom of our canoe, that we pulled up to the campground on the north shore just a little over an hour out of Paisley.

It would have been cheaper to continue on to some bush site located on one of the Crown land islands another hour downstream. But Alana and I thought it was worth it to splurge on a flush toilet, hot showers and clean drinking water (personally, I wouldn't even drink filtered water out of the Saugeen). We made use of one of the specially designed canoe campsites at the take-out, right beside the conservation area dock. The staff eventually wandered down to collect their fee.

The next morning we enjoyed bacon and eggs purchased in Paisley the day before and then set off on the seven-hour paddle to Southampton. The river widens its banks even more here and after the County Road 4 bridge, and especially after the County Road 17 bridge, it splits into definite channels around islands thick with willow and butternut trees. The rapids also continue, parting themselves around boulders, gravel bars and even the odd car tire and discarded living-room couch. And not far beyond the County Road 3 bridge, where a stunt man from the 1986 movie *One Magic Christmas* plunged a car into the river and didn't come back to retrieve it until a local canoe club sent some angry letters to the Walt Disney Corporation, is an excellent Class I rapid—the most challenging on the river.

Eventually the rapids calm down, around the next bend, and you'll begin to feel the cool wind coming off Lake Huron as you approach the take-out to the left of Denny's Dam.

It is possible to continue your tour of the river by portaging 50 meters left of the dam, and then take out at the public boat launch a little way downstream or directly on the public beach in Southhampton. By doing this, you're able to paddle past the historic meeting place where 700 Ojibwa war canoes gathered before heading inland and attacking the invading Iroquois in 1656.

Alana and I were informed by Thorncrest Outfitters, however, that the fast water past Denny's Dam was too dangerous to risk it, and the winds out on Lake Huron can cause problems at times, so we agreed to meet our shuttle driver at the first take-out instead. But somehow we managed to arrive three hours early, and rather than hang around the dam, we decided to ditch our gear in the nearby bushes and take a walk up to the outfitters.

Of course, that was a foolish move. The trip into town took an hour, and by the time we got back to the take-out, all of our gear had been stolen.

Words cannot describe the effect this incident had on us. I was furious. It wasn't just a pile of camping equipment that was taken from us; it was part of our life. The three-season sleeping bag Alana bought me for my birthday, a Therm-a-Rest® I bought her for Christmas, a compass I received from my father the day I graduated from college, a coffeepot that I had used since high school—all were now sitting in some idiot's car. And, believe it or not, this was the second time I'd been robbed that summer. Just a month before, the door of my truck was pried open with a crowbar while it sat in the parking lot in Algonquin. I was canoeing in the interior at the time, so my gear was safe. But everything else, including my collection of John Denver tapes, was stolen.

Mike, our shuttle driver, couldn't believe what had happened. Thorncrest had always stored their unlocked rental canoes at Denny's Dam and had never had a problem. Even when the police arrived, the officer couldn't understand who could have spotted our stuff hidden in the woods.

At any rate, it was late by the time Mike had us back to our vehicle, which was parked in Hanover, and really late by the time Alana and I got back to Peterborough. But here's the good news. Because we live in the modern age, we have insurance. With the help of the outfitting stores in Peterborough, very good friends, and a cooperative claims adjuster, we were able to put together enough gear to continue our adventures that summer (though we never could find a replacement for that coffeepot). To take away the unpleasant memories of that ill-fated trip, we returned to the Saugeen River. With the late John Denver's "Country Roads" playing on the truck stereo and Bailey now a seasoned paddler, we enjoyed a late-fall trip down the Saugeen River.

LONGEST PORTAGE 100 meters

FEE Apart from the shuttle, each designated campsite is at a municipal park, private park or conservation authority area where a camping fee is required.

ALTERNATIVE ACCESS The trip can be shortened by using a number of alternative access points. Lobies Town Park in Walkerton, the Municipal dock in Paisley and just downstream from Paisley at the County Road 3 bridge or the County Road 17 bridge are good options.

ALTERNATIVE ROUTE Between Hanover and Southampton there are at least nine possible access points to cut your trip short. Some canoeists even venture past Denny's Dam and out into Lake Huron.

OUTFITTERS
Thorncrest Outfitters
193 High Street
Southampton, ON, N0H 2L0
519-797-1608
or
258 Queen Street
Paisley, ON, N0G 2N0
519-353-9283
www.thorncrestoutfitters.com

Cowan Canoe / Kayak Livery
361 Victoria Street
Paisley, ON, N0G 2N0
519-353-5535

The Greater Saugeen Trading Co.
473 Queen Street
Paisley, ON, N0G 2N0
519-353-4453

FOR MORE INFORMATION
Saugeen Valley Conservation Authority
519-364-1255
www.svca.on.ca

Ministry of Natural Resources
519-376-3860
www.mnr.gov.on.ca

Saugeen Country Tourism Association
1-800-265-3127 or 519-371-2071
www.saugeencountry.ca

MAPS The Saugeen Country Tourism Association has produced a pamphlet titled *Saugeen River Canoe Route*. Andrew Armitage's guidebook, *The Sweet Water Explorer: A Paddler's Guide to Grey and Bruce Counties*, is also an excellent resource for the river. You can also refer to the Saugeen River map in The Adventure Map series by Chrismar.

TOPOGRAPHIC MAPS
41 A/3 & 41 A/6

GPS COORDINATES
44.159123, -81.036383

Thames River

🕐 1 day (4 to 5 hours)   None   ●----● 22 km   Some swift water that can be easily negotiated.

CANOEING HAS ALWAYS meant wilderness to me. So when my brother-in-law, Jim Harkin, and his two sons, Ryan and Keelan, asked me to take them canoeing on the Thames River—a not-so-wild waterway near their home in London—I couldn't help but feel a little hesitant, at first. The idea of paddling that close to development, past culverts spitting out tainted water and under major thoroughfares crowded with minivans holds little appeal: it's difficult for me to swallow the philosophy that any place with water could mean interesting canoeing. In fact, my only reason for agreeing to take on this non-wilderness route (the most southern watercourse in Canada) was that I had promised to take my nephews canoeing for a number of years, and they finally called me on it. So, keeping an open mind, I headed south with my wife, Alana, to guide Jim, Ryan and Keelan on their very first canoe trip, which, surprisingly, became one of my best times spent in a canoe all season.

The Thames River, originating northeast of London and flowing southwesterly to Lake St. Clair, offers more than 300 kilometers of navigable waterway. The upper river, between St. Mary's Dam and the city of London, is a quick stretch of water that remains confined by steep valley slopes. This is considered the most scenic portion of the river. By mid-June, however, the north branch quickly becomes a dried-up boulder garden. The lower half, named "La Tranche" by early French-Canadian explorers because of its wide, ditch-like appearance, begins south of the town of Delaware and is mostly characterized by a slow current bordered by cornfields and dusty country roads. It's an easy all-season paddle but most canoeists find it quite dull at times. Our group chose what's in between—a 19-kilometer section of shallow swifts and deep forested banks, beginning just below London's Springbank Dam and ending before the town of Delaware, along Highway 2. It was a perfect choice for us, first because it was more navigable than the north branch and much more natural than the lower half, and second, the access point happened to be only three blocks away from my brother-in-law's house.

To reach the put-in, head south on Sanatorium Road, make a right on Halls Mill Road and then a left on Old Bridge Road. There is a parking area beside a pump house, and a

Thames River

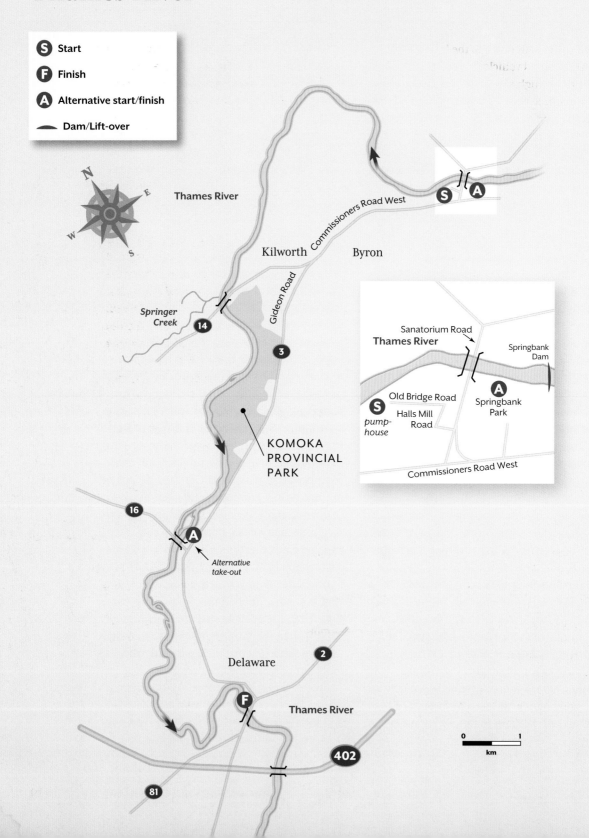

Legend:
- **S** Start
- **F** Finish
- **A** Alternative start/finish
- Dam/Lift-over

Thames River

Kilworth

Byron

Commissioners Road West

Gideon Road

Springer Creek

14

3

KOMOKA PROVINCIAL PARK

16

A

Alternative take-out

Delaware

2

F

Thames River

402

81

Inset map:

Sanatorium Road

Thames River

Springbank Dam

Old Bridge Road

A

Springbank Park

S

pump-house

Halls Mill Road

Commissioners Road West

0 1
km

rough road heads down to the launch area. To shuttle a second vehicle to the take-out on the east side of Highway 2, drive back to Sanatorium Road and turn right onto Commissioners Road West. Approximately 3 kilometers south, make a left onto Gideon Road (County Road 3) and then eventually a right on to Highway 2. The parking area is on the northeast side of the bridge.

There was a set of fast water about every 15 to 20 minutes of paddling throughout the day, and each time we would make a point of deciding which channel held less rock and more water. When in doubt, the rule was to choose the outside bend and make sure to keep the canoe pointed downstream.

Apart from the odd development encroaching on the river and the half-tame waterfowl, I was totally impressed with the wildness of the river. By the time we reached the County Road 14 bridge, our group had spotted five great blue herons, two belted kingfishers, an osprey, a longnose gar (a fish similar to a pike but with an elongated nose) and half a dozen turtles—including one of the rare Eastern softshell turtle. Surprisingly, the Thames River is home to 40 percent of Canada's endangered species and, in fact, holds more species of plants and animals today than when the aboriginals first settled here in 500 CE.

Actually, between 1920 and 1940, the Thames River was considered the richest clamshell bed in all of Canada and was heavily harvested for the commercial production of pearl buttons.

Downstream from our lunch spot Komoka Provincial Park offered a place for the gang to stretch their legs. My nephews seemed to prefer taking extended walks along the shoreline to sitting in a cramped canoe and paddling. So by late afternoon we were still a good hour away from the main take-out along Highway 2. Knowing Ryan and Keegan wouldn't last another hour in the canoe, Jim pulled out his cell phone from his daypack and called my sister for an early pickup at the Country Road 16 bridge.

Despite being cut short, our trip down the Thames was a great day out and a wild adventure for my nephews.

ALTERNATIVE ACCESS Canoeists can put in directly below Springbank Dam instead of at the pump house and take out earlier at either County Road 14 or County Road 16. Take note, however, that at the time of publication the City of London is in the process of deciding whether to repair or decommission (remove or repurpose) Springbank Dam.

ALTERNATIVE ROUTE A number of other day trips can be had on the north branch and the Lower Thames River. Contact the Upper Thames River Conservation Authority for information.

OUTFITTERS
London's Paddleshop
471 Nightingale Ave.
London, ON, N5W 4C4
519-455-6252
www.londonspaddleshop.com

FOR MORE INFORMATION
London Canoe Club
519-473-2582
www.londoncanoeclub.ca

The Upper Thames River
Conservation Authority
519-451-2800
www.thamesriver.on.ca

MAPS The Upper Thames River Conservation Authority has produced a pamphlet: *The Upper Thames Canoe Route: St. Marys to Delaware.*

TOPOGRAPHIC MAPS 40 I/14

GPS COORDINATES
42.963861, –81.336692

Cottage Country

Crab Lake

 2 days    1 portage   ●----● 10 km   **A novice route with one quick portage.**

My friend Noel's requests were quite demanding for his son's first canoe trip. He wanted a quick and easy route only a couple of hours drive from his home near Guelph; maybe a short portage so five-year-old Walker could experience, for a brief moment, what it felt to shoulder all your belongings on your back; and a choice campsite set on a remote lake that happens to be populated by monster-sized bass. Noel (the editor for my publishing company) had been on a number of trips with me before and I knew he wouldn't be at all surprised to hear that such a perfect trip didn't exist. But it did. A place called Crab Lake. And it's a gem I couldn't wait to share with him and Walker.

Crab Lake can be reached by Wolf Lake, which has an access point on its far eastern end. To reach the launch site, turn left off Highway 28, just south of Apsley, and onto Anstruther Lake Road. Then, exactly 3 miles (5 km) along, a dirt road to the left will lead you down to Wolf Lake.

Wolf Lake is a perfect destination on its own. Only a few cottages crowd the lake, mostly along the south shore, and a strip of Crown land along the north shore, as well as a number of small islands to the west, provide some excellent campsite possibilities. Crab Lake is much more isolated, however, and is easily reached by way of a short, 107-meter portage. The take-out is located at the far end of Wolf Lake's southwest bay, just before the last two cottages along the south shore.

Crab Lake has five main bays that head off in all directions (thus its local name, Star Lake) and it is much larger than it first appears. Each inlet also has one or two prime campsites, complete with an exposed chunk of granite to catch a breeze on to escape the bugs and a snug canopy of pine, maple and birch to pitch a tent under. Our group chose an out-of-the way spot directly below where a rough trail heads up to the top of Blueberry Mountain (an exposed hill that's literally covered in thick blueberry bushes), and after quickly setting up camp, we headed out in the canoe again in search of the lake's monster bass.

We cast our lines out the moment we entered the first weedy bay; Noel and I with our fancy plugs and spinners, and Walker with his half-dead worm stuck on a bare hook. It was my idea to give Walker the defunct

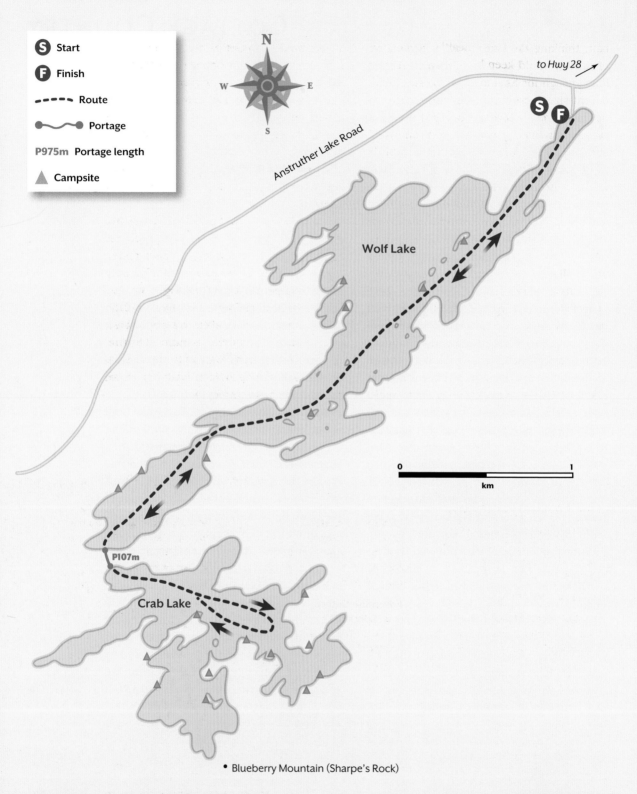

Crab Lake

S Start

F Finish

- - - Route

●—● Portage

P975m Portage length

▲ Campsite

N
W · E
S

to Hwy 28 →

Anstruther Lake Road

Wolf Lake

P107m

Crab Lake

● Blueberry Mountain (Sharpe's Rock)

0 — 1
km

bait, thinking the lake's healthy population of sunfish would keep him occupied at least long enough for Noel and me to catch some decent-sized bass for supper. Of course, in no time at all, Walker had caught three bass, averaging around 4 pounds each, and Noel and I hadn't even had a single bite. Quickly we switched to the decomposing worms and, in exchange, allowed Walker free rein on our lure boxes. Ten minutes later Walker had caught two more trophy bass (one on my scent-impregnated rubber frog and the other on Noel's pink-colored "Holla-Popper"). Noel and I still remained fishless.

I doubt that this lake had ever given up so many fish. In fact, Noel and I were quite mystified by Walker's success and had to blame it on beginner's luck to settle our egos. Walker, on the other hand, had a different reason for catching so many lunkers. Each time he lowered his line into the water, the intrepid angler would whisper a secret code—"Here fishy, fishy, fishy." Walker was insistent that without saying this magical phrase, no fish would ever bite the hook. So, we agreed to play along for the fun of it—or maybe we were just that desperate to catch a fish—and both tossed out our lines and repeated the expression "Here fishy, fishy, fishy." Ten minutes later Noel and I had caught a couple of bass each.

Thinking back, the trip to Crab Lake wasn't a complete success, not according to Noel's set criteria. The route was actually two-and-a-half hours' drive from his home; Walker only carried his personal pack halfway along the portage before handing it over to his father; and Noel and I never did catch a trophy bass. It did manage to fulfill his main objective, though—Walker can't wait until next year's trip—and according to Noel, a father can't ask for anything more perfect than that.

LONGEST PORTAGE 107 meters

FEE This route is now part of the new Kawartha Highlands Provincial Park and permits are now required to camp there.

ALTERNATIVE ACCESS None

ALTERNATIVE ROUTE Some canoeists prefer to stay on one of the Crown land sites on Wolf Lake.

OUTFITTERS
Wild Rock Outfitters
169 Charlotte Street
Peterborough, ON, K9J 2T7
705-745-9133
www.wildrock.net

Adventure Outfitters
County Road 18 at Highway 507
Lakefield, ON, K0L 2H0
705-652-7986
www.adventureoutfitters.com

FOR MORE INFORMATION
Ministry of Natural Resources
Bancroft District Office
613-332-3940
www.mnr.gov.on.ca

TOPOGRAPHIC MAPS 31 D/9

GPS COORDINATES
44.748879, -78.160703

Poker Lake Loop

 2 days  9 portages ●━━━● 10 km **This is a perfect introductory trip for novice paddlers.**

WHEN THE MINISTRY of Natural Resources maintained this route (now it's maintained by the Township of Algonquin Highlands under Haliburton Highlands Waterway Trails) they suggested that canoeists initiate their two-day trip on the Poker Lake Loop from Cinder Lake, north of Highway 118. I first canoed the loop during the summer of 1990, and I followed these directions and launched my canoe from Cinder Lake, but by the end of the weekend my opinion on the suggested access point differed from the Ministry's. Note: access is now designated to Poker Lake and parking is available on the south side of Highway 35.

While traveling the chain of lakes, I decided to camp on Bentshoe Lake, halfway along the loop. Here I made an unpleasant discovery: Every site had been previously occupied by groups of "party animals." The revelers had reached Bentshoe by simply carrying their boom boxes and coolers of beer down from the highway, which was just 100 meters away. Needless to say, the situation did not make me a happy camper.

It took a year before I was ready to give the Poker Lake route a second chance. This time,

I chose a weekend in late autumn when the only wildlife in the area was adorned with fur or feathers. And instead of driving to Cinder Lake, I simply drove 20 kilometers from the junction of Highways 118 and 35 and parked my vehicle in the designated parking area on the south side of the highway. A 100-meter portage took me to Bentshoe Lake, where I began a perfect trip through the Poker Lake Loop. (Be careful while crossing the highway from the parking lot to the portage leading down to Bentshoe Lake.)

Traveling clockwise, one must paddle the length of Bentshoe to the northern bay. A 325-meter portage, the longest on the route, takes you to scenic Poker Lake. Follow the north shore until you find the 50-meter portage into a small, weedy pond (Ooze Lake). At times, especially in low water, trying to navigate through this weedy, stump-infested body of water is next to impossible. It's best to keep to the right and follow a network of muskrat paths. The 75-meter portage into Quirt Lake from the north end of the pond may also have to be extended to avoid getting caught in swamp ooze.

Quirt Lake is divided in half, with a small

channel joining the south and north ends. Just before the narrow passage there is a nice lunch spot high up on a rock outcrop to the right. The site is secluded and high enough to offer a breeze as bug repellent. After a well-deserved break, paddle to the far western bay of Quirt Lake, where the last portage of the day (75 m) can be found marked at the northern tip of the swampy basin.

Once you finish the portage and begin to paddle across Cinder Lake, you will realize why I would much rather end the day than start it from this isolated lake. A large island and other smaller islands sprinkled across the lake make excellent campsites. My favorite place to spend the night is on the southern tip of the main island, halfway across Cinder. At this point the island appears to split the lake in two.

During my stay here, I watched a family of otters munch on crayfish on a small rock outcrop directly across from camp. After the feast they washed their paws and faces, slid into the water and bobbed up and down, watching me eat my dinner of freeze-dried stew.

If time permits, paddle to Cinder's north-west end and search for the hull of a sunken logging boat resting on some rocks, a small piece of evidence of Haliburton's logging days.

The trip begins the next day by taking the 175-meter portage southeast of the previously mentioned campsite, out of Cinder Lake and into another small pond. This section can be grueling in low water, and the last time I used the trail it was overgrown with thick patches of raspberry bushes. Unfortunately I was wearing shorts and a T-shirt that day—not the best apparel for bushwhacking.

The next portage, also 175 meters, is at the south end of the shallow pond, and if memory

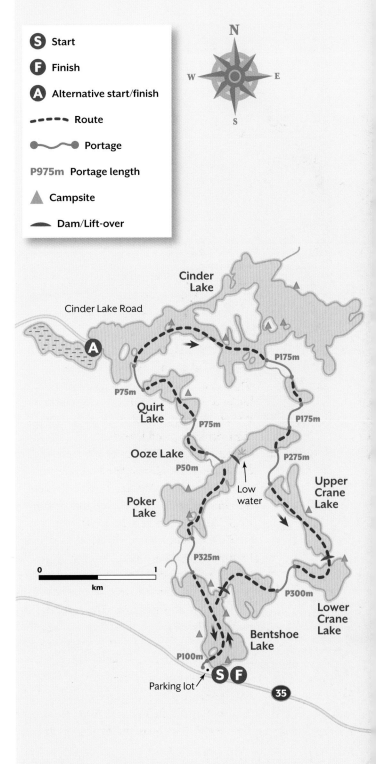

Poker Lake Loop

S Start

F Finish

A Alternative start/finish

- - - - Route

●━━━● Portage

P975m Portage length

▲ Campsite

━ Dam/Lift-over

serves me well, the time I traveled the route in midsummer I sank up to my knees in loon scat, trying to pull my canoe to the beginning of the poorly marked path. This muddy portage takes you to the eastern arm of Poker Lake, where you paddle directly across to reach yet another portage, this one being 100 meters longer than the previous ones.

The path into Upper Crane Lake is relatively easy, as is the 300-meter portage out of Lower Crane and into the eastern bay of the familiar Bentshoe Lake, located at the lake's western tip. Where Upper and Lower Crane join, however, can be quite an arduous passage if water levels are low. To make it through the junction, I once had to tie my bowline to my waist and jump from one floating bog mat to the other. If I hadn't spotted the curious family of otters furtively trailing behind me, I would have once again given second thought to returning to the Poker Lake canoe route. Thanks to the inquisitive otter family, as well as the scenic splendor of Cinder Lake, I have gone back many times to this enjoyable two-day loop on the western border of Haliburton County.

LONGEST PORTAGE 300 meters

FEE This route is now maintained by the Township of Algonquin Highlands under the Haliburton Highlands Waterway Trails. Camping permits and reservations can be made at www.algonquinhighlands.ca/water.

ALTERNATIVE ACCESS Cinder Lake can be accessed by using Cinder Lake Road, north of Highway 118. However, it is not recommended as it is no longer maintained.

ALTERNATIVE ROUTE Big East Lake, a much easier route, can be accessed directly across from the Poker Lake Loop.

OUTFITTERS
Haliburton Highlands Waterway Trails
20130 Highway 35
Algonquin Highlands, ON, K0M 1J2
705-766-9033
www.algonquinhighlands.ca/
water-trails.php

FOR MORE INFORMATION
Ministry of Natural Resources
Minden District Office
12698 Highway 35
Minden, ON, K0M 2K0
705-286-1521
www.mnr.gov.on.ca

MAPS Chrismar has produced an excellent map detailing the Poker Lake canoe route.

TOPOGRAPHIC MAPS 31 E/2

GPS COORDINATES
45.038864, -78.929184

Serpentine Lake Loop

 2 days    8 portages   ●----● 21 km   **Wind and waves can be a problem and the 1,584-meter portage is confusing to locate at times.**

MAGINE A CHAIN of lakes smack dab in the middle of the north Kawartha region, complete with cascading waterfalls, perfect island campsites, stout pine trees and excellent fishing. To be honest, when I first discovered the Serpentine route, I wanted to keep it all to myself. But eventually I couldn't stand to keep such a perfect paddle loop a secret.

This gem of a canoe route starts off from Anstruther Lake, just south of the town of Apsley. To reach the access point, turn left off Highway 28 onto Anstruther Road. Travel the rolling side road for approximately 10 kilometers and as the main road veers to the left, take the marked dirt road straight down to the government boat-launching site on Anstruther Lake.

From the access point, paddle north, up Anstruther until the lake narrows. After the shallow channel, head northwest to the first portage, located past a group of small rocky islands and to the left of the trickling waterfalls. The 162-meter path takes you overland from Anstruther to the more secluded Rathbun Lake. Campsites are available on the two islands in the middle of the lake and many

canoeists choose to set up base camp on one of these isles. I much prefer to continue traveling northwest toward North Rathbun Lake.

At the end of Rathbun's far northwestern bay, a portage follows alongside a small creek for 135 meters and leads into North Rathbun. Up until this point the forest cover consists of mixed stands of hardwood with a few stands of pine, hemlock and stunted oak rooted on exposed granite. From here, though, it changes to patches of spruce and tamarack growing through floating sphagnum mats. Where the sphagnum spreads across North Rathbun's southern shoreline, both of Canada's carnivorous plants, the sundew and pitcher plant, capture tiny insects to battle the bog's nutrient deficiency. The lake's northern shoreline is characterized by a large stand of white birch. These deciduous trees are beautiful during fall, with their bright yellow foliage crowning straight white trunks.

Otters frequent the waters of North Rathbun. While canoeing with friends from the city, I came upon the largest otter I've ever seen on this lake. It was playfully swimming close to my friends' canoe, but every time I went to point it out to them, the sly creature

Serpentine Lake Loop

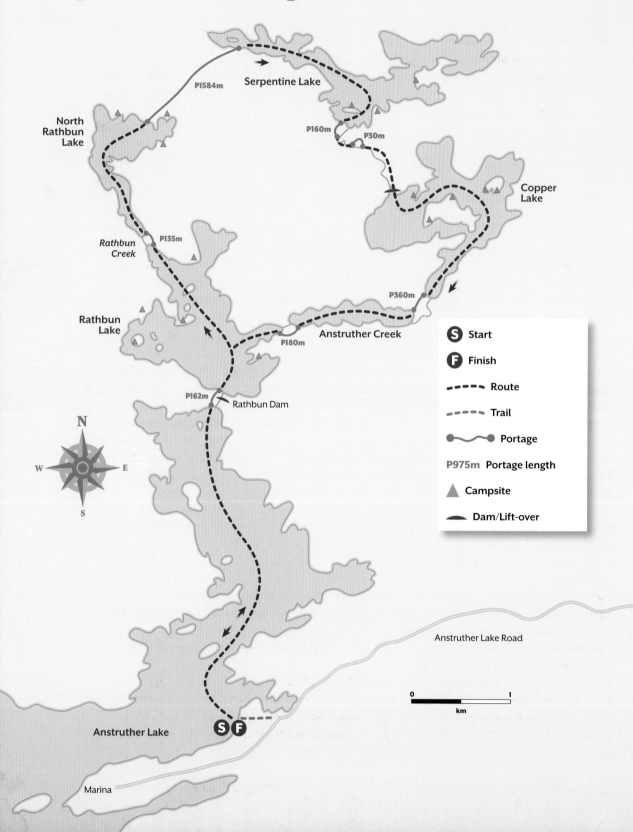

Serpentine Lake

North Rathbun Lake

P1584m

P160m

P30m

Copper Lake

Rathbun Creek

P135m

Rathbun Lake

P360m

P180m

Anstruther Creek

P162m

Rathbun Dam

S Start

F Finish

- - - Route

- - - Trail

●——● Portage

P975m Portage length

▲ Campsite

━ Dam/Lift-over

N
W E
S

Anstruther Lake Road

0   1
km

Anstruther Lake

S **F**

Marina

dove under their canoe and popped up on the opposite side. If my canoe partner hadn't verified my sighting, they would never have believed me.

The portage leading out of North Rathbun to Serpentine Lake is located by a natural sandy beach to the northeast. Before you get any ideas about taking a swim at the beach, however, I should warn you that in the past I've found North Rathbun's waters to be leech infested. But if the sun is out, you may want to risk it. If you do, have some salt handy on shore. If you sprinkle salt on leeches, they will usually loosen their grip.

Both Rathbun and North Rathbun lakes are named after a lumber baron who operated in the area. Just to the right of the portage, hidden among the brush close to where a creek enters North Rathbun, evidence of the area's logging era can be found. Among the treasures left behind are a tramway that once crossed a rocky crevice, and an old crosscut saw still bound in the trunk of a hemlock tree.

The portage to Serpentine is the longest on the route. It starts off on a groomed trail, then heads over patches of bare rock and through a woodland swamp. The most difficult portion of the 1,584-meter pathway is at its end, where the portage works its way down a fairly steep grade. Now you know why I travel clockwise rather than counterclockwise on the loop.

Because of the heavy minerals in the Serpentine Lake area, the water has a rusty tinge and at times a foul stench lingers in the air. Apart from the bad odor, however, Serpentine is the best lake to make camp on. Two excellent sites, one on an island to the south and the other on a point to the northeast, are equipped with a fire pit and a canopy of red and white pine.

To finish the canoe loop, paddle to Serpentine's southern bay, where a creek flows out of the lake. A portage is marked to the right of the creek and runs alongside it for 160 meters, until the waterway becomes deep enough to navigate with the canoe. Wend your way through the twisting creek until you are forced out of the canoe once more to make a 30-meter portage. After portaging, continue to follow the creek—lined with wild low-lying shrubs, clusters of wild iris, pickerel weed and the odd tamarack—until you come to where it enters Copper Lake. Depending on the water level, you may have to line or lift the canoe over into the lake's western bay.

The next portage, leading out of Copper Lake, is located at the southern tip of the opposite bay. The 360-meter path heads up an ATV trail for approximately 20 meters and then makes a sharp left turn, leading you through a mixed woodland and then down a steep grade to yet another shallow creek. It's essential to note that halfway along the portage the path cuts through another ATV trail. Make sure you don't go down the wrong path. I once found a family of four who had been lost for over an hour, having taken the wrong trail. Of course, I encountered the lost campers because I too had gone off in the wrong direction.

Joining Copper Lake with the familiar Rathbun Lake is an extensive marshland. Follow the creek, which snakes through the cattails and leatherleaf shrubs. You may have to stand up in the canoe to navigate through this lush wetland.

The marsh is home to dozens of red-winged blackbird families, but they're not the only species in abundance. On a hot summer day, I was quietly paddling through the cattails, heading for the portage into Rathbun, when I heard a faint sound of bells in the wind. At first I thought I was going bush happy; then, as I rounded a bend in the creek, I saw a herd of cows grazing in the wetland. Each one had a bell dangling from its neck, except for a solitary bull, who didn't seem to appreciate me gliding by his harem. I later discovered the cows belonged to a local farmer out on Highway 28 who leaves his livestock to graze freely throughout the area.

The next year I traveled through the same place with friends from the city. Already aware of the "wild" cows, I enjoyed keeping them a secret and amused myself by allowing my chums to puzzle over what appeared to be huge moose patties along the portage.

At the end of the marsh, the creek rushes over a beaver dam and marked to the left is a 180-meter portage leading to Rathbun Lake. A beautiful waterfall can be seen halfway along the portage. This is one of the most scenic sights of the entire loop. With the cold water tumbling over moss-covered granite, you can't help but put down your gear and cool off under the cataract.

The portage ends where the creek enters Rathbun Lake. To finish your two days on the Serpentine Loop, paddle the length of the eastern inlet and head for the familiar portage into Anstruther, almost directly across the lake. To reach the access, return via the same route across Anstruther Lake. And remember, if you return the next year with friends, keep Serpentine's cows a secret until your partners spot a giant patty or two.

LONGEST PORTAGE 1,584 meters

FEE This route is now part of the new Kawartha Highlands Provincial Park and permits are now required to camp there.

ALTERNATIVE ACCESS Marina, either right or left of the public access point.

ALTERNATIVE ROUTE It's possible to eliminate the long portage from North Rathbun to Serpentine by simply paddling/portaging in and out of Serpentine by way of Rathbun, Anstruther Creek and Copper Lake.

OUTFITTERS
Wild Rock Outfitters
169 Charlotte Street
Peterborough, ON, K9J 2T7
705-745-9133
www.wildrock.net

Adventure Outfitters
County Road 18 at Highway 507
Lakefield, ON, K0L 2H0
705-652-7986
www.adventureoutfitters.ca

FOR MORE INFORMATION
Ministry of Natural Resources
Bancroft District Office
613-332-3940
www.mnr.gov.on.ca

TOPOGRAPHIC MAPS 31 D/9

GPS COORDINATES
44.741577, -78.200031

Mississagua River

 1 to 2 days

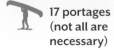 17 portages (not all are necessary)

 21 km

A moderate level of canoe-tripping skills and experience in whitewater canoeing are needed.

E VERY RIVER HAS a character of its own, but some have a more distinct personality than others. The Mississagua has a subtle charm that instantly bewitches the first-time river-runner and turns him or her into a lifetime whitewater fanatic.

The river flows between Mississagua Lake and Buckhorn Lake. To access the river you can leave behind a second vehicle on the shoulder where the Mississagua flows under Highway 36, just east of Buckhorn. However, the designated area is located just a few kilometers north of Buckhorn, along Highway 507. Look for the parking area to the right, where a snowmobile bridge crosses the Mississagua. From the 507 turn right onto Mississagua Dam Road. Follow the boat-launching signs for 3 kilometers until you come to a parking area beside the dam. Take the 50-meter portage from the lot to the base of the dam and the beginning of the Mississagua River. The waterway is open and shallow here, with cottages dotting the shore. Your paddle may frequently push into the sandy soil under the flow, digging up crayfish and clams.

The river soon changes character as it leaves the developed shorelines and begins to quicken its pace, flowing over a series of rocky staircases. Four sets of portages are presented in quick succession, ranging from approximately 45 to 170 meters. Due to the unavailability of detailed information on the Mississagua River route, all portage lengths are approximate. The first portage (170 m) is to the right and crosses a dirt road, avoiding a scenic split falls and a short swift flowing under a small bridge. Put in to the right of the bridge, paddle across a small pond and portage 45 meters to the right, around the third stairway. Almost immediately after the second portage the river twists to the south and flushes through a rocky chute. Portage 90 meters along the left bank, or if you feel a little adventurous and the water levels and your experience are up to snuff, line the canoe through the chute on the right bank and then run the rapids. Steep granite walls run along this section and a boulder garden awaits you at the end, so remember, once started, you are committed. Even though this set of rapids is among the best on the river, if in doubt, choose the portage. The portage finishes near the base of the rapids. If water levels are low, you may want to paddle directly across from

Mississagua River

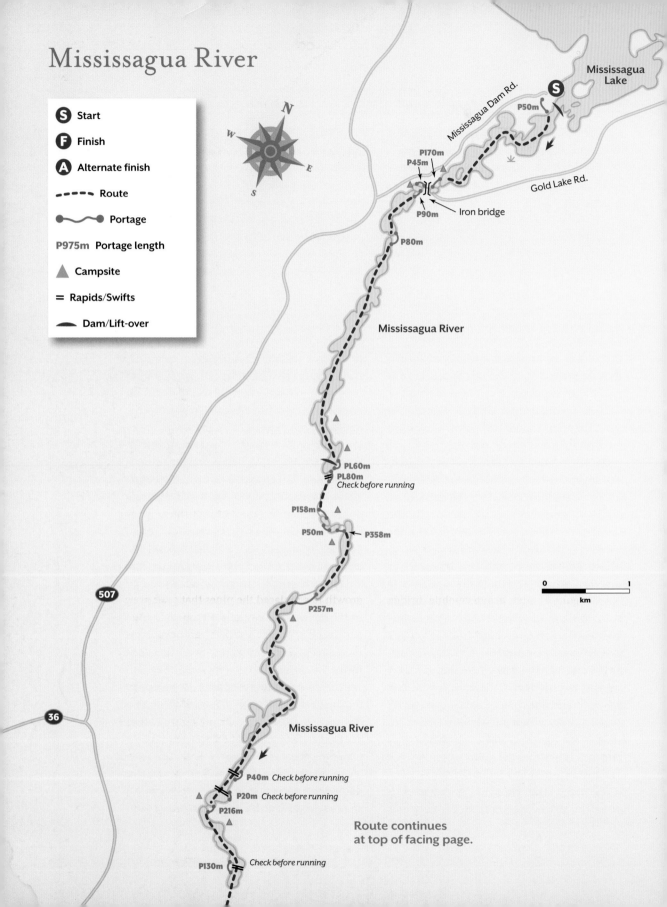

Legend

- **S** Start
- **F** Finish
- **A** Alternate finish
- - - - Route
- ●‿‿‿● Portage
- **P975m** Portage length
- ▲ Campsite
- = Rapids/Swifts
- ▬ Dam/Lift-over

Mississagua Lake

Mississagua Dam Rd.
P50m

P170m
P45m
P90m
Iron bridge

Gold Lake Rd.

P80m

Mississagua River

PL60m
PL80m
Check before running

P158m
P50m
P358m

P257m

507

36

Mississagua River

P40m *Check before running*
P20m *Check before running*
P216m

P130m *Check before running*

**Route continues
at top of facing page.**

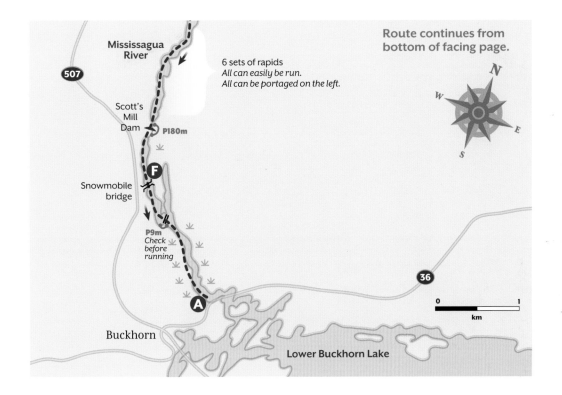

Route continues from bottom of facing page.

6 sets of rapids
All can easily be run.
All can be portaged on the left.

Mississagua River

Scott's Mill Dam — P180m

Snowmobile bridge

P9m
Check before running

Buckhorn

Lower Buckhorn Lake

this portage and use another portage (45 m) on the left bank to avoid decorating the rocks with canoe paint. The fourth portage (80 m) is a little farther downstream and again is located to the left, passing over a section of private property.

After going under a snowmobile bridge, the river stretches out its banks and calms its flow. The last section of fast water is hardly noticeable and can easily be run. A 40-meter portage is located to the right, however. During early spring, which is really the only time to run the Mississagua, the water along this section is alive with spawning suckers.

Since the river was once used to flush logs down to Buckhorn Lake and then down the Trent system, it is no wonder that the fish population has dwindled to schools of suckers, with the odd bass lurking in the lower,

deeper pools. Along this shallow section, one can plunge the blade of one's paddle into the river's seemingly sandy bottom and disturb the bark and wood chips left behind by the giant pines that once tumbled down the swollen spring river. Today a patchwork of second growth has replaced the pines that once grew in the low-lying areas, and a crop of stunted oak carpets the rock-strewn landscape that bears little resemblance to the wasteland left by the loggers.

For 2.5 kilometers the river moves slowly through a broad stretch of low, flooded vegetation. Eventually the surrounding scenery becomes more towering and a yellow portage marker appears on the left bank, indicating that the river once again drops down over hard granite. The first set of rapids can be lined and portaged or run by lifting your

gear over the beginning chute. You should put in immediately after and then maneuver through a straight channel filled with swirling water and jagged rocks. By running the rapids, you avoid two portages (60 m and 80 m in length) marked along the rocks to the left, but make sure to check the waterway beforehand. Only a few meters downriver, another portage, 158 meters long, is marked along the left bank. Don't miss it. The following set of rapids cannot be run unless you put in below where the river splits, forming three separate falls. By running or lining the last section, you can cut the portage in half.

A campsite that overlooks the triple falls is located along the portage, but I prefer to travel just a little farther and make camp at the most awe-inspiring site on the river. The Mississagua first tumbles over a steep ledge, down into a quiet pool, then crashes down a rocky gorge. A short portage (50 m) is marked to the right of the first falls, then a second portage (358 m) can be found almost immediately beside the first; just follow the shoreline to the western arm of the pool. To shorten this portage, the longest on the route, I simply paddle across the pool, keeping to the right of the second drop, then clamber up the rocky bank and bushwhack 20 meters until I meet up with the end of the extensive portage. The picturesque campsite is off to the left of the portage, alongside the gorge. You can set up camp here.

The next morning you can enjoy a relaxed 3-kilometer paddle through yet another meandering section of the river, which is interrupted halfway by a single set of rapids. The portage is marked to the left (257 m), but it is runnable if water levels permit.

Following the portage, the muddy banks are once again replaced with hard rock. Birch trees and trilliums give way to pine and columbine plants, and you'll soon hear the familiar roar of the river as it descends over granite. The next two portages are short (40 m and 20 m) and are marked along the left bank. You can easily run this section, but you must carry over the third set of rapids, using the 216-meter trail located along the left bank.

I know what you're thinking: not another portage! Well, to be honest, the first time I looked at the Mississagua River route on a map and counted more than 20 portages over a 16-kilometer stretch, I said forget it. But one early spring weekend my wife, Alana, talked me into attempting the river. We blindly set forth, with little whitewater experience, and soon discovered the magic of the Mississagua.

From the put-in to the set of rapids shortly after the previously mentioned 216-meter portage, the majority of the rapids are next to impossible to run. But as you make your way farther downstream, the rapids gradually become easier and easier. The magical part about all this is that while you are shooting more and more rapids, you think it's the skill you've gained along the way that has enabled you to conquer the river, not the ease of the runs themselves.

When Alana and I reached the halfway point, we came across a bend in the river where we could hear the roar of the rushing rapids just ahead. We went ashore so I could check the ease of the portage. After finding the 130-meter trail was blazed through a bug-infested swamp, I opted to look to see if the rapids were runnable. From my vantage point on a rocky ledge, I could gaze down at the rapids. The river squeezed itself through a narrow, boulder-strewn canyon, creating a series of deep-water haystack waves halfway through the run. But the boulder garden at the base of the rapids was swallowed by high water, so the only difficulty would lie in trying to balance the canoe through the haystacks.

I quickly returned to where Alana was holding the canoe and asked her if she wanted to attempt to run them. "Sure, let's go for it!" she exclaimed. So I tied down the packs, tucked my legs under my seat, zipped up my life jacket and pushed off from shore, allowing the current to take us around the bend in the river.

The moment I saw the sudden drop and swirling water, a lump formed in my throat. The rapids sure seemed a lot safer from the rocky ledge along the portage than at the brink of the tumbling river.

"Back paddle, back paddle," I called to Alana at the bow. It was too late. The current dragged us into the gut of the rapids and pushed our flimsy fiberglass vessel straight into the rolling haystacks. As the canoe bounced up and down the waves like a roller coaster, I began to panic. Luckily, with Alana still back paddling, I was able to shift the canoe away from the worst of it by making a series of pries and sculling draws. At the base of the rapids, a small eddy worked in our favor as we swung out of the rushing current to safety.

Before I was able to catch my breath and apologize to my bow partner for having chosen to run through all that foam and froth, Alana gave out a loud "Yaaa-hoooo!" and then asked, "Can we run it again?" There was nothing I could do for her now: the magical Mississagua had cast its spell and Alana was doomed to be a whitewater fanatic forever.

After the last set of rapids, the river tumbles over rock 12 more times. Most of these rapids can be run without difficulty in moderate water levels (all can be lined and/or portaged if necessary), except for the rapids that plunge over the ruins of the old Scott's Mill dam. The dam is a cement structure that was built by W.A. Scott in 1870 to flush his licensed timber along the Mississagua River down to Buckhorn Lake. Ownership of the dam has changed several times over the years, and in 1928 the dam was sold to the federal government, who use it to control water levels. The historic site appears soon after the sixth rapid, where Alana and I fought foam and froth. To avoid the turbulent waters crashing over the dam, hug the left bank. A portage trail (180 m) begins well above the falls.

After you have navigated through the last section of whitewater (five sections in total, with only the fifth having a marked 9-m portage to the right), the Mississagua slows and appears more like a long lake than a raging river. The banks are thick with green growth: willow, alder, dogwood, leatherleaf and bog-laurel. Yellow warblers, cowbirds and eastern kingbirds can be seen among the foliage. Gradually the signs of civilization make their appearance, marking the end of a spellbinding trip down a magical river.

LONGEST PORTAGE 358 meters

FEE This route is now part of the new Kawartha Highlands Provincial Park and permits are now required to camp there.

ALTERNATIVE ACCESS None

ALTERNATIVE ROUTE None

OUTFITTERS
Wild Rock Outfitters
169 Charlotte Street
Peterborough, ON, K9J 2T7
705-745-9133
www.wildrock.net

Adventure Outfitters
County Road 18 at Highway 507
Lakefield, ON, K0L 2H0
705-652-7986
www.adventureoutfitters.ca

FOR MORE INFORMATION
Ministry of Natural Resources
Bancroft District Office
613-332-3940
www.mnr.gov.on.ca

TOPOGRAPHIC MAPS 31 D/9

GPS COORDINATES
44.686006, -78.330570

COTTAGE COUNTRY

Nunikani Lake Loop

 2 days    4 portages   ●----● 19 km   A novice route except for possible problems with wind and waves on Big Hawk Lake.

BACK IN MY high-school days, a few classmates and I would gather every weekend to take a canoe trip. After graduation, however, we all went our separate ways, and I was the only one who continued the quest for great outdoor adventures.

Now that all my chums have grabbed hold of steady jobs, and some are even married and have children, we rekindle the old days by gathering once a year to go back in time, with paddles in hand. During the spring of 1992, I guided our group to one of my favorite lakes, Nunikani, set among the wilds of the Haliburton Highlands. After that memorable weekend we all decided that the '92 canoe trip had been one of the best reunions, and once you have tried the Nunikani Loop you will know why.

To reach the access point on Big Hawk Lake, follow Highway 35 north toward Dorset. Just past Halls Lake, turn right onto Road 13 and then left on Big Hawk Road. The paved road turns to dust and dirt halfway along, and at the dam on the Kennisis River you can view the historic log sluiceway. To put in, park your vehicle near the marina and push off from the beach to the left of the bridge, then paddle the length of the southwestern inlet and go around to the right, into Big Hawk Lake.

When canoeing the Nunikani Loop, I prefer to make the first day the longest and so head northeast, traveling counterclockwise. To reach the first portage, paddle the length of Big Hawk, keeping to the left inlet. Near the end of the far northeastern inlet (Little Clear Lake), along the western shoreline, a relatively flat 225-meter portage into Clear Lake is marked. Clear Lake is exactly that—clear. Its waters give off a turquoise glow at the surface, and the lake's bottom frequently flashes under your canoe, creating an effect that is quite dizzying and transfixing.

To reach the next portage, paddle out of the long inlet and then go straight across Clear Lake to the north shore. You have a choice of two paths (200 m or 276 m), both leading to Red Pine Lake. The longer portage on the right is only used when the middle section of the trail to the left becomes wet and muddy.

Red Pine is another big lake, and many canoeists choose to camp on its three large islands. The sites are scenic but can be a bit overused for my liking. I prefer to stay overnight on the more isolated Nunikani Lake.

Nunikani Lake Loop

Shoelace Lake

Caution: low water. Use rough portage on right.

Shoelace Creek

Wallace Pond

P150m

P387m

East Paint Lake

P1300m

Red Pine Dam

P30m

P440m

Red Pine Lake

Averoy Island

Side route for speckled trout and splake

Nunikani Lake

P200m

P276m

P194m

Nunikani Dam

Clear Lake

Cliffs

Cliffs

P225m

Big Hawk Lake

Little Hawk Lake

S Start

F Finish

- - - Route

······ Alternate route

●~● Portage

P975m Portage length

▲ Campsite

— Dam/Lift-over

S **F**

Kennisis River

Big Hawk Lake Road

N
W   E
S

0   1
km

It's one of my favorite lakes in the Leslie Frost Forest Reserve. To reach it from Red Pine, follow the western shoreline to the little channel directly across from small Averoy Island. Take out to the right of the dam and either cross over and take the 440-meter portage, following the left bank of the Kennisis River, or, if water levels permit and a little foam and froth doesn't scare you, simply lift over to the base of the cement structure and navigate your canoe down a short set of rapids. Make sure to stay clear of the tumbling water below the dam; the current is extremely powerful there. It's best to get your feet wet and wade your canoe down the right fork of the rapids.

In early spring, this section of fast water is clogged with lake suckers spawning on the riverbed. And during the summer months, the shoreline is decorated with a diversity of flora and fauna. Hummingbirds hum around the dark red cardinal flowers, and tiny wrens bounce across the shrubs that overhang the banks.

Nunikani's northern bay is cluttered with stumps and reeds, an excellent place to fish for bass with surface plugs come nightfall, but first make camp at one of the five designated sites. My favorite is on the northwest point. The camp is set among a neck of pines facing a rock slab, which is great for swimming or catching a breeze to keep the mosquitoes at bay.

This was the site my friends and I chose as a base camp during our 1992 spring trip. After a couple of years of guiding them to the more hard-to-get-to lakes, I decided to take them on this less strenuous route. I assured them that they would be able to pack a few luxuries. So instead of bringing freeze-dried stew, they brought frozen steaks, and Mike, the camp cook, was even allowed to pack a

grill for the fire. We also equipped ourselves with a wide assortment of lines and tackle in the hope of having fish for breakfast. Of course, who would have thought that a group of enthusiastic anglers would forget the most essential item. You guessed it—we left the landing net at home. Nobody really seemed too concerned about this because we didn't really think we would catch any fish. We never had on any of our other trips. But the moment we portaged into Wallace Pond, a small lake to the west of Nunikani that can be reached via a rugged 387-meter portage, we were shocked to see speckled trout darting at our shiny lures. (Take note that splake are now the species stocked in Wallace Pond.) We had great trophy fishing in Wallace Pond and got creative with our frying pan, using it as a makeshift landing net.

To head back to Big Hawk Lake and the marina where your vehicle is parked, take the 194-meter portage from the southern end of Nunikani Lake at the dam, following the right bank of the Kennisis River to the far northwestern inlet of Big Hawk Lake. Keep to the shoreline to your right. On your way along the western inlet, take note of the cliffs to your left. According to legend, one of the area's pioneers befriended a Native and was repaid with instructions as to the location of a hidden gold mine. However, the pioneer was unable to find it. Having read about the landmarks (two pines prominently situated on a mountain), I would guess the gold is somewhere on top of those cliffs.

At the mouth of the western inlet, keep following the shoreline to your right until you get to where the lake narrows; then paddle south, down the familiar inlet toward the marina and bridge. You will now have completed one of the best weekend loops in Haliburton.

LONGEST PORTAGE 440 meters (used only during low water levels)

FEE This route is now maintained by the Township of Algonquin Highlands under the Haliburton Highlands Waterway Trails. Camping permits and reservations can be made at www.algonquinhighlands.ca/water.

ALTERNATIVE ACCESS A public boat launch can be used at the Red Pine Lake Dam, reached by driving the Kennisis Lake Road.

ALTERNATIVE ROUTE Wallace Pond, reached by portaging in from the west end of Nunikani Lake, makes a great side route. It is also possible to paddle/portage in and out of Nunikani Lake from the Big Hawk access point.

OUTFITTERS
Haliburton Highlands Waterway Trails
20130 Highway 35
Algonquin Highlands, ON, K0M 1J2
705-766-9033
www.algonquinhighlands.ca/
water-trails.php

FOR MORE INFORMATION
Ministry of Natural Resources
Minden District Office
705-286-1521
www.mnr.gov.on.ca

MAPS Chrismar has produced an excellent map detailing the interior canoe routes of the Frost Centre Institute.

TOPOGRAPHIC MAPS 31 E/2

GPS COORDINATES
45.146957, -78.746442

Spider Bay Route

 2 to 3 days    2 portages   ●----● 36 km   **Moderate tripping skills are needed to deal with the heavy winds along the route.**

THE SPIDER BAY route is for the more experienced canoeist. Georgian Bay, a freshwater sea, can quickly sculpture waves to the height of hills, and these waves will roll with an unbridled violence against your canoe.

The route uses the access point at Three Legged Lake where you portage into Spider Lake. As the waters of Spider Lake head out into Georgian Bay, just keep going. Directly west, at the end of Spider Lake, a 130-meter portage leads you from the inland lake to the eastern tip of Spider Bay. The portage was once home to a log slide that lumber companies employed to flush logs down to the bay, where they were shipped out on three-masted schooners.

At the end of the portage, make your way through the shallow channel lined with thick aquatic greenery and mud-caked islands decorated with blue irises and red cardinal flowers. Farther out on Spider Bay, the waters open up, giving you a view of a distant skyline hovering over the waters of Georgian Bay.

The rocky islands and peninsulas of Spider Bay are covered with elaborate cottages. As you paddle by, terns play in the wind above you and cormorants sitting on top of the mounds of rocks eventually take off, leaving the islands covered in seabird dung. If you're like me, the majestic mood of Georgian Bay, with its flat blue horizon, will draw you forward like a magnet.

Once you navigate through Spider Bay, head out toward the expanse of open water, broken only by stark islands and steel-hulled tankers. Camp out along Spider Bay's north shore or search for a protected inlet to the south.

For the history buff, the north shore is a playground. Scattered remnants of a short-lived mining era around the turn of the century mark the graves of five known mine sites located to the north.

A few years ago, a friend and I paddled out to Spider Bay for the weekend. Unfortunately, constant downpour and heavy winds forced us to alter our plans to explore the isolated islands carpeted with ripe blueberry bushes. Like a couple of drenched dogs with tails between our legs, we paddled to the safety of Goose Neck Bay. Rains on Georgian Bay, especially during hot August days, always develop into magnificent thunderstorms. Gigantic

Spider Bay Route

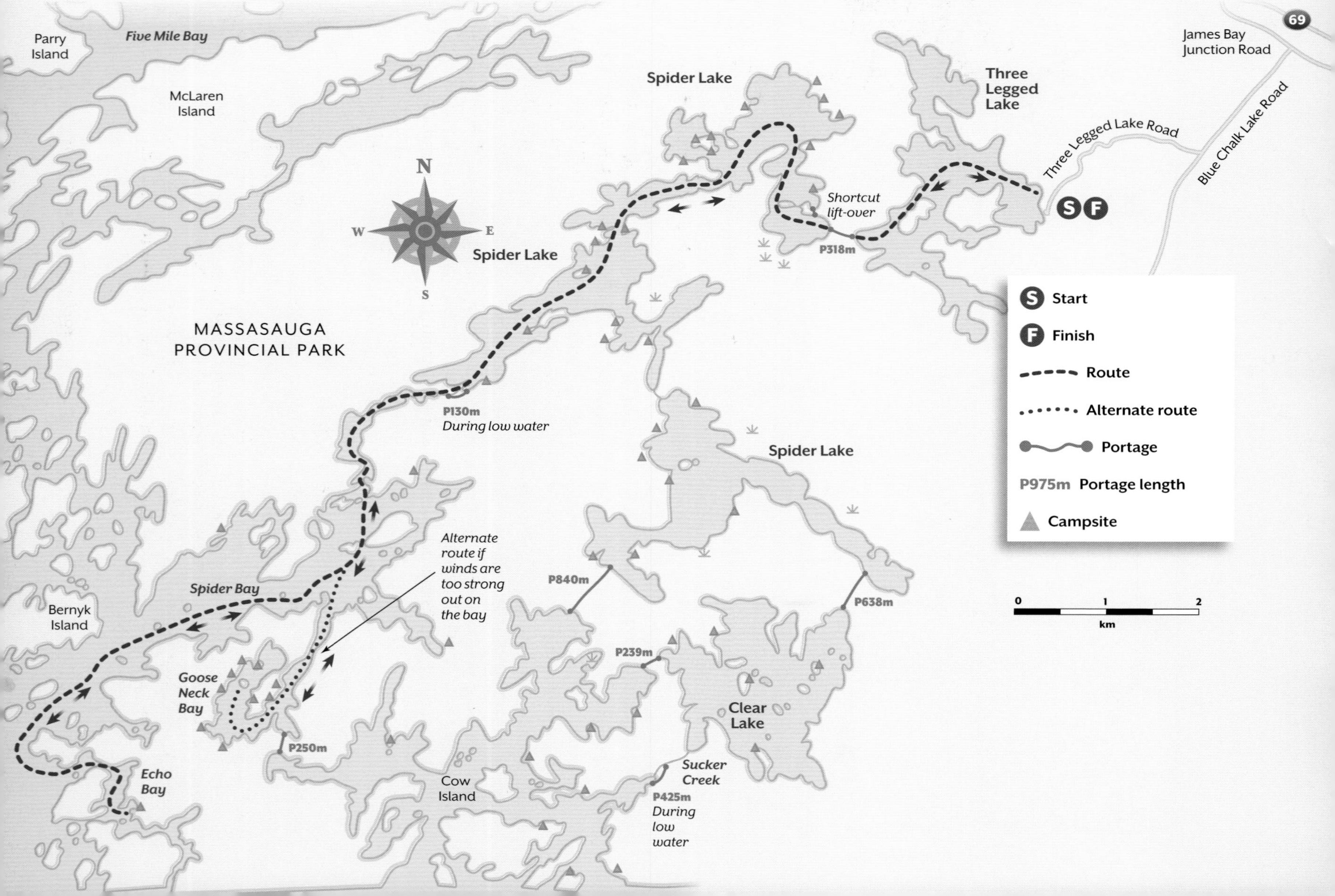

James Bay Junction Road

Blue Chalk Lake Road

Three Legged Lake Road

S **F**

Three Legged Lake

Legend

S Start
F Finish
- - - Route
· · · · Alternate route
•——• Portage
P975m Portage length
▲ Campsite

0 — 1 — 2 km

Shortcut lift-over

P318m

Spider Lake

Spider Lake

Spider Lake

MASSASAUGA PROVINCIAL PARK

N

P638m

Spider Lake

Clear Lake

Sucker Creek

P425m During low water

P239m

P840m

P130m During low water

Cow Island

Alternate route if winds are too strong out on the bay

P250m

Spider Bay

Goose Neck Bay

Echo Bay

Five Mile Bay

McLaren Island

Parry Island

Bernyk Island

clouds, frighteningly black, blow in with a vengeance. Brian (my canoe companion that weekend) and I sat in our canoe, hunched over, depressed by the change of weather. The raindrops struck the lake so hard that small columns of water erupted inches into the air. As a result, we had no choice but to beach our vessel on a rocky island covered in wet juniper bushes.

There we were, huddled under an outstretched tarp, eating soggy sandwiches and soup, feeling betrayed by the weather predictions that the announcer had given on the car radio before we headed out.

During the night, as I curled up in fetal position in my sleeping bag, I listened through the rage of the storm for the echoing blasts of ships' horns as they made their way up the arm of Lake Huron. Every time a ship bellowed its haunting sound, I would try to imagine the fear each sailor must have felt while attempting to navigate through such

a storm before wooden hulls were replaced with steel.

One of the most talked-about shipwrecks in the area was the *Waubuno*. Built in 1865, the vessel was the lifeline between Parry Sound and the outside world. On Friday, November 21, 1879, the ship was preparing to leave the port in Collingwood for its final northward journey of the season. A northwest gale ravaging Georgian Bay convinced Captain J. Burkett to stay in port until the storm subsided. Once the passengers heard of the delay, some opted to spend the night at a local hotel. But about 4:00 a.m., thinking the storm had eased enough for safe passage, the captain blew the whistle and headed into Georgian Bay, leaving behind those passengers in the hotel. They were the lucky ones. The 10 passengers, 14 crewmen and the captain traveled north toward Parry Sound. Past Christian Island the storm raged harder, forcing the *Waubuno* to weather it out around the islands south of Copperhead Island.

Only the ghosts of the wreck can tell what really occurred after the captain dropped anchor near Haystack Rocks. Historians speculate what happened next. According to Ron Terpstra's Historical Report: Blackstone Harbour Massasauga Wildlands Provincial Park, "The anchors held briefly, but the ship was battered by the rough seas, so bad that the upper works began to break, and the anchors tore loose from the anchor chains. The ship 'slid' downwind, and at Black Rock (near the Haystacks), she was picked up by the breakers in front of the shoal, and she turned on her side. She came over so hard that the ship's main engine was thrown through its side. She then broke longitudinally and the upper works, which held the victims, drifted downwind, sank, and was never seen again."

Two days later a tug was dispatched to search for the ship after it failed to arrive at its destination. On the shores of the Copperhead Islands, the crew found a metal lifeboat crushed at both ends, a life jacket with the ship's name on it and part of the ship's paddlebox revealing the letters WA. In 1880 the hull was finally discovered in the shallow water south of the Haystacks. Boaters still find remains of the *Waubuno* haunting the shoals of the bay to this very day.

To end the historic Spider Bay Route, simply return to the access point on Three Legged Lake via the same route. With luck you will be able to count on the same wind from Georgian Bay that once battled against your bow and use it to your advantage in sailing all the way to the eastern tip of Spider Lake.

LONGEST PORTAGE 318 meters

FEE A fee is required for overnight camping, and permits can be obtained at Oastler Lake Provincial Park or Blackstone Harbour entry point.

ALTERNATIVE ACCESS It is possible to access the park at Blackstone Harbour. Turn east off Highway 400/69 onto Muskoka Road 11. Then, after the town of MacTier (almost 6 kilometers from the highway), take the Healey and Kapikog Lake Road to reach the Petes Road and the Blackstone Harbour boat launch and fee station.

ALTERNATIVE ROUTE The Spider Bay Route can be reached by making use of the Blackstone Harbour access point, located at the south end of the park.

OUTFITTERS
White Squall Paddling Centre
53 Carling Bay Road
Nobel, ON, P0G 1G0
705-342-5324
or
19 James Street
Parry Sound, ON, P2A 1T4
705-746-4936
www.whitesquall.com

Swift Outdoor Centre (Georgian Bay)
Highway 400 North
Box 604
Waubaushene, ON, L0K 2C0
1-800-661-1429
www.swiftcanoe.com

FOR MORE INFORMATION
Massasauga Provincial Park
705-378-0685
www.ontarioparks.com

Ministry of Natural Resources
Parry Sound District Office
705-746-4201
www.mnr.gov.on.ca

MAPS Massasauga Provincial Park has produced an excellent map of the park's interior.

TOPOGRAPHIC MAPS
41 H1, 41 H8 & 31 E4

GPS COORDINATES
45.263737, -80.008140

York River

🕐 1 to 2 days　　　🛶 3 portages　　　●--- -● 72 km

The portages around Egan, Middle and Farm chutes are extremely steep but the river itself is a novice route.

OR COUNTLESS YEARS the York River was used as a major waterway. Algonquin tribes used it while retreating from the invading Iroquois. Fur traders used it as part of a transport route from Georgian Bay to the Ottawa River. Lumber companies based in Haliburton began flushing their logs down it before making use of any other neighboring tributary. Even the initial surveyors remarked it was a great-grandchild of the mighty St. Lawrence. But for a while now it's basically been forgotten. In fact, I can't recall ever seeing another canoeist while on the river. And for that reason alone, it definitely fits the "best canoe route" category.

The best section of the river to paddle is between Egan Chutes Provincial Park and Conroy Marsh. It's a perfect two-day outing for novice canoeists or advanced paddlers looking for a leisurely getaway.

Egan Chutes Provincial Park is 11 kilometers east of Bancroft, along Highway 28; the public access road is northeast of the highway bridge. Take note, however, that the park is no longer regularly maintained by the province and has only a small clearing below the remains of an old concrete dam acting as the put-in site. Also, since it's a river route, you'll have to shuttle a second vehicle to the public launch at the west end of Combermere, along Highway 62.

Not far from the starting point is Egan Chute itself, named after Lumber Baron John Egan, who, in the mid-1800s, built a number of timber chutes along the York River. He was in fact one of the first to hold a timber license in the district (1847), driving most of his logs down the river from nearby Baptiste Lake.

To the left of the cascade is a short but fairly steep 50-meter portage. It's used on a regular basis—not by canoeists, but by rockhounds. Bancroft is known as the Mineral Capital of Canada, and Egan Chute is one of the local hot spots, holding a high quantity of nepheline, sodalite, biotite, zircon and blue corundum.

Egan Chute also happens to be the place where my poor dog, Bailey, almost plummeted to her death. It was during my last trip down the York. The dog, for some unapparent reason, decided to go for a swim just above the falls. In seconds I found myself leaping down a rock face and grabbing her paw just as she was going over the brink. The dog came

York River

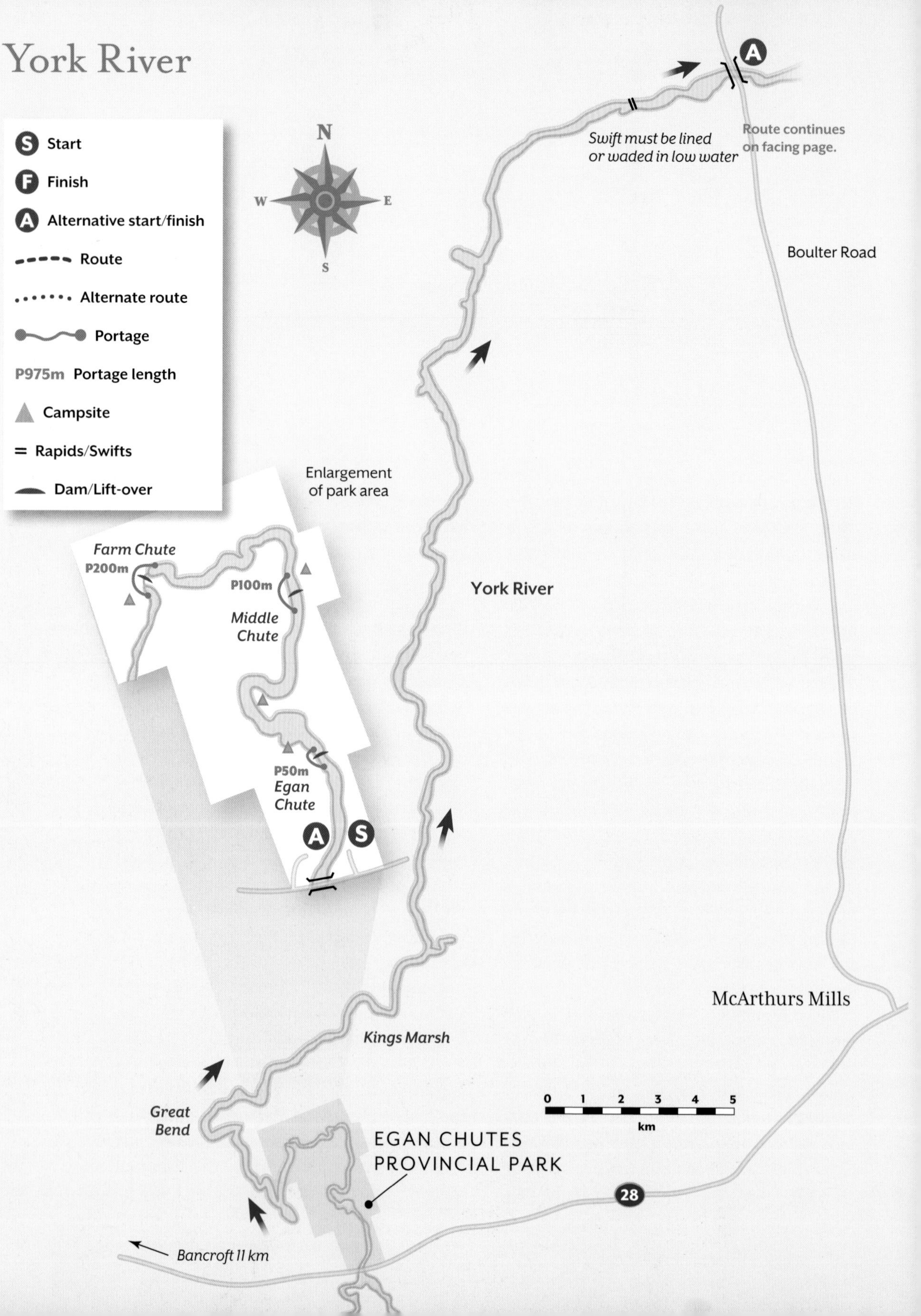

Route continues on facing page.

Legend

- **S** Start
- **F** Finish
- **A** Alternative start/finish
- - - - - Route
- ...... Alternate route
- •——• Portage
- **P975m** Portage length
- ▲ Campsite
- = Rapids/Swifts
- ━ Dam/Lift-over

N
W E
S

Swift must be lined or waded in low water

Boulter Road

Enlargement of park area

Farm Chute
P200m

P100m
Middle Chute

York River

P50m
Egan Chute

A **S**

McArthurs Mills

Kings Marsh

0 1 2 3 4 5
km

Great Bend

EGAN CHUTES
PROVINCIAL PARK

28

← *Bancroft 11 km*

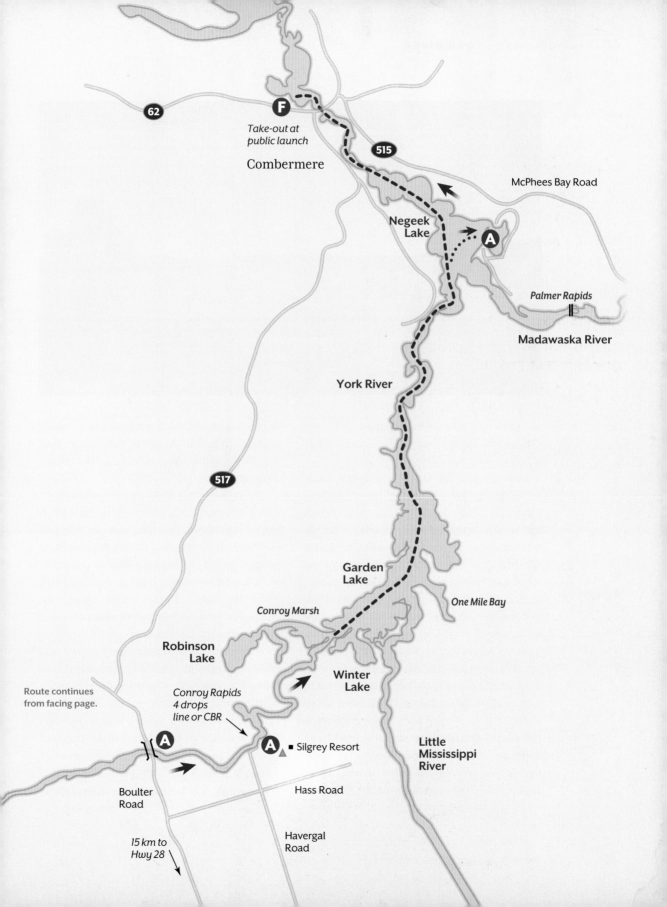

62

F

Take-out at public launch

Combermere

515

McPhees Bay Road

Negeek Lake

A

Palmer Rapids

Madawaska River

York River

517

Garden Lake

One Mile Bay

Conroy Marsh

Robinson Lake

Winter Lake

Little Mississippi River

Route continues from facing page.

Conroy Rapids 4 drops line or CBR

A

A ■ Silgrey Resort

Boulter Road

Hass Road

15 km to Hwy 28

Havergal Road

out of the ordeal without a scratch. I, on the other hand, suffered a split knee and cracked shinbone.

Just beyond Egan Chute are two more prominent drops—Middle Chute and Farm Chute. Both have portages (100 m on the left and 200 m on the right), but these are hardly used and can be difficult to follow at times. The first trail keeps close to the edge of the river, while the second heads almost directly up and over a knob of granite. Both also have campsites on the east bank. But again, they are rarely used.

Other sites are found not far downstream, situated on one of the many sandbars found between the Great Bend (where the river takes a dramatic twist to the northeast) and Kings Marsh. I've always arrived at these sites too early in the trip, however, and much prefer to make my own site farther downstream—making sure to practice low-impact camping, of course. This stretch, with its large sections of

deciduous swamps and forest levees, suits the York's Native name, Shawashkong (the river of marshes), and is my favorite place to paddle along the river.

If you're not that interested in making your own bush camp, it is possible to paddle a full six-to-eight-hour day and end your trip at the alternative take-out at the Boulter Road bridge. Better yet, you could also choose to book a cabin at Silgrey Resort, situated just below the Boulter bridge, on the south side of Conroy Rapids (four sets of swifts that can easily be run or lined down).

However, if you paddle only the first half of the route, you miss the most significant portion—Conroy Marsh—altogether.

This unique wetland, named after Robert Conroy, who held a timber license on land west of Robinson Lake, drained by the York River, was made famous some years ago after Group of Seven member A.J. Casson depicted it on canvas. And because of its richly diverse plant and animal life, as well its beautiful setting in the majestic hills of the Madawaska Highlands, the government soon made it a Crown Game Reserve. Recently, it was also designated a new park under the Living Legacy program.

Because of its size, it's also an easy place to find yourself lost in. Two kilometers downstream from Conroy Rapids the waterway spreads out over 6,000 acres, with Robinson Lake to the west and Winter Lake, Garden Lake, One Mile Bay and the mouth of the Little Mississippi River to the east. To help keep yourself on track, it's best to stay in the center of the main channel and eventually you'll meet up with Negeek Lake, where the York River flushes into the Madawaska River.

From here it's just a short paddle west, under the Highway 62 bridge, and then left toward the public launch in Combermere. Or, if you don't happen to have a not-so-bright dog prone to swimming above waterfalls, you could travel east on the Madawaska and take in a week of adventurous whitewater paddling all the way down to the Ottawa River.

LONGEST PORTAGE 200 meters

FEE No fee is required.

ALTERNATIVE ACCESS Put in from the Boulter Road bridge or Silgrey Resort, reached by turning east off Boulter Road onto Hass Road and then left on Havergal Road. You can also access the river at the end of McPhees Bay Road off Highway 515.

ALTERNATIVE ROUTE The route can be divided into two day trips by making use of the Boulter Road bridge access or Silgrey Resort.

OUTFITTERS
Silgrey Rustic Resort
1011 Havergal Road
Boulter, ON, K0L 1G0
613-332-1072
www.silgrey.ca

Trips and Trails Adventure Outfitting
258 Hastings Street N.
Bancroft, ON, K0L 1C0
613-332-1969

TOPOGRAPHIC MAPS
31 F/4 & 31 F/5

GPS COORDINATES
45.068752, -77.732180

Big Trout Lake Loop

 4 to 5 days   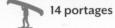 14 portages   ●----● 150 km

Moderate tripping skills needed to deal with possible wind and waves on Big Trout and other large lakes.

BIG TROUT LAKE has it all: breathtaking lakes, swamps teeming with wildlife, excellent campsites, fantastic fishing, easy portages and quick access. The only problem is that everyone seems to know about it.

By going out during early spring or late fall, however, you can avoid the crowds brought in by the neighboring camps during prime season.

To reach the access point, turn north off Highway 60 onto the road leading to the Portage Store. The gatehouse is down on the beach, near the parking area.

For your first day out, the route heads up from Canoe Lake to Burnt Island Lake. From here, you can either spend your first night on Burnt Island Lake or make the extra pilgrimage to Little Otterslide and Otterslide Lakes by way of the 790-meter portage. The trail is flat, but watch your footing on the exposed rocks near the put-in.

With no winds to slow our progress, Alana and I made it to Little Otterslide on our first night out. We chose an out-of-the-way campsite on the east side of the large island.

Early the next morning, we paddled on from Little Otterslide Lake into Otterslide Lake

by way of a weedy channel and then headed to the northwest corner and the beginning of Otterslide Creek. The first portage (250 m) is marked right at the entranceway to the creek, to the left of a giant logjam. It is soon followed by a 390-meter portage to the right and a 265-meter portage to the left.

Below the last series of portages is a 1.5-kilometer section dominated by sedge and tamarack. Here, Alana and I were lucky enough to spot a pair of otters—standing high in the water, their heads up like periscopes—spying on us from a swampy bay. A bull moose also blocked our way for a good 10 minutes, and we spooked three great blue herons that were feeding in the shallows.

Just before the next portage, the shoreline sedge is taken over by a patch of alder. The 730-meter trail is marked to the left of where the creek flushes alongside a towering cliff, which can be seen across the waterway halfway along the portage.

The last portage along Otterslide Creek is only 105 meters and works its way downhill to the right of a small cascade. A 10-minute paddle down a shallow inlet brings you out into Big Trout Lake.

Big Trout Lake Loop

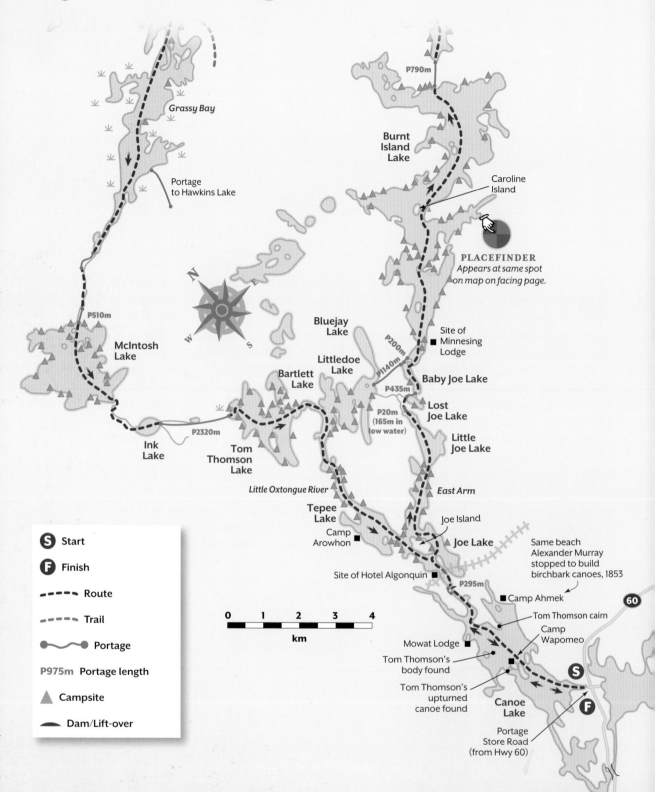

Grassy Bay

Portage
to Hawkins Lake

P510m

McIntosh
Lake

Ink
Lake

P2320m

Tom
Thomson
Lake

Bartlett
Lake

Bluejay
Lake

Littledoe
Lake

Little Oxtongue River

Tepee
Lake

Camp
Arowhon

Site of Hotel Algonquin

P790m

Burnt
Island
Lake

Caroline
Island

PLACEFINDER
*Appears at same spot
on map on facing page.*

P200m

P1140m

Site of
Minnesing
Lodge

Baby Joe Lake

P435m

P20m
(165m in
low water)

Lost
Joe Lake

Little
Joe Lake

East Arm

Joe Island

Joe Lake

Same beach
Alexander Murray
stopped to build
birchbark canoes, 1853

P295m

Camp Ahmek

Tom Thomson cairn

Camp
Wapomeo

Mowat Lodge

Tom Thomson's
body found

Tom Thomson's
upturned
canoe found

Canoe
Lake

Portage
Store Road
(from Hwy 60)

60

S

F

Legend

- **S** Start
- **F** Finish
- - - - Route
- - - - Trail
- ●━━● Portage
- **P975m** Portage length
- ▲ Campsite
- ━━ Dam/Lift-over

0 1 2 3 4
km

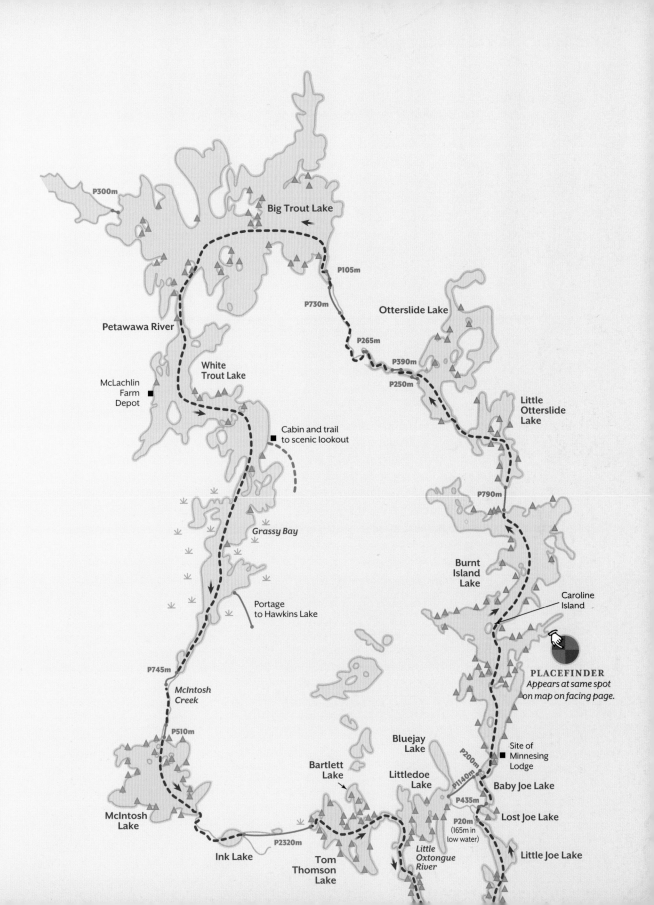

P300m

Big Trout Lake

P105m

P730m

Otterslide Lake

P265m

P390m

Petawawa River

P250m

White
Trout Lake

Little
Otterslide
Lake

McLachlin
Farm
Depot

Cabin and trail
to scenic lookout

P790m

Grassy Bay

Burnt
Island
Lake

Caroline
Island

Portage
to Hawkins Lake

PLACEFINDER
*Appears at same spot
on map on facing page.*

P745m

*McIntosh
Creek*

Bluejay
Lake

Site of
Minnesing
Lodge

P510m

Bartlett
Lake

P200m

Littledoe
Lake

Baby Joe Lake

P1140m

McIntosh
Lake

P435m

Lost Joe Lake

P20m
(165m in
low water)

Ink Lake

P2320m

Tom
Thomson
Lake

*Little
Oxtongue
River*

Little Joe Lake

The route now heads northwest to the third large bay, where a narrow channel joins Big Trout Lake with White Trout Lake. At this point in the trip, with the size of the lakes helping to spread out the crowds of canoeists, Alana and I were able to feel somewhat secluded. For two full days we explored the expanse of both lakes, and the wisps of smoke from distant campfires come dusk were the only sign of other human activity.

From White Trout's southwest end, the route continues through Grassy Bay (watch for the government signs and reflector tape marking the way through this massive wetland) and then up McIntosh Creek, complete with a 745-meter portage marked to the right and a 510-meter portage marked to the left.

We left the island site early the next morning, paddling through thick fog toward the south end of McIntosh Lake and the mouth of Ink Creek. As we entered the brown-stained waterway, we caught the sound of an elongated howl breaking through the mist. At first, we assumed it to be a performance by some wild campers. But after a second howl echoed across the lake, we began to consider the possibility that this baritone voice was that of a genuine Algonquin wolf.

Seconds later, two more wolves joined in, creating a chilling harmony of descending tones. We sat dumbfounded for at least 20 minutes before paddling on. Before long, we came across an open bog lined with miniature tamarack, clumps of insect-eating pitcher plants, and leatherleaf—all decorated with an irregular meshwork of spiderwebs. The morning was absolutely beautiful.

The creek ends at Ink Lake, and on the opposite shore is the longest and roughest portage en route. The 2,320-meter trail begins with an abrupt hill and then continues through muddy ravines, up a number of steep slopes, and finally, across a soggy field. Fortunately, each major obstruction is equipped with either a wooden staircase or a well-positioned catwalk to ease your way across.

The portage ends in a small bay hidden on the north end of Tom Thomson Lake. Once there, Alana and I ended the trip by heading south to Littledoe Lake and then southwest across Fawn, Tepee, Joe and Canoe lakes.

LONGEST PORTAGE 2,320 meters

FEE An interior camping permit must be purchased for Algonquin Provincial Park.

ALTERNATIVE ACCESS None

ALTERNATIVE ROUTE None

OUTFITTERS
Algonquin Outfitters
R.R. 1, 1035 Algonquin Outfitters Road
Dwight, ON, P0A 1H0
1-800-469-4948
www.algonquinoutfitters.com

The Portage Store
Box 10009 Algonquin Park
Huntsville, ON, P1H 2H4
705-633-5622 (summer) or
705-789-3645 (winter)
www.portagestore.com

FOR MORE INFORMATION
Algonquin Provincial Park
705-633-5572 (information) and
1-888-668-7275 (reservations)
www.algonquinpark.on.ca

MAPS The Friends of Algonquin, Chrismar as well as Backroad Mapbooks have produced excellent maps. There is also a free online map available at www.algonquinmap.com.

TOPOGRAPHIC MAPS
31 E/10 & 31 E/15

GPS COORDINATES
45.535103, -78.706791

The Brent Run

 8 to 10 days    46 portages   ●-----● 160 km   **The route is long and has some significant portages and some large lakes to paddle across.**

THE BRENT RUN Canoe Race was initiated after rumors that, during the early 1930s, the Stringer boys paddled their cedar-strip canoe from Canoe Lake to Brent and back again in 24 hours. Bill Stoqua and Bill Little, both former guides in the park, decided to try their luck and completed their trip in 32 hours. Then, on a dare from the two Bills, Hank Laurier and his brother, who were working for the Taylor Statten camps at the time, came in at 27 hours, fueled by only two peanut-butter-and-jelly sandwiches and two cans of orange juice.

The best recorded time to date is 23 hours, held by past members of Camp Ahmek Chuck Beamish and Bob Anglin. I'm not suggesting that you go out in a weighted cedar-strip and try to outdo Chuck and Bob. In fact, I recommend that you take a bit more time to complete the trip—eight days.

Canoe Lake is the starting line. To reach the access, turn north off Highway 60 toward the Portage Store. The gatehouse is down on the beach, near the parking area. From Canoe Lake, head north into Burnt Island Lake and either spend your first night here or portage 790 meters into Little Otterslide and Otterslide Lakes. (As Burnt Island is overused, I prefer going the extra stretch.)

From the northwest corner of Otterslide, the route continues north into Big Trout by way of Otterslide Creek using five flat but sometimes muddy portages (250, 390, 265, 730 and 105 m). Between the third and fourth portage, on the eastern side of the creek, is a scenic cliff; peregrine falcons were last seen nesting here in 1962.

The last of the portages on Otterslide Creek takes you to the right of a picture-perfect cascade. A short paddle from the put-in, up a narrow inlet, is the breathtaking Big Trout Lake.

Big Trout is a large lake, and if winds come up it may be difficult to paddle across to the northern end, so make sure you head out early. Cross the expanse of water to the 300-meter portage into Longer Lake, located just west of two small islands. Don't mistake the unmarked path on the opposite side of the islands as the portage; it leads into a small pond fed by twin creeks, and even though it will eventually take you into Longer Lake, the marked portage is much quicker.

There is a beautiful campsite on Longer

The Brent Run

A

N E W S

Grassy Bay

P790m

Burnt Island Lake

Caroline Island

🖐 PLACEFINDER
Appears at same spot on map on facing page.

McIntosh Lake

Bluejay Lake

Site of Minnesing Lodge

P200m

P1140m

Littledoe Lake

Bartlett Lake

P435m

Baby Joe Lake

Lost Joe Lake

P20m (165m in low water)

Little Joe Lake

Ink Lake

Tom Thomson Lake

Little Oxtongue River

East Arm

Tepee Lake

Joe Island

Camp Arowhon

Joe Lake

Same beach Alexander Murray stopped to build birchbark canoes, 1853

Site of Hotel Algonquin

P295m

Camp Ahmek

60

Tom Thomson cairn
Camp Wapomeo

Mowat Lodge

Tom Thomson's body found

S

Tom Thomson's upturned canoe found

Canoe Lake

F

Portage Store Road (from Hwy 60)

Legend:

- **S** Start
- **F** Finish
- - - - Route
- ●～● Portage
- **P975m** Portage length
- ▲ Campsite
- ⦀ Falls
- = Rapids/Swifts
- ━ Dam/Lift-over

0 1 2 3 4
km

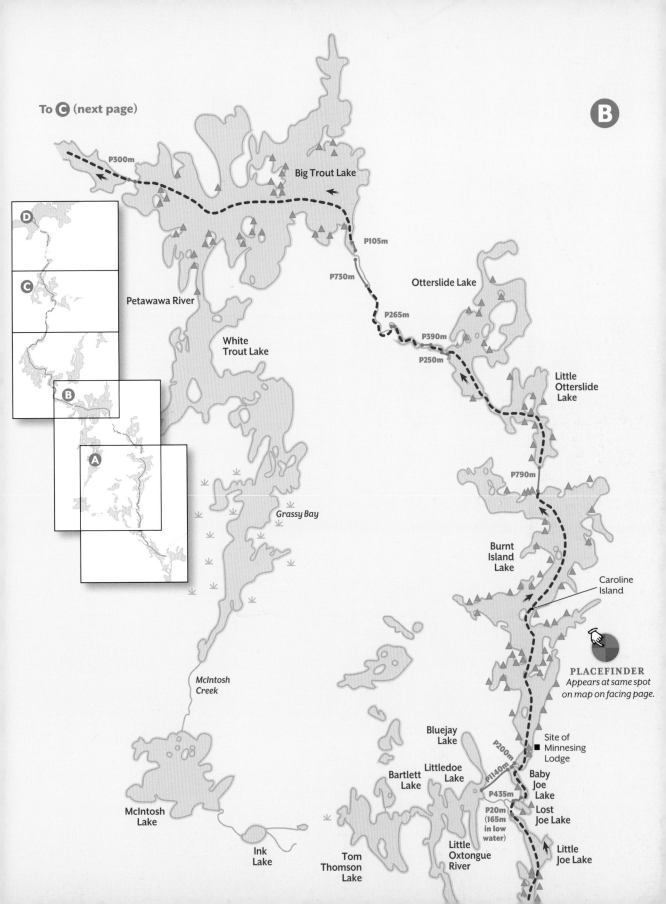

To **C** (next page)

B

P300m

Big Trout Lake

P105m

P730m

Otterslide Lake

D

C

B

A

Petawawa River

White
Trout Lake

P265m

P390m

P250m

Little
Otterslide
Lake

P790m

Grassy Bay

Burnt
Island
Lake

Caroline
Island

McIntosh
Creek

PLACEFINDER
*Appears at same spot
on map on facing page.*

Bluejay
Lake

Site of
Minnesing
Lodge

P200m

P1140m

Littledoe
Lake

Baby
Joe
Lake

Bartlett
Lake

P435m

Lost
Joe
Lake

P20m
(165m
in low
water)

McIntosh
Lake

Little
Joe
Lake

Ink
Lake

Tom
Thomson
Lake

Little
Oxtongue
River

The Brent Run (continued)

C

N
W E
S

Lynx Lake

Manta Lake

P1945m
P750m
P1105m

P365m
Catfish Rapids

Snowshoe Rapids
P320m
P90m
P420m
Cedar Rapids

Sunfish Lake

Petawawa River

PLACEFINDER
Appears at same spot on map on facing page.

Hogan Lake

Little Madawaska River
P685m

Osprey nest

Perley Lake

P155m

Burntroot Lake

Lake La Muir

Redpine Lake

P735m

P75m
P 40m

Redpine Bay

Barnet Depot Farm
(look for logging alligator on shore)

From B (previous page)

Petawawa River

Longer Lake

0 1 2 3 4
km

P300m

Big Trout Lake

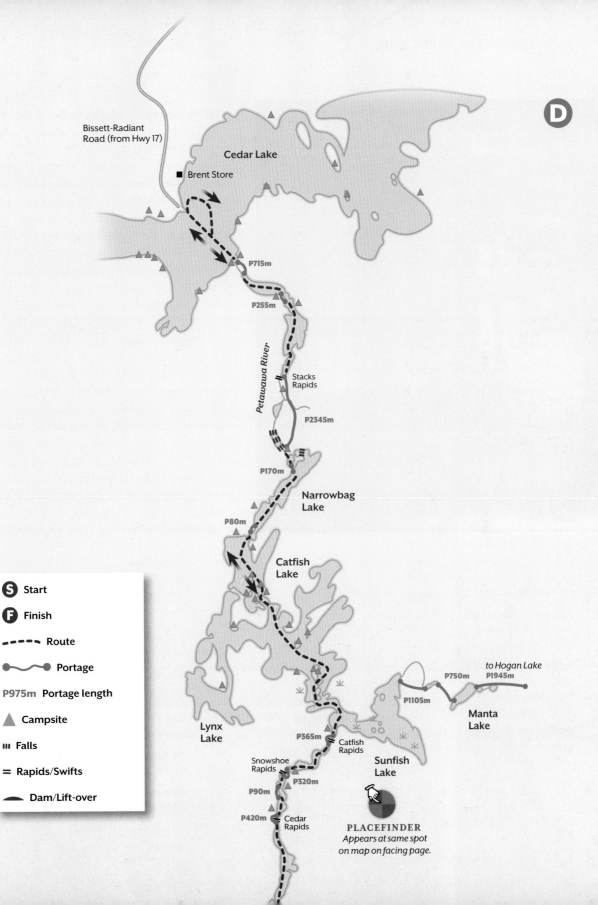

D

Bissett-Radiant
Road (from Hwy 17)

Cedar Lake

■ Brent Store

P715m

P255m

Petawawa River

Stacks
Rapids

P2345m

P170m

Narrowbag
Lake

P80m

Catfish
Lake

to Hogan Lake

P750m   P1945m

P1105m

Manta
Lake

Lynx
Lake

P365m

Catfish
Rapids

Sunfish
Lake

Snowshoe
Rapids

P320m

P90m

P420m

Cedar
Rapids

PLACEFINDER
*Appears at same spot
on map on facing page.*

S Start

F Finish

- - - Route

●—● Portage

P975m Portage length

▲ Campsite

⫶ Falls

= Rapids/Swifts

━ Dam/Lift-over

Lake, located at the mouth of the creek that flows out of the previously mentioned pond; however, it's next to impossible to find it unoccupied. I usually push on to Burntroot by way of two short portages (40 m and 75 m), both marked to the right of a double set of rapids. The second set is an easy swift, but running the first set of rapids is risky. The problem with portaging is that the trail is cluttered with poison ivy; it might be safer to wade or line your canoe down on the right.

From Burntroot, the route heads east down the Petawawa River to Cedar Lake (see Hogan Lake Loop for details). You should arrive on Cedar Lake by late afternoon on your fourth day and still have time to go for a soda and ice cream at the Brent Store before making camp.

To return, simply backtrack to Canoe Lake. But when you reach the finish line back at the Portage Store, don't expect a crowd cheering you on from the docks. After all, you've just completed the Brent Run in the worst time in the history of the race. Of course, it's not whether you win or lose, it's what you see along the way that counts!

LONGEST PORTAGE 2,345 meters

FEE An interior camping permit must be purchased for Algonquin Provincial Park.

ALTERNATIVE ACCESS The route could be accessed at the Brent side, beginning and ending at the Cedar Lake access point.

ALTERNATIVE ROUTE It's possible to do the route backward, beginning at Brent and ending on Canoe Lake.

OUTFITTERS
Algonquin Outfitters
R.R. 1, 1035 Algonquin Outfitters Road
Dwight, ON, P0A 1H0
1-800-469-4948
www.algonquinoutfitters.com

The Portage Store
Box 10009 Algonquin Park
Huntsville, ON, P1H 2H4
705-633-5622 (summer) or
705-789-3645 (winter)
www.portagestore.com

FOR MORE INFORMATION
Algonquin Provincial Park
705-633-5572 (information) and
1-888-668-7275 (reservations)
www.algonquinpark.on.ca

MAPS The Friends of Algonquin, Chrismar as well as Backroad Mapbooks have produced excellent maps. There is also a free online map available at www.algonquinmap.com.

TOPOGRAPHIC MAPS
31 E/10, 31 E/15, 31 E/16, 31 L/1 & 31 L/2

GPS COORDINATES
45.535103, -78.706791

Nipissing River Loop

🕐 8 to 10 days   33 portages   ●----● 180 km   **Due to the length of the route and long portages, moderate to advanced tripping experience is needed.**

It was mid-August, and Alana and I, eager to explore the isolated stretch of the Nipissing River between Allen Rapids and High Falls, had planned an extensive 10-day loop out from the Kawawaymog Lake (Round Lake) access point. It was the first time we had visited the north end of the park. The moment Alana and I entered the wood-framed gate-house, we noticed that the walls and counter tops were cluttered with snapshots—some of park wildlife, others of park regulars holding up record-breaking lake trout. The attendant, dressed in a wrinkled uniform and bright pink baseball cap, greeted us as long-lost relatives.

The warm welcome we received at the gatehouse that day helped set the mood for the rest of the trip—one of the best routes Algonquin has to offer.

To reach the Kawawaymog access point, located just outside the park's western border, turn east off Highway 11 on Ottawa Avenue, in South River. A 22-kilometer drive down a gravel road takes you to the parking area and gatehouse.

From the government docks, the route heads east. Cross the lake by following the left-hand shoreline. Next, travel down the Amable du Fond River, which marks the entry point to the park and links Kawawaymog Lake with North Tea Lake. This stretch of river is approximately 4 kilometers long and winds its way through tamarack swamp decorated with flowering pickerel weed and prickly rose.

Halfway along, the river splits. To the north, a narrow creek empties out of Pat Lake. Keep to the main route, which continues east. Soon after the fork, the river begins to straighten out; cedar and spruce take over the swamp tamarack, and lily pads grow out toward the center of the waterway.

Two portages (135 m and 255 m) are marked in succession just before the Amable du Fond River flows into North Tea Lake. This section can become quite busy. Alana and I were unaware of North Tea's popularity, and upon reaching the second portage, were shocked to see over a dozen beached canoes, their occupants all contending for room for their packs along the shore.

The route heads across North Tea and into the eastern inlet. Near the end of the inlet (Mangotasi Lake on the map), a series of three portages (240 m, 90 m and 140 m) are marked

Nipissing River Loop

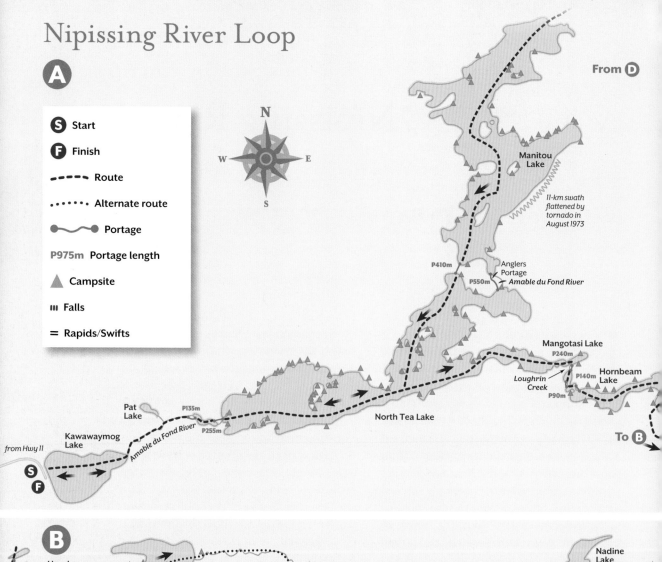

A

From **D**

S Start

F Finish

- - - Route

· · · · · Alternate route

●━━━● Portage

P975m Portage length

▲ Campsite

▥ Falls

= Rapids/Swifts

Manitou Lake

11-km swath flattened by tornado in August 1973

P410m

Anglers Portage

P550m *Amable du Fond River*

Mangotasi Lake

P240m

Loughrin Creek

P140m Hornbeam Lake

P90m

To **B**

Pat Lake

P135m

Amable du Fond River

P255m

North Tea Lake

from Hwy 11

Kawawaymog Lake

S
F

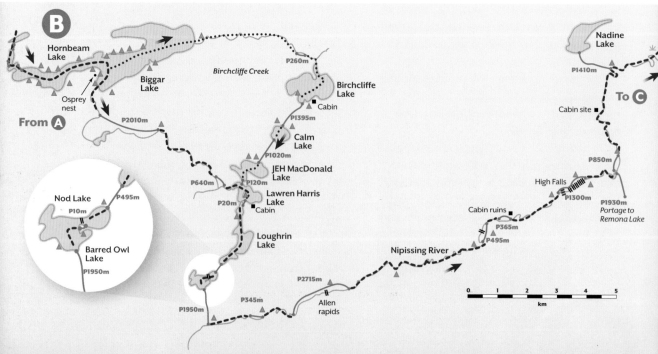

B

Nadine Lake

Hornbeam Lake

Biggar Lake

Birchcliffe Creek

P260m

Birchcliffe Lake

■ Cabin

P1410m

To **C**

Osprey nest

P2010m

P1395m

Calm Lake

P1020m

JEH MacDonald Lake

Cabin site ■

From **A**

P640m

P120m

P850m

P20m

Lawren Harris Lake

■ Cabin

High Falls

P1300m

P1930m *Portage to Remona Lake*

Loughrin Lake

Cabin ruins ■

P365m

P495m

Nipissing River

Nod Lake

P495m

P10m

Barred Owl Lake

P1950m

P1950m

P345m

P2715m

Allen rapids

0 1 2 3 4 5
km

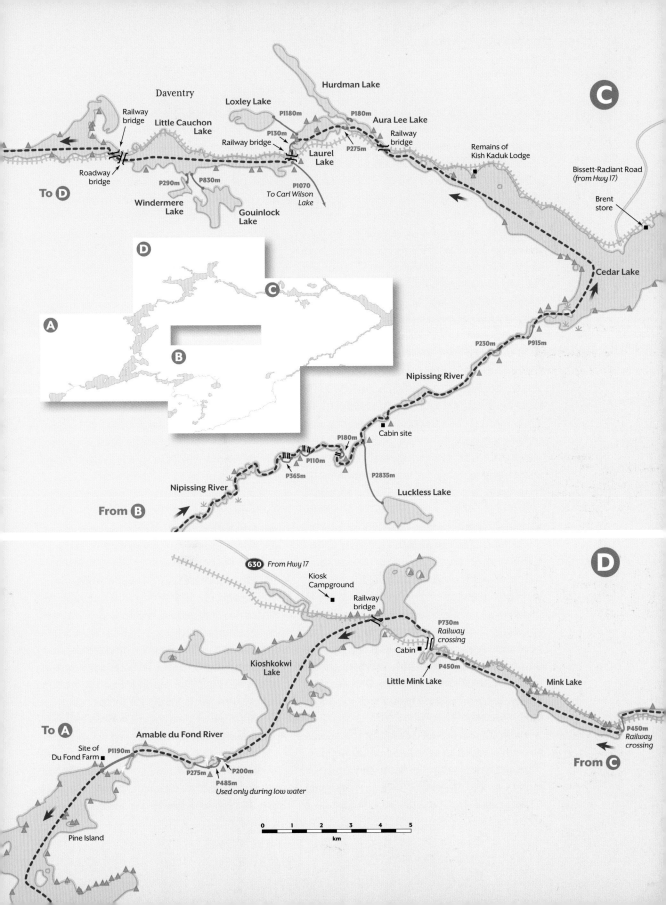

C

Daventry

Hurdman Lake

Loxley Lake

Little Cauchon Lake

Railway bridge

P1180m

P180m

Aura Lee Lake

P130m

Railway bridge

Laurel Lake

P275m

Railway bridge

Remains of Kish Kaduk Lodge

Bissett-Radiant Road *(from Hwy 17)*

Brent store

Roadway bridge

To D

P290m

P830m

Windermere Lake

Gouinlock Lake

P1070 *To Carl Wilson Lake*

D

C

A

B

Cedar Lake

P230m

P915m

Nipissing River

P180m

Cabin site

P365m

P110m

P2835m

Nipissing River

Luckless Lake

From B

D

630 *From Hwy 17*

Kiosk Campground

Railway bridge

P730m *Railway crossing*

Kioshkokwi Lake

Cabin

Little Mink Lake

P450m

Mink Lake

To A

Amable du Fond River

P450m *Railway crossing*

From C

Site of Du Fond Farm

P1190m

P275m

P200m

P485m *Used only during low water*

Pine Island

0 1 2 3 4 5
km

along the stream flowing out of Biggar Lake. The first and third portages are along the left bank, and the second is marked to the right of a stunted cascade that tumbles down into a small pond called Hornbeam Lake. Take note that the section between the second and third portage can become a rock garden if water levels are low.

Biggar Lake is a good place to camp for your first night out. The campsites on the west end, tucked away behind strands of heavily browsed cedar, are disappointing. But farther east, a number of prime tent sites are marked atop rock outcrops, directly opposite a breathtaking rock face, near the mouth of Loughrin Creek.

From Biggar Lake, the route heads south to the Nipissing River by way of either Loughrin or Birchcliffe creek. Some canoeists choose to wade up the sandy-bottomed Birchcliffe Creek provided water levels are low, as Loughrin can become a horrific mud bath. This will take you past the old ranger's cabin on the southwest shore of Birchcliffe Lake (see map for details). In general, though, Loughrin Creek is a more direct route, with swampy sections providing excellent opportunities to spot moose.

The entrance to Loughrin Creek is at the south end of Biggar's central bay. A short paddle up the creek takes you to the first portage along the narrow stream. This 2,010-meter trail, marked to the left, is relatively flat at first. Halfway along, however, two steep slopes slow your progress to a snail's pace. At the base of the second hill, the path meets back up with the creek and follows it along for a good distance, passing under gigantic white pine rooted along the bank.

From the put-in, the creek twists and turns through a wide stretch of swamp and eventually narrows at a stand of black spruce. Here, you're forced to drag the canoe over abandoned beaver dams and jagged rocks to the next

portage—an easy 640 meters across a logging road and into Lawren Harris Lake (named after the Group of Seven member, who painted in the park between 1914 and 1916).

At the south end of Lawren Harris Lake are the remains of an old ranger's cabin. The roof caved in a few years back, and now young birch and aspen trees have sprouted up through the center of the weathered shack.

The route continues into Loughrin Lake over a 20-meter portage, which passes near the cabin and to the left of a logjam. It then heads to the southwestern inlet, where a 495-meter portage takes you over a steep rise leading to Barred Owl Lake. Directly across from the put-in is a short lift-over into Nod Lake, and then, to the south, a 1,950-meter portage takes you to the tea-colored water of the Nipissing River. The trail is lengthy, but relatively flat, except near the put-in, where it makes a dramatic turn to the left and heads up a steep slope.

A campsite is marked at the end of the 1,950-meter portage. It's a poor site, though, and when Alana and I reached the spot, we decided to push on downstream to camp at the end of the 345-meter portage marked to the left of a rustic dam. Chilled from a long day of paddling and portaging in the rain, we cooked up a quick supper and headed into the tent early, with mugs of hot cocoa and a deck of cards. Three games of cribbage later, the cocoa kicked in and we both had to go out for a pee. When we unzipped the front tent flap, however, we came face to kneecap with a gigantic bull moose standing directly beside our flimsy nylon tent, browsing on the alder thicket on which our wet clothes hung to dry. For the sake of our bladders, we quietly slipped out the back flap. On our return, the only evidence of our visitor was a steaming moose patty blocking the entrance to the tent and a pair of socks missing from the alder bush.

We were on the river early the next morning, slowly drifting under the immense pines that spread out over the narrow waterway. By the time the hot sun chased off the looming mist, we began to hear the rush of Allen Rapids.

This stretch of rock-strewn rapids could probably be run, with care; the only problem is that it's impossible to scout from the 2,715-meter portage that runs along the left bank. Your best bet is to carry your gear three-quarters of the way down the trail, up to where a campsite is marked along the river. From there to the designated put-in is a series of simple swifts that can be easily navigated.

Approximately two hours downstream from Allen Rapids are two more portages (495 m and 365 m). The first is marked to the right of a scenic falls, and the second, equipped with a steep gravel slope at the take-out, is marked to the left and leads through a field littered with the remnants of several cabins left over from the logging era. The river spreads itself out from here, the soft current sifting through sedge and bulrush before eventually being pinched between canyon walls and tumbling over the twin ledges of High Falls.

The 1,300-meter High Falls portage, marked to the left, follows dangerously close to the cascade and has a steep take-out. With the rugged terrain comes a magnificent view, especially halfway along the trail. A picture-perfect campsite, situated on the south shore, is available at the base of the falls.

Downstream from High Falls, the river briefly stretches out again and then makes a dramatic turn north before another stretch of whitewater. Portages are marked on both sides of the river here. Be sure to take the 850-meter trail located along the left bank.

Once past the trail leading into Nadine Lake, the river heads east again and begins to meander uncontrollably through spruce lowlands. From here it takes approximately three and a half hours to reach the next series of portages. The first two (365 m and 110 m) are marked to the right, and farther downstream, the third portage (180 m) is marked to the left. One or two campsites are marked at each portage, but none compare to the scenic spots upstream at High Falls, which you should consider if you find yourself at the falls late in the afternoon.

What remains of the Nipissing before Cedar Lake is more of an elongated lake than a gurgling river, with only two portages not far upstream from the river's mouth. The first (230 m) is to the left of a runnable swift, and the second (915 m) is to the right of an old logging dam.

A weedy delta marks the end of your journey down the Nipissing, its pine-clad banks and tea-colored water quickly being replaced by the expanse of Cedar Lake. To celebrate your arrival at the halfway mark, a trip to the Brent Store, situated directly across from the river's mouth, is in order.

After a quick paddle across Little Cedar Lake the next morning, the route continues up a shallow creek and under a cement railway bridge to Aura Lee Lake. The crossing is the first of six spots where the route travels either under or over the now-abandoned CN line. The last train came through here on November 25, 1995, thanks mostly to the dedicated opposition of the Canadian Wildlands League. But our trip was four months before the closing date; so Alana and I were forced to put up with this noisy intrusion to the park's environment (mind you, both of us, after cursing the noise of the locomotive as it passed by, still instinctively waved at the conductor like a couple of schoolchildren).

There are two portages marked at the far end of Aura Lee Lake. Keep close to the left-hand shoreline and take the 275-meter trail that exits into Laurel Lake. Once across Laurel, continue to the left and take the steep, 130-meter portage into Little Cauchon Lake, marked to the right of a picturesque cascade.

A two-hour paddle up Little Cauchon and Cauchon lakes, and an easy, 450-meter portage remain before you make camp on Mink Lake.

The next day, two portages (450 m and 730 m) take you to the eastern end of Kioshkokwi Lake (*kioshkokwi* is Algonquin for "gull"). From the weedy put-in, stay close to the left-hand shoreline until you come to the last railway bridge en route. Once you reach the opposite end of the trestle, a 6-kilometer paddle west across the expanse of Kioshkokwi Lake will take you to the first of a double set of rapids at the base of the Amable du Fond River.

The ease of the trip upstream depends highly on water levels. In normal conditions, a series of three portages—200 and 275 meters, marked to the left, and a surprisingly easy 1,190 meters, marked to the right—takes you directly into Manitou Lake. During a dry spell, however, an extended 485-meter portage, marked between the first and second portages, may be necessary.

The winds on Manitou can be treacherous; so, when Alana and I reached the lake and found it to be surprisingly calm, we took full advantage. We paddled to the southernmost end, portaged over the steep 410-meter portage into North Tea Lake and finally called it quits on the first island campsite.

LONGEST PORTAGE 2,715 meters

FEE An interior camping permit must be purchased for Algonquin Provincial Park.

ALTERNATIVE ACCESS The route can also be accessed at Brent's Cedar Lake access point or the Kiosk access point on Kioshkokwi Lake.

ALTERNATIVE ROUTE It's possible to cut the route in half but you would have to organize a shuttle to the town of Brent on Cedar Lake through the local outfitters in South River.

OUTFITTERS
Algonquin Outfitters
R.R. 1, 1035 Algonquin Outfitters Road
Dwight, ON, P0A 1H0
1-800-469-4948
www.algonquinoutfitters.com

Voyageur Quest
22 Belcourt Road
Toronto, ON, M4S 2T9
416-486-3605 or 1-800-794-9660
www.voyageurquest.com

Voyageur Outfitting
Box 69
South River, ON, P0A 1X0
707-386-2813 or 1-877-837-8889
www.voyageuroutfitting.com

Northern Edge Algonquin
100 Ottawa Avenue
South River, ON, P0A 1X0
1-800-953-3343
www.northernedgealgonquin.com

FOR MORE INFORMATION
Algonquin Provincial Park
705-633-5572 (information) and
1-888-668-7275 (reservations)
www.algonquinpark.on.ca

MAPS The Friends of Algonquin, Chrismar as well as Backroad Mapbooks have produced excellent maps. There is also a free online map available at www.algonquinmap.com.

TOPOGRAPHIC MAPS
31 E/14, 31 E/15, 31 E/16, 31 L1, 31 L/2 & 31 L/3

GPS COORDINATES
45.922130, -79.184285

Barron Canyon

🕐 2 to 3 days   🚶 19 portages   ●----● 24 km   **The series of portages from St. Andrews Lake and Barron Canyon can be demanding.**

THE BARRON RIVER, named after Augustus Barron, a member of the House of Commons, is clearly the gem of Algonquin Park's east side. The waterway is lined with steep walls of hard, crystalline rock that tower far above the water (300 feet at their highest point), isolating the river and helping to defend its solitude.

The cliffs—sculpted by the waters of historic Lake Algonquin some 11,000 years ago, toward the end of the last Ice Age—dominate the primitive landscape. It took only a few centuries for the incredible volume of glacial meltwater, once equivalent to a thousand Niagara Falls, to retreat northward, from what geologists labeled the Fossmill Outlet, to a lower geological fault—the Lake Nipissing-Mattawa channel—reducing the Barron River to a mere trickle.

To reach the canyon (Access Point 22 on the Algonquin Park map), turn left off Highway 17 (approximately 9 km west of Pembroke) onto County Road 26. Then, after 300 meters, take the first right at the Achray Road and drive 26 kilometers to Sand Lake Gate, at the park boundary. Once you have received your interior camping permit (you may want to

phone ahead to reserve), continue for another 19 kilometers and make a left on a side road leading to the Achray Campground on the southeast tip of Grand Lake. On your way to Achray, you may want to make a quick stop at the Barron Canyon Trail (8 km before the turnoff to the Achray Campground). The 1.5-kilometer loop trail provides an excellent view—from the canyon's north rim—of your planned route.

If you arrive late in the day, the campground on Grand Lake is an excellent place to spend your first night, and if time permits, after dinner you can take a quick paddle to the east end of the lake to explore one of Tom Thomson's sketching sites.

Head out from the Achray Campground and portage 30 meters into Stratton Lake. Then, after paddling the full length of Stratton, portage 45 meters into St. Andrews Lake. It's best to set up a base camp here and then make the visit to the Barron River Canyon in a day trip. To reach the canyon from St. Andrews Lake, take the 550-meter portage into High Falls Lake. The trail is marked in St. Andrews' northeastern bay. From the northern tip of High Falls Lake, stay with the river

Barron Canyon

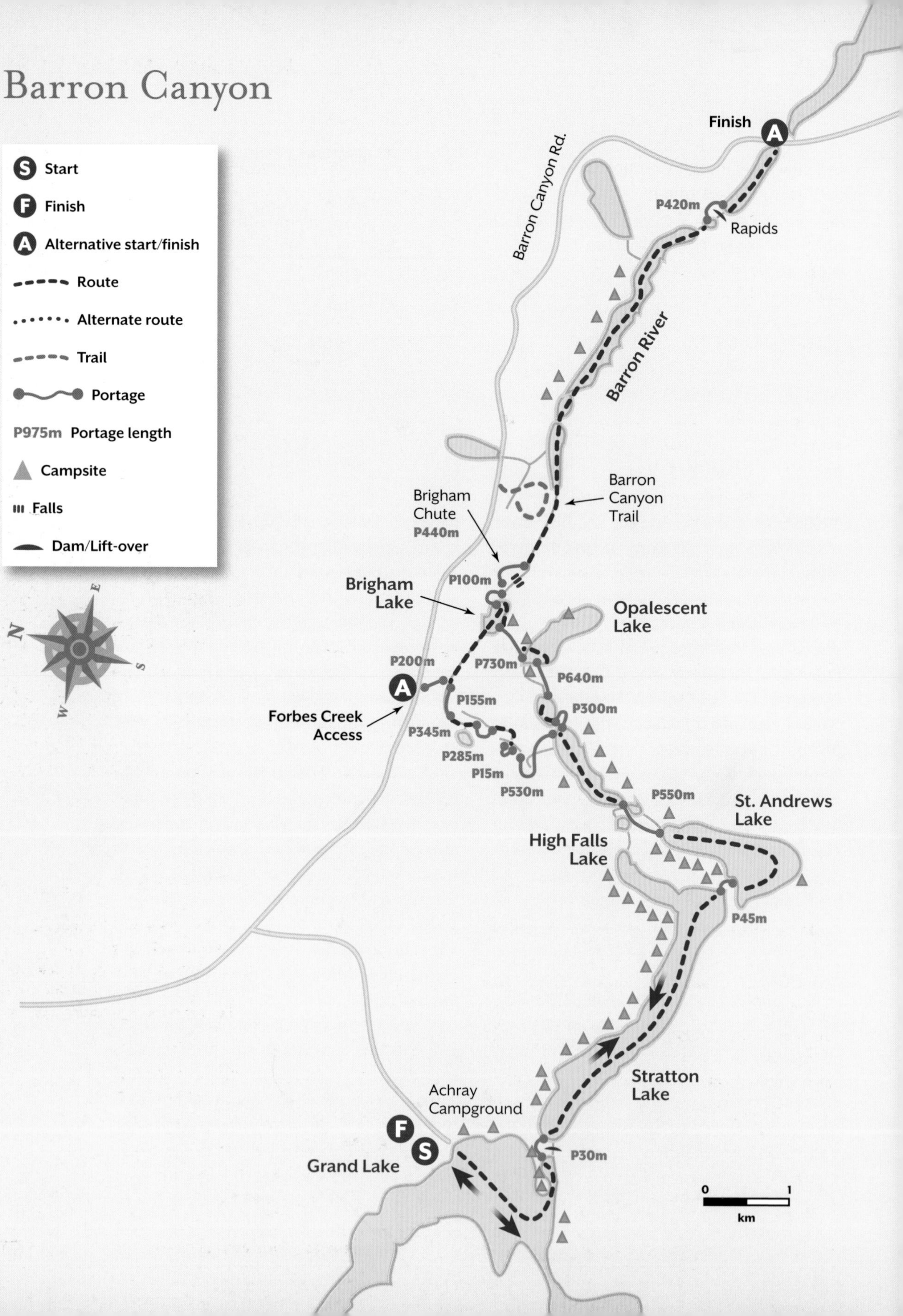

Legend

S Start

F Finish

A Alternative start/finish

- - - - Route

· · · · · Alternate route

- - - - Trail

●～● Portage

P975m Portage length

▲ Campsite

▥ Falls

▬ Dam/Lift-over

Finish **A**

Barron Canyon Rd.

P420m

Rapids

Barron River

Barron Canyon Trail

Brigham Chute **P440m**

P100m

Brigham Lake

Opalescent Lake

P200m

A

P730m

P640m

Forbes Creek Access

P155m

P300m

P345m

P285m

P15m

P530m

P550m

St. Andrews Lake

High Falls Lake

P45m

Stratton Lake

Achray Campground

F **S**

P30m

Grand Lake

0   1

km

by following the 530-meter portage to the left. Six more portages (the longest being 345 m, and all marked on the left bank except the fifth) lead you into Brigham Lake. Directly across the small pond, two more portages are marked to the left (100 m and 440 m), taking you around the Brigham Chute.

What lies ahead is spectacular: precipitous cliffs, with bright orange lichen (xanthoria) and lime-loving encrusted saxifrage rooted in the damp seepage areas. The canyon appears primeval, and it is easy to imagine that you have traveled back in geological time.

From here, the river is in no great hurry, and you can drift slowly between the granite walls, following the soaring ravens and red tailed hawks that nest high up on the rock cliffs. When it's time to head back to base camp, rather than lugging your canoe up the sequence of cascades, take the 730-meter portage, on the southwestern shore of Brigham Lake, into Opalescent Lake. Then head directly across to a 640-meter portage, followed by a short 300-meter portage, to reach High Falls Lake.

LONGEST PORTAGE 730 meters

FEE An interior camping permit must be purchased for Algonquin Provincial Park.

ALTERNATIVE ACCESS Forbes Creek access can be used to reach the Barron River itself more directly.

ALTERNATIVE ROUTE A much shorter trip can be had on Barron River itself by making use of the Forbes Creek access.

OUTFITTERS

Algonquin Portage Limited
1352 Barron Canyon Road
Pembroke, ON, K8A 6W7
613-735-1795
www.algonquinportage.com

FOR MORE INFORMATION
Algonquin Provincial Park
705-633-5572 (information) and
1-888-668-7275 (reservations)
www.algonquinpark.on.ca

MAPS The Friends of Algonquin, Chrismar as well as Backroad Mapbooks have produced excellent maps. There is also a free online map available at www.algonquinmap.com.

TOPOGRAPHIC MAPS 31 F/13

GPS COORDINATES
45.866684, -77.757461

Hogan Lake Loop

🕐 5 days   🧍 20 portages   ●– – –● 74 km   **The route has a couple of long portages where moderate tripping skills would be an asset.**

AFTER DRIVING THE dusty, washboard road leading into Brent, you'd think that town residents would want the park staff to fix it up a bit to boost business. But according to Jake Pigeon, the operator of the Brent Store, "If they fill in all those potholes, all the riffraff would come driving in and the canoeing up here would be the shits!"

To reach the remote access point, turn south off Highway 17 onto Bissett-Radiant Road, just west of Deux Rivières. Drive for 16 kilometers to the park gatehouse, at the fork in the road. You must pick up your interior camping permit here before continuing to the right for another 24 kilometers. The put-in is on the opposite side of the tracks, before Brent's main street. If you plan on arriving late in the day, you can use the campground adjacent to the access point.

The first day out is the hardest going. From the docks at the put-in, the route heads directly across Cedar Lake to a 715-meter portage marked to the left of where the Petawawa River empties out into the lake. Halfway along, the trail heads up two short hills and then forks. The side trail to the right leads to a dramatic waterfall, but the main portage continues to the left, ending just past a wooden cross that marks the gravesite of A. Corbeil, a logger who drowned at the base of the cascade while on a log drive in June 1888.

After a short paddle up a wide, weedy stretch of the river, another portage leads around another set of falls. The steep, 255-meter trail works its way to the right of the scenic cascade. The view is spectacular, but upstream there is an even more impressive stretch of whitewater called Stacks Rapids. A 2,345-meter portage—the longest en route—is marked to the left at the base of the rapids.

The river twists to the left, tucking itself under a low wooden bridge and into Narrowbag Lake. Your route to the lake, however, is somewhat different. From the put-in of the 2,345-meter portage, head directly across into a large back bay. Then, following the left-hand shoreline, locate the marked portage (170 m) leading up and over a timber-covered hill.

At the far end of Narrowbag—a rather inelegant name that does no justice to this pretty lake—is the last portage of the day, leading into Catfish Lake. The take-out of the 80-meter trail is marked to the right of a swift littered with debris left behind from past log

drives. A much more impressive logging arti-fact than the half-decayed log chute, however, is Catfish Lake's marooned alligator, located on the second of three islands clustered together at the north end.

Invented by John Ceburn West in 1889, the alligator was a powerful steam-driven tug capable of dragging booms of up to 60,000 logs for 10 hours on less than a cord of wood. It also had the unique ability to winch itself overland.

Both the upper and lower sections of Catfish Lake have excellent campsites. My preference, however, is the lower section, with my favorite site being directly east of the central island and south of Turtle Rock (a high rock ledge where Natives once came to worship).

An upstream battle on the Petawawa contin-ues the next day, beginning at the marshy south end of Catfish Lake. Soon, a short paddle against the slow-moving current, which gurgles past cedar-lined banks and clumps of sedge, brings you to where Cuckoo Creek empties out of Sunfish Lake, to the south. Here, the loop portion of the route begins.

It's best to travel in a counterclockwise direction here, remaining on the Petawawa and heading up toward Burntroot Lake. But just upstream from where the small tributary flows in from the south you'll find a number of rapids.

The first is Catfish Rapids, with a 365-meter portage marked to the right, followed shortly after by Snowshoe Rapids, with a shorter,

Hogan Lake Loop

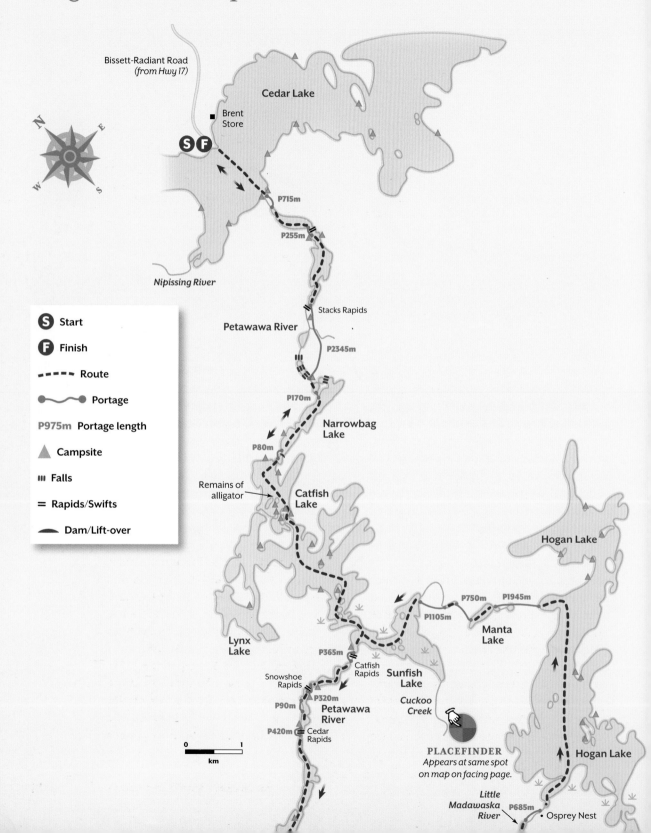

Bissett-Radiant Road
(from Hwy 17)

Cedar Lake

Brent Store

S **F**

P715m

P255m

Nipissing River

Stacks Rapids

Petawawa River

P2345m

P170m

Narrowbag Lake

P80m

Remains of alligator

Catfish Lake

S Start

F Finish

- - - - Route

●━━● Portage

P975m Portage length

▲ Campsite

⫼ Falls

═ Rapids/Swifts

━ Dam/Lift-over

Lynx Lake

Hogan Lake

P750m P1945m

P1105m

Manta Lake

P365m

Catfish Rapids

Snowshoe Rapids

P320m

Sunfish Lake

Cuckoo Creek

P90m

Petawawa River

P420m ═ Cedar Rapids

PLACEFINDER
Appears at same spot on map on facing page.

Hogan Lake

0   1
km

Little Madawaska River P685m

• Osprey Nest

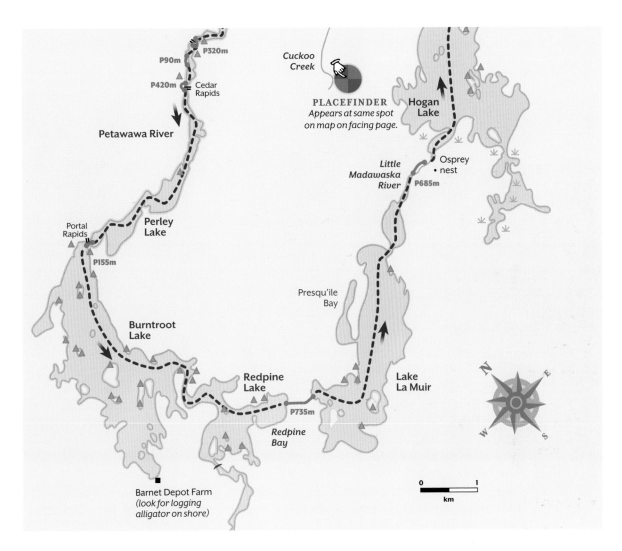

320-meter portage marked to the left. After Snowshoe Rapids, past the marked portage into North Cuckoo Lake, is a small, unnamed rapid with a 90-meter portage to the right. It may be possible to avoid this portage altogether and simply pole your canoe up the quick swift.

The last obstacle in this series of whitewater is Cedar Rapids. The flat but rocky portage (420 m) is marked to the right and heads into long, narrow Perley Lake. What remains before you make camp on Burntroot Lake, a lake randomly dotted with island campsites, is a 5-kilometer paddle across Perley Lake and a quick, 155-meter portage marked to the left of Portal Rapids (named after Lord Portal, a wartime marshal of the Royal Air Force, who visited the lake on a fishing trip in 1946). For a time, between 1964 and 1973, Burntroot Lake was also called Portal Lake. It eventually went back to its former title, derived from both Joseph Bouchette's 1846 map of Upper

Canada, upon which the lake was labeled Burnt Lake, and Dickson's 1886 account of an extensive burn site along a hillside to the north. The name was changed to Burntroot in 1931, however, to help distinguish it from Burnt Island Lake to the south.

The second day is somewhat shorter than the first, and you'll probably make camp on Burntroot Lake by mid-afternoon, giving you ample time to paddle down to the far end of the southwestern bay and explore the site of the Barnet Depot Farm. Not much remains of the original buildings, first occupied back in 1882 to keep a fresh supply of produce available for the neighboring logging camps.

But an alligator, much more intact than the tug left out on Catfish Lake, rests up along the shoreline here.

Your destination for day three is Hogan Lake, to the east. The route leaves Burntroot, heading southeast, all the way down into Redpine Bay. Here, a 735-meter portage works itself over a steep rise and into picturesque Lake La Muir.

Once on Lake La Muir, keep close to the north shore and paddle east toward the weedy shallows where the Little Madawaska begins. The waterway is lined with fallen dead cedar along most of its length, and just before a 685-meter portage to the left of where the river drops over a rock shelf is an active osprey nest.

From the muddy put-in of the 685-meter portage, the narrow river twists itself through a cattail marsh and then flushes out into Hogan Lake. Hogan is one of Algonquin's natural wonders. Forested hills crowd the shoreline, and an extensive marshland to the south hosts countless moose sightings. Peregrine falcons have even been sighted recently, nesting on an impressive granite wall to the east of the first large island. The wilderness appeal of the large lake is enhanced by a surprising lack of campsites (of course, this may not be such an appealing attribute if you arrive at the lake late in the day and find all the sites occupied).

After enjoying a night of seclusion, travel north back toward Catfish Lake. The first portage (1,945 m), located in a bay three-quarters of the way along the lake, is a rough trail, especially halfway along, where you have to clamber up a steep incline. At the crest of the hill, note the countless bear-claw marks left on the thin, seamless bark of the beech trees. These wounds are made when the bear shimmies up the trunk to get at the crop of beechnuts. If you take a closer look, you might see a "bear nest" in the crotch of the tree, where the bruin pulls in branches while feeding, breaking the limbs as they gorge.

After a short paddle across Manta Lake, you'll come to another portage (750 m), marked to the right of a small creek. It is flatter than the previous portage, but because of the lack of trail maintenance in the area lately, it can be just as rough.

Only a trip across the pond-like Newt Lake and an easy, 1,105-meter portage beginning under a giant white pine remain. A downward slope marks the end of the portage and the entrance to Sunfish Lake.

Two channels are marked to the west on Sunfish Lake. Take the one to the right, and work your way through the swampy maze back to the Petawawa River. The loop ends here, and it's a short paddle downstream to Catfish Lake, where you'll spend your last night out.

The next day it's downstream all the way from Catfish to Cedar. Of course, you'll have to endure the same lengthy portages you had to contend with on your first day out, as well as the long, bumpy drive back to the highway.

LONGEST PORTAGE 2,345 meters

FEE An interior camping permit must be purchased for Algonquin Provincial Park.

ALTERNATIVE ACCESS None

ALTERNATIVE ROUTE None

OUTFITTERS
Algonquin Outfitters
R.R. 1, 1035 Algonquin Outfitters Road
Dwight, ON, P0A 1H0
1-800-469-4948
www.algonquinoutfitters.com

FOR MORE INFORMATION
Algonquin Provincial Park
705-633-5572 (information) and
1-888-668-7275 (reservations)
www.algonquinpark.on.ca

MAPS The Friends of Algonquin, Chrismar as well as Backroad Mapbooks have produced excellent maps. There is also a free online map available at www.algonquinmap.com.

TOPOGRAPHIC MAPS
31 L/1, 31 L/2, 31 E/15 & 31 E/16

GPS COORDINATES
46.022853, -78.486600

ALGONQUIN

Kingscote/Scorch Lake

⊙ 2 to 3 days   6 portages   ●----● 22 km   **This is an easy trip except for a couple of long portages where some canoe-tripping skills would be an asset.**

SOMETIMES THE BEST places to paddle are right in your own backyard. Algonquin Park's Kingscote/Scorch Lake route is a great example. I paddle Algonquin a lot. Most of my trips there, however, start off from the north end, even though the southern access is just over an hour's drive away from my home in Peterborough. I'm not sure why I commonly ignore the more easy-to-get-to routes. Maybe it's because most paddlers think that the best places to travel are usually the most difficult to reach—which is most likely true, except when it comes to Algonquin's Scorch Lake. Its scenic splendor equals or even surpasses the majority of the park's more northern routes.

To reach the access, take Highway 648, 1.6 kilometers east of the village of Harcourt. Follow the Elephant Lake Road north for 12 kilometers and before turning left into the Kingscote Lake Road, pick up your permit at Pine Grove Point Lodge and Campground on your right. Then, go back to the Kingscote Lake Road and keep to that road for 7 kilometers and turn right to the access point.

Kingscote is a relatively new access point for Algonquin Park. Historically, there was

a cottage housed here, but in 1999–2000, under the Living Legacy Program, the Nature Conservancy of Canada helped Ontario Parks purchase and develop a mini campground at the south end of Kingscote. I've stayed at the campground and quite enjoyed the less-crowded drive-in or walk-in sites. The area boasts some incredible mountain-bike trails and a prime hiking trail along the York River. However, I much prefer paddling farther into the interior, north of Kingscote.

The area gained more protection due to the famous Kingscote "silver" lake trout. The trout differ from the common lake trout found throughout Algonquin by their uniform body color devoid of the common white spots or vermiculations. It's quite an amazing story, actually. These native subspecies of lake trout have somehow survived six decades of supplemental stocking. Basically, the local fish have adapted and outdone the captive species. It's a clear sign of biodiversity—something that desperately needs to be protected. Over time, Kingscote Lake has reduced its "cold water" habitat, and with it the high oxygen content. Rather than dying off, however, these trout adapted to the changing habitat. Some

Kingscote/Scorch Lake

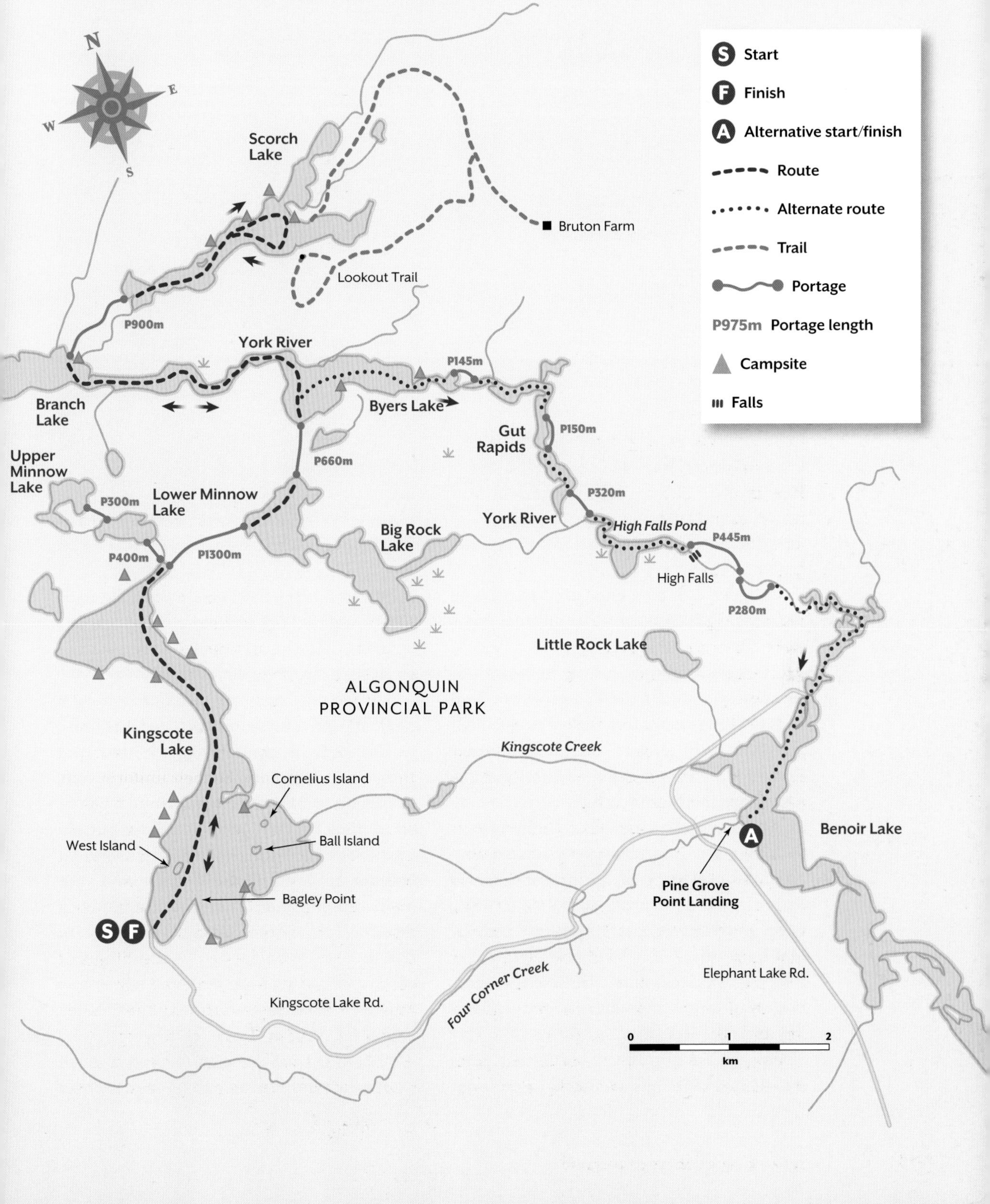

N **E** **S** **W**

Scorch Lake

■ Bruton Farm

Lookout Trail

P900m

York River

Branch Lake

P145m

Byers Lake

Gut Rapids

P150m

P660m

York River

P320m

High Falls Pond

P445m

High Falls

P280m

Upper Minnow Lake

P300m

Lower Minnow Lake

P400m

P1300m

Big Rock Lake

Little Rock Lake

ALGONQUIN PROVINCIAL PARK

Kingscote Creek

Kingscote Lake

Cornelius Island

Ball Island

West Island

Bagley Point

Benoir Lake

A

Pine Grove Point Landing

S **F**

Four Corner Creek

Kingscote Lake Rd.

Elephant Lake Rd.

S	Start	
F	Finish	
A	Alternative start/finish	
	----	Route
	····	Alternate route
	----	Trail
	●—●	Portage
	P975m	Portage length
	▲	Campsite
	⫶⫶⫶	Falls

0   1   2
km

fisheries experts have compared this to the difference between aurora trout and brook trout. It's a rarity for sure.

A few prime campsites exist on Kingscote, especially on the far northeastern shoreline. In general, it's not a busy lake, even though 20-horsepower motors are still allowed. However, I found that the majority of camp-sites on the lake were overly shaded in among a thick canopy of cedar.

The group I paddled with on the last outing, film friends Kip Spidell and Ashley McBride, was able to get to the access point early, and we were across Kingscote Lake by mid-morning.

The first portage of our trip was a lengthy one. It measures 1,300 meters and leads to Big Rock Lake. About a quarter of the way along, another trail forked to the left, lead-ing to Lower and Upper Minnow lakes—both

providing fair brook trout fishing. The rest of the trail to Big Rock had more than a few wet spots along the way and ended with a marshy stretch where it was impossible to keep our feet dry. And to add to the punishment, a good hill had to be dealt with near the end as well.

Most of Big Rock Lake is to the south, but our route went north and it wasn't a long paddle up to the top of Big Rock Lake before we reached the next portage. The Big Rock to Byers Lake portage measured 660 meters and had a good downhill slope to contend with (and an uphill slope to contend with on our return). It was here we stopped for lunch—a site that was good enough to stay the night at, but we had planned on going all the way to Scorch Lake, so we continued on up the York River.

Here, the York River resembles a small lake and it's unnoticeable that you're even on a river after leaving Byers Lake. Our group even second-guessed our whereabouts at one point due to Branch Lake looking more like a widening of York River than an actual lake. The good news, however, is that we lucked out on the way up the York by coming across a bull moose grazing in a marshy bay.

It took a good chunk of paddling for us to reach the portage leading to Scorch Lake. Scorch Lake is a real gem. We camped at a great site, on a rocky point toward the southeast corner of the lake. We were also the only ones there for the two days we base camped—a rarity in busy Algonquin Park. Our site even overlooked Scorch Lake Mountain, which we planned to ascend the next day.

We had an early supper and went to bed the moment it got dark. It had been a long day en route to Scorch Lake, a trip that should have been attempted in two short days rather than one long one. But by pushing all the way to Scorch Lake, we had a full day to climb the summit trail and overlook the incredible landscape we had traveled through to get there.

After a breakfast of flapjacks, bacon and a double dose of strong coffee, we all headed to the southeast corner of the lake to begin the hike to the top of Scorch Lake Mountain. The trailhead was easily found, tucked away in the far corner of the bay. Before taking the main path to the peak, we kept left where the trail forked and visited the old Bruton Farm. It wasn't a long hike and took us through some mature stands of maple and beech. An old stone fence marked the beginning of the old homestead and the forest trail continued across a logging road to the centerpiece of the farm. Not much was left of the farmhouse, four barns, blacksmith's shop and numerous smaller outbuildings, but it was an intriguing place and a good excuse to hike through some prime hardwood.

On our return we scrambled up the mountain trail, which went straight up a steep slope almost immediately and ended up on top with a moderate loop circling the crest. The viewing platform was a simple slab of rock covered in slippery moss. This was obviously not a well-visited spot. The view was definitely worth the 1-kilometer climb, but hordes of biting blackflies shortened our stay. We had returned to camp by late afternoon and all agreed that Kingscote/Scorch Lake makes up one of the best nearby paddle routes Algonquin has to offer.

LONGEST PORTAGE 1,300 meters

FEE An interior camping permit must be purchased for Algonquin Provincial Park.

ALTERNATIVE ACCESS None

ALTERNATIVE ROUTE It's possible to return by way of the York River and take out by the Road 10 bridge. A shuttle is needed to get back to the Kingscote access point.

OUTFITTERS
Trips and Trails Adventure Outfitting
258 Hastings Street N
Bancroft, ON, K0L 1C0
613-332-1969

FOR MORE INFORMATION
Algonquin Provincial Park
705-633-5572 (information) and
1-888-668-7275 (reservations)
www.algonquinpark.on.ca

MAPS The Friends of Algonquin, Chrismar as well as Backroad Mapbooks have produced excellent maps. There is also a free online map available at www.algonquinmap.com.

TOPOGRAPHIC MAPS 31 E/8

GPS COORDINATES
45.188469, -78.232080

Oxtongue River

 1 to 2 days   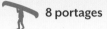 8 portages   ●----● 38 km   **Some knowledge of running rapids is required.**

THE OXTONGUE RIVER runs along the north side of Highway 60 and flows out of Algonquin's southwest boundary. Over a hundred years ago this river was a busy place. In 1826 Lieutenant Henry Briscoe became the first recorded explorer to travel it. He searched for a military route between Lake Huron and the Ottawa River because the government of Canada was growing concerned over Americans threatening the shipping areas along the southern border. Government surveyors Alexander Shirreff and David Thompson also traveled the Oxtongue in 1829 and 1837, respectively, to map the waterway as a possible navigational canal. They were followed in 1853 by Alexander Murray, the first chief ranger of Algonquin, and the well-known artist Tom Thomson, who camped along the Oxtongue during his first visit to Algonquin in 1912.

The Oxtongue was definitely a main canoe route, but at present you will be hard-pressed to spot another paddler traveling the river, especially the lower half that exits the park's southwest corner and forms a separate waterway park. I'm not sure why; the lack of use may have something to do with the river's proximity to Highway 60 (traffic can be faintly heard but not seen along some sections) or the assumption by some canoeists and kayakers that Algonquin Provincial Park has more to offer. Consequently, the river's relative quietness makes it a perfect weekend retreat for the avid paddler.

I spend three or four weekends per season traveling the Oxtongue River, sometimes in early spring or late fall to photograph moose (it is one of the best places in Algonquin to sight moose), but mostly I find myself traveling the river in the early part of the summer, when the waterway becomes almost dream-like. I'll spend an entire day floating down a gentle current, taking time to listen to the brook trout slurp bugs from the water's surface or count the number of wood turtles sunbathing on half-submerged logs. My favorite pastime, though, is to simply gawk at all the damselflies and dragonflies fluttering along the river's edge. This place is alive with these ancient insects. In fact, of the world's 5,000 members of the Odonata order, Algonquin Park has just under 100 recorded species—the majority of which were sighted along the Oxtongue.

There are various access points to begin and end your trip. The favorite, however, is to put in at Algonquin's familiar Canoe Lake access and take out at the Algonquin Outfitters on Oxtongue Lake. You'll need to shuttle a vehicle first. Algonquin Outfitters provides a shuttle service, dropping you off at the access point so your vehicle is waiting for you at the take-out.

The road leading off Highway 60 to Canoe Lake access point is marked on the north side of the highway, 14 km past Algonquin Provincial Park's West Gate. You can put in at the beach or the docks beside the Portage Store.

Not far out on Canoe Lake, the route heads southwest across Bonita Lake and Tea Lake. Don't be concerned about the usual crowds here. Tea Lake Campground and Camp Tamakwa make good use of this area. However, the moment you take the first portage (240 m) to the right of Tea Lake Dam, the crowds quickly disappear.

Tea Lake Dam was where artist Tom Thomson made camp while on his first visit to Algonquin. The trip was a warm-up to his two-month expedition down the Mississagi River (see the Mississagi River chapter for details). He later returned to Tea Lake Dam in 1914 and even guided fellow Group of Seven artist A.Y. Jackson to the very same spot.

You'll encounter only a couple of small swifts on the river before reaching another historic stop—Whiskey Rapids. Here, sometime during the turn of the century, two log drivers lost a three-gallon keg of whiskey. They were appointed by their fellow workers to head up the Oxtongue to pick up the precious cargo at the Canoe Lake railway station. Everything was going as planned, that

Oxtongue River

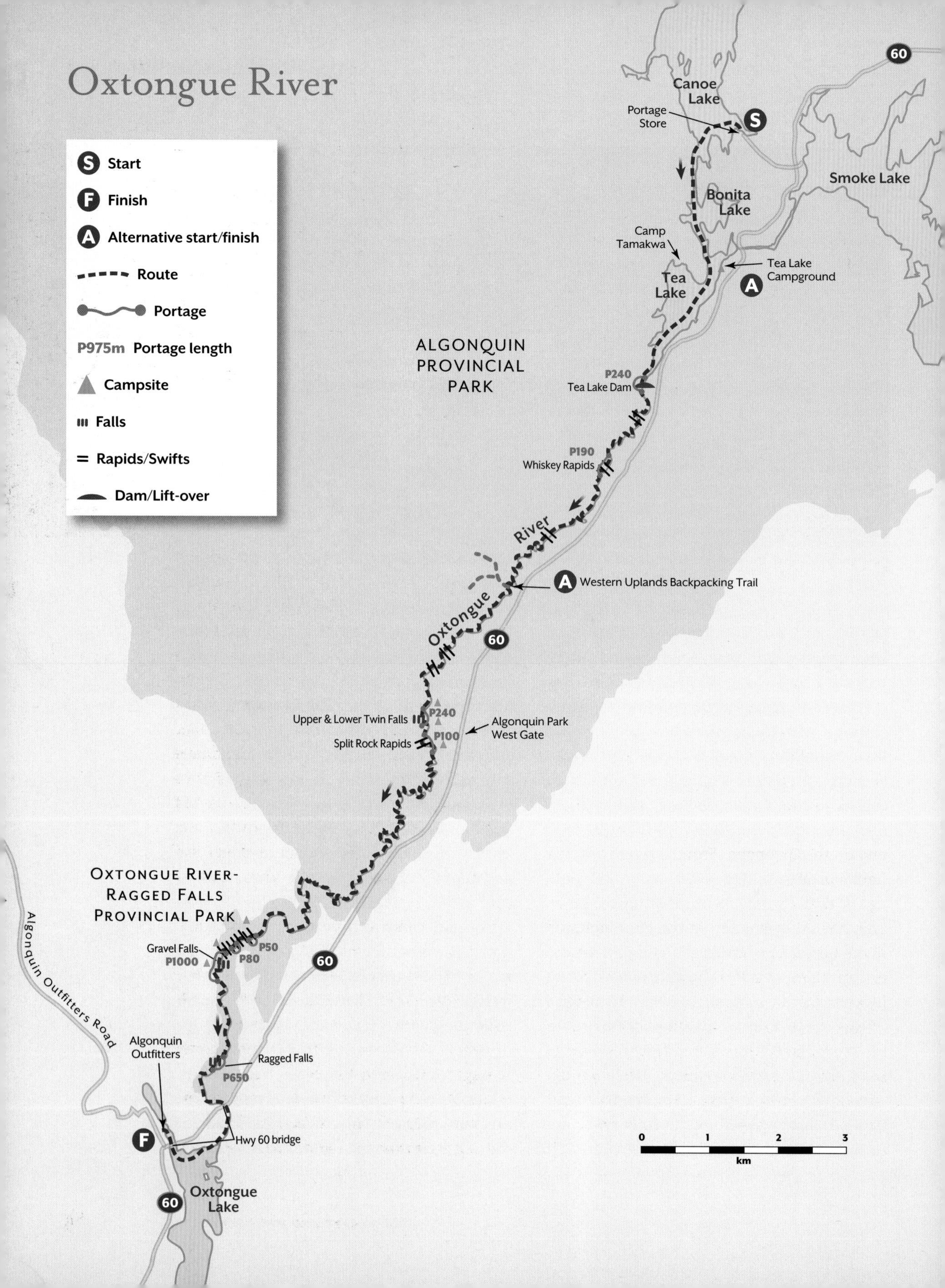

S Start

F Finish

A Alternative start/finish

- - - Route

Portage

P975m Portage length

▲ Campsite

⫶⫶⫶ Falls

= Rapids/Swifts

⌒ Dam/Lift-over

Canoe Lake

Portage Store

S

Smoke Lake

60

Bonita Lake

Camp Tamakwa

Tea Lake Campground

A

Tea Lake

ALGONQUIN PROVINCIAL PARK

P240 Tea Lake Dam

P190 Whiskey Rapids

River

Oxtongue

60

A Western Uplands Backpacking Trail

Upper & Lower Twin Falls

P240

P100

Algonquin Park West Gate

Split Rock Rapids

OXTONGUE RIVER– RAGGED FALLS PROVINCIAL PARK

60

Gravel Falls

P1000

P80

P50

Algonquin Outfitters Road

Algonquin Outfitters

Ragged Falls

P650

Hwy 60 bridge

F

Oxtongue Lake

60

0   1   2   3

km

is, until they decided to stop for a drink or two on their return trip. It was dark by the time they reached the rapids, and having spotted the take-out for the portage too late, the drunkards chose to run down the whitewater while it was in spring flood. They made it, but the barrel of whiskey was never found.

The present-day portage around Whiskey Rapids is an easy 190 meters and is marked on the right. Just be sure to keep to the left when the trail forks halfway along.

Downstream, not far past another set of rapids that can either be run or waded down depending on water levels, the waterway begins to meander in every direction. This calm stretch of river, which winds its way around pine-clad bluffs on one side and spills quietly past islands covered in alder and dogwood on the other, is a great place to spot a moose, especially in early spring when almost every salt-deprived moose in the park is attracted to the road salt left along the highway close by.

It takes about an hour's paddle from Whiskey Rapids before the footbridge for the Western Uplands Backpacking Trail comes into view. This is another possible access point for canoeists looking for a much shorter weekend on the Oxtongue. From here, it's another hour's paddle before the river picks up speed again, first at a series of insignificant swifts and then, shortly after, at the more noteworthy Upper and Lower Twin Falls and Split Rock Rapids. Both cascades have short portages (240 m and 100 m), each marked on the left. However, the take-out for Split Rock Rapids is incredibly steep and uncomfortably close to the edge of the falls, especially during high-water levels. You may want to play it safe and head for shore a few meters farther upstream to make use of an extended bush trail.

The river continues to meander for another three hours, passing by what Alexander Shirreff perfectly described in his 1829 journal as "A level, sandy valley, timbered chiefly with balsam, tamarac and poplar, beyond which, however, the hardwood rising grounds are seen seldom a mile distant on either side." Then, not far past where Algonquin Provincial Park ends and Oxtongue River-Ragged Falls Provincial Park begins (the border is marked by a small creek on the left that leads to the nearby highway), the river drops down five sets of shallow rapids before plunging over the 10-meter Gravel Falls.

All five rapids can be run. The first and fourth both have portages (50 m and 80 m) marked on the left just in case. You may also want to wade down the fifth set, which is only a few meters above the brink of the falls.

Gravel Falls comes with a 1,000-meter portage, marked to the right. Don't worry— moderately experienced whitewater paddlers can put in directly below the falls (reducing the portage to 200 m) and paddlers with even

less experience can run the remaining swift water.

The current continues its fast pace all the way to Ragged Falls—which is a drop that is three times the height of Gravel Falls. Ragged Falls is also a day-use area, and I find the trip quickly loses its wilderness appeal the moment you run into the crowds of tourists who walk in from the highway. As well, the network of trails leading back and forth from the falls make finding the exact whereabouts of the 650-meter portage (which is marked on the left) extremely frustrating. There are, however, small florescent squares on the trees to help point you in the right direction.

From Ragged Falls it's an easy paddle to the Highway 60 bridge. Continue for another 20 minutes until you arrive in the expanse of Oxtongue Lake. Keeping to the right-hand shore, you'll eventually paddle under the Highway 60 bridge again and then take out at the Algonquin Outfitters on your left.

LONGEST PORTAGE 1,000 meters. This portage can be reduced to 200 meters by running some moderate rapids below Gravel Falls.

FEE The upper section of the river runs through Algonquin Park so an interior camping permit must be purchased for Algonquin Provincial Park as well as a parking permit for Canoe Lake.

ALTERNATIVE ACCESS You can put in at Tea Lake Campground or Western Uplands Backpacking Trail access area.

ALTERNATIVE ROUTE A number of alternative access points along the river can create a shorter trip.

OUTFITTERS
Algonquin Outfitters—
Oxtongue Lake
1035 Algonquin Outfitters Road
Dwight, ON, P0A 1H0
705-635-2243 or 1-800-469-4948
www.algonquinoutfitters.com

FOR MORE INFORMATION
Algonquin Provincial Park
705-633-5572 (information) and
1-888-668-7275 (reservations)
www.algonquinpark.on.ca

MAPS The Friends of Algonquin has produced a good map for the park. Jeff's Map has also produced an interior route map of the Algonquin.

TOPOGRAPHIC MAPS
41 E/7

GPS COORDINATES
45.363544, −78.923231

Wendigo to Radiant Lake

 3 days

 16 to 18 portages

●- - - -● 32 km

Some canoe-tripping skills are required.

I'VE PADDLED FROM the Wendigo access point to Radiant Lake a couple of times on the way to trips down the notable Petawawa River. The problem was my mind was always on the whitewater awaiting me in the river section that starts after Radiant, not on the series of lakes leading up to it. So I decided to return to the area and paddle from Wendigo Lake to Radiant Lake and back to see all I had missed along the way. By doing so I discovered one of the best quick and easy trips Algonquin's east end has to offer.

My canoe mate, Andy Baxter, and I chose the first weekend in October for the trip. Trout season had just closed but some of the lakes en route were populated with bass and walleye, and the fall is prime for fishing either species.

To reach the access point, turn south off Highway 17, just west of Deux-Rivières, onto Brent Road. The permit office is just a half-kilometer down the gravel road. From there it's a 16-kilometer drive down Brent Road and then left onto the Wendigo Lake access road. Drive another couple of kilometers to the launch site.

From Peterborough, Ontario, it was a solid drive for us to reach the east end of the park,

which made it mid-morning by the time we paddled off from the canoe launch. Wendigo Lake isn't part of the Algonquin yet. The park border doesn't start until the first portage on the far eastern end of Wendigo, which takes you to Allan Lake. The portage measures 180 meters and is an easy carry. In fact, we found most of the portages on this route relatively straightforward, including the next one (255 m) that leads into North Depot Lake. (In higher water levels I'm guessing you can avoid this portage completely.) A problem with the ease of access was the campsites on the first couple of lakes (Allan and North Depot) showed some abuse. The sites themselves were nice but the majority of them, especially the ones on the main islands, were devoid of good firewood. They are likely easy targets for when trout season opens in early spring. The scenic atmosphere here is still spectacular, with the typical stout white pine rooted along the granite shoreline and loons serenading us while we paddled—some of the many gems Algonquin offers.

It was lunch by the time we reached the end of North Depot Lake, and Andy and I snacked on cheese and dried salami before taking

on the longest portage—770 meters running along the left side of a set of rapids and ending at an old dam. The put-in marks my favorite part of the route: the North River. You're almost guaranteed to see a moose here. Andy and I saw two; a bull and later a cow. I've seen a lot of moose in my previous canoe journeys but these two were special to me. Prior to the trip my daughter, who was seven at the time, reminded me how she had yet to see a moose (and she's been paddling the north with me since she was six weeks old!). I'm not sure why we've never spotted a moose on our trips together but she was always disappointed when we didn't. So before my trip I promised her I would see one and take a few photos for her. I also read out a quote from Bill Bryson's book *A Walk in the Woods* to help characterize their appearance: "Hunters will tell you that a moose is a wily and ferocious forest creature.

Nonsense. A moose is a cow drawn by a three-year-old." She giggled uncontrollably after hearing that and was insistent that I see one for her and take a picture. That day she got her wish and I became the best dad ever—for a whole week at least.

After a short paddle down the river you'll come upon three portages (230 m, 230 m and 310 m), pretty much one after the other, along the right side before you reach a small pond called Clamshell Lake. Just make sure to keep to the trail of the second portage to the very end and don't be misled by a faint trail that leads you back to the river too early.

There was only one campsite on Clamshell, on the east end of the lake on top a big mound of rock, and even though it was small, with room for one tent, it seemed perfect. We had planned to get all the way to Radiant, however, so we paddled quickly across to the other side,

Wendigo to Radiant Lake

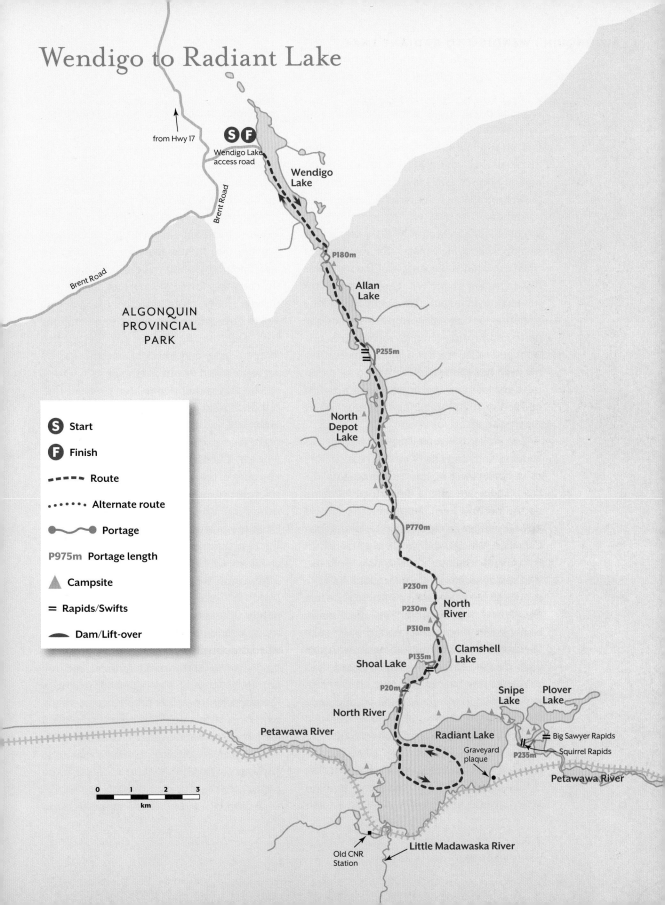

from Hwy 17

S **F**
Wendigo Lake
access road

Brent Road

Brent Road

**ALGONQUIN
PROVINCIAL
PARK**

Wendigo
Lake

P180m

Allan
Lake

P255m

North
Depot
Lake

P770m

P230m

P230m   North
                River
P310m

P135m   Clamshell
                  Lake

Shoal Lake

P20m

North River

Snipe   Plover
Lake   Lake

Big Sawyer Rapids

Squirrel Rapids
P235m

Radiant Lake

Graveyard
plaque

Petawawa River

Petawawa River

Little Madawaska River

Old CNR
Station

Legend

S Start

F Finish

- - - - Route

· · · · · Alternate route

●~~● Portage

P975m Portage length

▲ Campsite

= Rapids/Swifts

— Dam/Lift-over

0   1   2   3
km

stopping briefly to cast a line for smallmouth bass. (We caught four good-sized fish.) Then we took on two more short portages—135 meters to Shoal Lake and a very quick 20 meters around a beaver dam—to access the remaining North River that flows into Radiant Lake.

Radiant Lake was worth the effort, but it took a while to realize it. It's a big, round, shallow lake, which makes for rough water when the wind is blowing. And the wind was blowing when we arrived. Exploring the lake was next to impossible. We simply hugged the shoreline looking for a campsite, and on the north end we discovered an incredible beach-front and called it a day. Later in the evening the wind had calmed and we ended up spending a glorious evening sipping bush martinis on the beach and watching the sunset along the west shore.

We awoke to a motorboat buzzing across Radiant. Andy and I had forgotten that motors of 10 horsepower or less are allowed on the lake. There are also a few rustic cottages on the northwestern shoreline. The owners arrive by either an old road or the abandoned Canadian National Railway line. Personally, I felt this intrusion didn't take away from our wild surroundings at all. In fact, Radiant Lake is far less busy now than in the past. When the railway was running this was a main access point for canoeists entering the park. The authors of the well-known Algonquin book *The Incomplete Anglers* (1944) began their trek across the park by jumping off the train here. In 1847 J. MacDonell, the original land surveyor of the Algonquin region, recorded numerous Algonquin camps on Radiant Lake (then called Trout Lake) when he stopped to purchase a canoe from them. It was during the logging era, however, that Radiant Lake saw the most traffic. Various lumber

companies, including J.R. Booth, Gillies Bros. and Harris and Bronson Co., occupied the lake—especially in the 1930s. A large depot farm was constructed along the west shore and a steam-powered tug boomed logs into the bay of the North River.

Andy and I spent the entire next day exploring Radiant Lake, which I recommend you do, too. In the morning we fished for smallmouth bass and walleye at the mouth of the Petawawa River. We even took a 235-meter portage downstream on the Petawawa to Plover Lake where we caught some amazing bass. Later in the day we circumnavigated Radiant Lake and checked out the loggers' gravesite noted on our park map.

The graves themselves aren't easy to find, but we found the memorial plaque easily enough. It was located on the southeast corner of the lake, placed on a large boulder up from a beach. The plaque states, "In this enclosure are buried the bodies of more than twenty rivermen drowned in the nearby waters before 1916 when the railway was completed." From the plaque we followed a faint trail to the east through an alder thicket that ends at Bissett Creek/Radiant Road. According to information I had gathered from Donald L. Lloyd's book *Canoeing Algonquin Park*, an even fainter trail to the left of the plaque will lead to a wooden staff that marks the whereabouts of a single wooden cross held together with binder twine. Andy and I found the side trail but no evidence of a wooden staff or graves. I'm guessing too much time has passed and any traces at this point have blended in with the forest, but maybe you'll have better luck!

Our third night was to be our last, and Andy and I paddled the same route back and stayed on an island site on North Depot Lake. This allowed us to be closer to the Wendigo

Lake access point and get an early start on the long drive home. It also provided a nice change. North Depot Lake is much smaller than Radiant, and it was satisfying to be away from the harsh winds. However, we already missed Radiant Lake. Around the campfire on our last night out, while sipping bush martinis and watching the sunset again, we planned a return trip to Radiant. It's a captivating place—and besides, next time we just might find the hidden gravesites that escaped us the first time out.

LONGEST PORTAGE 770 meters

FEE An interior camping permit must be purchased for Algonquin Provincial Park online or at the Wendigo Gate House.

ALTERNATIVE ACCESS None

ALTERNATIVE ROUTE None

OUTFITTERS
Algonquin Bound Outfitters
525 Barron Canyon Road,
Pembroke, ON, K8A 6W7
613-637-5508
www.algonquinbound.com

FOR MORE INFORMATION
Algonquin Provincial Park
705-633-5572 (information) and
1-888-668-7275 (reservations)
www.algonquinpark.on.ca

MAPS The Friends of Algonquin has produced a good map for the park. Jeff's Map has also produced an interior route map of Algonquin Provincial Park.

TOPOGRAPHIC MAPS
42 L/4, 41 L/13 & 41 L/16

GPS COORDINATES
46.144637, -78.291836

Noganosh Lake

🕐 3 to 4 days

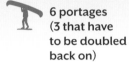
6 portages
(3 that have
to be doubled
back on)

●----● 40 km

Since this is an
unmaintained
route, moderate
tripping experience
is recommended.

I'M ALWAYS ON the lookout for that unsung canoe route—some obscure river or lake that other paddlers seem to know little about; a secret spot that has miraculously remained undeveloped and enticingly wild. Then, after spending hours glancing over maps, reading guidebooks, browsing the Web and then heading out and "testing the waters," I most likely will find the portages overgrown, water levels unnavigable, and the shoreline taken over by private ownership. On that rare occasion, however, I manage to hit the jackpot. An obscure route with short portages, pristine campsites and unbelievable fishing. A place like Noganosh Lake.

Alana and I, along with our hyper springer spaniel, Bailey, discovered this route in late August 1999. I had just got back from a lengthy trip in Wabakimi—a wilderness park in the far north—and Alana was a little jealous that her summer canoeing was only a few weekend jaunts to busy recreational parks in the south. Of course, the size of the Noganosh area couldn't come close to that of Wabakimi. But the feeling of remoteness was pretty darn close at times.

We used the Ess Narrows access point on the northeast side of Highway 522, 21 kilometers west of the town of Loring. From here, we paddled under the highway bridge and began the long 3-kilometer paddle down the length of Dollars Lake to Kawigamog Lake (named after the steamboat that worked the area lakes in the early 1900s). This is the most boring section en route, especially with the dozens of cottages dotting the shoreline and heavy motorboat traffic racing down the waterway. Alana and I made the best of it, waving at each cottager sitting on their dock and gesturing a thank-you to all the passing boats that slowed down to reduce their wake. Actually, in slowing down, the chop increases, but it's the thought that counts.

Once at the junction of Dollars Lake and Kawigamog Lake, we took the more isolated channel along the north side of the Elbow and Cincinnati Island rather than heading straight out to the center of the lake. There's no cottage development here and little boat traffic. There are even a number of makeshift campsites that have been developed on Crown land for canoeists who arrive late in the day and need a place to stay before heading all the way into the Noganosh area. Be

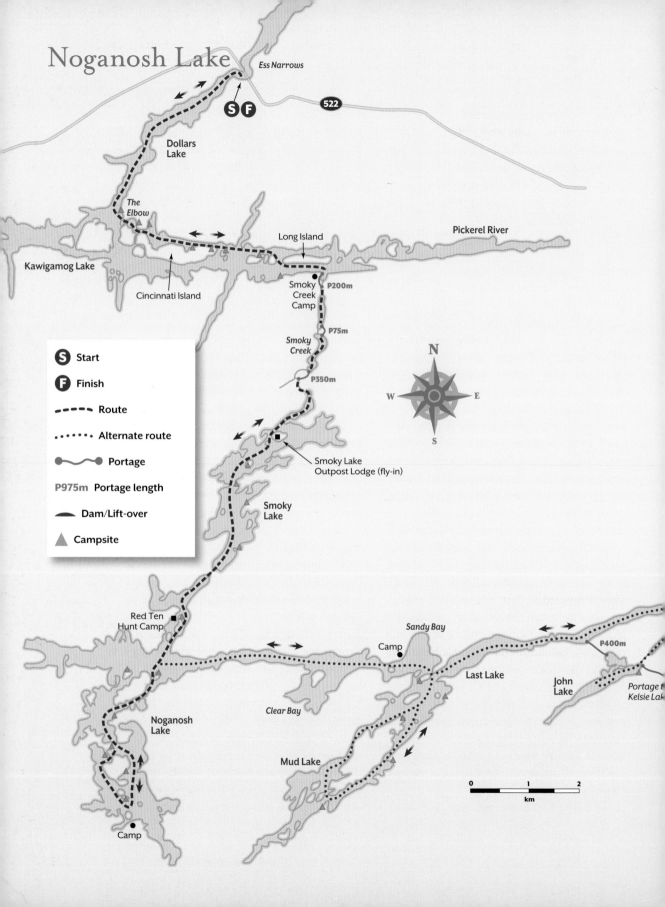

Noganosh Lake

Ess Narrows

S **F**

522

Dollars
Lake

The Elbow

Long Island

Pickerel River

Kawigamog Lake

Cincinnati Island

Smoky
Creek
Camp

P200m

P75m

*Smoky
Creek*

P350m

S Start

F Finish

- - - Route

······· Alternate route

●‿● Portage

P975m Portage length

⌒ Dam/Lift-over

▲ Campsite

Smoky Lake
Outpost Lodge (fly-in)

Smoky
Lake

N

W   E

S

Red Ten
Hunt Camp

Sandy Bay

Camp

Last Lake

John
Lake

P400m

*Portage to
Kelsie Lake*

Noganosh
Lake

Clear Bay

Mud Lake

0   1   2
km

Camp

warned, however, that these sites become party central on a long weekend.

Approximately 2 kilometers east, the out-of-the-way channel, now called the Pickerel River, opens up. After reaching the west side of Long Island, Alana and I slowly made our way across to the south shore to search for the outlet of Smoky Creek and the first of three portages.

Eventually we located the take-out between the Smoky Creek Hunt Camp and the creek itself. It's a clear, 200-meter trail, chewed up by constant ATV use coming out of the hunt club, and it avoids a giant beaver dam that keeps the water level on Smoky Creek navigable throughout the season. Even in high water, though, the next 2 kilometers of upstream paddling to reach the next portage—a 75-meter path heading up and over a steep knoll to the left of another large beaver dam—can be extremely frustrating (take note that the dam now has a makeshift ladder if you'd prefer to lift directly over it). Countless times the creek snakes back on itself, and by the end you've covered more than three times the distance.

The third and final portage is to the right of the last 75-meter lift-over. The route looks straightforward at first, with a weed-choked passageway meandering through to the west. But Alana and I found ourselves at the end of at least two dead-end channels before we finally pulled up at the proper take-out to the left of the creek.

The trail was the longest en route—measuring a little over 350 meters—but it was relatively flat and straightforward. About a quarter of the way along, however, we took some time out to follow a side trail across from where a weathered sign was nailed to a pine tree to commemorate a local hunter who

was killed in the area. The path crossed the creek and made its way slowly up a winding hill toward the remains of an old broken-down pickup. A wide assortment of rusted trucks and dilapidated hunt camps can be found throughout the area, reminders of how well traveled the region has been throughout the years, mostly due to the abundance of deer. To this day, this section of forested land south of Lake Nipissing holds the largest gathering of white-tailed deer in the province. Known as the Loring herd, it consists of 8,000 to 14,000 individuals.

After the last portage, the creek runs directly south, eventually snakes around to the west, and then opens up into Smoky Lake. Here, on an island, is Smoky Lake Lodge, a fly-in camp owned by Tornado's Canadian Resorts. It's mostly American fishermen who come here to try their luck for a trophy small-mouth bass or monster pike. When Alana and I passed the docks of the camp, we said hello to some of the occupants sitting out on the main porch. I guess after spending a good bit of cash to be flown into the remote lake, they were all a little taken aback, witnessing our leisurely paddle in on our own. One of the customers, an elderly man dressed in full Elmer Fudd costume, yelled out to us, "How the hell did y'all get into this godforsaken lake?" Not wanting to ruin his "wilderness experience," we babbled some crazed story of spending hours on muddy portages and bug-infested swamps. It was an outright lie, but the man felt sorry enough for us that he handed Alana and me each a beer before we headed down the lake to make camp.

Our choice of sites was a secluded spot, tucked into a back bay on the southeast end of Smoky Lake. Noganosh Lake itself has far more ideal places to camp but I caught a

would have been best to bring along our camp gear and stay overnight on a second site. There's so much open water to explore here, with the remains of a ranger station and firetower to search for in the bush along the north shore of the western inlet and a scattering of islands across the southern bay offering perfect spots for a shore lunch, that you could spend an entire week on Noganosh Lake alone. But Alana and I had only planned a quick weekend getaway for this trip and, with it being the summer solstice, we decided to take advantage of the extended light of the longest day of the year and explore as much to the east as possible.

In the early morning calm, we quickly paddled through the shallow channel joining Smoky Lake with Noganosh Lake, slowed down only to check out a couple of rustic hunt camps and then made haste down the long eastern inlet toward the first adjoining lake.

The channel remained unaltered all the way to the entrance to Clear Bay, Sandy Bay and then Last Lake (all great places to troll for bass or pike). We kept to the north shore for most of the route, staying close to the massive outcropping of rock that would block the wind and made for easy paddling.

By midday we found ourselves roaming the lower portion of Mud Lake, and we stopped for lunch at a makeshift campsite.

It was getting quite late by the time we circled around back to the top of Last Lake. So we chose to leave John Lake, located just over 4 kilometers farther east, for another trip. It was a good call. By the time we got back to our base camp on Smoky, it was getting dark and we had to resort to a quick dinner of macaroni and cheese before heading off to bed.

By late morning the next day we managed to crawl out of our tent and start packing up to

4-pound bass while drifting by the spot on Smoky Lake and quickly decided it would be a good place to stay.

The next day, Alana, Bailey and I headed out early to explore, not only Noganosh Lake, but also three other connecting lakes (Last Lake, John Lake and Mud Lake). Ideally, it go home. Even poor Bailey, who I don't recall paddling a single stroke the day before, was totally exhausted and was quite slow taking in her morning routine—a leisurely swim and a game of tag with the camp chipmunk.

On our return trip we stopped to say hello to the Elmer Fudd look-alike who was fishing at the entrance to Smoky Creek. Alana and I pulled alongside his aluminum fishing boat and asked the age-old question "Having any luck?" The American simply smirked and reported he had caught nothing all morning—even though I caught a glimpse of a full stringer of fish dangling off the back-side of his boat. I kept quiet about his catch, thinking he was just an average angler who was trying to keep his newly found fishing hole a secret (something I totally respect). Either that or he was just feeling sorry for two canoeists who had to deal with hours of battling bugs and muddy portages while he waited comfortably for a plane to pick him up at the end of the day.

We wished him a pleasant flight and he wished us good luck on the portages, neither of us knowing that we would all meet again that same day. It was the craziest thing. After Alana and I padded back out to the Ess Narrows access point and headed down the highway for home, we stopped at the local coffee shop in the town of Loring. There, sitting at the counter, was the American fisherman. At first, he didn't quite recognize us. After all, we had him believing that the trip out of Smoky Lake was a painstaking ordeal that would take us at least a full day, not a three-hour pleasure cruise. But then he heard our dog Bailey barking at us to get a move on, and it finally dawned on him who Alana and I were. "My God!" he said "How the hell did you get back so soon?"

There was nothing I could do but lie again. This time it was a doozie. I told him that we had actually met a bush pilot in the next lake and paid him for a quick lift back to Loring. Thinking about it, the fib wasn't all that terrible a thing to do. After all, in the end, the American's concept of wilderness was left intact and our easy and inexpensive paddle route into the Noganosh system was kept a secret—unless he reads this book, that is.

LONGEST PORTAGE 300 meters

FEE This is an unmaintained provincial park and no fee is required.

ALTERNATIVE ACCESS Tornado's Outpost Camp provides a fly-in service to their lodge on Smoky Lake.

ALTERNATIVE ROUTE Rough portages can be used at the south end of Noganosh to connect to other routes along the Magnetawan River and to the east of Last Lake to link Island Lake.

OUTFITTERS
Grundy Lake Supply Post
R.R. 1
Highway 69 and Highway 522
Britt, ON, P0G 1A0
705-383-2251

FOR MORE INFORMATION
Ministry of Natural Resources
Parry Sound District Office
705-746-4201
www.mnr.gov.on.ca

Tornado's Canadian Resorts
Box 26
Port Loring, ON, P0H 1Y0
1-800-663-2277 or 705-757-2050
www.tornadosresorts.com

TOPOGRAPHIC MAPS 41 H/16

GPS COORDINATES
45.919314, -80.243804

Magnetawan River Loop

🕐 3 to 4 days    14 portages   ●----● 80 km   **This is a perfect novice trip except for a handful of long portages that paddlers will find difficult.**

M Y FIRST TIME ever paddling the Magnetawan River loop I made the mistake of heading out in mid-June, when blackflies, mosquitoes and deerflies joined forces to plague each and every portage. John Glasgow (my canoe companion that week) had been so badly bitten by insects (I counted a total of 22 bug bites on John's left kneecap) that he looked like a walking pincushion. The insanely long portages en route (the longest 2,285 m) were blocked with either mud puddles or sharp granite slopes. And, to make matters worse, a pre-summer heat wave hit the area; with the humidity, temperatures soared as high as 40 degrees. By the time the ordeal was over we both agreed wholeheartedly that our first trip would be the last. Three months later, however, John and I found ourselves talking over the trip at a local bar, declaring how cheated we both felt after it was all over. We agreed that if it wasn't for the excessive heat and bugs we encountered along the way, the Magnetawan itself wouldn't have been a total disaster.

So, believe it or not, we gave the route a second chance, this time in mid-September when the air was cool and the portages were free of bugs. And our second time around, we came out unscathed. In fact, John and I had such a good trip that we can honestly say that the Magnetawan Loop, when paddled at the right time of the year, of course, is at the top of the list when it comes to Ontario's canoe routes.

The Magnetawan River Loop has three possible access points: Naiscoot Lake and Harris Lake, both off Highway 69, and Wahwashkesh Lake, off Highway 124 and Highway 520.

John and I chose the Wahwashkesh Lake access point. The public boat launch can be reached by taking Highway 124, turning north onto Highway 520 just east of Dunchurch and turning north again onto Wahwashkesh Lake Road (before the town of Whitestone). The parking lot and dock site are 8 kilometers along this road, just past Linger Long Lodge.

Wahwashkesh Lake is a large lake with countless islands and bays that can easily confuse any navigator. To reach the Magnetawan River, paddle to the northwest bay (Deep Bay).

The first and longest portage of the trip is downriver at Canal Rapids. Where the river forks before the rapid, follow the right-hand inlet. The portage begins just right of the Deep Bay Hunt Club dock. It then follows an old tote road built by loggers in 1868 and ends where a bridge crosses the river.

Looking upstream from the bridge you can catch a good glimpse of Canal Rapids, where canyon walls 50-feet sheer on either side direct the flow of the river over a series of rock staircases.

A short distance downstream is Graves Rapids. Local people say there is a graveyard here for the log drivers who drowned in the rapids. The Magnetawan Archives contain this description from James MacArthur, a lumberman and settler of the South Magnetawan, as he saw the site in 1926: "Not far above the shallows where the creek enters the Magnetawan, is a plot of ground on a sunny slope, with a cedar fence surrounding it. Here are the graves of two river drivers drowned in the canal thirty years ago [1896] running a pointer boat through. The spot is tended to each spring by the passing drivers. Gone are most of the curios left by fellow workers—the corked shoes, pipes, broken watch cases and other knickknacks. The carved doves that rested over the head of the pieces, miniature 'peaveys' and pike poles, marauding tourists have lifted."

Canoeists have three options at Graves Rapids: continue along the tote road for another 500 meters, paddle from the bridge to the foot of the rapids and use a separate 200-meter portage found to the right, or if your whitewater skills are up to it, cautiously run the set.

West of Graves Rapids is Trout Lake, an incredible, scenic lake with a number of perfect campsites, each with rock outcrops and lush canopies of red and white pine. I can guarantee that spending your first night

camped on the lake will be one of the highlights of the entire trip.

From Trout Lake the regular route follows the South Branch. But if you're in the mood for more long, wet, muddy portages, it is possible to extend the trip for another day by continuing to paddle west across Island Lake, portaging 2,380 meters around Thirty Dollar Rapids (so named after an entire drive of logs jammed and cost the dollar-a-day loggers a month's pay) and then looping back to the South Branch by way of a 1,370-meter portage.

The added day brings you through some major historic sites. You may find the long portages too grueling, however, and opt to keep to the main route to the south. Look for Eagle Rock, a prominent cliff marking the entrance to the narrow inlet leaving Trout Lake.

Magnetawan River Loop

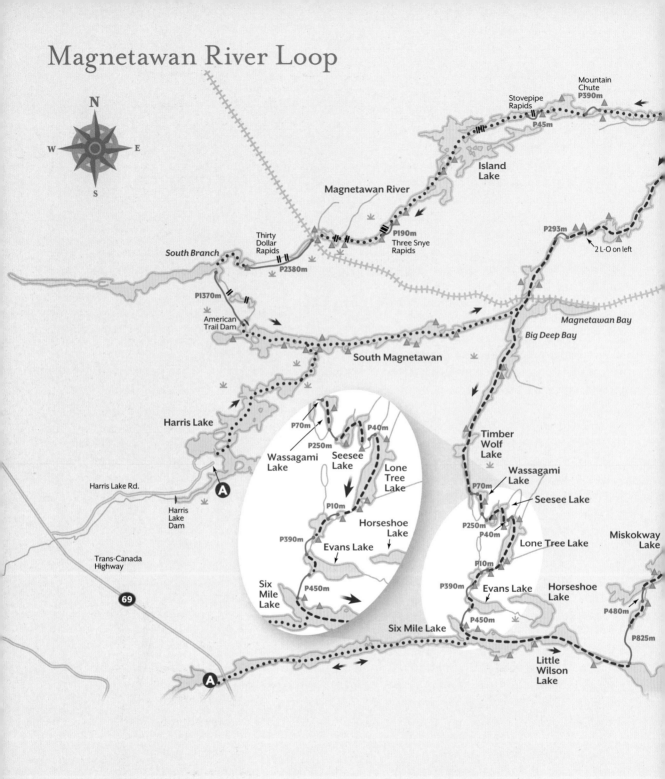

N W E S

Mountain Chute **P390m**

Stovepipe Rapids

P45m

Island Lake

Magnetawan River

P190m

Three Snye Rapids

P293m

2 L-O on left

Thirty Dollar Rapids

South Branch

P2380m

P1370m

American Trail Dam

Magnetawan Bay

Big Deep Bay

South Magnetawan

Harris Lake

Harris Lake Rd.

Harris Lake Dam

(A)

Trans-Canada Highway

69

Timber Wolf Lake

P70m

P250m

Wassagami Lake

Seesee Lake

P40m

Lone Tree Lake

Wassagami Lake

Seesee Lake

P10m

Horseshoe Lake

P40m

Lone Tree Lake

Miskokway Lake

P390m

Evans Lake

P250m

P10m

P390m

Evans Lake

Horseshoe Lake

Six Mile Lake

P450m

P480m

P825m

(A)

Six Mile Lake

P450m

Little Wilson Lake

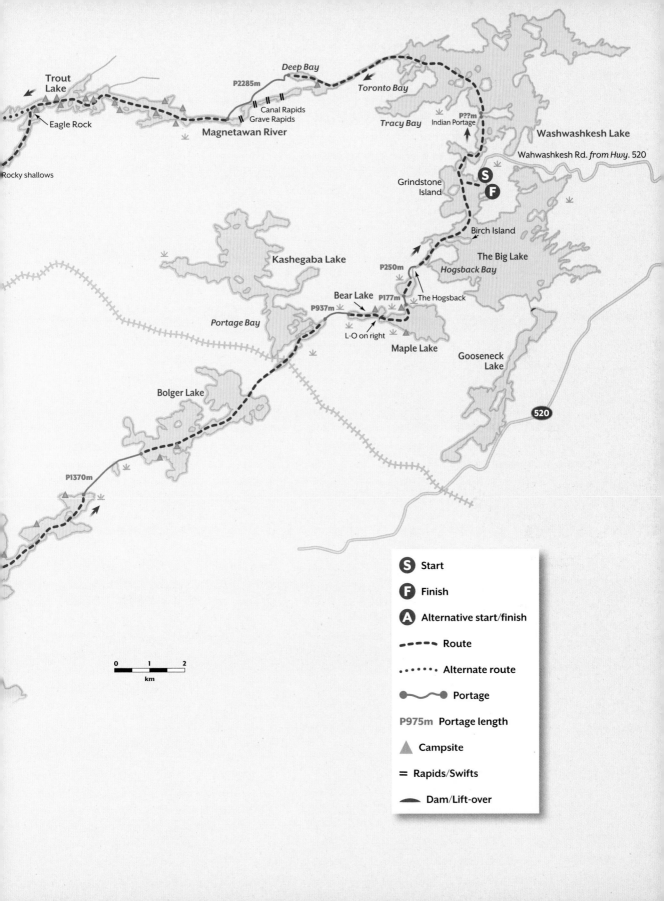

Trout Lake

Eagle Rock

Rocky shallows

P2285m

Deep Bay

Canal Rapids
Grave Rapids

Magnetawan River

Toronto Bay

Tracy Bay

P??m
Indian Portage

Washwashkesh Lake

Wahwashkesh Rd. *from Hwy.* 520

Grindstone
Island

S
F

Birch Island

Kashegaba Lake

P250m

The Big Lake

Hogsback Bay

Bear Lake

P177m
The Hogsback

P937m

Portage Bay

L-O on right

Maple Lake

Gooseneck
Lake

Bolger Lake

520

P1370m

0   1   2
km

S Start

F Finish

A Alternative start/finish

--- Route

⋯⋯ Alternate route

●～● Portage

P975m Portage length

▲ Campsite

= Rapids/Swifts

━ Dam/Lift-over

Many riffles, too minor to be called rapids, speed your progress to the spot where the hydro line crosses the river. The rocky shoreline smoothes out here, and clumps of lush white birch begin to replace the red and white pine. Depending on water levels, you may have to make a double lift-over where the current flushes over two rock ledges in succession, directly below the power lines. And shortly downstream, a 293-meter portage on the right bank must be taken to avoid a stunted cascade.

The landscape regains its rugged appeal south of the Canadian National Railway bridge. Here, where the waterway forks, the South Magnetawan River travels west toward Harris Lake; to the south, where you will be paddling, is Big Bay.

The next portage (70 m) is located along the eastern shoreline, just before the southern tip of Big Bay. Wooden steps have been put in place at the take-out to help you scramble up a steep slope. Keep a sharp look out for where the path forks. A well-maintained trail continues to the left. That's not the way you want to go. Trust me! I've learned by mistake. Follow the faint path to the right to Clear Lake (Wassagami Lake).

From Clear Lake a series of six small lakes follow, each one enclosed by walls of hard granite and separated by short, but steep and rugged, portages. The third lake (Lone Tree Lake) and the sixth lake (Evans Lake) are miniature versions of Trout Lake, providing yet again picture-perfect campsites.

Special note should be made of the 390-meter portage into Evans Lake. I'm sure that during low water the entire portage is necessary, but when John and I paddled the route we shortened the path by at least 200 meters by navigating the shallow creek.

From Evans Lake's southwestern shore, a good 450-meter portage takes you to where Naiscoot Lake and Little Wilson Lake join. The route heads east down almost the entire length of Wilson Lake, until another portage, located on the northern shoreline, heads overland to a small, unnamed lake.

It was on this particular steep portage that both John and I came to the logical conclusion that the map we were following, produced by the Ministry of Natural Resources and entitled *Magnetawan River Canoe Route*, was somewhat inaccurate in its portage measurements. The MNR pamphlet recorded the path out of Wilson Lake as 825 meters in length. It seemed to us more like 1,000 meters. To make matters worse, the even longer portages that follow also appeared to be incorrectly reported.

On the left-hand shore in the unnamed lake's northern bay, a 480-meter (more like 600-meter) portage works down a precipitous slope to Miskokway Lake. Paddle east across the length of Miskokway to yet another portage. The 1,370-meter (more like 2,000-meter) trail begins at a local hunt club's boat launch area, crosses over a small creek and then follows a rough road all the way to the Bolger Lake boat launch. The halfway mark along the portage is at a hydro line, just after a second dirt road crosses your path.

Bolger Lake has only a scattering of cottages and is not a bad choice for a place to spend your last night en route (the two campsites at the mouth of the southern bay, right of the put-in, are the best on the lake). More secluded campsites can be found, however, if you have time, by continuing east across Bolger Lake, up Bolger Creek. From there, cut across the south end of Portage Bay, portage 937 meters into a small unnamed lake, and then lift over a beaver dam or portage 9 meters into Maple Lake, where you will find three campsites on the north shore. Despite the few developed sections, this entire stretch is rich in wildlife. Great blue herons stalk the weeded bays, ospreys perch high on top of dead snags and crows swoop from island to island, echoing out their caws.

The crow-sized broad-winged hawk, identified by the distinct black and white bands across its tail feathers, also populates the dense mixed woods. In mid-September dozens of these raptors can be spotted soaring high above, waiting to catch a warm air thermal to help them on their long journey to the Amazon rain forests.

A shallow and marshy creek lined by pitcher plants rooted on islands of sphagnum moss takes you north, out of Maple Lake and into a small pond. The MNR canoe route booklet has a 177-meter portage marked to the right of the creek. When we paddled through we saw no sign of the trail anywhere. The water level was high at the time, so we had no trouble paddling up the swampy creek and into the small pond.

Directly across from the creek's mouth is the last portage of the trip. A 250-meter path leads you to Wahwashkesh Lake by running alongside a creek on the north side of the bridge, left of the take-out. Near the put-in, submerged debris left from the logging days can be seen on the lake's mucky bottom. The rusted iron and rotten timbers signify the last of the Magnetawan's lumber boom. When the supply of timber dwindled along the Ottawa River and Lake Ontario, the lumber barons moved inland. By the late 1860s the Magnetawan was clogged full of prime pine being driven down to Georgian Bay to be cut in the mills or transported to far-off markets.

Once on Wahwashkesh Lake, paddle east out of the inlet and then into the northern bay. A grassy narrows on the bay's northeast point will lead you back to the familiar sight of the government dock.

LONGEST PORTAGE 2,285 meters

FEE The route travels through Crown land and there is no fee required for Canadian citizens.

ALTERNATIVE ACCESS The route can be accessed from Highway 69 by way of Naiscoot Lake (the parking area is west of the highway and on the south shore of Naiscoot Lake) and Harris Lake, east of the highway, almost 5 kilometers along Harris Lake Road.

ALTERNATIVE ROUTE Two slightly easier weekend trips can be made by either accessing the campsites on South Magnetawan River by way of Harris Lake or, after organizing a car shuttle, paddling from the Harris Lake access point to the Naiscoot Lake access point.

OUTFITTERS
White Squall Paddling Centre
53 Carling Bay Road
Nobel, ON, P0G 1G0
705-342-5324
or
19 James Street
Parry Sound, ON, P2A 1T4
705-746-4936
www.whitesquall.com

FOR MORE INFORMATION
Ministry of Natural Resources
705-564-7823
www.mnr.gov.on.ca

MAPS The Ministry of Natural Resources has produced a canoe route pamphlet: *Magnetawan River Canoe Route.*

TOPOGRAPHIC MAPS
41 H/9 & 41 H/16

GPS COORDINATES
45.716268, -80.039717

Island Lake

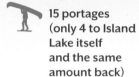

🕐 2 to 4 days   15 portages (only 4 to Island Lake itself and the same amount back)   ●----● 34 km   Possible high wind and waves on Wahwashkesh Lake, and a long day of portaging and lift-overs along Farm Creek.

I HAVE AN UNWRITTEN code before I write up a route (or fishing hole): if the route isn't set in a protected park or part of a historic travel route, or it can't withstand high use from paddlers, I respect the "secret" spot and move on to investigate another paddling area.

When I mentioned to Mike Kipp about a possible canoe trip to Island Lake, he suggested we have a look at an old government Forest Branch map, dated 1933, stored in a metal cylinder inside his cabin. How could I resist? It was like a pirate being told of a map pointing to long-lost treasure.

Mike and I used the public launch on Wahwashkesh Lake to start and end our journey. The access is reached by taking Highway 124, turning north onto Highway 520 just east of Dunchurch and turning north again onto Wahwashkesh Lake Road (before the town of Whitestone). The parking lot and dock site are 9 kilometers along this road, just past Linger Lake Lodge.

Wahwashkesh Lake is a large piece of water to paddle across, with a good number of islands to confuse the navigator along the way. But you head generally northwest, toward Deep Bay and where the Magnetawan River flushes out of the lake. Just before the river, on the north shore, off the tip of Sandy Hook Island, you'll see where Farm Creek empties out into Wahwashkesh.

The first of four portages along the creek begins right away with a 100-meter carry to the left, avoiding a small section of rocky rapids. Then, after a quick paddle across a widening of the creek, there's a second 100-meter portage, also to the left of a rockbound rapid. From here the creek opens up again, and to the right you enter a narrow section that veers to the left into another widening of the creek. It's here where you'll see the Hysert Hunt Camp, to the left of where the creek flushes through a miniature granite gorge.

The cabin is on leased land and the third portage en route (250 m) is to the left, between the outhouse and the main building. The club has eight members, with the oldest being 73 and the youngest (Mike) being 40. Mike's father started hunting in the area by canoe tripping up Farm Creek and then Cramadog Creek. And when he and other hunting pals made up the hunt club at the cabin, they all

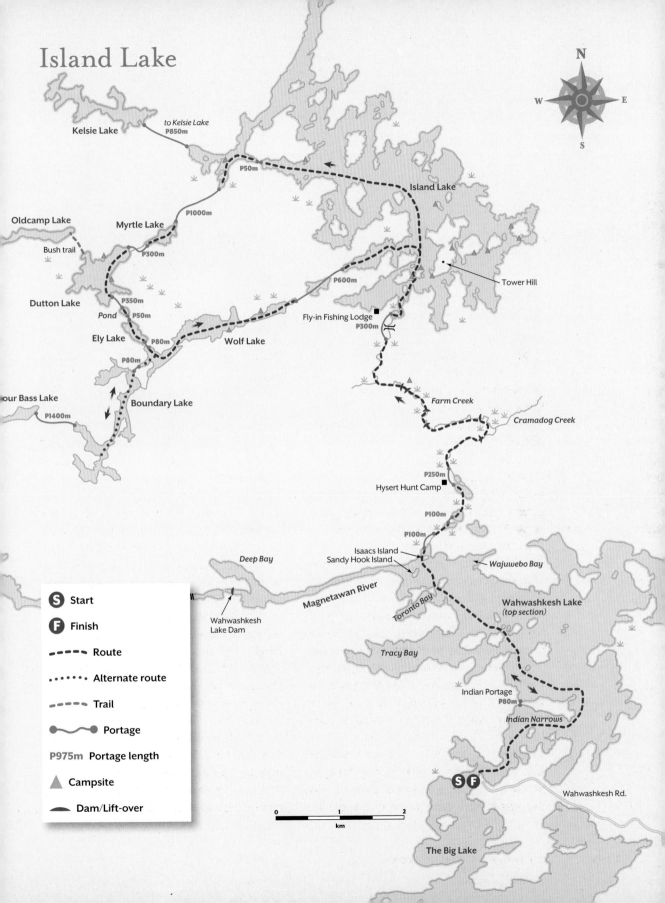

Island Lake

N
W E
S

Kelsie Lake

to Kelsie Lake P850m

P50m

Island Lake

P1000m

Oldcamp Lake

Myrtle Lake

Bush trail

P300m

Tower Hill

Dutton Lake

P350m

Pond P50m

P600m

Fly-in Fishing Lodge

P300m

Ely Lake

P80m

Wolf Lake

P80m

our Bass Lake

P1400m

Boundary Lake

Farm Creek

Cramadog Creek

P250m

Hysert Hunt Camp

P100m

P100m

Deep Bay

Magnetawan River

Isaacs Island
Sandy Hook Island

Wajuwebo Bay

Wahwashkesh Lake Dam

Toronto Bay

Wahwashkesh Lake
(top section)

Tracy Bay

Indian Portage
P80m

Indian Narrows

S Start

F Finish

- - - - Route

· · · · · Alternate route

– – – Trail

●～● Portage

P975m Portage length

▲ Campsite

━ Dam/Lift-over

S **F**

Wahwashkesh Rd.

The Big Lake

0   1   2
km

insisted on always canoeing to the cabin due to the amount of ATV abuse the area is getting.

We stayed our first night in the cabin so we could scan over the old map and record the old portages neighboring Island Lake, and we shared our bunks with a dozen or so mice. It's more of a shack than a cabin, but has a cozy feeling to it, decorated with deer and moose antlers, logging relics found in the creek (and pinups dating back to the 1960s). Sadly, the cabin was broken into a year after our trip. I had written a story on my blog about the map and a group of idiots trashed the place and stole the map.

Mike and I were paddling up what remained of Farm Creek before 8:00 a.m., lifting over the first of five beaver dams not far past the cabin. Not long after, we also made a dramatic turn left where Cramadog Creek flows into Farm Creek from the northeast. The four remaining beaver dams were farther up, in the last remaining quarter of the creek, with the third being a more prominent lift-over to the left of a major rock outcrop. From here, Farm Creek makes a major twist northwest, then north. It's a maze of dead-end channels where a distance of less than 2 kilometers as the crow flies took us over two hours to paddle.

Eventually a bridge comes into view, and the last portage before Island Lake is reached. The 300-meter trail is to the left of the bridge and heads across an ATV/snowmobile trail, then cuts through some impressive old-growth pine and hemlock before crossing a patch of swamp grass and more old-growth trees. Near the end, it joins the last bit of another ATV trail that leads down to the water's edge.

Island Lake on its own is a paddler's paradise. The lake is over 6 kilometers long and

3 kilometers wide and is covered in islands, most of which make prime campsites. Even with a fly-in fishing lodge located in the southwest bay and a handful of private camps, this lake still provides an exceptional place to hang out and enjoy a wild setting. And that's exactly what Mike and I did. We spent the rest of the day navigating through the labyrinth of islands, catching monster smallmouth and largemouth bass, and surprisingly, we only got confused as to our whereabouts once. Both Mike and I thought we were paddling in a bay to the northeast but our compass showed us traveling westward. However, by getting lost we ended up finding a 50-meter carry-over, creating a shortcut to the far northwestern bay we wanted to enter the next day.

Mike and I camped on a bush site snuggled in a back bay where a rugged portage leads into Kelsie Lake, to the west of Island Lake.

We were on the water again the next day just before 8:00 a.m. Mike gets up quite early on trips, which is fine by me.

The night before we had walked the 1,000-meter unmaintained portage from Island to Myrtle Lake—which leads into Dutton (Cross) Lake—so we knew what we were getting ourselves into.

Myrtle Lake is teardrop shaped, very clear, with the bottom covered completely in aquatics, mostly coontail. It was also a decent bass lake. Mike and I caught quite a few moderate-size fish before heading onto Dutton (Cross) Lake. The portage was at the very end of the southern inlet. We were confused for a bit at first though when we noticed the snowmobile/ATV trail prior to the inlet, on the left. That trail eventually linked up with the original portage, but we would have walked a bit farther by taking it.

The portage out of Myrtle was far clearer then the one in—not sure why that was. It did, however, fork once again near the end. The portage, measuring 300 meters, seemed to end where the snowmobile/ATV trail went left and right. We went right and soon came to where the creek empties into Dutton (Cross) Lake. And there to help us across was a make-shift bridge made from three TV antennas, frost fence and chicken wire. It had to be the oddest overpass I've ever seen, and Mike and I were a little nervous carrying over it. A sandy beach marked the put-in to Dutton (Cross) Lake, just to the left of the bridge.

Mike and I caught more bass (smallmouth and largemouth) while making our way across Dutton (Cross) Lake and then checked out an old cabin on the far south end. Our progress was slow, not only due to fishing far too much but by checking out every bay and inlet for possible bush trails. We located a very over-grown path linking up to Oldcamp Lake to the northwest and a very old trail heading off toward Duck Lake. Mike and I nearly missed the second portage and only discovered it by stopping for lunch on a rock outcrop to the left of the entrance to the southeastern inlet. It was like solving a mystery; the clues being an oddly placed rock, a grown-over blaze scar and rusty nails hammered in an old pine that obviously once held the portage sign. The portage itself was very difficult to follow, however, and Mike and I opted to look for an alternate route around to Duck Lake by using Wolf, Boundary and Four Bass lakes.

We headed south on Dutton (Cross) Lake to where a marshy creek flowed in. Here we met a local trapper guiding a group on a fishing trip. They were camped to the left of the creek and Mike and I stopped to ask if the watercourse was passable. The trapper didn't know, but advised us to just take the ATV trail

behind them to the connecting beaver pond. We thanked him for his advice and tried the creek anyway.

We should have listened to the trapper!

Mike and I were able to paddle up the creek for about 30 meters; then we carried through patches of sedge and dogwood bushes for another 100 meters or so before coming to where the ATV trail crossed over. Another 20-meter walk got us to a giant beaver dam. From here we paddled across a small pond and then, to the right of a creek, walked through a 50-meter bush trail, hidden by young red pine and large patches of raspberry bushes, to reach Ely Lake.

Wolf Lake was our destination for the day

and Mike and I only had to paddle across Ely and carry 80 meters over to reach Wolf. Once there, we found the first makeshift campsite and set up for the night—hoping to relax before taking on more "undiscovered" portage routes the next day.

Wolf Lake was difficult to leave the next morning. It had everything a canoe tripper could ever want. Morning mist shrouded the pine-clad shoreline, loons wailed off in the distance and a fish breakfast could easily be caught by simply casting a line from the campsite. But Mike and I had a lot of "unsolved" portages to search out and we were off before 8:00 a.m. once again.

Boundary Lake, the next lake in the chain, was easily reached by an 80-meter portage located at the end of the first of two bays at the southeast end of Wolf Lake. Another ATV trail crosses the portage to confuse things once again, but it was more straightforward than what we had to deal with the previous day.

Boundary Lake was just as nice as Wolf Lake, and it had more bass to catch as well. Needless to say, it took Mike and I awhile to start looking for a way out of the lake.

We first went to where the original portage was marked on Mike's 1933 map, traveling south from the portage that took us into Boundary; then once through a narrow channel that linked us into a much broader section of the lake, we paddled to the top end of the first northern bay. It was here that a portage measuring approximately 1,400 meters supposedly went to Four Bass Lake. And from there the plan was to follow a creek out to the Magnetawan River's Trout Lake, with a side trip to Duck Lake, and then upriver on the Magnetawan back to Wahwashkesh Lake. Simple enough we thought; that is, if we could find the portage.

Truth be told, Mike and I did find the portage. It took us a great amount of "mystery solving," locating old blaze marks, rock cairns, even the odd beer can and a broken paddle to find the trail's whereabouts. But no mere mortal would ever want to carry a canoe and gear across what we found—that is unless some portage crew came to re-mark and clear it out. So we searched for an alternate route that some canoeist who posted his trip online told us about. He supposedly followed an ATV trail across from the other bay adjacent to the one we were at.

Mike and I paddled around to the other bay, then lifted and dragged our canoe along a dried-up creek, to the right of where the survey boundary marker was placed long ago on "Boundary" Lake. We eventually came to a large beaver dam, some floating logs and then a small, weedy pond. And on the far shore, after some severe bushwhacking, we located what seemed to be an old wagon road. Mike and I assumed this was the ATV trail that the other paddler had referred to on his online post. The problem was, the trail was grown over with raspberry bushes armed with pencil-sized thorns. To portage along this trail for what seemed to be over 2 kilometers was not doable at all. The old portage was still an option, and we did return to it and began unpacking the canoe for the nasty walk ahead of us. But then Mike made a brilliant point. "Kevin, no one is going to want to do this portion of the route until a proper portage is marked. So, why not return to Island Lake through Wolf Lake and call it a trip?" I agreed totally. We repacked the canoe and retraced to Wolf for our third night out.

We headed back to the familiar Island Lake by using a moderate 600-meter portage to the right of the creek on the eastern inlet of Wolf Lake. From there Mike and I paddled to the lower islands to make camp our last night out. Retracing our route back to Island Lake was the best choice overall. Mike and I spent our extra time catching more fish, portaging into other side lakes to the east and north of Island Lake and taking a hike up to Tower Hill to check out the remains of a forest fire tower constructed here back in the 1930s. From the ridge top we could pick out the terrain we had paddled through for the last week, and also set our sights on possible trips farther afield, linked with the "secret" Island Lake.

LONGEST PORTAGE 1,000 meters

FEE The route is situated on Crown land and an unmaintained Conservation Reserve and no fee is required. A Crown land fee may be required for non-Canadian citizens.

ALTERNATIVE ACCESS None

ALTERNATIVE ROUTE It's quite possible to extend this trip into a full-week loop by linking up to the Noganosh Lake system to the west of Island Lake by way of Kelsie and John lakes and then south to Magnetawan River and then upriver back to Wahwashkesh Lake.

OUTFITTERS
White Squall Paddling Centre
53 Carling Bay Road
Nobel, ON, P0G 1G0
705-342-5324
or
19 James Street
Parry Sound, ON, P2A 1T4
705-746-4936
www.whitesquall.com

FOR MORE INFORMATION
Ministry of Natural Resources
705-564-7823
www.mnr.gov.on.ca

TOPOGRAPHIC MAPS
41 H/9 & 41 H/16

GPS COORDINATES
45.716268, -80.039717

Big East River

🕐 1 to 2 days   None   ●----● 34 km   **Some introductory canoe-tripping skills are required.**

THE BIG EAST River is an absolute oasis for any wilderness paddler looking for a quick getaway. I've never understood why this place doesn't get much traffic from canoeists. Maybe it's because it borders on the west side of the well-known Algonquin Provincial Park. It also might have something to do with the upper reaches being a bit of a nightmare to paddle. The first time I attempted this waterway I started the downstream run from the river's headwaters in the interior of Algonquin. That was a mistake. The upper reaches were pristine and remote,

but the low water levels had me dragging my boat more than paddling it. I cursed the route, that is, until I reached downstream of Distress Dam. From there to the town of Huntsville the river widens, slows down and meanders through some of the best scenery the area has to offer.

Despite neighboring cottage developments, the landscape that surrounds the lower Big East River is unexpectedly wild. A good portion of the river is part of Big East River Provincial Park and a fair amount of land upstream of Highway 11 is Crown land.

The common two-day outing on the Big East is from Distress Dam access to Williamsport Road bridge and then from Williamsport Road to Huntsville. Through the years I've altered my route slightly. I find the Distress Lake access road a little bumpy to drive and water levels a little too low after mid-June for the first stretch to Williamsport Road. Also, from where the river empties out into Lake Vernon to the town docks in Huntsville is a little over developed for my liking. So now either I do a full day trip from Williamsport Road access to the take-out at Hutcheson Beach off Ravenscliffe Road (Muskoka Road 2), or I

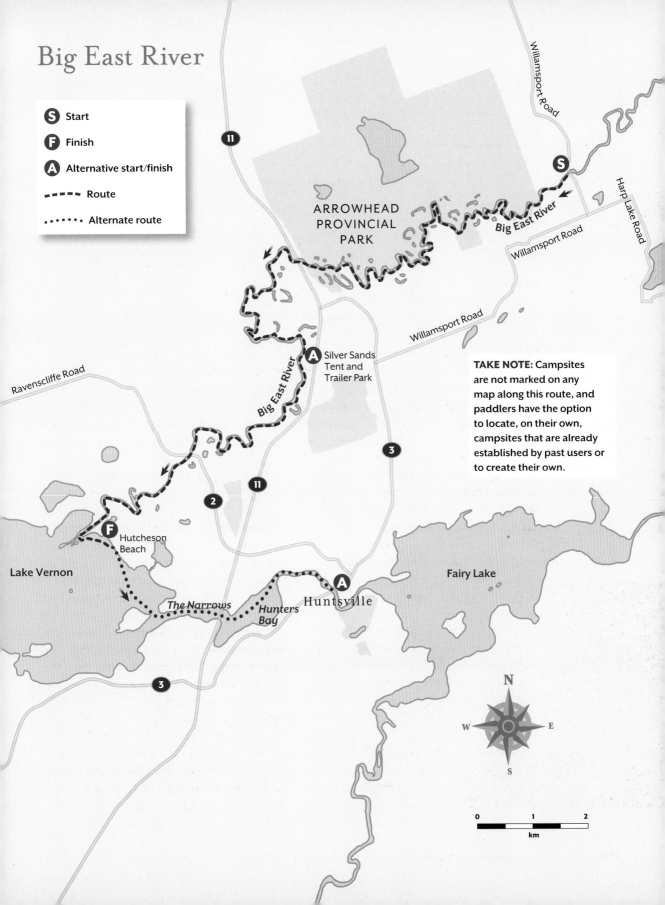

Big East River

S Start
F Finish
A Alternative start/finish
- - - - Route
· · · · · Alternate route

ARROWHEAD
PROVINCIAL
PARK

Big East River

S

Willamsport Road

Harp Lake Road

Willamsport Road

Willamsport Road

A Silver Sands
Tent and
Trailer Park

Ravenscliffe Road

Big East River

TAKE NOTE: Campsites
are not marked on any
map along this route, and
paddlers have the option
to locate, on their own,
campsites that are already
established by past users or
to create their own.

11

2

3

11

3

F Hutcheson
Beach

Lake Vernon

The Narrows

*Hunters
Bay*

A

Huntsville

Fairy Lake

3

N

W   E

S

0   1   2
km

begin at Hutcheson Beach, paddle upstream to camp on one of the many sandbanks near Arrowhead Provincial Park and then paddle back downstream the next day.

Williamsport Road bridge is reached by taking Muskoka Road 3 to Williamsport Road. Parking and the access point are on the southwest corner of the bridge. The first couple of kilometers downstream are made up of shallow swifts that you may have to get out and wade through. The next section consists of oxbows that snake along the fringes of Arrowhead Provincial Park and reveals the river to be part of a 10,000-year-old glacial spillway that cuts through 35-meter-high sandbanks. It's an amazing paddle.

After drifting by Arrowhead Provincial Park the river straightens, deepens and flows under a few bridges, including Highway 11, which marks the halfway point on your trip downriver. If you wish to make camp at this point there are a number of possible bush campsites along the sandbanks upstream and downstream from Arrowhead Provincial Park.

The river harbors an abundance of wildlife, especially songbirds. On every trip, my bird list increases by several more species, including one or two uncommon species. The last time I drifted down the Big East, a willow flycatcher fluttered across the bow of my canoe, so close I could see the distinct cat whiskers on its beak. I also spotted a red-shouldered hawk as it glided high above a spruce grove behind my tent site. It is not unusual to see and hear bird species typical of the north—such as dark-eyed juncos, black-backed woodpeckers, gray jays, Swainson's thrushes and Lincoln's sparrows—as well as southern species, like the eastern towhee and the yellow-throated vireo. At nightfall I sat by the campfire and listened to the distinct call of the barred owl—"Who-cooks-for-you? Who-cooks-for-you-all?"—and the familiar wail of loons calling to each other on nearby lakes.

As you approach the end of your trip, you'll feel the breeze coming off Lake Vernon. This is the largest of four lakes surrounding Huntsville, and it still retains a good amount of undeveloped shoreline. Vernon offers a scenic paddle with a picturesque backdrop of the Canadian Shield's sweeping hills. Wind is usually an issue out on this big lake, but you'll get a break as you make your way through the delta system at the mouth of the river. The mounds of sediment flushed out by countless floods have created an ecological masterpiece: a rare deciduous swamp forest of birch, ash and red and silver maple. This area is a water-logged haven for a variety of birds and a perfect ending to an exceptional river paddle.

If you decide to continue paddling across Lake Vernon to end at the town docks in Huntsville, you will get to soak in more of Vernon's scenery and have a chance to splurge on a hot meal washed down with a cold refreshment at the local pub. Not a bad option, either.

LONGEST PORTAGE None

FEE The route travels through an unmanaged conservation reserve and Crown land. No camping permit is required.

ALTERNATIVE ACCESS If you wish to shorten the route, you can start or finish at the Silver Sands Tent and Trailer Park access point.

ALTERNATIVE ROUTE To avoid a vehicle shuttle, you can begin the route at Hutcheson Beach, paddle up Big East River to camp along one of the many sandbanks near Arrowhead Provincial Park and then paddle back downstream the next day.

OUTFITTERS
Algonquin Outfitters –
Huntsville Store
86 Main Street East
Huntsville, ON, P1H 2C7
705-787-0262
www.algonquinoutfitters.com

Silver Sands Tent and Trailer Park
58 Silver Sands Road
Huntsville, ON, P1H 2J4
705-789-5383
www.visitmuskoka.com

FOR MORE INFORMATION
Arrowhead Provincial Park
451 Arrowhead Park Road
Huntsville, ON, P1H 2J4
705-789-5105
www.ontarioparks.com

MAPS Jeff's Map has produced an interior route map of Algonquin Provincial Park that covers this section.

TOPOGRAPHIC MAPS
31 E/6 & 31 E/7

GPS COORDINATES
45.388331, -79.192499

Charleston Lake Provincial Park

 2 days   None   ●----● 6 km   **This is definitely a novice trip where the main campground is a stone's throw away in case of an emergency.**

MANY CANOEISTS ASSOCIATE true wilderness paddling with the Canadian Shield—a great slab of ancient rock more obvious in northern parks such as Algonquin or Quetico. To the east, however, this two-billion-year-old rock also dominates the landscape by way of a southern extension known as the Frontenac Axis. And because of this, Charleston Lake Provincial Park is also added to the list of the province's prime canoe destinations.

The rugged, northern character of the Charleston Lake area has always been best suited for the pursuits of outdoor enthusiasts, as settlers found the thin soils unproductive. As far back as the 1860s, the lake itself had become a well-known retreat for upper-class vacationers from Ottawa, Toronto and Upper New York State who found pleasure in exploring the lake by steamer, fancy sailboats or cedar-strip guide boats rowed by a single oarsman.

Present-day canoeists now seem to dominate the recreational scene by making use of a number of lakes, rivers and creeks in the area. (Charleston Lake–Red Horse Lake–Gananoque River–Wilts Creek is the most popular weekend loop.) However, the provincial park, situated on the southwest corner of Charleston Lake, does offer the best canoeing overall, especially when low water levels can make the extended routes unnavigable throughout most of the paddling season.

Charleston Lake Provincial Park is located northeast of Kingston and can be reached by County Road 3 from Highway 42 and Highway 15 and the Lansdowne turnoff from Highway 401.

The main campground maintains 238 sites, but the park also offers 13 interior sites organized into clusters grouped together at Bob's Cove, Hidden Cove, Buckhorn Bay, Captain Gap, Slim Bay and Covey's Gap. Each cluster has one to three campsites and can hold six people and three tents per site. There is a canoe launch and parking lot at the far end of the main campground, past the interpretive center and second beach.

It's wise to reserve well in advance for the more remote sites, especially the cluster site located in Slim Bay, where powerboats have been banned because the area is the only known nesting site for loons in the park. (The southern portion of Runnings Bay is also

Charleston Lake Provincial Park

Legend

- **S** Start
- **F** Finish
- - - - Trail
- ▲ Campsite
- ▼ Historic Native camp
- ⬤ Historic Native rock shelters
- No-motorboat zone

Green Bay

Deer Island

Buck Island

La Rose Bay

Republican Island

Tallow Rock Bay

Beaver Pond

CHARLESTON LAKE PROVINCIAL PARK

Charleston Lake

Hedgehog Island

Frizzle Island

Petries Island

Mud Bay

Tallow Rock Bay Trail West

Shoreline Centennial Trail

Runnings Bay

Croziers Island

Slim Bay

S **F**

Tallow Rock Bay Trail East

Sandstone Island Trail

Slacks Bay

Hemlock Island

Narrows Island

Whitefish Island

Huckleberry Island

↓ *To County Road 3 and park entrance*

Pine Island

0 ⸻ 1
km

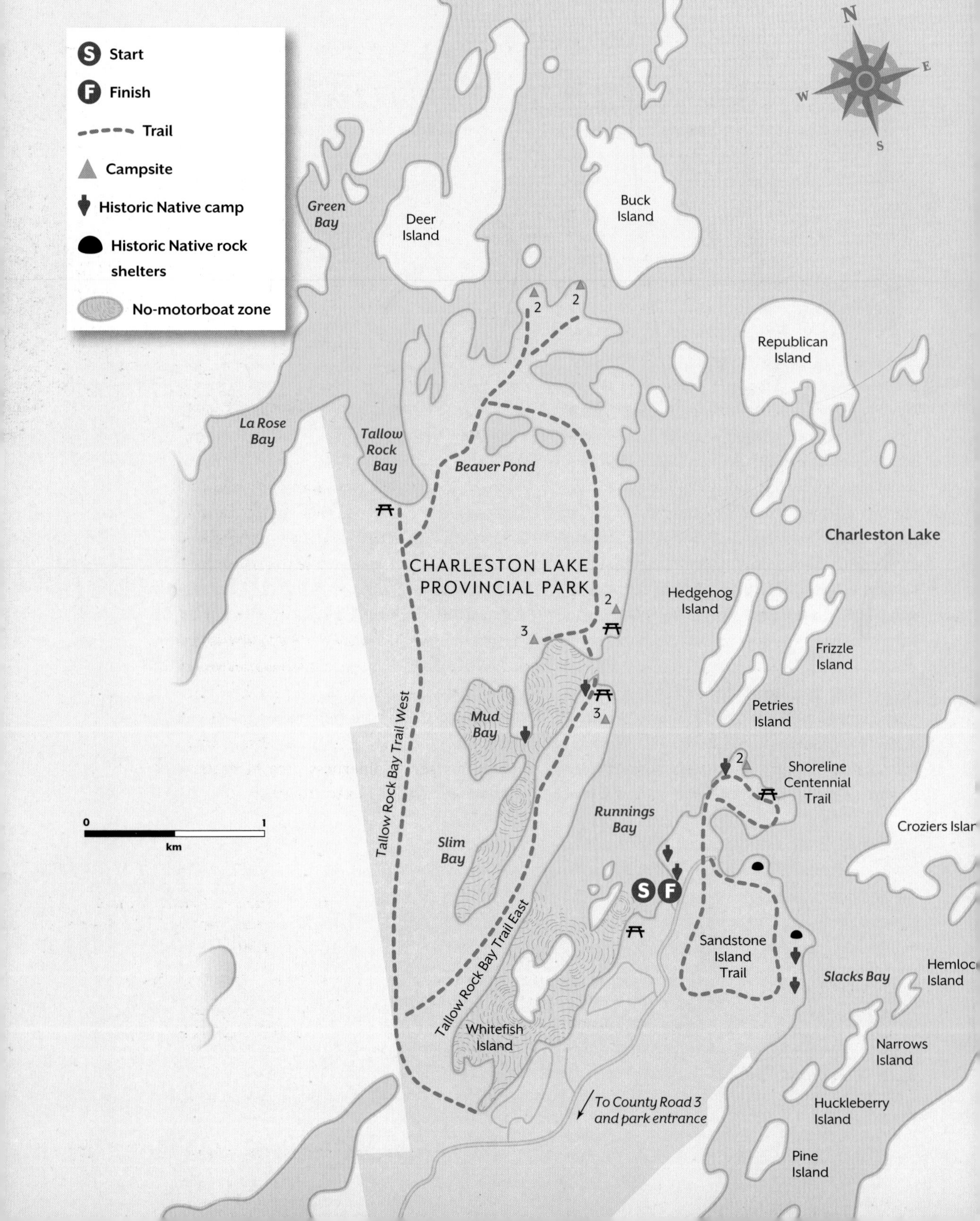

off-limits to powerboats.)

Conveniently connected to each interior site is a hiking trail upon which visitors can head off to explore the area's wide assortment of flora and fauna. Since the Frontenac Axis is the most southern part of the Shield, the various habitats that are found here create what biologists call a transition zone. Here, a large selection of plants and animals occur either beyond the normal southern or northern extent of their range, and Charleston Lake has some of the rarest finds in the province. Rooted along a narrow valley in Tallow Rock Bay, as well as a southern portion of Slim Bay, is a collection of showy orchis growing at the base of mature hemlock. Pitch pine, which was once used to seal wooden boats and is one of Canada's scarcest tree species, is also found in good concentration on the quartzite ridge north of Duck Bay. And Charleston Lake's unofficial mascot is the black rat snake—a harmless but good-sized tree-climbing constrictor that, when startled, will flatten out its neck and vibrate its tail.

Three main archaeological sites that you can easily visit by canoe include the pictographs in Slim Bay and the mysterious rock shelters found at Jackson's Point and Gordon Rock. The rock paintings have become harder to spot over the years, but the rock shelters,

thought to be used by primitive man, are quite noticeable to canoeists cruising the shoreline. The caves were formed when weaker layers of quartzite pebbles crumbled beneath the more resistant sandstone.

These biological and cultural treasures abound in Charleston Lake, but it's still the scenic appeal of the rugged landscape, much like the land more to the north, that has influenced both the natural and human history of the area and that will continue to draw canoeists to this semi-wilderness area of eastern Ontario. Believe me, it's worth a visit!

FEE A fee is required for overnight camping.

ALTERNATIVE ACCESS None

ALTERNATIVE ROUTE You can plan a circle route by canoeing Charleston Lake, Red Horse Lake, Gananoque River and Wilts Creek. (Ask the park staff for information.)

OUTFITTERS The main campground offers canoe rentals.

FOR MORE INFORMATION
Charleston Lake Provincial Park
148 Woodvale Road
Lansdowne, ON, K0E 1L0
613-659-2065
www.ontarioparks.com

MAPS Charleston Lake Provincial Park has produced a map: Charleston Provincial Park.

TOPOGRAPHIC MAPS 31 C/9

GPS COORDINATES
44.515553, -76.024840

Grants Creek/Pooh Lake

🕐 3 to 4 days   🧍 11 portages   ●━━━● 24 km   **Moderate canoe-tripping experience is needed if you wish to travel upstream on Grants Creek.**

I T DOESN'T SEEM to matter how busy work gets, I always manage to make it down to the coffee room at least once a day. Not for the coffee, of course. The stuff tastes like shoe leather. It's the conversations with my fellow workmates that draw me down to the basement. You see, there's a group of us who have promised never to talk about anything except canoeing while taking in our daily caffeine fix.

One instructor, Hugh Banks, takes this pledge very seriously. Whenever someone mentions a problem with his students or makes some political statement about the college administration, he changes the subject by quickly blurting out, "So where's our next canoe trip, Kevin?" To help his scheme, I simply fire back the name of some obscure place that no one has ever heard about, and the conversation is quickly turned back toward the desired subject—canoeing.

A number of great adventures have been formed this way. Of course, the best one to date was when I mentioned a possible trip to Pooh Lake—named by a former Algonquin Park ranger after author A.A. Milne's 1926 story, *Winnie the Pooh*. That definitely got everyone's attention. I remember it took three cups of coffee to explain all the details to a very fixed audience.

There are two ways to reach Pooh Lake, located just outside of Algonquin Provincial Park's eastern boundary. The first is to paddle up Grants Creek—a new and unmaintained Waterway Park developed through the Lands for Life (Ontario's Living Legacy) project of 1999. And the second is a bumpy ride down the Menet Lake Road, marked on the left side of Highway 17, just north of Driftwood Provincial Park and about 3 kilometers south of where Grants Creek flows into the Ottawa River.

If you happen to be in a hurry to reach Pooh Lake, and your vehicle can manage the rough ride, then the Menet Lake Road is your best bet. Simply follow the main dirt road for approximately 10 kilometers and then take the side road to the left just before the main road crosses Grants Creek. A short portage is marked on the right side of the roadway, just past where a bridge crosses over the creek to a cabin owned by the Grants Creek Hunt Club. It's another 20-minute paddle upstream from here to Pooh Lake, with a few exposed rocks and a large beaver dam to lift over just before you get to the lake.

Grants Creek/Pooh Lake

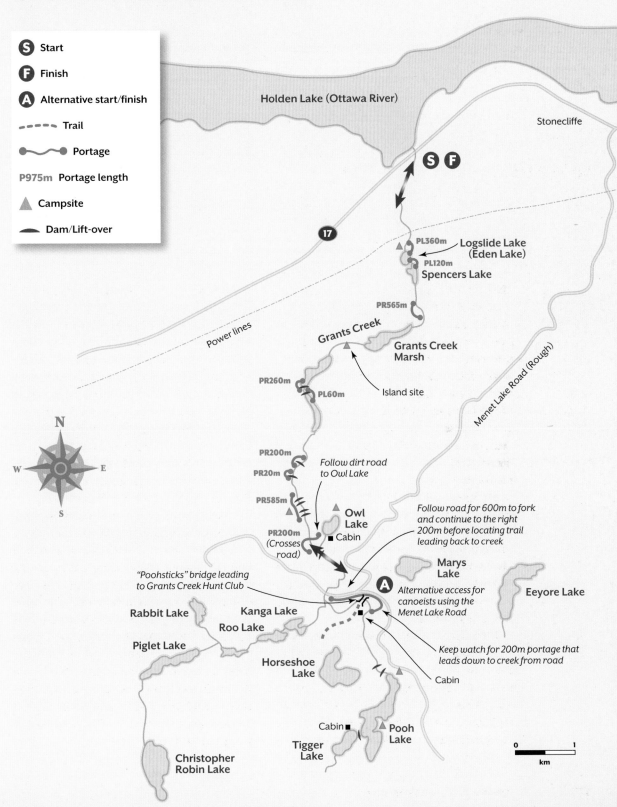

Legend

S Start

F Finish

A Alternative start/finish

- - - - Trail

●—————● Portage

P975m Portage length

▲ Campsite

➤ Dam/Lift-over

Holden Lake (Ottawa River)

Stonecliffe

S **F**

17

PL360m **Logslide Lake (Eden Lake)**

PL120m **Spencers Lake**

PR565m

Grants Creek

Grants Creek Marsh

Island site

PR260m

PL60m

PR200m

Follow dirt road to Owl Lake

PR20m

PR585m

PR200m *(Crosses road)*

▲ **Owl Lake**

■ Cabin

Follow road for 600m to fork and continue to the right 200m before locating trail leading back to creek

Marys Lake

Eeyore Lake

"Poohsticks" bridge leading to Grants Creek Hunt Club

Rabbit Lake

Kanga Lake

Roo Lake

A *Alternative access for canoeists using the Menet Lake Road*

Piglet Lake

Keep watch for 200m portage that leads down to creek from road

Horseshoe Lake

Cabin

Cabin ■

Pooh Lake

Tigger Lake

Christopher Robin Lake

N / W / E / S

Power lines

Menet Lake Road (Rough)

0   1
km

Hugh and I decided to paddle the entire stretch of Grants Creek, however. We were accompanied by Hugh's 10-year-old son, Jeremy, and we thought the unmaintained route up Grants Creek would introduce the youngster to the realities of canoe tripping. Besides, the cold-water stream looked awfully promising for brook trout fishing.

Well, we were wrong about the fishing. None of us caught a single trout. But the trip up, and eventually back down, Grants Creek happened to be Jeremy's first real adventure in a canoe.

The escapades began almost immediately. The government sign that marks the parking area north of the Grants Creek bridge and on the left side of Highway 17 was hidden by brush, and we ended up parking south of the bridge and wading up a series of rapids before realizing our mistake. Then, after a long, 2-kilometer section of river blocked by three consecutive beaver dams, we endured the first of the route's 10 rough and incredibly steep portages. The first portage is marked to the left and climbs alongside a scenic cascade for a short 360 meters.

After a quick paddle across Logslide Lake (once used to hold logs before being flushed down into the Ottawa River come spring), the second portage is marked to the left of yet another waterfall. The path measures only 120 meters but it heads directly up a slab of granite and happens to be the steepest portage en route.

Soon a third portage, to the right, is marked at the end of Spencers Lake. It's not as abrupt as the first two, but it's difficult to locate at times and measures a full 565 meters.

From here it's a leisurely hour's paddle across the expanse of Grants Creek Marsh, alive with various species of ducks, great blue herons, muskrat and beaver. Throughout the expansive marsh a few outcrops of rock carpeted in white pine present themselves as places to pull up on shore for a lunch break. A prime campsite is even marked on a central island and can be a great place as long as the bug population stays down.

The next series of portages begins close to the far west end, where the creek empties into the marsh. There are two trails here. The first measures 260 meters and is marked on the right of a minor waterfall, and the second is only 60 meters and marked on the left of a large rock pile.

After a good 10 to 15 minutes of paddling through almost stagnant water, the shoreline grows rugged once again and another string of portages now avoids one of the most impressive drops along Grants Creek. The first portage is a straightforward 200-meter path leading around the right of a gigantic water slide. The next is a mere 20-meter carry to the right of a rock-strewn chute. But the third portage, also found to the right, is an extensive 585-meter, poorly maintained pathway squeezed through a miniature canyon. This is the most frustrating portage along the creek, both because the rough path is dangerously steep in places, not to mention blocked by a number of fallen trees, and because a series of side trails heading back down to the creek makes the main trail almost impossible to locate at times.

Disgruntled about accidentally exploring three of the five side trails, Hugh strongly suggested that we make camp halfway along the portage. It was a bush site (since the route is no longer maintained, the selection of designated campsites is an almost impossible task), but the cleared area came with a plot of soft moss to erect the tent on and a flat rock to use as a handy dinner table. In fact, it was

such a perfect, out-of-the-way spot along the flooded creek that we decided to make it our base camp and make tomorrow's paddle up to Pooh Lake into an easy day trip. This would rid us of dragging all our gear upstream through the unexplored route and reduce our trip from four days to an easy three.

So early the next morning, after hanging our food pack between two old pine trees, we loaded our canoe up with our lunch bags and fishing gear and continued our upstream journey.

Another portage, a 200-meter trail marked to the right of an iron bridge, is quick to block the route again. The path crosses a dirt road about three-quarters of the way along, and a five-minute walk across the bridge and up the road will take you on a side trip into Owl Lake. Keeping with the Winnie the Pooh theme, our group took time out to explore the oval-shaped pond. We even took a few casts from shore to try and catch at least one of the many good-sized brook trout that are rumored to hole up on the bottom of Owl Lake.

However, an hour later, not even Jeremy, the best angler among us, had hooked a fish, and so we decided that we would continue on up the creek and spend our energy on the not-so-renowned rainbow trout stocked in Pooh Lake.

Except for a quick swift, followed by a large beaver dam, both of which have to be dragged over almost immediately after the last portage, the creek remains sluggish right up until the Menet Lake Road crossing.

Hugh, Jeremy and I were a little confused as to our whereabouts at this point. An old Algonquin map, dating back to 1971, was the only thing that we could find before heading out on our trip that had a description of the Grants Creek canoe route, and so far the map had proved only somewhat accurate. At this point, however, it became totally useless. The map showed a 200-meter portage and 345-meter portage on the left bank and no sign of any road crossing. We figured that splitting up was our best option, with Hugh and Jeremy walking the dirt road to the south and me paddling farther up the creek.

An hour later, after finding no portages and having to slug over boulders and gnarled spruce trees fallen across the creek like matchsticks, I finally met Hugh and Jeremy sitting on top of a metal bridge, enjoying a game of "Poohsticks." (The game originated in A.A. Milne's *The House at Pooh Corner* and involves dropping sticks into the stream and seeing which one appears on the other side of the bridge first.)

Obviously, the road is the better route. First, go left from the bridge and walk uphill for approximately 600 meters until you reach a fork in the road. Then go right to where you'll eventually see the old Poohsticks bridge crossing over to the Grants Creek Hunt Camp. Here, remain on the main road on the left side of the creek and look to the right where a 200-meter path will lead you back down to the water.

From here it's only a 20-minute paddle through a large marsh, followed by another shallow swift and beaver dam that must be lifted over (we couldn't find another 300-m portage that the old map had marked to the left), before you reach the very scenic Pooh Lake. (Christopher Robin, Piglet and Eeyore lakes are also nearby but far too difficult to reach by canoe.)

There is a campsite on a pine-clad point about halfway across Pooh Lake. Our group's plan, however, was to troll our fishing lines directly across the lake, then make a quick "bounce" into Tigger Lake (a short lift-over connects this small pond with Pooh Lake's northwest bay) for a well-deserved shore lunch of fried trout. But even with our trip's mascot—a stuffed Winnie the Pooh bear—tied onto the canoe's bowplate for good luck, we remained fishless and had to resort to stale honey sandwiches for our afternoon meal.

By midday we gave up any hope of catching fish (Jeremy figured they were taken by a gang of Heffalumps) and headed back to base camp. Along the way, rejoicing at finally being able to travel with the current, our spirits remained surprisingly high for three avid anglers returning with an empty stringer. After all, as Winnie the Pooh once said about his "Expodition" to the North Pole, "We might find something that we weren't looking for, which might be just what we were looking for, really." To me, that's what canoe tripping on Grants Creek was all about.

LONGEST PORTAGE 1,000 meters

FEE This is an unmaintained provincial park and no fee is required.

ALTERNATIVE ACCESS You can avoid most of Grants Creek by using Menet Lake Road to access Pooh Lake.

ALTERNATIVE ROUTE A side trip to Owl Lake can be had by following the dirt road that crosses the ninth portage en route.

OUTFITTERS
Dumoine River Expeditions
613-586-2562
www.dumoine-exp.ca

FOR MORE INFORMATION
Ministry of Natural Resources
Pembroke District Office
613-732-3661
www.mnr.gov.on.ca

TOPOGRAPHIC MAPS
31 K/4 & 31 L/1

GPS COORDINATES
46.210787, -77.926531

Upper Ottawa River

 5 to 6 days   None   ●----● 74 km   **Possible high winds and waves and the lack of designated campsites are the only problems that could arise.**

OUR FAMILY TRIP down the upper Ottawa River was made by complete chance. I had just come back from a work trip in the far north when my wife, Alana, announced she was able to gather an extra week of holidays. Her criteria for the unanticipated time off was to take our five-year-old daughter, Kyla, on a canoe trip—an easy route, with limited or no portages, and somewhere we had yet to travel. I had two days to figure it out. Obviously, it wasn't an easy job. I've paddled most of the province. However, I remembered a workmate had mentioned the upper Ottawa River, from the town of Mattawa to Driftwood Provincial Park. He said it was an ultimately easy and yet remote canoe trip. Admittedly, I ignored him at the time, basically because I couldn't imagine a portage-free route along a portion of a well-known river like the Ottawa, where everyone in Canadian history once traveled, being a nice "get away from it all" paddle trip. Truth is, the only reason I chose the trip was that I couldn't come up with another plan in time for our departure. Thank goodness I did. My workmate was right about the upper Ottawa—it's an ultimate paddling destination.

I'd never been so unprepared for a canoe trip in my life. We organized our car shuttle the night before the trip, and thankfully we found someone. Algonquin North Outfitters provided the service. The plan was to drive my vehicle to the put-in at Mattawa's public boat launch, on the north side of the town bridge that crosses the Mattawa River. The outfitter would then pick up our vehicle and later in the week drive it down to Driftwood Provincial Park's designated parking area near the take-out.

We drove the six hours from our home in Peterborough, dropped the key off to the outfitters along Highway 17, at the entrance to Algonquin's Kiosk Lake access, and then spent the first night at the nearby Samuel de Champlain Provincial Park. Surprisingly, my poorly laid plan was coming together.

After a breakfast in the town of Mattawa, we packed our canoe with more gear than usual. It was a good feeling. There were no portages to worry about, so lawn chairs, extra snacks and a mini-cooler were stored in front. Our new dog Ellie even got extra treats and a chew-toy.

Before heading downriver we took a hike

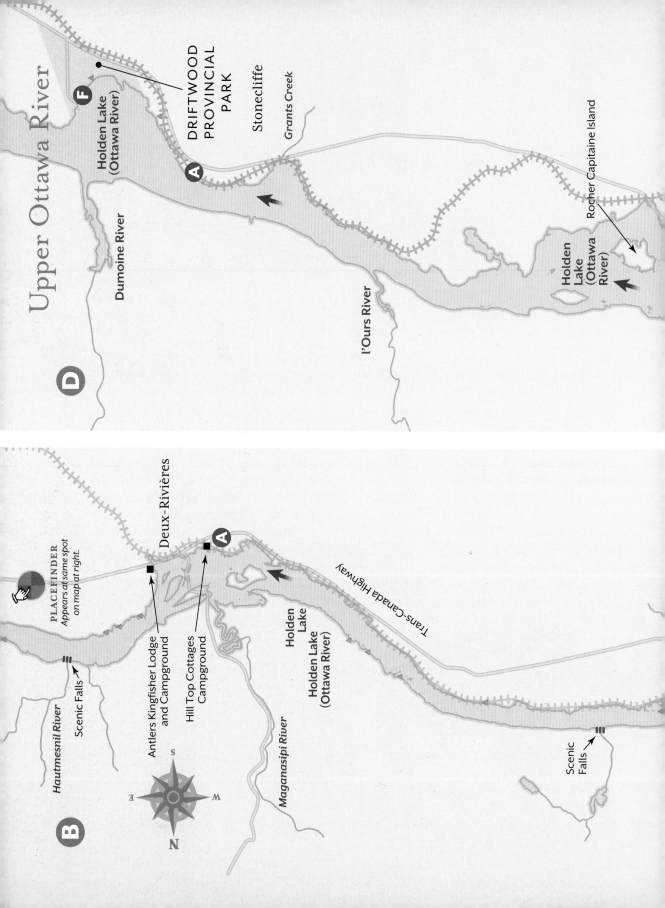

Upper Ottawa River

D

Dumoine River

Holden Lake (Ottawa River)

F

DRIFTWOOD PROVINCIAL PARK

Stonecliffe

Grants Creek

l'Ours River

Holden Lake (Ottawa River)

Rocher Capitaine Island

A

B

Hautmesnil River

Scenic Falls

PLACEFINDER
Appears at same spot on map at right.

Deux-Rivières

A

Antlers Kingfisher Lodge and Campground

Hill Top Cottages Campground

Holden Lake

Holden Lake (Ottawa River)

Maganasipi River

Trans-Canada Highway

Scenic Falls

N
S
E
W

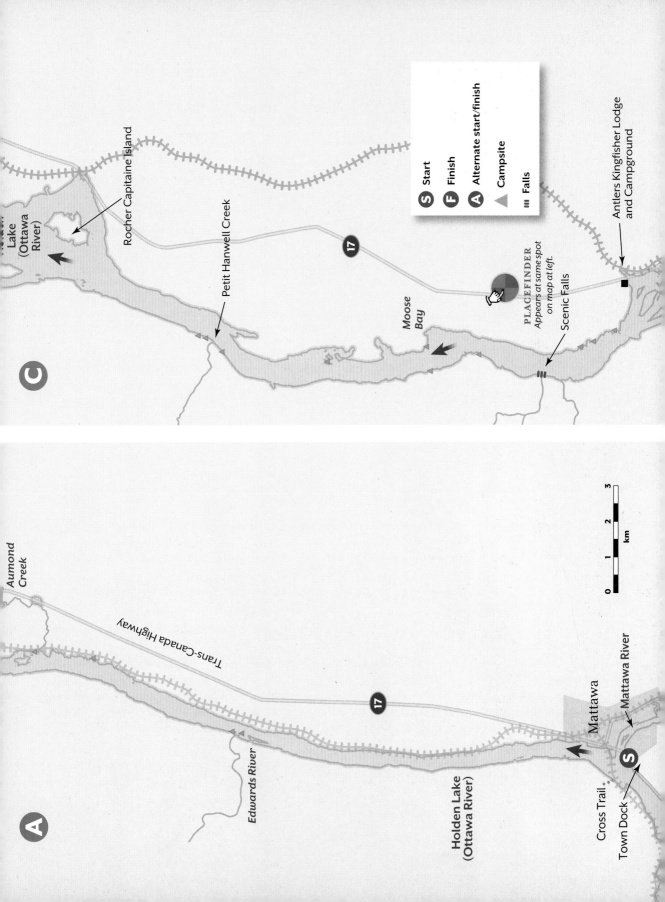

A

Aumond Creek

Trans-Canada Highway

17

Edwards River

Holden Lake (Ottawa River)

Mattawa

Mattawa River

Cross Trail

Town Dock

S

0 1 2 3
km

C

Lake (Ottawa River)

Rocher Capitaine Island

Petit Hanwell Creek

17

Moose Bay

PLACEFINDER
Appears at same spot on map at left.

Scenic Falls

Antlers Kingfisher Lodge and Campground

S Start

F Finish

A Alternate start/finish

▲ Campsite

▮▮▮ Falls

up to the notable three white crosses affixed on a ridge across the Ottawa River, on the Quebec shore. The original markers were thought to have been erected in 1686 by order of Sieur de Tryes, a missionary priest, during his journey up the Ottawa River to celebrate the first mass in Mattawa. Other reports state it was three local priests who put them there in 1917 to show their support for WWI. Whoever first placed them there was a moot point for Alana, Kyla, Ellie and I, however. It was the scenic splendor we all witnessed while standing on the ridge, overlooking the river we were about to paddle down, that inspired us and made the pilgrimage up the hill worthwhile.

Less than an hour into our trip I was totally enthralled with the upper Ottawa as a canoe route. The scenery was amazing, with the steep-walled corridor of Quebec's Laurentian hills to the left and the surprisingly undeveloped Ontario forested shoreline to the right. The width of the river was just under a kilometer at best. We saw two motorboats, both anchored where Edwards River flushes into the Ottawa on the Quebec side. The anglers were there practicing for a bass tournament scheduled for the next day. They weren't catching much and had a good laugh at their bad luck when we paddled a little farther up the creek mouth, and Kyla hooked into the largest smallmouth bass I've seen in my life. It was caught on her Barbie fishing rod, and I ended up pulling the line in hand over hand while she reeled in the loose line. I plopped it back into the pool below the rapids and on cue Kyla looked over at the anglers in the boats and said "That's how you do it, boys." I've never been so proud.

The fishermen let us know that the two campsites to the right of the cascade, one small bush site directly beside the mouth of the river and another around the corner at a small beach, were better campsites than the ones a bit farther downstream. So we pulled up early to camp our first night out, paddling only 11 kilometers. We chose the smaller of the two sites. Mid-morning on our second day of floating down the Ottawa, we came across the alternative campsites we originally thought of taking our first night out. They were on the Ontario side this time; one was a bush site just before Aumond Creek and the other was directly after Aumond Creek. Another site was about 1.5 kilometers downriver, on a small island. The anglers were right—the two sites upstream were better choices and we were glad we stopped when we did. In general, none of the sites were all that nice. And in retrospect, the only major problem with paddling the upper Ottawa River was the lack of good campsites and, for the last portion of the trip, the lack of any campsites. Prior to the trip, I had found no information at all about the location of campsites on the river and if it wasn't for the staff at Algonquin North Outfitters who marked some known campsites on the river, we'd have been paddling blind. It wouldn't have been my first time doing that. On many of my more northern trips I simply found a place in the bush to spend the night. But when you're traveling with a five-year-old, a campsite has to be more kid-friendly if you ever want her to go on a trip with you again.

Not far from the small island site where we stopped for brunch was the first of many scenic cascades tumbling down the Quebec side of the river. It was an incredible spot and while floating at the base of the falls, filtering water from the clearer water of the small tributary rather then the expanse of the Ottawa River, I soaked in the vista around us. It was truly an amazing backdrop, especially

considering that Highway 17 was a stone's throw away from the Ontario shoreline, and even closer was the railway line. However, the rail line is presently closed, which may add a bonus for paddlers wanting some peace and quiet along the river, but may not be the best thing for the local economy.

Having the train track not in service happened to be a godsend for us. The scorching weather brought in a major storm later in the afternoon that crept up on us very quickly. By sheer luck we were paddling close to the Ontario shore, nearing the old rail town of Hodgson, and minutes before the storm hit, spotted a very old and rarely used campsite once used by rail workers. I put up the tarp and Alana and Kyla tied up the canoe, while our dog Ellie took cover under the nearby brush.

The foul weather stayed for the rest of the day, and it wasn't until around dinner time we could crawl out from under the tarp to check out our surroundings. We then took the time to walk the abandoned rail line all the way to Hodgson before dusk. It was a nice walk, especially since we had no reason to portage during the entire trip. Not much was left behind at the old station, but Kyla found enough rusted rail ties and weirdly shaped globs of rock slab to keep her amused.

Our alarm clock the next morning was a motorboat speeding downriver, then another and another. The bass tournament had begun. We counted five boats in total, which was not bad for a river of this size. We were still in awe of how little the upper Ottawa River was used.

The morning mist that had hugged the Quebec Laurentian hills the day before until well after breakfast, wisped away a lot quicker due to more hot weather approaching. We were hoping for a slight breeze to build up by midday but nothing happened. It even felt at times that the excessive heat was making us paddle slower than if we had to fight against gusts of wind and heavy trough.

We just weren't in a hurry to go anywhere. We had brunch drifting along the more shaded Quebec side of the river, soaking in complete solitude until we interrupted a group of nesting terns along a cluster of tiny islands. We really weren't that close to the nesting area, but the hyped-up birds launched, flocked up and then dove straight down at us. Ellie became quite upset about the attack, and she hid under my seat each time the birds screeched just above us. By doing so, the dog was able to escape the poop-bombs. The first splatter hit the top of the packs, the second landed on Kyla's lap (she wasn't impressed) and the third assault struck the brim of my favorite canoe hat. Kyla and I fought back by unpacking our water guns but it did little. On the fourth strike, the terns got poor Alana on the head as well. Unfortunately, she wasn't wearing a hat.

As we approached the town of Deux Rivières, the river had more of a Huck Finn feel to it. The wild shorelines were replaced by a few cottages and the boat traffic doubled. Rather than gawking at wildlife, we watched people enjoying their time on the river. We stopped to talk to a group of anglers with a pimped-out bass boat participating in the bass tournament, a middle-aged couple in a leaky sailboat and a bunch of rowdy guys drinking beer on top of their rental houseboat.

Deux Rivières was the only town en route, and we took advantage of it. We pulled up on the Ontario docks of Hilltop Cottages and

Campsites to place an order of coffee and muffins at their Gingerbread Café. If it had been later in the day, we would have stayed here, renting one of their teepees for the night. Kyla would have loved that. Meeting the new owners, Sue and Eppo v. Houten, was one of the highlights of our trip down the Ottawa. They had just recently moved from Holland and were busy fixing up the cabins. Sue and Eppo fell in love with the place at first sight. They happened upon Hilltop during a family holiday when they stopped along the highway to gawk at the striking scenery. That's when they noticed the old fishing lodge was for sale. Sue went over and shook the owner's hand and said "It's not for sale anymore." It changed their life completely, and the only regrets they have are dealing with the blackflies in the spring—Sue hates blackflies—and the fact that it's not really on a hill. "If you want to be pedantic about it," Sue told us, "it's a hillside, not a hilltop; but I love it just the same."

Our next stopover was Antler's Kingfisher Lodge, about a 20-minute paddle directly downriver from Hilltop, where we stopped to pick up important supplies such as chocolate bars, potato chips, cold pop and fresh water.

Not long after leaving the dock of the private campground we met our first and only canoe group en route. It was a church faction from Ottawa and like us, it was their first but definitely not their last trip down this underutilized route. They were a larger group, totaling six, and moving much faster than we were as well. We had planned six to seven days to paddle the route, and they were completing it on a long weekend.

It wasn't until Ontario's Moose Bay, past where another scenic waterfall plunges in on the Quebec side, that we made camp. It wasn't a true campsite, and many paddlers would have passed it by without even knowing it was there. But we lucked out when I stepped out of the canoe to pee. Once we pulled the canoe up and I walked around a bit, it was obvious the site had once been a common place for people to camp. After pulling the grass out from the old fire pit and clearing a couple of fallen trees away from the tent site, we put up the bug shelter to help Kyla's fear of deerflies (she had been bitten earlier) and made dinner.

Our fourth day out, the river grew wider and deeper. We spent the morning drifting down the center, taking advantage of the still-strong current. The river is more lake-like here, and without the obvious flow, you wouldn't know it was an actual river. The Ottawa measures over 1,200 kilometers in length, drains an area of 146,300 square kilometers and is the second-longest river in Canada (St. Lawrence being the first, flowing into the Atlantic). The Algonquin called it Kitchissippi meaning "Great River" and the deepest part is roughly 330 feet. Still, we saw only one boat racing across it before lunch. Unfortunately, the boater sheared a pin after hitting one of the many pulp logs that randomly float up to the surface and become a real hazard.

Seeing the floating pulp logs was a good reminder of how busy this place would have been during the massive log drives that happened on the Ottawa River. Driving logs downriver began around 1830, and it's estimated that over 14 billion logs were floated down the Ottawa during the logging era and 2 to 5 percent of those were lost each year to the bottom of the river. No wonder a few pop up now and then.

To share the logging history of the Ottawa with Kyla, Alana and I sang a few verses of the famous Stompin' Tom Connors' song "Big Joe

Mufferaw" who "paddled into Mattawa, all the way from Ottawa in just one day." Mufferaw was a French-Canadian folk hero from the Ottawa Valley who was characterized as Canada's version of Paul Bunyan. After hearing a few verses, Kyla claimed Mufferaw was better than Bunyan. After all, Bunyan didn't have a pet frog that was bigger than a horse, or drown out a forest fire over 50 kilometers away with spit balls.

Driving the logs would have been a dangerous job, even for the likes of Joe Mufferaw. Before the construction of Des Joachims Dam in 1950, where 46 kilometers of river was flooded and called Holden Lake, a number of substantial rapids existed along the stretch we were paddling. Deux Rivières had a massive flow of water, and Rocher Capitaine was even bigger.

It was less than an hour's paddle upriver of Rocher Capitaine Island that we ran into our first occupied campsite. It was about a two-hour paddle downriver of our last campsite, and it was the best campsite on the river so far. It even came complete with a picnic table. The two guys making use of it, who had a motorboat smaller than our canoe, were a joyful duo and even invited us to share the site. We declined, however. Actually it was Kyla who declined. They were French and she replied to them in French because she understood better than us. Kyla is in French immersion, and it came in handy more than once on our trip.

Alana and I figured we could get to the area around the flooded Rocher Capitaine rapids. It seemed, however, that our whole timing was off when looking for a campsite on the river. Nothing existed at all on the Quebec side near Rocher Capitaine. Most likely some type of campsite existed on the large island in Bissett Bay itself, but the paddle across to check it out was about 1.8 kilometers. Alana and I seriously thought we'd find a spot farther downriver. We didn't. We had kept to the Quebec side most of the time to gain as much shade as possible from the tall Laurentian hills, but the abruptness of shoreline limited any possible flat spot to erect a tent. However, even when we paddled over to Ontario, the bush was generally too thick. We may have missed a site somewhere along the way, but with the river so wide at this point we couldn't paddle back and forth as easily as we did the first couple of days of the trip.

Around 5:00 p.m. we were getting desperate and had to make the decision to paddle all the way to Driftwood Provincial Park, our take-out point, to book a campsite. Going all the way to Driftwood was a huge issue for us. If it had been just Alana and I, then paddling faster and farther the last day wouldn't have been much of a problem. With Kyla, however, we knew we would soon run out of songs and games to play to keep her from getting bored.

The last section was the most tedious of the trip. From the mouth of Rivière à l'Ours to the hamlet of Stonecliffe, the river seemed to go on forever. Calm waters at least allowed us to cut across Driftwood Bay rather than stick to the shoreline, cutting off a good 3-kilometer distance. And by 7:00 p.m. we pulled the canoe up on Driftwood Provincial Park's day-use beach, the furthest beach to the left. From here it was a casual walk up the hill to retrieve our vehicle and then load up back at the beach before booking a gorgeous campsite at the park.

It was a simple end to a simply planned but incredibly enjoyable trip. Alana and I even shared ideas on the drive home of returning and paddling more of the Ottawa the following summer, either from Lake Timiskaming to Mattawa or from Driftwood to Pembroke. Kyla agreed, but asked for conditions—we don't go in deerfly season and she enters the bass tournament so she can win the prize for biggest fish next time. You can't beat that for prerequisites coming from a five-year-old.

FEE The route travels through an unmanaged area and no fee structure is in place.

ALTERNATIVE ACCESS The trip can be shortened by beginning in the town of Deux Rivières, using Hilltop Cottages or Antler's Kingfisher Lodge and Campground as a put-in.

ALTERNATIVE ROUTE The trip can be shortened into a 2–3 day trip by paddling from Mattawa to Deux Rivières or from Deux Rivières to Driftwood Provincial Park.

OUTFITTERS
Algonquin North Outfitters
The corner of Hwy 17 and Hwy 630
Mattawa, ON, P0H 1V0
1-877-544-3544 or 705-744-3265
www.algonquinnorth.com

FOR MORE INFORMATION
Ministry of Natural Resources
705-564-7823
www.mnr.gov.on.ca

TOPOGRAPHIC MAPS
31 L/1, 31 L/7, 31 L/8, 31 K/4 & 31 K/5

GPS COORDINATES
46.320240, -78.710225

Mattawa River

 13 portages

●----● 46 km

This is a novice route, since all rapids come with well-marked portages.

I HAVE TO GIVE an editor friend of mine, Noel Hudson, a lot of credit. Noel has read over every misadventure I've ever had in a canoe. Yet not only does he still agree to tag along with me on our annual paddling trip, he chooses to be my canoe partner as well.

This trip started off innocently enough. Noel and I, along with the rest of our group, met in the town of Mattawa and then had Fudge Doucette at the Petro-Canada gas station on McConnell Drive (just across the road from the town's tourism building) shuttle us back up to the top end of the river. We took Highway 17 and, deciding to bypass Trout Lake in order to begin directly at the entrance to the Mattawa Waterway Park, turned right at Corbeil Corners (Highway 94) on Centennial Drive. From there we followed MacPherson Drive almost 6 kilometers to the road's end.

After loading the canoes at the government docks, we headed east and paddled through the narrows to the left, passing the historic Portage de la Tortue. Originally there was a shallow, rocky section here that Natives, explorers, missionaries and voyageurs had to carry around when traveling on the Mattawa. The obstruction was later blasted open to connect Trout Lake and Turtle Lake.

At the end of Turtle Lake there's a choice of two routes that will take you to Talon Lake—the largest lake en route. You can keep with the river and make use of five portages (none of which measures over 150 m), or continue east and portage in and out of Pine Lake. We chose the second of the two (the traditional route of the voyageurs), hoping to spend our first night out on one of the islands of Pine Lake.

So we paddled up a muddy creek (which, oddly, drains in the opposite direction to the Mattawa), lifted over a beaver dam, made use of the 200-meter Portage de la Mauvaise Musique on the right and then set up camp on the north side of Pine Lake's largest island.

Portage Pin de Musique, 450 meters long and marked in a weedy bay to the northeast, led us out of Pine Lake and into Talon Lake's McCool Bay the next morning. The wind was coming from the northwest, but caused us some concern only while paddling toward the far point off to the right. As soon as we rounded the corner, we were able to speed down to Talon Chutes at the southeast end.

Portage de Talon (named after the governor

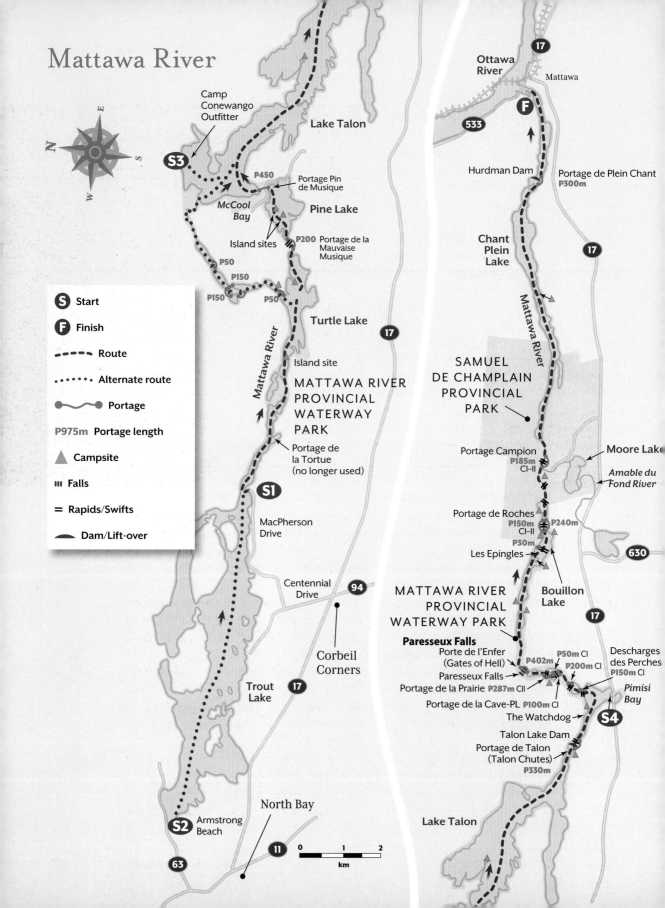

Mattawa River

Legend

S Start

F Finish

- - - Route

.... Alternate route

●～● Portage

P975m Portage length

▲ Campsite

╫╫ Falls

= Rapids/Swifts

◠ Dam/Lift-over

Left map

Lake Talon

Camp Conewango Outfitter

S3

P450

Portage Pin de Musique

McCool Bay

Pine Lake

Island sites

P200 Portage de la Mauvaise Musique

P50

P150

P150   **P50**

Turtle Lake

17

Mattawa River

Island site

MATTAWA RIVER PROVINCIAL WATERWAY PARK

Portage de la Tortue (no longer used)

S1

MacPherson Drive

Centennial Drive   **94**

Corbeil Corners

Trout Lake   **17**

North Bay

S2 Armstrong Beach

11

63

0   1   2
km

Right map

17

Ottawa River

Mattawa

F

533

Hurdman Dam

Portage de Plein Chant **P300m**

Chant Plein Lake

17

Mattawa River

SAMUEL DE CHAMPLAIN PROVINCIAL PARK

Moore Lake

Amable du Fond River

Portage Campion **P185m** CI–II

Portage de Roches **P150m** CI–II   **P240m**

P30m

Les Epingles

630

Bouillon Lake

MATTAWA RIVER PROVINCIAL WATERWAY PARK

17

Paresseux Falls

Porte de l'Enfer (Gates of Hell)   **P402m**   **P50m** CI   Descharges des Perches

Paresseux Falls   **P200m** CI   **P150m** CI

Portage de la Prairie **P287m** CII

Portage de la Cave-PL **P100m** CI   *Pimisi Bay*

The Watchdog   **S4**

Talon Lake Dam

Portage de Talon (Talon Chutes)   **P330m**

Lake Talon

of New France, Jean Talon) is one of the most difficult portages en route. Marked to the right, just before a dam, the 330-meter trail makes its way over a series of precarious rock ridges and then descends steeply down toward a small beach. Of course, thinking back to when the voyageurs carried monstrous packs weighing no less than 180 pounds, a modern-day canoeist burdened down with lightweight canoes and packs shouldn't really complain.

Difficult portages aside, Talon Chutes is an incredibly historic place. Natives held vision quests in the 6-to-16-foot-deep potholes scoured out of the rock on the north side; a section of the 100-foot-high cliff below the chutes was used as a lookout when the invading Iroquois ambushed the Nipissing people. A rock formation above the potholes, called the Dog Face, appeared in Ripley's *Believe It or Not* in the 1950s. Well-known canoeist and cinematographer Bill Mason shot footage here for the portage scene in his film *The Voyageurs*. And William and Jacques, the two characters from the popular television commercials for Labatt's Brewery, jumped off the south side of the chute. (Jacques lost his wig on the first take, and the whole scene had to be redone.)

Not far downstream, just before the river empties into Pimisi Bay, is another historic gem — a humpbacked rock on the north bank called the Watchdog. There, Natives and voyageurs left an offering of tobacco to appease the spirits and ensure safe passage. Noel and I should have taken heed of this, for it was on the third set of the five upcoming rapids where we took our ill-fated dump.

The first rapid begins where the river heads north out of Pimisi Bay. A 150-meter portage is on the right. It's called Descharge des Perches, being the place where the voyageurs discarded their poles used for traveling

upstream. We all ran through, rushing over the remains of an old logging dam and then down the left channel of a rocky Class I rapid (be ready to make a sharp right turn at the bottom).

The second rapid, with an unnamed 200-meter portage found at the end of the small bay on the southeast side, as well as the third set, with the 100-meter Portage de la Cave marked on the left, were far more difficult Class Is. We still managed to run them, however, with a tight squeeze between the rocks near the bottom of the third set being the most challenging part.

Then, after heading down a quick swift (there's an unnecessary 50-meter portage on the right), we approached the last run before Paresseux Falls. Everyone headed for the

287-meter Portage de la Prairie (also known as Petite Paresseux) marked on the left—everyone except Noel and me, of course. I'm not sure if it was arrogance, laziness [Editor's note: *paresseux* does mean "lazy"] or just plain stupidity, but I suggested to Noel that we run down the first drop and have a look at what was around the corner. What a mistake!

Halfway down we found ourselves caught up in the current and tried to power toward shore. That failed miserably. Then we tried to eddy in behind a small boulder. That also failed. And it wasn't long before we found ourselves drifting sideways to the current, heading toward a miniature fall.

It wasn't a dramatic flip. Noel and I just slid sideways down a smooth piece of rock, miraculously staying upright until the very end. There was a brief moment of panic when Noel's foot became wedged in a rock and held him under, but he eventually recovered and we began swimming downriver after our packs and canoe. Miraculously, the only item lost was Noel's favorite baseball cap.

The rest of the group, who had all safely walked around the rapid, arrived at the put-in just in time to witness us coming ashore, looking like a couple of drowned rats. I don't think they had much sympathy for us, but they did point out that there was a campsite halfway along the portage if we wanted to stop for the day. Noel and I refused, however, and insisted that they just allow us time to change into some dry clothes before continuing on. It was a humbling experience, to say the least.

The 26-foot-high Paresseux Falls, with a mandatory 402-meter portage on the right, is absolutely breathtaking. What's even more impressive, however, is Porte de L'Enfer—a narrow cave located just around the corner on the north side of the river.

The site is actually an old Native mining site dating back three thousand years. Lured here by the sounds of spirits singing at the base of the falls, the Native people found the rich veins of hematite, an oxide of iron that when refined was used as the basis for the rock paintings known as pictographs. The superstitious voyageurs, however, interpreted this as the living quarters for a flesh-eating demon (its blood made up of the red ocher) and named it the "Gates of Hell."

The first campsite after Paresseux Falls is where our group stayed for our last night on the river. In the morning, Noel and I, wary from our dump the day before, had to be coaxed out of our tent by the smell of bacon, eggs and fresh coffee.

The first rapid of the day, Les Epingles, was a mere swift leading into Bouillion Lake. Noel and I regained a bit of confidence by making a clear run down the center (a 30-meter portage does exist on the left). After one look at the rapids flowing out on the other end of Bouillion Lake—a Class I–II that had become quite technical due to the low water levels—we panicked, however, and headed straight for the 150-meter Portage de Roches marked on the left (for some reason there is also a portage, 240 m long, on the right).

Portage Campion, measuring 185 meters and found on the right (just past where the Amable du Fond River, coming from the upper reaches of Algonquin Park, enters the Mattawa), marks the next set of rapids. Noel and I scouted the set first and classed it as another technical Class I–II. But since it was the last navigable whitewater of our trip, we convinced ourselves it was safe to run. So, after talking over our planned route (starting center and then going a tad to the right to avoid most of the shallow stuff), we ran it not only once, but three times.

Portage Campion also marks the river access to Samuel de Champlain Provincial Park. This makes for an excellent alternative take-out point, especially since the Mattawa Waterway Provincial Park ends soon after the provincial campground and cottage development begins to appear just before the Hurdman Dam. (A 300-m portage—Portage de Plein Chant—is marked to the right of the dam.) The traditional end point, however, is in the town of Mattawa, at a municipal park located on the south side of the river just before the cement bridge. We chose the customary route, basically because that's where our shuttle driver had stored our vehicles.

The extra three-hour paddle was worth it, though. The section before Hurdman Dam, where the river spreads itself into a placid sheet and surrounds itself with high walls of granite, was quite scenic. You may enjoy a sense of history by ending at the confluence of the Mattawa and Ottawa Rivers (mattawa is actually the Ojibwa word for "meeting of the waters"). We enjoyed the poutine and cold drinks we bought at a restaurant on the main street of Mattawa. And by storing our vehicles back at the Petro-Canada gas bar and not having to pay for parking at Samuel de Champlain Provincial Park, I was able to save enough money in the end to buy poor Noel another baseball cap and a comical pair of water wings to match.

LONGEST PORTAGE 450 meters

FEE No interior camping permit is required for Mattawa Provincial Park. A moderate shuttle fee is required, however.

ALTERNATIVE ACCESS There are a number of options to begin the trip. Armstrong Beach on Trout Lake (in the town of North Bay), Camp Conewango Outfitters on Lake Talon and Pimisi Bay and Highway 17.

ALTERNATIVE ROUTE By starting out at North Bay's Armstrong Park, on Lakeside Drive just off Trout Lake Road (Highway 63), you can add an extra few hours of paddling across Trout Lake.

OUTFITTERS
Algonquin North Outfitters
The corner of Highway 17 and Highway 630
Mattawa, ON, P0H 1V0
1-877-544-3544 or 705-744-3265
www.algonquinnorth.com

Fudge Doucette
Mattawa Petro-Canada
290 McConnell Drive
Box 774
Mattawa, ON, P0H 1V0
705-744-2866

North Bay Canoe Company
2822 Highway 17 East
Corbeil, ON, P0H 1K0
1-800-927-1290
www.nbcanoe.com

FOR MORE INFORMATION
Samuel de Champlain Provincial Park

1-888-668-7275 (reservations)
www.ontarioparks.com

Friends of the Mattawa River Heritage Park
705-744-2276

MAPS The Friends of the Mattawa River Heritage Park have produced a very detailed canoe map for the Mattawa River. Hap Wilson's guidebook, *Rivers of the Upper Ottawa Valley: Myth, Magic and Adventure*, is also an excellent resource. You can also refer to the Mattawa River map in The Adventure Map series by Chrismar.

TOPOGRAPHIC MAPS
31 L/6 & 31 L/7

GPS COORDINATES
46.312632, -79.257703

Bonnechere River

🕐 2 days   🧍 2 portages   ●----● 26 km   **This is a novice route, although some canoe-tripping skills are required.**

THE BONNECHERE RIVER is situated in the northern portion of the Mada-waska Highlands, between the Ottawa River and the southeast corner of Algonquin Park. This route's put-in is at Algonquin's Basin Depot access point.

Basin Depot can be reached by turning off Highway 58 onto Turner's Road, which is 7.3 km north of Round Lake Centre. Before heading up Turner's Road, you will need to drop off a second vehicle at either Bonnechere Provincial Park or the outfitters at Round Lake Variety, just over 1 km south of the park. Parking and park permits for Basin Depot can be purchased at Bonnechere Provincial Park. After dropping off the second vehicle, follow Turner's Road (which will turn into Basin Depot Road) for 16 km to the park boundary and six more to Basin Depot.

The Bonnechere River is managed by two separate authorities: the upper portion is protected by Algonquin Provincial Park and the lower stretch is defended by Bonnechere River Provincial Park. I've paddled both sections, and both make possible weekend outings. The Algonquin portion that is upriver from Basin Depot, however, can be an absolute nightmare—a place where I walked, portaged and lifted over logjams more than paddled. For me it was a slog, not an adventure, and a route I vowed never to repeat. But the section of river that exits Algonquin and flows into Round Lake, a river route I've returned to many times, is much more manageable. It's the more scenic of the two, being a part of the Ottawa Valley watershed and equipped with rich forested uplands that roll up from the basin floor.

Algonquin's Basin Depot is a historical site that holds the ruins of an old logging shanty-town dating to between 1850 and 1913. One of the 10 original buildings is still intact: a well-constructed log home built by the McLachlin Lumber Company in 1892 (making it the oldest standing building in the Algonquin region). It served as a hospital during a diph-theria epidemic in 1911, and at least seven gravesites hidden in a nearby poplar grove endure as signs of the outbreak.

Park your vehicle near the slab of cement that marks the remains of two farm sites in the area and continue down to the Bonnechere River by walking a narrow path overgrown with grass and raspberry cane.

A quick glance at the river here will tell you what your journey down the upper section, to Couchain Lake, will be like. If the tea-colored water is flowing easily over the cobblestone, then you're in luck. If not, there's likely not enough water to paddle this section. You'll have to drive back south along Basin Depot Road and make use of the Couchain Lake access point, 1.7 km outside Algonquin's boundary. (No provincial park permit is required here.)

Why even bother with the upper section then? It's the most scenic portion of the river. This is where two diverse habitats collide—a place where a couple strokes of the paddle take you from the province's near-north climate, which is almost savannah-like, to the far south, where spruce trees and columbine plants give way to birch and white trilliums.

What gives you this impression of the south the most, however, are the bird species spotted along the shore. Belted kingfishers swoop down across the river, the pileated woodpecker's hysterical call echoes throughout the back woods, American bitterns sound out from patches of sedge where the river widens its banks and an endless assortment of warblers flutter across your bow. It only takes a five-minute paddle downriver from the put-in to have Algonquin's regular calls of boreal chickadees and gray jays change over to the sounds of great crested flycatchers, northern flickers and gray catbirds.

However, it's not only birds that provide entertainment along the way. My most memorable trip on the Bonnechere was during an early morning paddle when I spotted a moose cow and calf, a white-tailed deer and a family

of otters all sharing the same back bay of the river. Then, a few strokes around the next bend, I heard the faint whimpering of baby beavers inside a gigantic lodge. As I drifted closer to the stick-and-mud structure, the mother swam out, dove directly under my canoe, surfaced not far from my stern and loudly slapped her tail against the surface of the water. I was awestruck. I've never had so much drama unfold in such quick succession on a trip, and the memory of the wildlife encounters I had that morning will never be forgotten.

Two portages along the upper section (110 m to the left and 520 m to the right) are required to avoid a double set of shallow rapids, but at good water levels it's quite easy to run both rapids.

If you intend to make this a multi-day trip, Couchain Lake has three of the four possible campsites along the route. The two largest are found on the southeast end of the lake, just before the waterway narrows; the third site is

off on its own on the northwest side, overlooking the scenic bluff called Egg Rock.

Beyond Couchain Lake is easy paddling across Curriers Lake, White Mountain Bay (named after the steep rock wall to the right), Beaverdam Lake and Enos Bay. Then the river narrows again, twisting and turning its way toward Turner's Road bridge. Once past the bridge the river forks. Go right here (the left channel is much shallower) and paddle out into Stevenson Lake.

The fourth designated campsite is marked on the top end of Stevenson Lake, just past where the Pine River empties into the Bonnechere. Depending on how much time you have, camp here or continue on downstream to Bonnechere Provincial Park on Round Lake. There's not much to contend with directly after Stevenson Lake, only two shallow swifts and a small drop called Jack's Chute. The swifts can be run, lined or waded. Jack's Chute can be run—by experts—or lifted

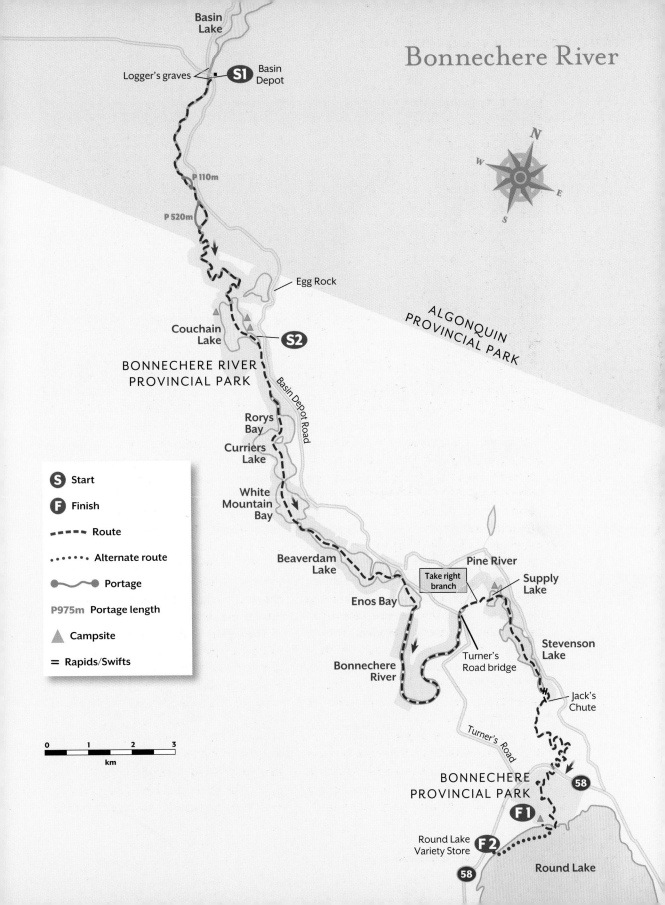

Bonnechere River

Basin
Lake

Logger's graves ••• S1 Basin
Depot

P 110m

P 520m

Egg Rock

ALGONQUIN
PROVINCIAL PARK

Couchain
Lake

S2

BONNECHERE RIVER
PROVINCIAL PARK

Basin Depot Road

Rorys
Bay

Curriers
Lake

White
Mountain
Bay

Beaverdam
Lake

Pine River

Take right
branch

Supply
Lake

Enos Bay

Stevenson
Lake

Turner's
Road bridge

Jack's
Chute

Bonnechere
River

Turner's Road

BONNECHERE
PROVINCIAL PARK

58

F1

Round Lake
Variety Store

F2

58

Round Lake

Legend

S Start

F Finish

- - - - Route

• • • • Alternate route

•~~• Portage

P975m Portage length

▲ Campsite

= Rapids/Swifts

0   1   2   3
km

over on either side. Just keep in mind that the land on both sides of the chute is private and should be respected.

Farther downstream the river continuously winds back on itself. In 1861, surveyor Robert Hamilton made note of this "exceedingly torturous" stretch of the Bonnechere. He avoided this stretch by using a long portage, which no longer exists. Because of this you'll have to grin and bear the monotonous paddle and hope the fry-truck is open for business outside the park gate when you're done.

LONGEST PORTAGE 520 meters

FEE A parking permit and interior camping permit is needed for Basin Depot and the section of river that runs through Algonquin Provincial Park. An interior camping permit is not required for camping on Couchain Lake or at the top of Stevenson Lake.

ALTERNATIVE ACCESS Couchain Lake access point, 1.7 km outside the park boundary on Turner's Road (no provincial park permit is required here), can be used.

ALTERNATIVE ROUTE If you wish to shorten the route, it's possible to skip the upper section and just paddle from the Couchain Lake access point to Bonnechere Provincial Park on Round Lake.

OUTFITTERS
Round Lake Variety
3740 Round Lake Road
Killaloe, ON, K0J 2A0
613-757-2162

FOR MORE INFORMATION
Bonnechere Provincial Park
4024 Round Lake Road
Killaloe, ON, K0J 2A0
613-757-2103

MAPS You can also refer to the Bonnechere River map in the Adventure Map Series by Chrismar.

TOPOGRAPHIC MAPS
31 F/12

GPS COORDINATES
45.662824, -77.570899

Lake Timiskaming/Ottawa River

🕐 6 to 8 days    2 portages   ●-----● 120 km   Canoeists must be experienced in paddling rough water.

LIKE THE LOWER stretch of the Ottawa River below the town of Mattawa, the upper section that flows from Lake Timiskaming to Mattawa gets little use from paddlers. I haven't a clue why. The scenery is exceptional, with thick boreal forest rooted on the western Ontario shoreline and the Laurentian Mountains jutting up behind the eastern Quebec border. And the best part is you get to travel a total of 120 kilometers and only portage once. The notably rough waters of Lake Timiskaming—the same that drowned 12 boys and one leader from St. John's Anglican School of Ontario in 1978—may keep paddlers away. But when approached with caution and logic, this entire route makes a perfect journey on one of Canada's most historic waterways.

The last time I paddled this route, my group (which included my daughter, Kyla, and another family) stayed the night before and the night after the trip at Nature's Harmony, a totally off-the-grid retreat that has a choice of rustic log cabins or cozy canvas yurts to sleep in. It's a glamper's paradise. We had Jen and Tzach, the owners, drop us off at the launch in Ville-Marie, Quebec, and rather than take

out at the dam before the town of Mattawa, Ontario, we exited close to their eco-lodge, which is northeast of Mattawa.

To reach the launch at the marina in Ville-Marie from the south, follow Highway 101, turn left on Rue Notre Dame Sud in Ville-Marie and left again on Rue Sainte Anne.

Our first camp—an island site a few kilometers along the eastern shore of the lake—wasn't too far from the put-in. The waves weren't breaking yet but it made sense to end the day early before conditions got worse; they definitely did. I should note that the entire route has no designated campsites so we had to find our own, ensuring we practiced low-impact camping as we journeyed along the route.

Part of the Ottawa River, Lake Timiskaming definitely deserves the highest respect; any big lake does. However, it's the lower half that you really have to watch out for. It's narrower than the upper section, but don't be fooled by that. The high cliffs along the shoreline create a tunnel effect, and with the prevailing winds blowing across the wider upper section, you may find yourself dealing with some massive troughs in a matter of minutes.

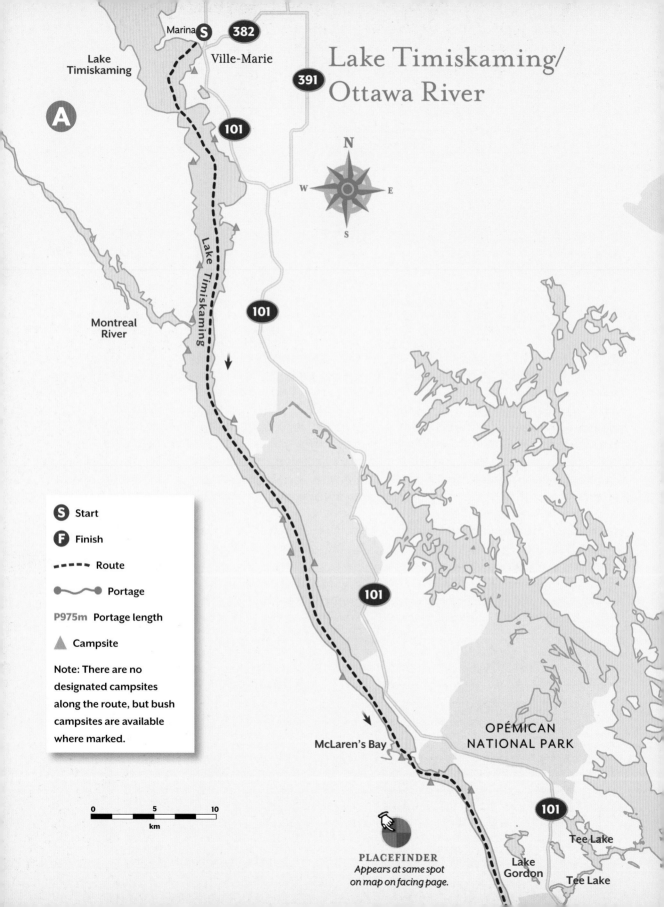

Lake Timiskaming/Ottawa River

Marina

S Ville-Marie

382

391

101

Lake Timiskaming

A

N

W   E

S

Montreal River

Lake Timiskaming

101

101

101

101

OPÉMICAN NATIONAL PARK

McLaren's Bay

Lake Gordon

Tee Lake

Tee Lake

S Start

F Finish

- - - - Route

•——• Portage

P975m Portage length

▲ Campsite

Note: There are no designated campsites along the route, but bush campsites are available where marked.

0   5   10

km

PLACEFINDER
Appears at same spot on map on facing page.

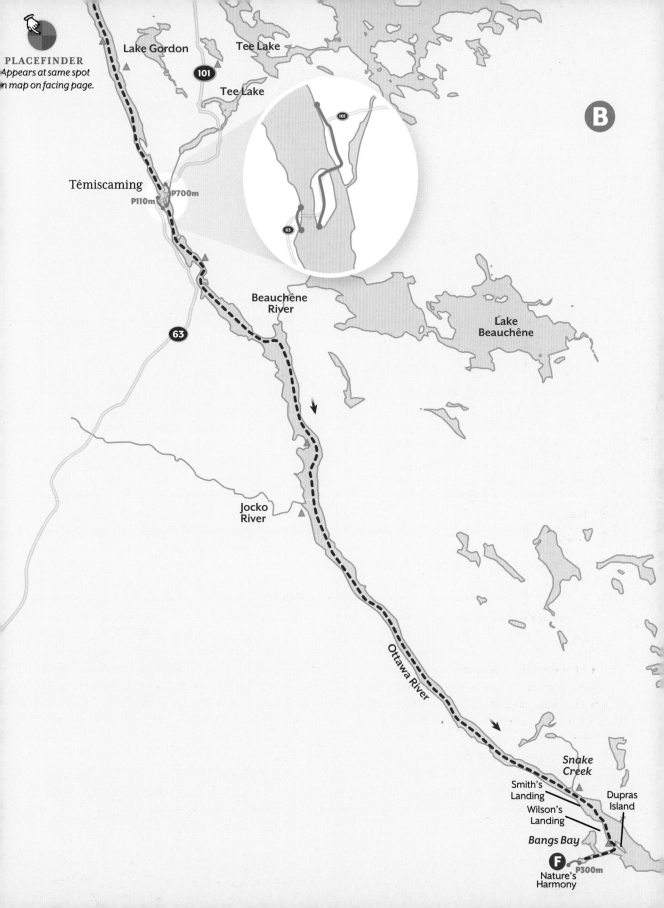

PLACEFINDER
Appears at same spot
on map on facing page.

B

Lake Gordon

Tee Lake

101

Tee Lake

Témiscaming

P700m

P110m

101

63

Beauchêne
River

Lake
Beauchêne

63

Jocko
River

Ottawa River

Snake
Creek

Smith's
Landing

Dupras
Island

Wilson's
Landing

Bangs Bay

F

P300m

Nature's
Harmony

The worst-case scenario, however, is when the winds come from the south and blow against the downstream current. Though it behaves like a big lake, Timiskaming is comparatively smaller and shallower, which means it sculptures waves closer together and with steeper sides.

Its smaller size doesn't preclude it from having its own legendary monster, called the "Mugwump" (which supposedly means fearless sturgeon) or "Tessie" (a Timiskaming-style play on "Nessie"). It is believed the serpent that haunts these waters is over 6 meters long—a creature I'm relieved to say we didn't run into on our journey.

Averaging about 12 kilometers (5 to 6 hours) a day, we took four days to paddle down Lake Timiskaming to where the lake narrows and finally ends at the town of Temiscaming, Quebec. Our group generally kept to the less-rugged Ontario shoreline to find campsites each night. As mentioned, no campsites are marked or maintained, but we always found

a place to pitch our tents at the end of every day.

The town of Temiscaming is the only place you will need to carry your canoe and gear because a hydro dam blocks your path. It's also where the Ottawa River portion of your trip begins. There's a short 110-meter portage on the Ontario side, which is found to the right, once you've paddled over the protective floating buoys before the dam. The carry ends at the base of the dam. Personally, I think the Quebec side provides a far better choice. The portage on the eastern shore is longer (700 m), but it passes by a gas station and corner store; and as anyone from Ontario knows, you can buy beer at corner stores in Quebec. It was also a hit with the kids, who loved the idea of stopping along a portage for chips, pop and ice cream.

For the longer portage, take out at the public marina on the left shoreline, carry along Du Lac Promenade, which merges into Chemin Kipawa (Highway 101), cross the bridge at the Tembec sign, cut through the municipal depot area and put in at the public launch not far from the Algonquin Canoe Company and Outfitter store. (Take care crossing the busy roads, especially if you decide to stop at the gas station.)

Past Temiscaming, options for possible campsites become sketchy. I had an old map that indicated one site among weedy islands just downstream from the town, where Highway 63 winds away from the river. When we got there the site was surrounded by swamps and a little too close to Temiscaming. After paddling a couple of hours past the mouth of the Beauchene River, our group still hadn't located a possible tent spot. Just before sunset we did finally locate a place—an island at the mouth of a good-sized bay on the Ontario side that is a couple kilometers before you pass Jocko River. It was a perfect site and around the fire that night the adults enjoyed some nice, cold beer purchased in Temiscaming.

From there the Ottawa takes you past a few cottages, but the majority of the river is left to its natural state—patches of maple and birch are scattered among the dominant stands of conifer trees, and lush blueberry bushes carpet the forest floor. You'll come across a couple of good spots to camp, each marked with a knob of granite and a cluster of pine. If you feel it's too early to stop for the day, the next possible bush campsite is a good distance (at least three hours) downstream, at a public launch at the mouth of Snake Creek, on the Quebec side. In my opinion, though, it's best to stop early at the better sites and extend your last day's journey.

From Snake Creek it's a short distance to the take-out. Paddle a few more kilometers of the Ottawa River and then take a sharp turn into Bang's Bay, just to the west of Dupras Island, to reach a rough road close to Nature's Harmony. This bay is an excellent place to end the trip—a pristine spot that is much more tranquil than the wider banks of the Ottawa.

We followed a 300-meter trail up to the rough road where the owners of Nature's Harmony had parked our vehicles. Even if you choose not to use Nature's Harmony to organize your shuttle, this is still the better option for a take-out point than the dam in the town of Mattawa.

LONGEST PORTAGE 700 meters

FEE This route travels through Crown land and no camping permit is required for Canadian citizens.

ALTERNATIVE ACCESS The trip can be shortened by putting in at the public boat launch in the town of Temiscaming.

ALTERNATIVE ROUTE You can shorten the trip into 4–5 days by either taking out or putting in at the town of Temiscaming and dividing the route into the upper or lower half.

OUTFITTERS
Nature's Harmony
Box 240
Mattawa, ON, P0H 1V0
705-223-4340
www.naturesharmony.ca

Algonquin North Outfitters
The corner of Highway 17 and Highway 630
Mattawa, ON, P0H 1V0
1-877-544-3544 or 705-744-3265
www.algonquinnorth.com

FOR MORE INFORMATION
Ministry of Natural Resources
705-564-7823
www.mnr.gov.on.ca

TOPOGRAPHIC MAPS
42 M/5, 42 M/3, 42 M/14, 42 M/11, 42 L/7

GPS COORDINATES
47.327282, -79.459723

Chiniguchi/Donald Lake Loop

🕐 4 to 5 days  7 portages ●----● 74 km **Moderate tripping skills are needed because this is an unmaintained route.**

OUR DAUGHTER, KYLA, was only two when Alana and I took her on her first extended two-week canoe trip—through the Chiniguchi area, near Sudbury. It was such a perfect trip that we decided to take Kyla back there when she was three, making only two slight changes: we reduced the trip to a week and altered it to take a route we hadn't tried before—a loop southeast of the main route we had completed the year before. Chiniguchi is an addictive place for Alana and me to paddle. The landscape is similar to Killarney Provincial Park with its white quartzite hills and turquoise waters. It also lacks a busy reservation system. Being part of an unmaintained park, there are no permits required at this particular time—something we really enjoy when trying to organize a family canoe trip.

Our canoe-trip portion got an early start due to the fact that we stayed the night directly at our access—Sportman's Lodge on Kukagami Lake. This was an ideal setting. Rooms were nicer (and cheaper) than a hotel, and we were able to park our vehicle in a safe area for a mere $5 a day (the lodge also offers shuttles to other access points for $20–$30 and rents canoes if you need them).

To reach the Sportsman's Lodge we drove on Highway 17 east of Sudbury for approximately 20 minutes and turned left (north) on Kukagami Road. The road is gravel and full of washboard but isn't too bad overall. At the 22-kilometer mark, the road takes a major fork. Stay on the main road, veering right, which leads to the lodge on the west shore of Kukagami Lake.

The morning of day one was spent paddling from the beach put-in and across to the far side of the lake, where a narrow inlet joins the south end of the lake with the central portion. Cottages line the banks on both areas of the lake, but there are a few island campsites situated en route, all of which were surprisingly clean for such a busy area.

The lake kept calm the entire morning and Alana and I were able to paddle to the far northeast bay of the central portion of Kukagami Lake, Carafel Creek and Outlet Bay by 11:00 a.m. The only problem was that Kyla and our 12-year-old dog Bailey were having their naps in the canoe, and we had to wait until just before noon to attempt the first portage.

Chiniguchi/Donald Lake Loop

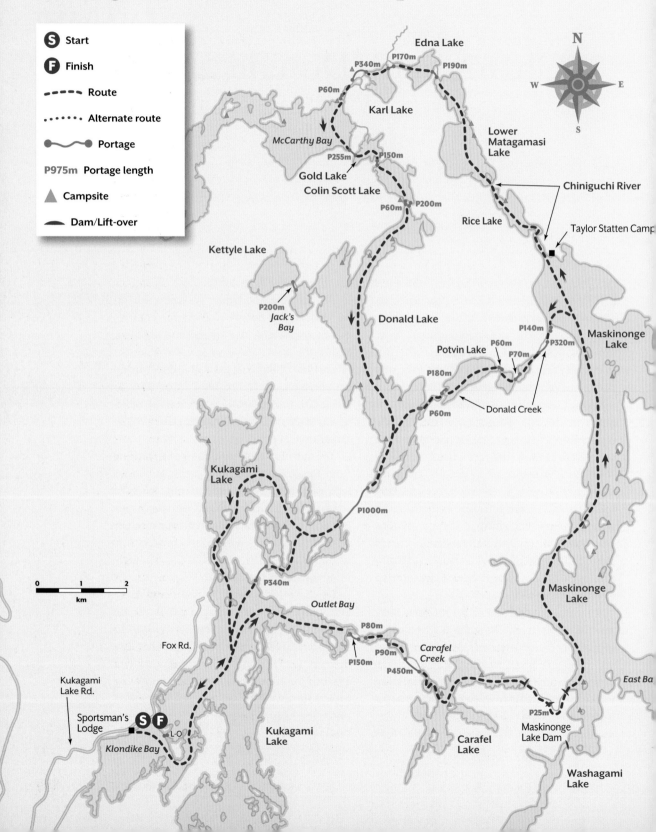

Legend:
- **S** Start
- **F** Finish
- Route
- Alternate route
- Portage
- **P975m** Portage length
- ▲ Campsite
- Dam/Lift-over

Edna Lake

P340m P170m P190m

P60m

Karl Lake

McCarthy Bay

Lower Matagamasi Lake

P255m P150m

Gold Lake

Colin Scott Lake

P60m P200m

Rice Lake

Chiniguchi River

Taylor Statten Camp

Kettyle Lake

P200m

Jack's Bay

Donald Lake

Potvin Lake

P60m

P140m

P70m P320m

Maskinonge Lake

P180m

Donald Creek

P60m

Kukagami Lake

P1000m

Maskinonge Lake

P340m

Outlet Bay

P80m

Carafel Creek

P90m

P150m

P450m

East Ba

Fox Rd.

Kukagami Lake Rd.

Sportsman's Lodge

S **F** L-O

Klondike Bay

Kukagami Lake

Carafel Lake

P25m

Maskinonge Lake Dam

Washagami Lake

0 1 2
km

N
W   E
S

This portion of the route — Carafel Creek to Maskinonge Lake — was completely new to me. In fact, I hadn't even considered it until the lodge owner mentioned it to me that morning. The portage showed little sign of use, but it was a clear route. The only issue was near the beginning of the 150-meter trail (found to the right of the creek), where it forked. Bailey wanted to keep right but I insisted we keep to the left. I should have listened to Bailey. The trail to the left did actually lead to a proper put-in and measured only 70 meters or so. But it only led to a small pond. From there we had to lift-over, drag, line, wade and bush portage through a series of shallow rapids that snaked around the corner, from right to left. It was all doable, but taking the rough trail Bailey found would have avoided all that and saved a lot of bottom paint on our new canoe.

The second portage, found not far from the first and also on the right of the creek, was an easy 90 meters. But the third, a longer 450-meter trail beginning on the right, was a rougher path and came complete with another confusing fork in the trail, this time closer to the end. I managed to go the wrong way again and carried the canoe down below the base of a falls (nice falls, though). That wasn't correct. Bailey continued to the right and simply barked at me to clamber back up and keep right. How embarrassing. My three-year-old daughter and wife were smart enough to keep with Bailey.

A weed-choked creek mouth eventually opened up to reveal Carafel Lake, where we had planned on camping our first night out.

Our second day out was much easier than the first. After a leisurely morning of flapjacks and bacon, we drifted up to the northeast corner of Carafel Lake and took the marshy creek out to Maskinonge Lake. The only obstructions along the way were two beaver dams, one in the very beginning of the creek and the second three-quarters of the way along, where a logging road bridge had been recently removed by order of the Ministry of Natural Resources. As well, a small set of shallow rapids also had to be waded down, just past the second dam.

It was a beautiful morning to paddle the creek. Mist still hung low over the water until well after 9:00 a.m., highlighting the spiderwebs dangling from the countless dead snags rooted along the bank. It also seemed to keep our presence hidden from the local inhabitants longer than normal. While en route, we saw great blue herons, kingfishers, beaver, mink, muskrat and otter.

The calm continued as we made our way out into the expanse of Maskinonge Lake, making paddling easy for Alana and I as we headed north on this gigantic lake. Having rough waters on a big lake is tough on any trip, but it's an extra pain when you have a three-year-old (and a 12-year-old dog) stored in the boat. Alana and I have found that it's not the portages and obstructions found along them that's the difficult part of canoe tripping with young children; it's finding enough songs to sing and stories to tell Kyla while we make our way across large bodies of water, especially when that water crossing gets delayed due to wind and waves. Anxieties are sure to build.

By noon we had reached the cluster of islands halfway along Maskinonge and decided to start looking for one to camp on. On one of the last large islands, I discovered an old campsite hidden from view, way up on a ridge. A fallen tree had to be removed from the tent site and the fire ring had to be rebuilt, but the scenery, swimming area and overall charm of the site was unbelievable. In fact, we liked our hidden oasis so much we ended up camping there for two days rather than one.

It wasn't easy leaving our perfect site on Maskinonge. We even considered at one point camping the entire week there. But we also knew there were even better places to camp farther to the north. So, we left our little retreat early that morning to avoid any possible high winds on the large lake.

Our route from there hadn't really been planned out; there are just too many options in Chiniguchi. We knew, however, that a visit to Donald Lake was a must. Not only was it a perfect link back to Kukagami but it also had striking scenery. To get there we had two main options: enter from the top end by a series of small lakes linked to Matagamasi Lake (Gold and Colin Scott)—with Matagamasi being linked to Maskinonge by the Chiniguchi River—or a shortcut to the southeast end of Donald Lake from the northwest end of Maskinonge.

We originally considered the shortcut to Donald. Problem was, I hadn't traveled the portages yet and was worried they'd be a little tough for Kyla, or more realistically, a little tough for poor dad who had to carry most of the gear across them. We had an older map that showed a 1,000-meter portage along the left bank of the rock-strewn creek. The trail exists but it's more common now for paddlers to try out three shorter portages that follow closer to the left shoreline of the creek into Triangle Lake (140 m, 320 m and 70 m). After Triangle Lake, a 60-meter portage to the right leads into Potvin Lake and two more portages (180 m on the right and another short 60 m) remain along the creek coming out of Donald. Not too bad, I guess. Alana and I decided, however, that for Kyla's best interest, and ours, we would take the northern route, one that we already knew.

The route from Maskinonge to Matagamasi, where we camped for the fourth and fifth nights, was quite simple. First there are a series of swifts connecting the upper portion of Maskinonge Lake with what's called Lower Matagamasi Lake. From there the first portage is found, an easy 190 meters marked to the left of where the Chiniguchi River flushes into Lower Matagamasi. The trail leads into Edna Lake. Next was an even easier 170-meter portage, this time to the left of the river and into Karl Lake. The third carry, which was one of the most scenic trails on the entire route, was a 340-meter portage, found on the right and tucked away in a small bay where the river squeezes through a pile of rock. And the fourth, and last, was a quick 60 meters to the right of an old dam.

Prior to all that, we decided to paddle by Taylor Statten Camp, located at the north end of Maskinonge, to the right of where the first swift appears when you go toward Lower Matagamasi.

The Camp's history originates in Algonquin Park and was opened up by Taylor Statten, a veteran of the Boer War who, working with youth for the YMCA, decided to open up a children's camp in the Park's Canoe Lake in 1921. By doing so, he established the first Canadian-owned private summer camp in Algonquin Park.

We spent two full days hanging around Matagamasi before moving on to Donald Lake and I have to say that the idea of "hanging around" took a bit of getting used to for me. So many of my trips before Kyla was born were made up of traveling from point A to point B as fast as possible, mostly because I was always writing a guidebook and always found myself trying to get as much mileage in before the season ended. With that said, however, I think traveling slower can definitely make you far more connected to your environment, and the relaxed pace is far more addictive than trying to paddle as fast as humanly possible.

Alana and I visited areas neighboring Matagamasi Lake. Apart from favorite haunts like Wessel Lake and the native paintings farther west on Matagamasi, we also bushwhacked our way into Big Valley Lake and ridge-climbed to the northeast.

Our relaxed pace continued while tripping into Donald Lake. We left Matagamasi mid-morning and reached Donald a couple of hours later.

To reach Donald, we paddled to the southeast corner of the eastern bay of Matagamasi and took a 255-meter portage leading into Gold Lake. The take-out was tucked away in a patch of weeds and the trail, which went directly uphill, ended in a shallow, rock-strewn bay. But it wasn't a bad trail overall. Gold Lake was small and lacked any true place to camp but it had a charm all to itself. Even better was Colin Scott Lake, reached from Gold Lake by a straight 150-meter portage. The color of the water was turquoise and the surrounding landscape was identical to the quartzite mountainside of Killarney Provincial Park.

There are two portage choices to go from Colin Scott into Donald. The original trail was hidden back behind a rough campsite, found up on a rock slab in a small bay to the southwest. It measured only 60 meters but the route itself disappears near the end and you end up walking through brush to reach the lakeshore. The second option is better: a 200-meter portage going up and over a knob of granite and found to the right of the most southern bay of Colin Scott.

We were pleased to find that the campsite

on the first point along the south shore wasn't taken (actually, we had the lake to ourselves). It's the best site on the entire lake. And once situated, we all went in for a refreshing dip and had a nap before setting up camp for two more full days of "hanging around."

We had a perfect campsite on Donald, something that became more apparent during our tour of the lake on the second-last day of the trip. The lake itself was gorgeous everywhere we went, but the campsites were only moderate throughout, except maybe one site near the entrance to the southeast inlet and a bush site we discovered while checking out Kettyle Lake—an out-of-the-way oasis reached by a hard-to-find 200-meter portage from Donald's Jack's Bay.

A 1,000-meter portage exited Donald Lake to the southeast, and we were somewhat concerned over the length, especially with three-year-old Kyla tagging along. And our anxiety grew while we searched and searched for the darn take-out. Problem was our map indicated the portage started on the left side of the small inlet and it actually started on the far right shore. Once we found the starting point, however, we discovered the trail was pretty easy. The path was relatively level and midway, a massive crop of blueberries were ripe for picking. The only downfall was the abundance of bear poop mixed in with the blueberry patch and a strong wind on Kukagami that kept us windbound at the put-in for over an hour.

The wind was bringing rain, so we made the decision to quickly head across to the opposite shore and make camp at a designated site. And we made it just in time. The moment the tarp was set up a heavy downpour began and didn't end until around midnight.

It wasn't until morning, when I searched the backwoods for wood to start a fire that I learned that we had camped at an old logging site and homestead. In fact, the tent site was directly beside the foundation of the main building. Scattered through the backwoods were all kinds of treasures.

It was a cold and damp morning and Kyla and Bailey slept most of the time while Alana and I paddled Kukagami's northern bay—a place so scenic and full of possible campsites that we considered coming back to the following year.

A couple of hours' paddling brought us to the familiar section of Kukagami, and the beginning of where cottages lined the shoreline. And by noon we found ourselves back at our starting point at Sportsman's Lodge where we celebrated our trip by having a beer (and milk for Kyla) on the porch of the dining hall.

What a fantastic trip. The only problem is to better it next time. I've paddled a lot of places in Ontario, and it would be difficult to find a more perfect route for a family paddling trip.

LONGEST PORTAGE 1,000 meters

FEE The route travels through an unmanaged and newly proposed provincial park and a fee structure is not yet in place.

ALTERNATIVE ACCESS Matagamasi Lake public launch can also be used; at the main fork on Kukagami Lake Road go left onto Matagamasi Lake Road for another 5 kilometers, then head right and drive for another 1.4 kilometers.

ALTERNATIVE ROUTE On the northwest end of Maskinonge follow the series of portages to Donald Lake rather than going north and linking up to Donald from Matagamasi Lake.

OUTFITTERS
Sportsman's Lodge Wilderness Resort
240 Kukagami Lake Road
Wahnapitae, ON, P0M 3C0
705-853-4434 or 1-877-708-8882
www.sportsmanslodge.net

FOR MORE INFORMATION
Ministry of Natural Resources
705-564-7823
www.mnr.gov.on.ca

TOPOGRAPHIC MAPS
41 I/15 & 41 I/16

GPS COORDINATES
46.721760, -80.579753

Chiniguchi/Sturgeon River Loop

 6 to 8 days  28 portages ●----● 125 km **Moderate canoe-tripping and whitewater skills are required.**

M Y WIFE, ALANA, has a specific rule that must be met on our canoe trips. I can't work. That means no picture taking for magazines or stopping throughout the day to document information for another guide book. Her reasons are simple enough; unlike myself who paddles most of the season for employment, Alana has a normal job with limited holidays. Her time out there is precious.

I generally respect her one condition, but a few years back, I made the mistake of inviting a group of canoe colleagues on a trip with Alana and me. The act was innocent enough. I figured they'd keep work-related stuff to a minimum. They didn't. A lot of time was spent taking promo photos and talking about article ideas. Alana was not a happy camper. To pay her back I quickly planned another trip for her remaining holidays and promised it would be the best trip of our lives. The route was perfect. I combined two of our favorite places to paddle—Sudbury's Chiniguchi region, which resembles Killarney's white quartzite mountains and turquoise lakes, and Temagami's Sturgeon River, characterized as the big sister of the Spanish River for its continuous CI and CII rapids.

Alana and I (and our dog, Bailey) booked a hotel in Sudbury the night before our trip, and we were at the access on Matagamasi Lake early. To reach the put-in, we drove 20 minutes east of Sudbury on Highway 17 and turned left on Kukagami Lake Road. At the first fork in the road (made up of gravel and full of washboard) at the 22-kilometer mark, we went left and followed Matagamasi Lake Road for another 5 kilometers; then headed right and drove for just over 1 kilometer to reach the small and poorly maintained government launch.

Matagamasi Lake is a good two-hour paddle. Along the way, the shoreline is dotted with a few cottages and camps and is made up of typical northern pink granite outcrops topped with stout white pine. The lake also has a few prime campsites in case you arrive later at the access point. However, the scenery gets better and better the farther you go. The white quartzite begins to show itself in small clumps in Matagamasi's north arm, and after the first portage, the scenery becomes identical to Killarney Provincial Park. Shimmering quartz hills surround crystal clear turquoise water.

Chiniguchi/Sturgeon River Loop

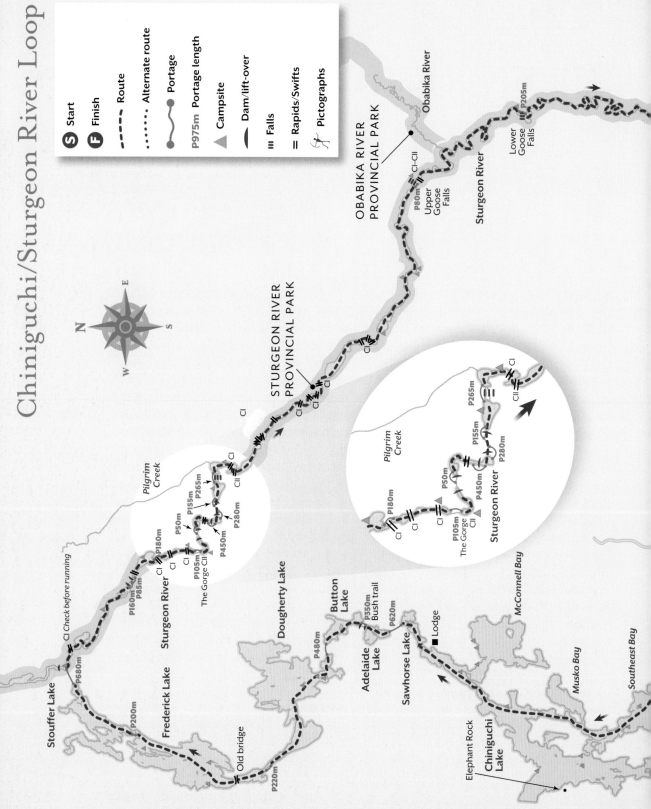

Legend

- **S** Start
- **F** Finish
- - - - Route
- ······ Alternate route
- ●—● Portage
- P975m Portage length
- ▲ Campsite
- ▬ Dam/lift-over
- ||| Falls
- = Rapids/Swifts
- 🏃 Pictographs

N E S W

OBABIKA RIVER PROVINCIAL PARK

Obabika River

STURGEON RIVER PROVINCIAL PARK

P80m CI-CII
Upper Goose Falls

Sturgeon River

Lower Goose Falls ||| P205m

CI

CI
CI
CI

Pilgrim Creek

P155m P265m
P50m
|||
CII CI
P280m
P450m
The Gorge CII
P105m
CI
Sturgeon River
P180m
P85m
P160m
CI Check before running
P680m
Stouffer Lake
P200m

Frederick Lake

Dougherty Lake

Old bridge

P220m

P480m

Button Lake
P350m Bush trail
Adelaide Lake
P620m
Sawhorse Lake
■ Lodge

Elephant Rock

Chiniguchi Lake

McConnell Bay
Musko Bay
Southeast Bay

Pilgrim Creek

P180m
CI
CI
P265m
|||
P155m
P50m
P280m
P450m
The Gorge
CII
P105m
CI
CII
CI
Sturgeon River

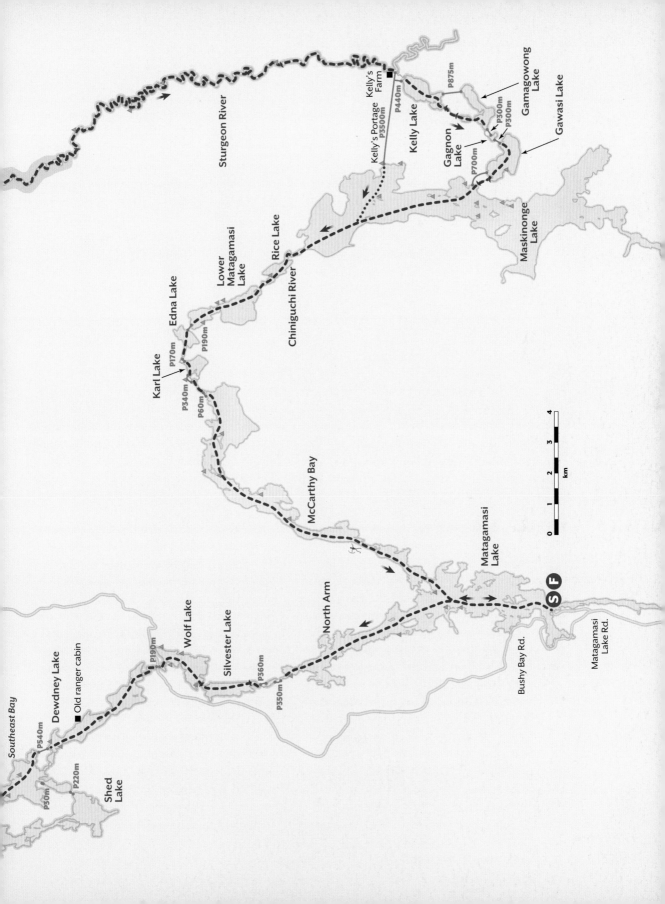

The first day was relatively easy. At the top end of Matagamasi Lake were two short consecutive portages. The first was to the left and measured 350 meters. The second was soon after, on the right and measured 360 meters. It was much steeper than the first portage, but Alana and I took a rest halfway and walked left off the trail to take a quick dip in Paradise Lagoon, an oval-shaped basin at the base of a beautiful cascade. This is an incredibly picturesque spot and has been used for years by canoe trippers.

When we returned to the trail to finish the portage, Alana and I met up with another group of paddlers. I immediately recognized them as the canoe club from Barrie, Ontario, who I had presented to a few days before our trip. And while chatting with them, another canoe group I knew from London, Ontario, portaged past us. Both groups were on their way to camp on Wolf Lake. It was a busy spot. In fact, this portion of the route has continually become busier and busier, which is why Alana and I chose the hotel the night before the trip option. That way we weren't racing for a campsite the first night out.

We stuck with the two groups, paddling up a strong swift shortly after the Paradise Lagoon portage and across Silvester Lake where lining up two more swifts brought us into Wolf Lake. They spread out on the two prime campsites along the eastern shoreline and Alana and I continued on and took the 190-meter portage on the northwest corner of Wolf Lake, to the right of the bridge crossing the rapids coming out of Dewdney Lake. It's an uphill climb to the roadway, an old logging road that was supposed to be eliminated once the new Chiniguchi River Waterway Park was formulated back in 2006. The road is still there, but the protection of Wolf Lake itself is now in question.

During the province's Living Legacy park program, the Wolf Lake area was protected under the Chiniguchi Waterway Provincial Park, but the Wolf Lake area was later separated from the waterway provincial park and given a "forest reserve" status. This was due to the heavy interest in mining claims on Wolf Lake. A provincial park would protect the area from mining claims but a forest reserve wouldn't. For now, however, the road is still there, splitting the portage to Dewdney Lake.

Alana and I paddled across Dewdney Lake, split into two sections, and stopped for a late lunch at the old ranger cabin along the east shore of the upper section of the lake. It was where the caretaker of the nearby fire tower stayed and is where his ghost, Bob, haunts the grounds. Ghost or not, Alana and I still enjoyed our cheese and cucumber sandwiches before heading to the next and final portage of the day—a 540-meter trail linking the north end of Dewdney Lake to the southeast bay of Chiniguchi Lake.

Our plan was to try and reach the campsite on McConnell Bay—an inlet located on the far northeast end of Chiniguchi that comes complete with a 1.5-kilometer sand beach. It was getting late, however, and we saw a large group from a girls' camp ahead of us who, we guessed, were racing for the same site. So we opted for an island camp to the west, titled Blueberry Island and across from a notable ridge labeled the Elephant, the most prominent knob of quartz in the area, that rises a good 1,312 feet over the lake.

In the morning we paddled back over to the northeast corner of Chiniguchi to continue our trip toward the Sturgeon River, and on the way past the entrance to McConnell Bay we took a side trip to check out the beach. Alana hadn't seen this part of the lake yet and I was excited to show it to her.

We continued on toward the remote lodge at the end of the northeast bay and crossed over an ATV trail (leading to the lodge) to reach Sawhorse Lake. From there we paddled to the northeast bay of Sawhorse to locate the 620-meter portage to Adelaide Lake. The take-out was easy enough to find. It was marked with a plywood sign with the letter "P" painted on it. Keeping to the trail itself, however, was a challenge. It begins along a rough trail (old logging road) that links up to a newer road where you veer to the left. Then you'll come to another road/ATV trail. We went right here and portaged for approximately 100 meters before turning left onto another lesser-used old logging road/ATV trail.

At the north end of Adelaide Lake, our map showed a lift-over to the left of a beaver dam and a second lift-over at an old bridge to reach Button Lake. When we arrived, however, the water level was too low to use the creek, and we had to resort to carrying over a 350-meter bush portage that hugged the right side of the creek.

Alana and I portaged the 480 meters over from Button into Dougherty. The trail has a steep incline at first and then a quick descent.

Dougherty was connected to Frederick Lake by a large beaver dam and an easy 220-meter portage on the left. Then Stouffer Lake was reached by portaging another easy 220 meters.

We arrived on Stouffer Lake alone and set up camp on the only campsite, located on the northern tip of the large island. After supper we sat out by the rock point and soaked in the solitude. Alana had us up at 4:30 a.m. the next morning, and it was just getting light when we portaged the 680 meters over to the Sturgeon River. The trail headed up slope for the first

part, but for the remainder it went downhill to the river. Once at the put-in, it felt good to be at the river, knowing we'd be paddling with the current for a few days before looping back to Chiniguchi's Matagamasi Lake. To me, a river is a totally different experience than paddling across a series of lakes and ponds. It takes you on a journey that somehow reconnects you with your surroundings much more than any other type of canoe trip.

Alana and I prepared the canoe for our downriver paddle, making sure the throw bag, extra paddle and bailer were easily accessible, and that the packs were properly stored. Then we shoved off from shore and almost immediately ran a quick section of water. It was rated a Class I rapid but it seemed bigger. A series of standing waves was a sign of high water, higher than I'd expected. I'd been down this section of river before on a solo canoe trip, beginning at Scarecrow Lake, and this particular rapid had been a mere swift with a few rocks to avoid.

The river gushed through a narrow stretch soon after, before emptying into a small pond where the route twisted to the far right. Then there was a long section of the river, flowing past thick forested banks, before we took out for two consecutive portages at a place our map labeled "The Canyon." Both trails were on the right, with the first (160 m) avoiding a large chute and the second (85 m) a highly technical, ragged rapid. The portages were short but excessively rocky and steep. I was constantly thrown off balance by the weight of the canoe on my shoulders while clambering, crawling and teetering over to the second put-in. The Sturgeon River truly is one of my favorite rivers to paddle, but the majority of portages are mere goat trails.

For a good stretch it seemed every turn of the river held rapids and all our concentration was put toward deciding which tongue of water to take and what pile of rocks to avoid. We ran four Class I–II rapids, all made easier with the higher water, and a Class II at a place called "The Gorge" that came equipped with a 105-meter portage on the left shore. Then, around a sharp bend were three more Class I rapids (the second having a 50-m portage on the left) before the river flushed into a small pond. We took a short break here, drinking from our water jugs and munching on

some bannock and peanut butter, before we rounded the next corner after the pond and ran yet another Class I rapid prior to a necessary portage found on the right. The trail measured 450 meters and had an incredibly steep dip midway along.

It was along this portage that Alana and I met another camp group. It was a group of eight young boys, six of them aged 14 and two 17-year-old leaders. They were polite and courteous to us and were in the process of cleaning up some garbage found along the trail. We stopped to chat with them for a while and learned they were on their last few days of a 26-day canoe trip across Temagami. To me, they represented the typical youth camps that have traveled throughout Chiniguchi–Temagami ever since Camp Keewaydin led the first outing in 1905. It was groups such as Keewaydin, and later Taylor Statten, who used the Chiniguchi and Sturgeon Rivers as a main route and kept the portages open and campsites clean when no one else seemed to bother.

Alana and I allowed the camp group to go first on the portage, being courteous in return. They thanked us and began hauling their wooden Wanigans and cedar-canvas canoes across the rocky portage. Two minutes later, one of the younger boys, who was carrying a large pack directly in front of me, slipped on a steep slab of rock and immediately began screaming in pain. We all quickly dropped our packs and ran over to assess his injuries. It was his leg that seemed to cause him the most grief and when one of the leaders went to move him, the boy nearly passed out in agony. It was a good guess that the leg was broken.

Alana and I assisted in setting the leg with two paddles and duct tape while the two group leaders gathered together, out of earshot of the boy, and calmly went over possible scenarios. The big question was should they try to move the boy and paddle to the nearest lodge with a satellite phone (I let them know of a place about a day's paddle away) or have two of the better paddlers go ahead and call for help. At first they voted on carrying him out. There was no real sign of a break, and the boy seemed to be feeling better. He even ate a piece of bannock for lunch. But when they went to move him, he again nearly passed out in pain.

While the leaders gathered once more to discuss options, even having a helicopter come in to complete a rescue, I started over to take part in the discussion. Alana stopped me, however. She asked me why I was getting involved. "It's routine for me to do so," I said. After all, I had worked as a guide for youth camps for a number of years and dealt with similar issues. Alana disagreed. "You're wanting to get involved to get a good story," she commented. Even though I desperately wanted to disagree with her, she was right. Being involved with the rescue would make an ultimate narrative, and that would obviously break her rule of not working during our holidays. But that wasn't the main reason she wanted me not to be involved directly with the group's actions. "Let them have their own adventure, Kevin," she whispered to me. Alana was right again. The two leaders were amazing. They were making the right choices and doing all the right things during a very stressful event. There was no real need for me to be directly involved. I grudgingly stepped back and let them plan out their own rescue. The decision was made. One of the leaders partnered up with one of the younger boys, the best paddler in the group, and headed downriver for the lodge equipped with the satellite phone. The rest of the group made

camp along the portage, making the patient as comfortable as possible.

Alana and I paddled downriver, portaged another steep 280-meter portage on the right, ran through a Class I–II rapid (there was an optional 155-m portage on the left) and then made camp on a site on the far side of a pond.

Meanwhile, the boys had some incredible luck. Not far downstream they met a couple of anglers at the outflow of Pilgrim Creek who agreed to drive the boys to the lodge on their ATVs. A helicopter was then called in from Sudbury, and the rescue was on.

The rescue was amazing. Or at least that's what the boys' camp later told me. We were too far downstream to witness it all (yes, I secretly cursed Alana for me not being on their site to capture photos). To enable the helicopter to evacuate the boy, his buddies made a raft out of two canoes, placed him on a stretcher and floated the raft to a hump of rock at the foot of the mini-falls along the portage. Here, the pilot was able to lower cables and lift the stretcher up and take the boy to the hospital. The boys truly had their own adventure. (The boy ended up being okay after they put a few pins in his leg.)

Alana and I were quick to get back on the river early the next day, hoping that the rest of the trip would be uneventful. And it was. We still had plenty of rapids and portages to finish up on the Sturgeon River, however. The first was just around the corner from our campsite. A 265-meter portage avoided a falls on the left bank. From there until Upper Goose Falls, and where the Yorkston River flushes into the Sturgeon River just upstream, it was a free float down over a dozen almost continuous rapids, passing by high gravel banks and deep forest of jack pine flats. The difficulty of this stretch varies with

water levels. Class I rapids become Class II rapids when the river is more swollen in the spring, but become a bump-and-grind boulder garden in midsummer.

Due to the high water when we traveled the river, the take-out for the 80-meter portage on the right of Upper Goose Falls was dangerously close to the lip of the cascade. Alana and I even approached it wrong. She stepped out of the canoe first, allowing the strong current to pull the stern away from the shore. Not wanting to be swept over the falls, I leapt out of the canoe and grabbed the stern and bow rope to hold the canoe steady. All that time our dog Bailey sat in the center of the canoe wondering what all the excitement was about.

The portage goes down a steep gravel bank and ends right at the bottom of the falls, leaving a series of Class I–II rapids to run through just before where the Obabika River joins the Sturgeon. From here it was another half hour of paddling, on a much calmer river, to Lower Goose Falls where we portaged 205 meters on the left.

The river twisted and turned uncontrollably after Lower Goose Falls, and it became almost impossible to know exactly where we were most of the time. There was the odd swift that I noted on my map, but a couple more bends in the river and some more highly eroded sandbanks and we were confused about our whereabouts once again. Alana and

I haven't a clue where we camped that night. It was somewhere on a small beach on the inside bend of the river. Actually, it was nice not to know where we were. At dusk we heard wolves howl in the distance, and around midnight a very upset beaver hissed outside our tent because we mistakenly pitched camp on top of its regular travel route.

To make amends with the neighborhood beaver, Alana and I were on our way earlier than usual in the morning. We followed the meandering river for another hour and located the portage route taking us back toward the landscape of Chiniguchi. The take-out was on the right shore and just before where a small creek emptied into the Sturgeon. We hoisted our gear and canoe up the steep muddy bank to a clearing that was once a farmstead. It was here we had to make the decision of which way to take to Maskinonge Lake. The common route was to follow a 3,500-meter portage (labeled Kelly's Portage) beginning behind an abandoned prospector's cabin and ending on the east shore of Maskinonge Lake. The alternative was to follow a series of portages through Kelly–Gamagowong–Gawasi to Maskinonge. Alana and I chose the secondary route, hoping it would be easier than the long but direct carry-across. In retrospect, I'm not sure it was the right choice.

The route started off with a 400-meter portage veering not far off to the left of the 3,500-meter portage. The trail hadn't been used much but it wasn't too bad to follow. We then paddled to the far southeastern corner of Kelly Lake to begin an 875-meter portage to Gamagowong Lake. Twenty minutes of searching and we finally found it. Actually, it was our dog Bailey who found it. The portage resembles more a moose trail leading through the bog than an actual portage. We later found

out that some canoeists have been successful navigating the creek that joins Kelly Lake and Gamagowong Lake, lifting over only two giant beaver dams. Problem is, those paddlers went through in spring conditions and in lower water it might not be possible.

After the long haul through the faint portage, we paddled the full length of Gamagowong Lake to start another portage. It was marked on our map as a full 825 meters but is actually made up of two 300-meter portages leading in and out of a small pond called Gagnon Lake. Keeping to the actual trail was a bit of a puzzle, however. To the left of the original take-out we saw an overturned boat and an ATV trail leading off into the bush. Alana and I were confused about which trail to take. So we tried both. The ATV trail forked and another ATV trail to the right led to the shoreline of Gagnon Lake. The original portage, found to the right of the ATV trail, runs pretty much parallel with the ATV trail, with its take-out about 10 meters from the ATV take-out. We still had to haul our canoe and gear over some floating islands of sphagnum moss and tussock grass to get to Gagnon and then paddle across to complete the remaining 300-meter portage to Gawasi Lake.

When I looked at the map and saw we had another 700-meter portage, located to the right of a creek linking Gawasi to Maskinonge Lake, I regretted not taking the 3,500-meter portage at this point; that is until we discovered the 700-meter trail wasn't necessary. We couldn't locate it at first anyway, so we took a chance at paddling the creek between the two lakes. One beaver dam lift-over and we were in Maskinonge. What a stroke of luck! Alana and I paddled up Maskinonge, then through a series of swifts to adjoining Rice Lake and Lower Matagamasi Lake. We finally made camp on a prime site along the east shore. It was a long haul, wading through mud, pulling over sphagnum bogs, being confused about the portage route more than once. But it was a good day, too—sunny, a nice breeze to keep the bugs down, and it was the third day we hadn't seen a single person.

The scenery was striking our last day en route. We were heading back to the familiar Matagamasi Lake by paddling up the Chiniguchi River. The first portage was an easy 190 meters to the left of where the Chiniguchi River empties into Lower Matagamasi. It goes to Edna Lake. Next was an even easier 179-meter portage to the left and into Karl Lake. It was on the third carry, a 340-meter portage on the right, where we spotted pockets of Killarney-like white quartz again along the portage, and by the time we had carried over the final portage, a quick 60 meters to the right of an old dam, Alana and I made the decision to stay just one more night to soak it all in.

By staying one more night on the trip, we had the entire day to drive back to our home in Peterborough. Ironically, it was the same day of the largest power outages in decades (August 14, 2003). It affected much of Ontario and the northeastern United States and a state of emergency was called. Problem was, Alana and I never had the radio on during our drive and knew nothing of the outage until we reached our home. My neighbor at the time, John, who was in his late 80s, came over and said, "The world has come to an end—please help me drink my beer!"

Alana and I didn't seem to react as much to the event, maybe because we had been living without power for a couple of weeks already. So, we took our neighbor up on his request and helped him with his beer storage issue and then invited him over for a blueberry pie we cooked in the backyard, made from berries we picked on our trip and baked with our camp stove. What a perfect way to end a canoe trip.

LONGEST PORTAGE 3,500 or 875 meters depending on alternative route choice.

FEE The route travels through an unmanaged and newly proposed provincial park and a fee structure is not yet in place.

ALTERNATIVE ACCESS Sportsman's Lodge on Kukagami Lake. Turn left (north) on Kukagami Road. The road is gravel and full of washboard but isn't too bad overall. The 22-kilometer mark on Kukagami Lake Road takes a major fork. Stay on the main road, veering right, instead of going left.

This leads to the lodge on the west shore of Kukagami Lake.

ALTERNATIVE ROUTE You can combine this route with the Chiniguchi/Donald Lake route to use Sportsman's Lodge as your access.

OUTFITTERS
Sportsman's Lodge Wilderness Resort
240 Kukagami Lake Road
Wahnapitae, ON, P0M 3C0
705-853-4434 or 1-877-708-8882
www.sportsmanslodge.net

FOR MORE INFORMATION
Ministry of Natural Resources
705-564-7823
www.mnr.gov.on.ca

TOPOGRAPHIC MAPS
41 P/1, 41 P/2, 41 I/15 & 41 I/16

GPS COORDINATES
46.742851, −80.612980

Lady Evelyn Loop

🕐 6 to 8 days    19 portages   ●----● 102 km   **There are some rugged portages, and novice whitewater skills are needed.**

MY WIFE, ALANA, (and dog, Bailey) and I hadn't been to Temagami for a couple years and figured we'd try to plan a route out that combined a bunch of the area's prime scenic spots. That's not an easy task. Temagami is full of natural wonders and deciding on which ones to visit can be an ordeal. However, choosing Maple Mountain, prominent stands of old-growth white pine, and the cascades along the north and south Lady Evelyn River was a good start. So, one look at the map and we were able to join the dots and create one of the best trips we've ever had.

Mowat Landing is the access point we started and finished our loop from. It's not as busy as the central access on Lake Temagami. Lady Evelyn Lake itself isn't as busy either. Don't get me wrong; this lake has a number of fishing lodges, camps and even a few houseboats using the lake. But due to its sheer size and elongated shape, it's also quite easy to find solace here as well.

The access is reached by driving Highway 11, 45 kilometers north of the town of Temagami to Highway 558. Mowat Landing is 20 kilometers west on Highway 558. There's a public parking area and boat launch, and from here it's a very short paddle southeast on the Montreal River to Matawapika Dam, where a 260-meter portage along a rough road/trail will take you past Mitchell's Camp and to the shores of Lady Evelyn River.

It's said that the prevailing winds on this lake are from the southwest. Alana and I quickly found out how right that was. We were paddling hard against the wind in the first few minutes, pushing our way up the 5 kilometers of what remained of the Lady Evelyn River, the most northerly tributary of the Ottawa River, and our first day out we only got to a small island campsite just before the lake begins to open up. Our short paddle wasn't too upsetting. It had been a long drive for us, and we took advantage of setting up a tarp, lighting a fire and relaxing in comfort our first night out. The campsite, even though it was set in the middle of a heavy traffic area, wasn't too dirty. The Friends of Temagami had even constructed a thunderbox (treasure chest, poop box, mini-outhouse or whatever you want it call it...). Problem was, it was heavily guarded by a wasp nest and we decided not to make use of it.

Lady Evelyn Loop

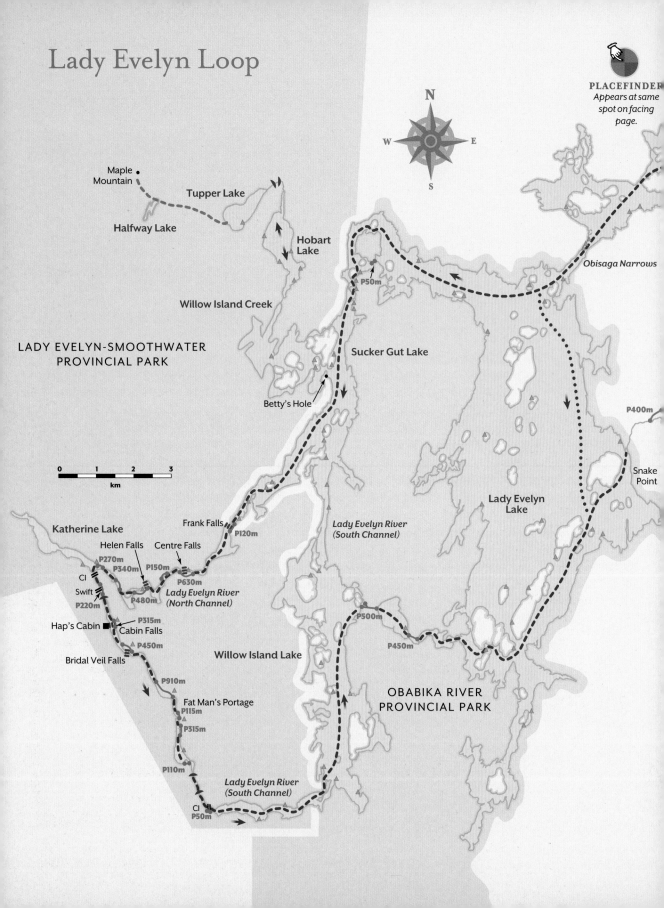

PLACEFINDER
Appears at same spot on facing page.

N
W   E
S

Maple Mountain

Tupper Lake

Halfway Lake

Hobart Lake

Willow Island Creek

P50m

Obisaga Narrows

LADY EVELYN-SMOOTHWATER PROVINCIAL PARK

Sucker Gut Lake

Betty's Hole

P400m

0   1   2   3
km

Snake Point

Lady Evelyn Lake

Katherine Lake

Frank Falls

P120m

Helen Falls   Centre Falls

Lady Evelyn River (South Channel)

P270m
P340m   P150m
CI
Swift   P630m
P220m   P480m   Lady Evelyn River (North Channel)

P315m
Hap's Cabin   Cabin Falls

P450m

P500m

Bridal Veil Falls

Willow Island Lake

P450m

P910m

Fat Man's Portage
P115m

P315m

OBABIKA RIVER PROVINCIAL PARK

P110m

Lady Evelyn River (South Channel)

CI
P50m

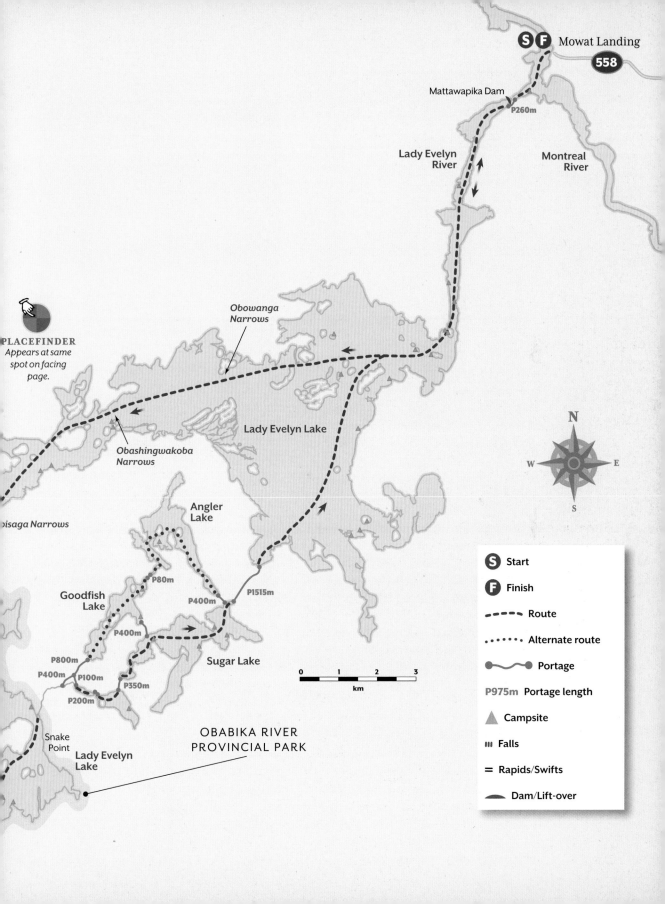

S F Mowat Landing
558

Mattawapika Dam
P260m

Lady Evelyn
River

Montreal
River

Obowanga
Narrows

PLACEFINDER
Appears at same
spot on facing
page.

Obashingwakoba
Narrows

Lady Evelyn Lake

N
W   E
S

bisaga Narrows

Angler
Lake

P80m

P400m   P1515m

Goodfish
Lake

P400m

P800m

P400m   P100m

P200m   P350m

Sugar Lake

Snake
Point

Lady Evelyn
Lake

OBABIKA RIVER
PROVINCIAL PARK

0   1   2   3
km

S Start

F Finish

- - - Route

· · · Alternate route

●~~● Portage

P975m Portage length

▲ Campsite

⫼ Falls

= Rapids/Swifts

━ Dam/Lift-over

The original name of Lady Evelyn Lake was Monzkananing Lake ("haunt of the moose"). The European label was given sometime in the 1870s for the Earl of Erne's daughter who never visited, nor for that matter, ever even knew of its whereabouts or its beauty. Paddlers consider the lake "Temagami North" and it is thought to provide a totally different element than the lake system in southern Temagami. After witnessing the sun set over our campsite the first evening, Alana and I had to agree.

The high winds continued to blow all night and even though Alana and I forced ourselves to get out on the water by 6:30 a.m. we still had a difficult time making our way up Lady Evelyn Lake. Keeping close to the north shore helped, but it also forced us to paddle close to double the distance across the first quarter of the lake. We were safe, however. And it was either extra paddling or being windbound our second day out a stone's throw away from the access point.

An hour of pushing through the waves brought us near the entrance to the geological fault line titled the Obowanga Narrows (Ojibwa for "sandy narrows") and the most noteworthy place on Lady Evelyn Lake, known as the sand dunes. These eskers were formed thousands of years ago, long before the Hydro Electric Dam flooded the bottom of the dunes back in the 1920s. These are some amazing geological features and even the campsites were removed from the clutter of islands a few years back to help protect the ecologically sensitive area.

Alana and I continued to keep close to the north shore up until we came to a fishing camp. Here, we went directly across to the south shore to save us time and distance. It also happened to be the narrowest place to cross for a good stretch. The decision was

a bad one, though. The south side was full of whitecaps; waves with dark, menacing troughs that dunked the bow of our canoe deeper and deeper as we went along. We were forced to brace every fourth or fifth stroke and eventually we had to give up and beach at a campsite where we boiled up two pots of tea, waiting for the winds to subside.

It wasn't until midday that we were able to escape back out onto the water, and with a fresh breeze rather than howling winds, we made good time reaching the far side of Lady Evelyn Lake and then south into Sucker Gut Lake.

Campsites were dirtier here than on Lady Evelyn itself. It was disheartening. Every time Alana jumped out onto the shoreline to check out a possible campsite for the night, she came back with total disgust and reports of toilet paper mounds and food scraps scattered about. We had to make the best of it, though. Not only was Sucker Gut a good scenic place to camp, with lots of weedy bays and rocky outcrops, it was also the entrance to the waterway linking to the base of Maple Mountain. The scenic hike was to be one of our highlights of the trip and we made the decision to clean up our chosen site as best we could and leave for the mountaintop at first light.

From Sucker Gut to Maple Mountain, Alana and I paddled west, through Betty's Hole and the entrance to Willow Island Creek to Hobart Lake. Lots of scenic campsites overlooking Maple Mountain are on Hobart and are prime spots to stay over before heading up to the summit. I'd stayed here once before. Not only does the place get crowded with large groups, but I had a bear visit my site during the night. So I had no interest in staying here a second time.

To exit Hobart, Alana and I used the small creek to the north, which soon twisted to the west and took us into Tupper Lake. The creek got shallow in a few spots, and we had to complete a few lift-overs before we reached Tupper. The water level was even down somewhat at the southwest end, where the base of the trail leading to Maple Mountain is.

The climb is about a three-hour round trip, and Alana and I figured we'd better fill our water bottles before clambering up the mountain. We used a spring located about 50 meters east of what remains of the original ranger's cabin, a spot told to me by Hap Wilson, an author and preservationist who wrote the first (and best) guide to Temagami. There is a spring up top Maple Mountain, and some campers who decide to overnight on the crest have used it. I've only been to the top

three times, but I've never considered this spring a good source of drinking water. It is, however, the reason why you see a group of black spruce oddly rooted so high in elevation. The main ridge itself, however, is pretty much bare, except for a massive carpet of blueberries. This tundra-like appearance is due to a forest fire ignited a numbers of years ago by the children of the forest ranger who operated the fire tower bolted to the top of Maple Mountain. Ironic, isn't it—the result of kids playing with matches near a fuel barrel now allows for a panoramic view of the surrounding landscape.

Alana and I lingered way too long on the summit of Maple Mountain, not to mention it took some doing to get our dog Bailey down the "Hillary Step," a section of old steel fire tower ladder put in place long ago for hikers to climb up and down the rock face just prior to the top of Maple Mountain. We even stopped for a swim in Halfway Lake, a tranquil bit of water found closer to the three-quarter mark than halfway along. Our tardiness in getting back to the canoe made it too late in the day to paddle back to Sucker Gut, and we had to take one of the unoccupied sites on Hobart Lake. It was actually a nice site but the phobia of having a bear visit me again while camping on this lake made a deep sleep that night pretty much impossible.

Our next step of the trip was to paddle up the North Lady Evelyn River and down the South Lady Evelyn. We were up early and on the water by 7:00 a.m. An early start for sure, but we were rewarded by spotting a gathering of loons at the far southwest inlet, near where the Lady Evelyn River's north channel flushes into Sucker Gut. The group totaled 22 birds and was a clear sign that the summer season was quickly coming to an end. Loons gather in great numbers in both spring and fall, and I've been lucky enough to witness a total of 96 birds that once gathered on Lady Evelyn Lake a number of years back. It was awe-inspiring to say the least. Ornithologists have figured out the spring groupings have to do with some type of courtship ritual, but they are still puzzled about why they would gather again in the fall. Alana and I decided it was just an excuse for a big party before migration starts.

The first portage, a 120-meter trail to the left of Frank Falls, was good practice for what lay ahead. The majority of portages along the Lady Evelyn River are short, but they are extremely rocky (and slippery). The next portage en route around Centre Falls (nicknamed the "Golden Staircase") is a good example. The 630-meter path, marked on the left, has a number of sharp inclines and jumbles of rock to scramble over. The falls, found halfway across the portage, are spectacular though and well worth the effort.

Not long after Centre Falls, Alana and I had to get our feet wet while lining and tracking up a rock-strewn rapid. We noticed a short 150-meter portage on our right but it seemed safer (and quicker) to wade our canoe and gear upstream rather than dance across the pile of wet rocks spread out on the trail.

Helen Falls was next. Wow! What a climb! The portage, a moderate 480 meters marked with rock cairns and found on the left bank, twisted its way up a ridge made of sharp quartz. The last bit seemed to be the worst. The trail kept uncomfortably close to the steep river bank and across a clump of massive boulders. But again, gawking at the cascade was well worth the hassles of portaging up the picturesque pool and drop-style river the Natives titled Men-jamma-ga-sibi ("the trout streams").

Just upstream from Helen Falls, past where the current slows enough to allow water lilies to take root, was a small swift where we witnessed a mink snatch a frog and then swim past our canoe with its catch, and seconds later an otter slipped into the current not far from the bow of the canoe.

Another portage waited for us upstream. It was right of a shallow rapid and measured 340 meters. It was also a lot easier than the last two previous carries but by no means a good walking trail. Huge boulders were scattered everywhere and there was a solid incline along the way as well. The worst of it was I remembered running the rapid last time I paddled the river. It's a Class I–II rapid that's navigable in high water. I was traveling downstream at the time, of course, but it bothered me more than a bit to walk past a runnable rapid.

Alana and I took on one more portage, a 270-meter trail to the right that was just as rocky as the one previous, before we ended our day on Katherine Lake. It was only 3:00 p.m. but we wanted a full day to paddle down the south branch of the Lady Evelyn River and decided to make it an early day to relax and soak in the surroundings. This is one of my favorite places in Temagami and there was no need to rush through the experience. Besides, this was also the first time on the river where I wasn't guiding. On the previous trips I was always on guard, keeping the clients safe and happy. There was never a solid amount of time to enjoy the area I was traveling through; or at least I believed that to be the case. My last trip here was also my last time guiding for quite some time. I took a sabbatical of sorts after guiding a particularly demanding group.

A shroud of mist still blanketed Katherine Lake when Alana and I began our journey down the south channel of the Lady Evelyn the next morning. Only 10 minutes' paddling brought us to the entrance where we slipped down a Class I rapid filled with a number of rocks that made us feel as if we were the steel ball in a pinball machine. Shortly after, we were getting out of the canoe to carry around the first true set of whitewater. The portage was on the left and measured only 220 meters. How we made across it without injury is surprising, however. It was if someone dropped a bag of marbles across the path and we were forced to balance on each one, with a full load of packs and canoe. The morning dew had also greased each rock, making it seem that the portages around the falls the previous day were far easier. The portage truly characterized the south branch of the Lady Evelyn. This is a much more rugged stretch then the north branch—but it's also less used by canoeists and even more scenic.

A section of quick current then took us to where the river widens and to the take-out for another portage (315 m) marked around a second cascade. It seemed possible to shorten the carry by lifting over some rock piles twice before portaging around the main drop, but Alana and I figured it would be a lot easier just to walk the entire trail. The portage heads uphill almost straight away and then, from a small campsite, it leads immediately downhill. The cascade is titled Cabin Falls and is home to Hap Wilson's cabin and ecological retreat located on the opposite shoreline. The original cabin was built here in 1931 by Adrian Newcomb and a group of cottagers from Lake Temagami. Katherine Hyde was the last surviving member of the group, which is why some canoeists label this cascade as Hyde's Cabin Falls. Hap keeps this cabin open for paddlers to use in case of emergency and it contains a guest book. He built the extension

back in 1999 to operate Sunrise Eco-Lodge Adventure Post.

The next carry was Bridal Veil Falls or what some call Twin Sister Falls. The second name makes some sense due to the double cascades, but as far back as 1953 it's been more commonly documented as Bridal Veil Falls because the main drop resembles a bride's veil. Whatever the name, this was a major highlight for Alana and I. The drop is significant and according to countless other Temagami paddlers, it's the best waterfall in the district.

To carry around Bridal Veil Falls was not a highlight, however. The take-out was to the left, just after we paddled through a shallow, rocky section uncomfortably close to the lip of the falls. The 450-meter trail is very rough throughout but the ending is insane. Alana and I managed to carry everything to the last portion and ended up sliding the canoe and packs down toward the water's edge. In the process, my main pack got loose and rolled out of control all the way to the bottom. It was a hectic moment watching what contained a good portion of our gear head straight for the river. Fortunately it came to rest a few inches from shore and only my camp mug was damaged in the ordeal.

Five minutes of paddling brought us to another portage, found on the left hidden among a grassy bay. It was probable to lift-over the first bit of the rapid and run the rest. However, the water level that Alana and I had made that not entirely possible and we decided to walk the entire length. The distance measured 910 meters but it thankfully was the best trail, with the best footing, we had all day.

Before stopping for lunch, Alana and I decided to take on one more portage—a 115-meter trail on the left labeled "Fat Man's

Portage" due to a granite fissure that's a bit of a squeeze to get a canoe through. It avoids Fat Man's Falls and has also been titled "Fat Man's Misery" and "Fat Man's Squeeze." The take-out was dangerously close to the brink of the falls, which gushed through a narrow gorge, and the trail was difficult to locate at times, wandering all over the slab of rock alongside the gorge. And once again, the last stretch went pretty much straight downhill. Here I ended up falling. Maybe we should have stopped for lunch earlier. I was tired and wasn't watching my footing as closely as I should have. It was when the tail end of my canoe got caught on a rock during the almost vertical drop in the trail. A quick yank backwards and I found myself falling hard on a pile of rock. I suffered a sore wrist and minor cuts to the forearm. Our dog Bailey also took a tumble near the end of the trail and suffered worse, however. The buckle of the pack of kibble she carries on portages became caught up, shifting the weight enough to take her for a tumble down the steep slope. Alana and I missed most of the accident. We just witnessed where her pack was abruptly left behind on the trail with a clump of her hair and some blood still attached. It was her paws that suffered the most, and we were thankful to have a separate dog first-aid kit packed along. Some gauze, horse tape and aspirin got her through the trip.

The next obstacle was a double set of rapids flushing out not far downstream from Fat Man's Falls. The plan was to lift over the first major drop and then take on the rapids below. The water levels, however, were way too shallow and too many rocks were exposed to allow safe passage. So Alana and I portaged once again. We made use of an okay 315-meter trail on the left.

What remained was another double set of rapids. Again, the first we portaged around (110 m on the right) due to low water levels, and the second we managed to bump and grind down, losing a bit of canoe paint as we went.

Only a shallow swift remained (a 50-m rough portage exists on the right) before the Lady Evelyn emptied out into the southwest corner of Willow Island Lake. We took some time out to check what remained of an old lumber camp and found that not much was left to see. Then we chose a campsite for the night on Willow Lake. It reminded us of Sucker Gut for its scenic rock outcrops—but also for its trashed sites. The one we ended up staying on wasn't bad though and for humor 's sake, Alana and I sat around the campfire that night and made a note of all the camp gear we had found left behind on a campsite or lying at the end of a portage: 33 socks, two pairs of underwear, one sweatshirt, two T-shirts, one running shoe, two towels, three PFDs, one paddle and a canoe. Most of what we found must have been from the large youth camp we came across on the river. They had pitched their tents at the rapids near Katherine Lake and when we arrived, the camp councilor was screaming bloody murder at them: "If you don't pick up your gear I'll throw it in the river." A few minutes later and into the river it went. The kids retrieved the gear—well, maybe not all of it.

Alana and I woke up to a fantastic morning. The sun rose at 6:00 a.m., and we were up early enough to sip on our morning coffee and watch it rise over the treetops. Loons gathered again, this time adding up to 26. After a second cup of coffee and bannock with honey for breakfast we headed up Willow Island Lake, cutting through the morning mist. In an hour

we were taking on the first of two portages that would take us back over to the lower end of Lady Evelyn Lake. The trail take-out starts out on the east shore, in a back bay, and the portage measures 500 meters. The second is straight across a moderate-sized unnamed lake and measures 450 meters.

It would have been possible to just keep paddling up Willow Island Lake and link up with the familiar Sucker Gut Lake and the upper Lady Evelyn Lake. The bottom end of Lady Evelyn Lake, however, is an incredible place; it's dotted with islands and surrounded by majestic white pine. It was only midday when we found ourselves drifting by the main cluster of islands but we couldn't resist the temptation to stay here. It would mean adding an extra day onto our trip but we had lots of food left on our pack-barrel and nowhere to be after our trip, so the decision was made to pitch

our tent at the south end of an elongated island.

Staying over an extra night was a bit of a blessing in disguise. At first I cursed our decision. The prevailing southwest wind the next morning was causing us some major anxiety as we made our way along Lady Evelyn's eastern shoreline. A tailwind seems okay at first, helping to speed your progress, but as the waves increase in size, and you begin to surf, the chance of water slopping into the boat's stern and sinking the canoe increases dramatically. We hugged the eastern shoreline as best we could but continuing on to the north end of Lady Evelyn seemed impossible. Problem was, we couldn't afford another day off. But that's when luck prevailed. While taking a break behind an island on the top end of an eastern bay, Alana bailed the excess water from the bow and I glanced at our map for our escape options. And I found one. Sugar Lake route, a chain of small lakes and portages, could be taken directly from where we were and across to the far side of Lady Evelyn Lake. The route (part of the Sugar Lake Conservation Reserve) would definitely be safer than attempting to continue up the expanse of Lady Evelyn and, we would soon discover, Sugar Lake route was a pure oasis that ended up being the highlight of our trip.

Alana and I located the creek mouth that marked the beginning of the route not far from the island we hid behind, north of Snake Point. We paddled up the marshy creek for a good 10 minutes before reaching the first take-out. From here there were two ways to go. The trail heads off for approximately 400 meters and then splits. To the left a path continues for another 800 meters to Goodfish Lake (yes, fishing is good for smallmouth bass and pike). To the right it's just another 100 meters that will take you in the direction

of Sugar Lake. If you decide on Goodfish Lake, then a 400-meter portage located at the southeast inlet will take you into Sugar Lake; or you could take a side trip in and out of Angler Lake to the northeast by way of an 80-meter and a 400-meter portage. Alana and I chose right, however. It seemed easier on the map but I'm not sure it actually was. We entered a widening in the creek and then took on another 200-meter portage at the far end to an unnamed lake. Both the take-out and put-in were cluttered with slippery boulders that made for a treacherous carry.

A late lunch was had on the one campsite of the unnamed lake and then we moved on toward Sugar Lake. A 350-meter portage took us out of the north end of the unnamed lake, a portage that ended up being much worse then the previous rock-strewn trail. It was a risky balancing act getting the packs and canoe over to the other side. And when the portage was done, Alana and I found ourselves gently maneuvering through boulder gardens in mid-creek at the beginning and the end, wading a good portion of it before entering Sugar Lake.

By the time we flushed ourselves out into Sugar Lake the winds had brought in bad weather and the decision was made to camp here on Sugar Lake rather than continue on to Lady Evelyn Lake. The campsite near the portage that would lead us out of Sugar Lake was well protected from the winds but it was already taken, leaving us to pitch our tent up on an exposed bush site on a ridge top across the lake. The view was glorious, however, and I've come back to make use of this site many times after.

The wind continued to blow rough and noisy in uneven gusts all through the night, howling through the stand of pine trees rooted around our flimsy tent. In early morning, however, we woke to sun and silence. The winds had mysteriously stopped and the lake was calm and inviting. Alana and I skipped breakfast, except for coffee and granola, in fear the winds would pick up again midday and slow our progress again on Lady Evelyn. We packed up quickly and paddled directly over to the take-out of the 1,515-meter portage to Lady Evelyn. And then we wasted a good chunk of time clambering up a steep slope toward a hunt camp before we realized we weren't on the portage—just an ATV trial.

Eventually the proper portage take-out was found through an inlet more to the northeast of Sugar Lake, lined with chunks of granite. The first section was confusing at times, taking us over a barren slab of bedrock where the trail seemed to disappear at times. Halfway along, the trail dropped down a respectable slope and wandered through some wet patches. Overall, however, it wasn't bad and it didn't take us long to carry over to a large bay on Lady Evelyn Lake.

It took us a few hours to paddle across what remained of Lady Evelyn Lake. We took a break at a fishing camp in hopes of getting some ice cream. It was a hot afternoon on the water and in the distance we saw a large sign posted on the camp's boathouse advertising ice cream. How could we resist? Problem was, the lodge had no ice cream. The sign was something that floated into shore one spring, and they nailed it up to keep the boathouse roof from falling down. What a disappointment!

After Alana and I finished the familiar 260-meter portage back over to Mowat's Landing we took note of the common site all paddlers dread—the sight of the boat launch, parked cars and people rushing about. It had an effect on us. It meant the trip was over; something that both Alana and I (and I think our dog, Bailey) weren't quite ready for.

As we beached the canoe at the launch we saw others preparing for their canoe trips, exhilarated but anxious, just as we were when we headed out. The only difference between them and us, however, was that the anxiety part had long faded away.

LONGEST PORTAGE 1,515 meters

FEE The route is part of the Lady Evelyn–Smoothwater Provincial Park and an interior camping fee is required.

ALTERNATIVE ACCESS None

ALTERNATIVE ROUTE The trip can be shortened into a 4–5 day trip by eliminating the Lady Evelyn River portion.

OUTFITTERS
Smoothwater of Temagami
Box 40
Temagami, ON, P0H 2H0
705-569-3539
www.smoothwater.com

Temagami Outfitting Company
6 Lakeshore Drive
Temagami, ON, P0H 2H0
705-569-2595
www.temagamioutfitting.ca

FOR MORE INFORMATION
Ministry of Natural Resources
Temagami District
705-569-3622
www.mnr.gov.on.ca

MAPS Chrismar has produced an excellent map of this route and many other paddling routes throughout Temagami.

TOPOGRAPHIC MAPS
41 P/1, 41 P/7 & 41 P/8

GPS COORDINATES
47.471696, -79.979196

Nellie Lake Loop

 2 to 3 days    4 portages   ●----● 28 km   There are a number of long, very steep portages.

I PREFER THE NORTHWESTERN entrance to Killarney Provincial Park. It's more isolated, gets far less use than the main access point at the George Lake campground, the mountain range is more rugged than the hills to the south (and more scenic, in my opinion), and it was here that members of the Group of Seven often chose to paint. There are disadvantages, of course. A little more driving time is required for the majority of park users, and the portages seem a little more strenuous. But the view is absolutely stunning.

One of the best quick trips is the Nellie Lake loop—the same trip that artist Frank Carmichael referred to as "a painter's paradise." His brother-in-law, E.R. Went (Uncle Willy), discovered this beautiful area while working for Inco. Went told Carmichael that he must see it for himself. Carmichael was hesitant to take his brother-in-law's advice at first, resisting the idea that an artist could be told where to find his inspiration, but in 1926 he finally gave in during a visit to Uncle Willy near Whitefish Falls. He climbed the fire tower on Tower Hill, where he viewed the hills and islands and fell in love with the landscape.

The canoe route begins at the government-assigned access point at Widgawa Lodge, where park permits can be obtained (reservations are highly recommended). The lodge is located just off Highway 6 south of Espanola. From here it's a day's paddle to Grace Lake by way of Frood and Cranberry lakes. The two lakes are joined by a shallow channel, which happens to be littered with the rubble remains of a dam built by Frank Carmichael himself. The Group of Seven member had built a cottage in 1934 to the east of the narrows and became frustrated with not being able to get to some of his favorite sketching sites because the dam at nearby Whitefish Falls leaked constantly. (To the south, Carmichael sketched *Bay of Islands*, and to the north, *Twisted Pine*.) He decided to correct the problem by constructing a makeshift dam between Frood Lake and Cranberry Bay.

Carmichael's daily routine consisted of rising at dawn, having breakfast, and then heading out from his cabin to the neighboring ridges to sketch. He would return by noon and would sometimes go out again, this time with the entire family—his wife equipped with a good book, his daughter with a pail for blueberries, and him with

Nellie Lake Loop

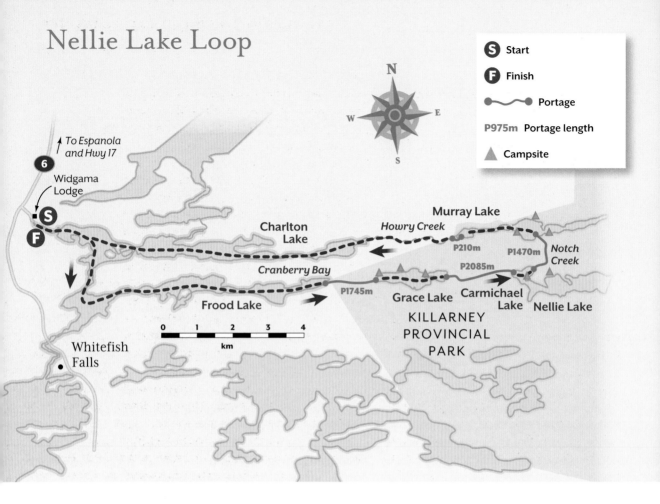

his sketchpad. Carmichael's daughter, Mary Matson, remembers the joy of the family's annual extended canoe trips: "We would fish in Murray, swim at Grace and sometimes visit Mr. Jackson and his artist friends on Nellie. I'll never forget the time A.Y. stood beside a blazing fire—this was during the heat of the day—and he actually offered me a cup of tea. I thought the man was mad."

If the wind is at your back here, which it usually is, the trip doesn't get too difficult until you reach the 1,745-meter portage leading from Cranberry Lake's far eastern bay to Grace Lake. The trail runs alongside a small stream and, compared to the rest of the portages on the route, it's the least strenuous.

There are only three campsites on Grace.

The one closest to the east end of the lake is the nicest and is more suitable for larger groups, but the one situated right at the put-in of the portage was a favorite of Carmichael's. From here he would head up the ridge to the north or clamber up the steep incline to the south and sketch the mound of quartzite separating Grace and Nellie lakes. He also liked to paint the many hidden waterfalls in the deep valleys between Cranberry and Grace and Nellie and Murray lakes.

Most of the second day of your canoe trip is spent working your way up the steep 2,085-meter portage from Grace Lake to Carmichael Lake, which is actually the western bay of Nellie Lake. This is one nasty portage, and the only thing that makes all the anguish and torment worthwhile is Nellie Lake's stunning beauty. The water of Nellie Lake is the clearest of all Killarney lakes.

The route heads north from Carmichael Lake. Before continuing on, however, make sure to take time out to paddle to the far end of Nellie and have lunch or even camp out for an extra day; and along the way keep an eye out for the old scow sunk at the bottom of the eastern bay. It's rumored to be the same boat used by A.Y. Jackson during his visits here. In his autobiography, he noted: "Swanson proposed we should go to Nellie Lake the next day. It was some miles away, nestled in high hills. There [were] a couple of portages on the way, and at the first Swanson, a giant of a man with a small head and sharp eyes, picked up a canoe and stuck it on his head as though he was putting on a hat. There was a scow on Nellie Lake that we embarked instead of our canoes. Two of the professors each took an oar and laboriously started rowing down the lake that was long and narrow, enclosed by big

hills. After a while Swanson said, 'Give me the oars,' and he sent the scow along like a racing shell, calling our attention to the scenery as we went along."

Jackson loved to paint at Nellie Lake, and one of his most famous paintings, entitled *Nellie Lake*, was based on the view from the ridge just to the east of the take-out for the portage leading to Murray Lake. He captured a view of Carmichael Lake with the "saddle portage" leading to Grace Lake as a backdrop, immortalizing the rolling mound of quartzite that characterizes so much of Killarney Park.

Two other members of the Group of Seven—Arthur Lismer and A.J. Casson—also showed interest in Killarney. They worked throughout the area, hiking along its ridges and canoeing the chain of lakes and bays, all the while transferring the spirit of the land onto to their sketchpads.

Killarney's rugged landscape has been a drawing card for artists for quite some time—Joachim Gauthier, Eric Aldwinckle,

J.E.H. MacDonald, Robert Bateman, Bill Mason—but it was members of the Group of Seven who first exposed this painter's paradise to the world. They were searching for Canada's true "wild country" so as to convey its beauty and environmental importance to the Canadian people, and it was here, in the heart of La Cloche, the Group found what they were looking for.

The canoe route continues, and the 1,470-meter trail that takes you to Murray is rough, forcing you to cross over Notch Creek three or four times along the way, but it's not as rough as any of the previous portages. This one is downhill and is the main reason why I choose to do this loop counterclockwise rather than the other way around. Going uphill, from Murray to Carmichael and Nellie, would hurt far more.

Once you reach Murray Lake, the mountains of La Cloche seem to disappear and the glorious vistas give way to a diverse system of swamp and fen. You're in the lowlands here, where the quartzite changes to granite and the hemlock and pine change to mostly maple and birch. This also marks the original northern boundary of the park. From here it's either Crown land or portions of the newly extended park boundary proposed through the Living Legacy program.

It's also your last night out en route, with the best site being to the east of the portage put-in, not far from where Notch Creek tumbles into the lake.

The final day is now spent paddling down Howry Creek, located to the far west end of Murray Lake. Howry Creek finally winds its way to the open expanse of Charlton Lake, which, of course, can be a good or bad thing, depending on the wind direction. Usually the same wind that helped you sail down Frood Lake will now stop you in your tracks while paddling up Charlton Lake. Thankfully, a few islands dot the lake and provide at least some protection against the headwind, and eventually the moment arrives when you round the next bend in the shoreline and spot your vehicle at the take-out, marking the end of yet other excursion into the heart of the northern La Cloche range.

LONGEST PORTAGE 2,085 meters

FEE An interior camping permit must be purchased for Killarney Provincial Park.

ALTERNATIVE ACCESS None

ALTERNATIVE ROUTE None

OUTFITTERS
Widgawa Lodge
Box 19
Whitefish Falls, ON, P0P 2H0
705-285-4966 or 1-800-562-9992
www.widgawa.ca

Charlton Lake Camp
1086 Willisville Lake Road
Whitefish Falls, ON, P0P 2H0
705-285-4281 or 1-877-587-3474
www.charltonlakecamp.com

FOR MORE INFORMATION
Killarney Provincial Park
705-287-2900 (information) and
1-888-668-7275 (reservations)
www.ontarioparks.com

Friends of Killarney
705-287-2800
www.friendsofkillarneypark.ca

TOPOGRAPHIC MAPS 41 I/4

GPS COORDINATES
46.146372, -81.739184

To the Crack and Back

 2 to 3 days

 6 portages

●----● 54 km

Moderate canoe-tripping skills are required due to the long portages.

KILLARNEY PROVINCIAL PARK'S Silver Peak has always been the hot spot from which to view the La Cloche mountain range. Personally, however, it's not my favorite. My preference is "the Crack," a large split in the rock on top of Blue Ridge. From here you can get an incredible view of Killarney and OSA Lake. It's not as panoramic as Silver Peak, but in my opinion it's far more breathtaking. And what makes it even more special is that it's possible to design a canoe route that includes the hike halfway en route. The access point is the main campground on George Lake, and the first day's route is to paddle across George, portage the 80 meters to Freeland, and then the 455 meters to Killarney. Most paddlers choose Killarney Lake to camp on the first night. It is possible, however, to make it all the way to Norway Lake. The portage (1,390 m) is located in Killarney Lake's northeastern arm and is not a bad carry; it's just the length that's the problem. A few years back it was possible to cut off a good chunk of it by paddling the creek to the right of the portage. Not long ago I recall having only to carry around to the right of a logjam at the mouth of the creek, then to the left of a high beaver dam,

and then portage another couple hundred meters at the end, joining up with the regular portage where the creek narrows. Recently, however, the beaver dam broke and the creek was completely unmanageable, making the long portage the only option.

A small stream meanders down from Sandy Lake on the east side of Norway. I once used this creek as a handrail while bushwhacking with a group of high-school students all the way from Silver Lake. We were on a backpacking trip and were forced off the regular hiking trail due to a buildup of spring snow and slush. Detouring through the thick brush, we set our compass bearing for Norway Lake, where we planned to make camp. On the way, one particular student stepped in some swamp ooze along the creek and lost his shoe to the foul-smelling muck after we yanked him free. Several attempts were made to retrieve his shoe, but the student eventually had to resort to hiking the rest of the way out with one mud-caked sneaker and one very worn woolen sock.

The advantage of making it to Norway the first day out is that you have the morning to hike a section of the La Cloche Silhouette Trail.

To the Crack and Back

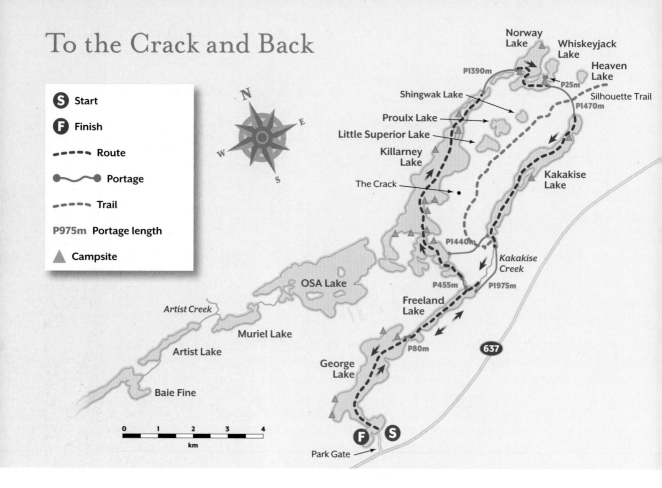

Legend:
- **S** Start
- **F** Finish
- - - - - Route
- ●～● Portage
- - - - - Trail
- P975m Portage length
- ▲ Campsite

Norway Lake
Whiskeyjack Lake
Heaven Lake
P1390m
P25m
Shingwak Lake
Silhouette Trail
P1470m
Proulx Lake
Little Superior Lake
Killarney Lake
Kakakise Lake
The Crack
P1440m
Kakakise Creek
OSA Lake
P455m
P1975m
Artist Creek
Freeland Lake
Muriel Lake
P80m
637
Artist Lake
George Lake
Baie Fine
0 1 2 3 4 km
F S
Park Gate

On your way out of Norway and in to Kakakise, the La Cloche Silhouette Trail cuts across the 1,470-meter portage. The trail meets up with the portage shortly after the take-out and is marked to the right. It leads to views of Shingwak, Proulx and Little Superior lakes. It takes a good portion of the morning to reach the lakes, however. A shorter option might be to continue along the portage to the halfway mark, where the hiking trail heads off to the left and takes you to Heaven Lake. This was once thought to be the highest lake in the province, and even though it's not, it sure feels that way once you look out at the distant views from the south shore campsite.

The portage itself has a few steep inclines along the first quarter, but eventually it's a moderate downhill slope the rest of the way.

From Kakakise Lake the route heads to the east. This is the lake you should spend your second night on, because you've just spent the morning hiking off the Kakakise portage, and because you really should complete another hike up to the Crack (located at the east end of Kakakise Lake) the morning of day three. The problem is, Kakakise Lake has only two campsites. It used to have three, but one was closed due to abuse. Both present campsites are nice spots, but good luck reserving them. If you don't get a campsite on Kakakise and still want to walk up to the Crack, you have a few alternatives. You could portage 1,440 meters out of your way and camp on Killarney Lake; you could forget the morning hike off the Kakakise portage, walk up to the Crack instead and then head for home that same

day; or you could choose to spend the last night on George Lake itself, after completing the walk up to the Crack. However, each of these options makes for a very long day. Whatever you choose, make sure the Crack is part of your trip.

To walk up to the Crack, use the take-out at the 1,440-meter portage to Killarney Lake. After you store your canoes off the trail, you then head north along the Silhouette Trail, past Kidney Lake, and then eventually up to the giant rock fracture. The entire center of the park can be viewed from just beyond the split. You can see OSA and Killarney lakes below, with the entire South La Cloche Range as a dazzling backdrop. It's by far the best place to ponder the geological development of this incredible vista.

The story behind the creation of the La Cloche range is quite unique. It all began about three and a half billion years ago, when scalding stream and poisonous gases burst from openings in the earth's surface. Quake activity constantly shifted layers of sediment, and finally rock pierced the rolling waves of the gigantic ocean that covered what is now called Northern Ontario. This land formation, an island referred to by geologists as "the Superior Province," underwent dramatic changes during the next several hundred million years. Large chunks of its southern shore were eroded, creating "the Southern Province." In the Killarney region, sediment exceeded 11 kilometers in depth, and these layers, caught between rising land and the weight of the ocean, formed different varieties of rock, which eventually buckled, thrust upward and became what we now call the La Cloche mountain range, one of the oldest mountain ranges in the world. Approximately 75 percent of Killarney Provincial Park is made up of ancient quartzite. Another 15 percent of the park is part of the Laurentian Mountains, largely comprised of pink granite peaks formed roughly two billion years ago.

The La Cloche Range once towered as high as the Rockies, but about a million years ago an ice age caused glaciers to advance and retreat four times over, each time scouring the quartzite peaks, stripping them of soil, grinding and scarring their surfaces, and leaving behind sand, gravel and boulders. As the ice melted, a huge lake was formed, with a water level well above that of present-day Lake Huron. The La Cloche Range was thus transformed into a cluster of white-capped islands.

Today, the younger Rockies boast higher elevations than the La Cloche, as do sister peaks the Laurentians, but if the hills of Killarney could talk, they would spin a historic tale far more grand and ancient. There are only two more portages to get you from Kakakise Lake and back to the George Lake access point. One is the familiar 80-meter trail connecting Freeland to George, the same portage you carried over on your first day out. First, however, you have to complete another 1,975-meter portage, taking you from Kakakise to Freeland. The take-out is located in the southwest corner of Kakakise, where a small creek flushes out of the lake just to the left of the 1,440-meter portage leading to Killarney Lake. The trail is to the south of the creek. If water levels are up, you might be able to paddle through the narrow, weed-choked creek with lifts over a few beaver dams. Either way, it's an easy trek back when compared to all the hiking you've done so far, and it's a pleasant way to finish up an astonishing trip to some of the best highlights of Killarney Provincial Park.

LONGEST PORTAGE 1,975 meters

FEE An interior camping permit must be purchased for Killarney Provincial Park.

ALTERNATIVE ACCESS The loop can also be linked up from Carlyle or Johnnie Lake access points using a relatively flat 940-meter portage from Terry Lake, which is actually the northwest bay of Carlyle Lake, to Kakakise Lake. Carlyle Lake access is reached by turning north off Highway 637, 50 kilometers in from Highway 69, the put-in adjacent to 637. Johnnie Lake access is at the end of Johnnie Lake Road. Turn north off Highway 637, 45 kilometers in from Highway 69 (just past the West Mahzenazing River bridge). Permits must first be picked up at the main office at George Lake Campground.

ALTERNATIVE ROUTE None

OUTFITTERS

Killarney Outfitters
Killarney, ON, P0M 2A0
705-287-2828 or 1-800-461-1117
www.killarney.com

Killarney Kanoes
Box 66, Stn. B
Sudbury, ON, P3E 4N3
705-287-2197 or 1-888-461-4446
www.killarneykanoes.com

FOR MORE INFORMATION

Killarney Provincial Park
705-287-2900 (information) and
1-888-668-7275 (reservations)
www.ontarioparks.com

Friends of Killarney
705-287-2800
www.friendsofkillarneypark.ca

TOPOGRAPHIC MAPS 41 I/3

GPS COORDINATES
46.018264, -81.397580

Eighteen Mile Island Loop

 4 to 5 days

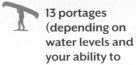 13 portages (depending on water levels and your ability to run whitewater)

●----● 74 km

Novice to moderate experience needed in running whitewater and lining a canoe up and down rapids.

THE FRENCH RIVER'S Eighteen Mile Island Loop, located east of Highway 69, is an excellent five-day trip. It provides a chance to practice the art of lining upstream (guiding the canoe along from the shore with ropes tied to bow and stern) and the skills of navigating fast-moving whitewater.

Loon's Landing Resort, on Dry Pine Bay, is where the upstream battle begins. To reach the put-in spot, drive north of the French River bridge on Highway 69 and turn right onto Highway 607. Turn right at the T-intersection, just after the railway, and then turn again at the next left. Keep left on the side road until you reach the lodge on the west shore of Dry Pine Bay.

There are campsites and cabins at Loon's Landing, handy if you arrive late in the day. However, phone the resort ahead of time to ensure a place to spend the night.

From the put-in, head directly across Dry Pine Bay to Meshaw Falls (formerly called "Michaud Falls"), where you can connect up with Eighteen Mile Bay. You could travel up Stony Rapids, just south of the falls, as an alternative route to Eighteen Mile Bay, but the two portages en route are poorly marked and overgrown. The path around Meshaw Falls, beginning at the private beach of Meshaw Cottages Ltd., is by far the best choice.

As you follow the Meshaw Falls portage up the resort owner's laneway and over a dirt road, notice the cut stone wall built around the perimeter of a swirl hole. The natural hole, measuring 6 feet across and 16 feet deep, was created by the swirling action of a large stone made of hard granite. The 150-pound stone, which looks something like a jumbo-size bowling ball, is on display in the camp's store.

From Meshaw Falls, paddle the length of Eighteen Mile Bay and then head northeast between the two white quartzite islands. Here, the journey up the French River's North Channel begins. If luck is on your side, the prevailing winds coming off Georgian Bay will counteract the river's current.

The first rapid along the North Channel can be easily lined or waded. There is, however, a 50-meter portage to the left. Shortly after, a small swift flows under a metal bridge, and if water levels are high you may have to carry your gear up and then back down a steep bank to the opposite side.

Eighteen Mile Island Loop

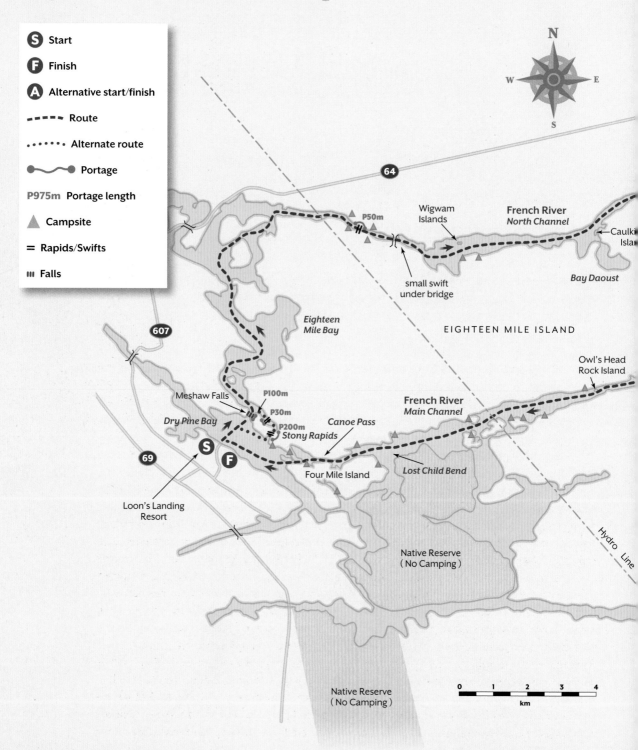

Legend

- **S** Start
- **F** Finish
- **A** Alternative start/finish
- - - - **Route**
- · · · · **Alternate route**
- ●~● **Portage**
- **P975m** Portage length
- ▲ **Campsite**
- = **Rapids/Swifts**
- ⫴ **Falls**

N
W — E
S

64

French River
North Channel

P50m

Wigwam
Islands

Caulki
Isla

small swift
under bridge

Bay Daoust

607

*Eighteen
Mile Bay*

EIGHTEEN MILE ISLAND

Owl's Head
Rock Island

Meshaw Falls

P100m

P30m

Dry Pine Bay

P200m

Stony Rapids

Canoe Pass

French River
Main Channel

69

S **F**

Four Mile Island

Lost Child Bend

Loon's Landing
Resort

Native Reserve
(No Camping)

Hydro Line

Native Reserve
(No Camping)

0   1   2   3   4
km

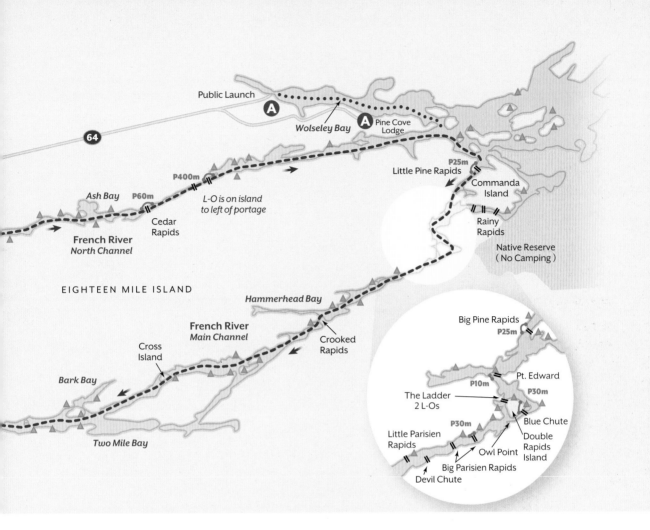

The map includes the following labels:

Public Launch
Wolseley Bay
Pine Cove Lodge
64
Ash Bay
P60m
P400m
L-O is on island to left of portage
Cedar Rapids
French River North Channel
Little Pine Rapids
P25m
Commanda Island
Rainy Rapids
Native Reserve (No Camping)
EIGHTEEN MILE ISLAND
Hammerhead Bay
French River Main Channel
Crooked Rapids
Cross Island
Bark Bay
Two Mile Bay

Big Pine Rapids
P25m
Pt. Edward
P10m
P30m
The Ladder 2 L-Os
Blue Chute
Little Parisien Rapids
P30m
Double Rapids Island
Owl Point
Big Parisien Rapids
Devil Chute

After the bridge, the French opens up looking more like a lake than a river. South of the Wigwam Islands, at the base of an abrupt granite cliff face, you will find the first campsite. Since much of the North Channel is made up of Crown land, and it is not part of the provincial park, campsites are not marked or maintained on a regular basis. As a rule, however, prime sites are easily found by searching out well-placed fire rings. If you still can't figure out where to make camp, ask one of the local cottagers to point out a good site.

I prefer to bypass the sites south of the Wigwam Islands and paddle past the southern Baie Daoust and Caulkins Island, to where the shoreline closes in once again.

Day two paddling the North Channel offers time out to explore a number of secluded bays and hidden lakes. Abundant bird life—osprey, broad winged hawks and even the uncommon sandhill crane—take advantage of these protected pockets just a stone's throw from cow pastures and cottage lots.

Only Cedar Rapids, divided into two main sections, interrupts the river, halfway to Wolseley Bay. The first section can be lined or portaged 60 meters to the left. Farther up the river, the second section (a double set of rapids) requires a little more effort. First, complete a lift-over on an island in the center of the rapids. Then paddle a short distance upstream to where a challenging 400-meter portage is necessary to avoid the final stretch.

The trail is on the left side of the river, running along the top of a ridge. To find it, however, you must first haul your gear up to the top of the rock face and then search out a series of rock cairns that mark the way.

Spend your second night on the river either along the last stretch of the North Channel, where points of pink granite make ideal campsites when the bugs get bad, or on one of the many pine-clad islands that dot the expanse of Wolsley Bay.

The channel gets less motorboat traffic than Wolsley Bay, but from any of the island sites you can lie in your tent at night, listening to the low roar of nearby Little Pine Rapids, and anticipate the upcoming downstream run.

The Main Channel runs directly parallel with the North Channel, flushing out of Wolsely Bay in two directions, to the right and left of Crane's Lochaven Wilderness Lodge (opened for business by the CPR in 1925) on the northern tip of Commanda Island. Little Pine Rapids, the first of seven major rapids known collectively as the Five Mile Rapids, is the preferred route around the island. There is a 25-meter portage in a small bay to the right, but many canoeists choose instead to line their canoe down or run straight through the rapid's center V. During a trip in late spring, I took the large curling white waves formed at the base of the rapid for granted and paid the price. The canoe plowed straight into the foam and froth, bogged itself down with water and submerged like a submarine. It was two full days before my gear was dry.

The next set of whitewater, Big Pine Rapids, is a little more challenging to run or line, especially where a large boulder juts out three-quarters of the way down the run. I have always opted to take the 25-meter portage to the right instead of risking an upset halfway along the trip.

Next come Double Rapids, which is nothing more than a double swift and can usually be easily run. You can also choose to carry around 10 meters to the right. Just downstream, the river splits, making its way around Double Rapids Island by way of the Ladder to the right or the Blue Chute to the left. The Ladder can be avoided by lifting over the two ledges on the right bank. A steep 30-meter portage works its way over the center of Double Rapids Island to bypass the Blue Chute.

The base of the Ladder was the first site chosen by a group of treasure hunters searching the French River for voyageur artifacts in 1961. They speculated that the voyageurs avoided the more turbulent Blue Chute by negotiating their large cargo canoes down the twin ledges, but that with such a small area to turn between the two ladders, some of the 36-foot vessels would have swamped on their way down. Their hunch was right. The divers swam to the surface with axe heads, brass kettles, glass beads, knives, a musket, flint, balls and shot. After a decade of increased archaeology exploration on the river, the base of the Ladder was one of the two most productive sites for voyageur artifacts.

Downriver from Double Rapids Island, the river continues to drop, forming Big Parisien Rapids, Devil Chute, Little Parisien Rapids, and later, west of Hammerhead Bay, a double set called Crooked Rapids. All can be run, except possibly for the unnamed channel preceding Big Parisien Rapids. There the water gushes through a narrow slice of river bordered by walls of dull granite. The whitewater can be avoided completely by a 30-meter portage that follows the rocky bluff to the right.

Farther downstream, after Big Parisien Rapids, where water levels allow for safer passage over the rock-strewn river, keep to the left to navigate Devil Chute, Little Parisien Rapids and Crooked Rapids.

After Crooked Rapids, the final drop of the staircase ledges, the river is without whitewater and the remaining two days are spent paddling a calm and serene strip of water back to Dry Pine Bay.

As the current changes, so does the landscape. Gradually the shoreline vegetation alters from forests of stout red and white pine to runty jack pine. Islands with obscure shapes jut out in the center of the river, each with a story behind its name. Cross Island is said to be the place where a group of Jesuit missionaries in the 17th century were massacred, most likely by Iroquois raiding parties from the south on their way to attack the Nipissing band in 1649. Crosses have been erected on the western tip of the island. It's a peaceful spot for a shore lunch, but be warned that the island is still shunned by local Natives who consider it cursed.

It can be difficult to choose a place to spend your last night on the river. Most of the campsites past Owl's Head Rock Island come complete with a massive hydro line humming overhead; no camping is allowed on Cantin Island Indian Reserve; and the sites west of the reserve, along Lost Child Bend (where the crying of a lost child was heard for six days while searchers hunted the woods), are ugly as sin. There are a few places to make camp, however, hidden back in the bay on the north side of Four Mile Island and just west of Canoe Pass. They will leave you less than an hour's paddle away from the put-in at Loon's Landing and allow time for a hearty breakfast before the drive home the next morning.

LONGEST PORTAGE 400 meters

FEE An interior camping permit must be purchased for the French River Provincial Park.

ALTERNATIVE ACCESS Since this is a loop route, it is possible to begin your trip at a number of other lodges along the way. Some options are the put-in at the public launch at Wolseley Bay, Wolseley Bay Lodge or Pine Cove Lodge. Drive east on Highway 64/528 and follow the signs.

ALTERNATIVE ROUTE The route can be shortened by simply paddling downstream to Blue Chute and then back up to the access point.

OUTFITTERS
Grundy Lake Supply Post
Highway 69
Britt, ON, P0G 1A0
705-383-2251

White Squall Paddling Centre
53 Carling Bay Road
Nobel, ON, P0G 1G0
705-342-5324
www.whitesquall.com

The Lodge at Pine Cove
Box 91
Noelville, ON, P0M 2N0
705-898-2500
www.frenchriver.com

Loons Landing Resort
263A Hass Road
Alban, ON, P0M 1A0
705-857-2175
www.loonslanding.ca

FOR MORE INFORMATION
French River Provincial Park
705-857-1630 (visitor center)
www.ontarioparks.com

MAPS French River Provincial Park Canoe Map

TOPOGRAPHIC MAPS 41 I/1 & 41 I/2

GPS COORDINATES
46.043187, -80.581802

The French River's Old Voyageur Channel

🕐 4 to 5 days   🚶 3 portages   ●----● 84 km   **Perfect for the novice canoeist. Just watch out for the heavy winds on Georgian Bay.**

I'VE ALWAYS WANTED to paddle down the Old Voyageur Channel on the lower half of the French River, not just for its sense of history but also for its reputation for small-mouth bass, walleye, pike and even monster muskie. And what better partner than Peter Fraser, a fellow angler I've gotten to know well through countless other canoe adventures.

The trip begins on the docks of Hartley Bay Marina, located at the end of Hartley Bay Road. To access the starting point turn left off Highway 69, just north of the Hungry Bear Restaurant. The put-in can be crowded, especially on a long weekend. But after you pay for your permit at the main office (located directly across the railway tracks), the marina staff will park your vehicle and help you quickly get on your way.

The route heads west along Hartley Bay for 3 kilometers and then south, down Wanapitei Bay. It's best to keep to the western shoreline here, staying clear of the confusing set of islands and shallow inlets.

Ox Bay marks the most southern end of Wanapitei Bay and also where the river spreads out into a series of outlets. The Main Outlet is directly south and the Western Outlet

is to the west. Take the Western Outlet, leaving the Main Outlet for your return trip back from Georgian Bay.

If you keep to the left-hand shore, it's a straightforward run from here to Crombie Bay, where the river eventually twists its way southwest. Designated campsites are marked along the way, but because this area is busy with cottage and motorboat activity, you may want to wait until just after Crombie Bay to make camp.

You'll spend a good part of the next morning paddling an elongated stretch of the French before it splinters off into yet another set of channels, outlets and exits. To the east is the Bad River Channel, which eventually breaks off into a series of smaller outlets, all with fast swifts and boiling rapids. The Voyageur Channel is to the west and is a fairly straight passage out to Georgian Bay. However, water only flushes down this channel when river levels are high. The Old Voyageur Channel, situated between the other two outlets, was thought to be the principal route of the voyageurs and was the route of choice for Peter and me.

We first had a difficult time locating the

exact entranceway to the channel, but by making good use of the detailed topographic map we packed along, Peter and I eventually began to make our way through the chasm.

The first is the East Channel of the Rock Circus. Here we had to choose to navigate our craft through the area with the fewest jagged rocks; as the water level was rather low, obvious route choices became few and far between.

The next obstruction is Petite Faucille, or Little Sickle, a knee-high rock ledge just to the right of Morse Bay (a great place to fish for bass and pike). A 20-meter portage is marked to the left, but Peter and I just lifted our gear over and then lined our canoe straight through, which is what we assumed the voyageurs had done as well. In fact, my post-trip research found that several notations of this carrying place had been written up in old journals and that several artifacts were taken out from the base of Petite Faucille in the late 1960s. Even an 1845 painting by Paul Kane, titled *French River Rapid*, is thought to be of voyageurs portaging around the same location.

Two noteworthy sections remain—Palmer Rapids and La Dalle—both located not far downstream from Petite Faucille. A series of angled rocks can make Palmer Rapids difficult in low or moderate water, but La Dalle is no problem at any water level.

Once past La Dalle, the river flows into what is called the West Cross Channel. From here the voyageurs had two ways to reach the expanse of Georgian Bay: travel west on the same channel or paddle directly out by way of the Fort Channel. Of course, Peter and I chose neither. We were traveling east, back toward our vehicles at Hartley Bay. We made sure to keep close to the right shoreline so as not to get lost while traveling up the West

Cross Channel; this was especially important just before we lined up the Cross Channel Rapids. By discovering a few dead ends along the way and asking the odd boater for directions, we eventually found ourselves at the base of the three cascades emptying out of the Bad River—Back Channel, the Jump and Lily Chute.

Other anglers had gathered here to fish, so Peter and I took time out to jig for walleye. The spot looked ideal, but we caught only a couple of perch. An hour later the sun was close to setting, and with more boats beginning to gather, it seemed a prime time to fish the rapids. But we had yet to set up camp and decided to continue on to a protective cove just east of the Devil's Door Rapid.

At low water the Devil's Door was easy to run. I could well imagine, however, that during spring runoff it would be next to impossible. There is a short portage to the north, but because of its location, it doesn't seem safe at all. I would rather line or run Big Jameson, located directly to the south, or even make use of Little Jameson's portage, which is marked at the end of the inlet to the right of the Devil's Door.

Peter and I were amazed at how crowded the harbor was just beyond the Devil's Door; an assortment of fancy speedboats, yachts and outboard runabouts had moored for the night at the same place we had planned on staying. It's not that we expected to be totally alone while out on the Bay. We just never thought that we'd have to camp alongside of them. But Peter and I made the best of it by pitching our tent behind some trees, trying to ignore the humming of generators and the crackle of short-wave radios.

The next morning Peter and I made the decision to stay clear of the crowds by

The French River's Old Voyageur Channel

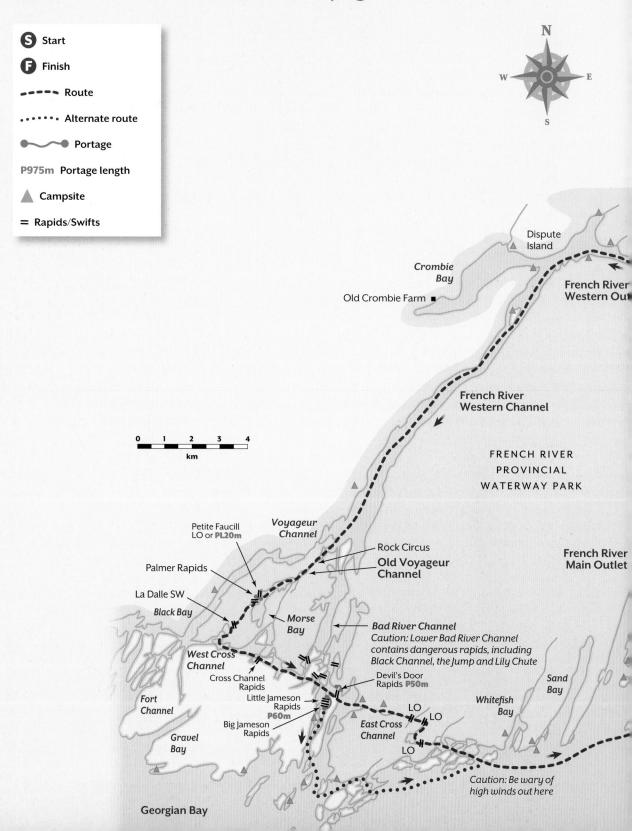

Legend:
- **S** Start
- **F** Finish
- - - - Route
- ····· Alternate route
- ●—●　Portage
- **P975m** Portage length
- ▲ Campsite
- = Rapids/Swifts

N

0 1 2 3 4 km

Dispute Island

Crombie Bay

Old Crombie Farm ■

French River Western Outlet

French River Western Channel

FRENCH RIVER PROVINCIAL WATERWAY PARK

Petite Faucill LO or **PL20m**

Voyageur Channel

Rock Circus

Old Voyageur Channel

French River Main Outlet

Palmer Rapids

La Dalle SW

Black Bay

Morse Bay

Bad River Channel
Caution: Lower Bad River Channel contains dangerous rapids, including Black Channel, the Jump and Lily Chute

West Cross Channel

Cross Channel Rapids

Devil's Door Rapids **P50m**

Sand Bay

Fort Channel

Little Jameson Rapids **P60m**

LO　LO

Whitefish Bay

Big Jameson Rapids

East Cross Channel

LO

Gravel Bay

LO

Caution: Be wary of high winds out here

Georgian Bay

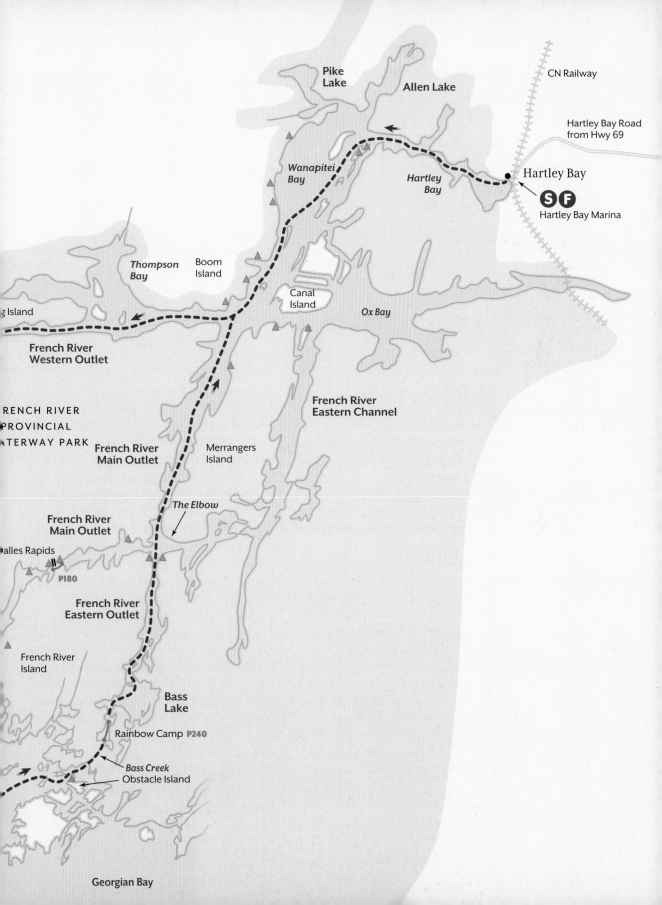

Pike
Lake

Allen Lake

CN Railway

Hartley Bay Road
from Hwy 69

*Wanapitei
Bay*

*Hartley
Bay*

Hartley Bay

S **F**
Hartley Bay Marina

*Thompson
Bay*

Boom
Island

Canal
Island

Ox Bay

g Island

**French River
Western Outlet**

**FRENCH RIVER
PROVINCIAL
WATERWAY PARK**

**French River
Eastern Channel**

**French River
Main Outlet**

Merrangers
Island

The Elbow

**French River
Main Outlet**

alles Rapids

P180

**French River
Eastern Outlet**

French River
Island

**Bass
Lake**

Rainbow Camp **P240**

Bass Creek
Obstacle Island

Georgian Bay

following the East Cross Channel, a narrow passage navigable only by canoe. At first the route was straightforward enough. But by mid-morning we had lifted over two large beaver dams, waded through a number of rocky shallows and become "confused" about our location at least half-a-dozen times. The bottom of our canoe suffered greatly, but we neither saw nor heard another boat.

Georgian Bay was surprisingly calm when we finally reached it, and Peter and I took advantage of the openness by paddling far out past the reefs to troll for a monster pike. At one point we even thought seriously of making the crossing to the Bustard Islands — a collection of 559 rocks over 3 kilometers out from the mainland.

The group of islands — named after a European game bird that made a habit of frequenting isolated areas — has long been a favorite anchorage for boats traveling out on Georgian Bay. The most popular stopover is the Bustard Island Lighthouse. The navigation beacon was first manned in 1875 by

Edward B. Barron, who, surprisingly enough, was a canoeist. Besides his commission at the lighthouse, the keeper was hired by the government to make exploratory trips to the James Bay area by way of canoe.

Peter and I had reached about the halfway point when we felt a breath of wind blow across the water. That was all we needed to make us come to our senses and head back for shore. The canoe rose easily on the waves at first, but as we approached the mouth of the Main Channel the breeze had turned into a steady gale. The boat began to tip and wobble in the troughs. Luckily, my wife, Alana, and I had traveled in the same area a year earlier and found ourselves in a similar dilemma. We had escaped by finding shelter in a circuit of islands and coves not far to the east, so Peter and I decided to make a run for it.

The islands seemed close enough, but midway across, the winds were steadily building and our canoe began to take on water. To help brace, we both jammed our knees tight against the gunwales and headed farther downwind. That lengthened the distance but seemed to keep us drier. Eventually we glided into flat, calm waters and made camp on the lee side of Obstacle Island.

The winds had made us nervous of Georgian Bay, and the next day we found ourselves on the water quite early. Taking full advantage of the morning lull, we quietly escaped back upriver by way of the Eastern Outlet's Bass Creek Tramway. This 240-meter long boardwalk, originally constructed of rails mounted on large timbers, was first established as a way for the lumber companies, which were phasing out operations at French River Village (just below Dalles Rapids), to move their mills elsewhere out on Georgian Bay. The skidway has been rebuilt over the years and used for a number of purposes, from transporting firefighting equipment for the Department of Lands and Forests to providing a shortcut to the Bay for boaters and canoeists. A cluster of cabins at the end of the tramway marks the remains of Rainbow Camp, one of the first of many bustling fishing lodges that operated along the French River in the early 1900s.

From the put-in at Rainbow Camp, the route heads across to the northeast of Bass Lake. From there, it continues up the Eastern Outlet, to the intersection with the Main Outlet called the Elbow, and then directly up the Main Outlet to the familiar Wanapitei Bay.

Peter and I took time out to fish while paddling this entire stretch. It had rained on us since Bass Lake, but we figured the change of weather would bring on the fish—and we were right. By the time we reached Ox Bay we had caught a mess of pike—the biggest weighing in at 16 pounds. The rain, though, had now changed to a constant downpour and a lather of whitecaps formed across the water.

Once again we made the right choice by heading for shore. We immediately set up camp. It took only minutes for us to erect the tent and tie down the canoe, but by then hurricane winds had whipped the water into a frenzy and we could hear nearby trees snapping like matchsticks.

The skies quickly darkened overhead. Peter and I ran for the relative safety of our flimsy nylon tarp to watch as great forks of lightning set the air crackling with electricity. We were a bit shaken by the event but, except for a soggy tent (Peter forgot to zip up the front flap), we came out of it unharmed. Little did we know, however, that a twister had touched down nearby, forcing two men to swim almost 100 meters back to shore after their house was tossed into the lake by a funnel cloud. Oblivious to the nearby destruction, we mourned the loss of dry sleeping bags and a good night's sleep, then headed back to the marina the next morning.

LONGEST PORTAGE 240 meters

FEE An interior camping permit must be purchased for the French River Provincial Park.

ACCESS Hartley Bay Marina, at the end of Hartley Bay Road. Turn left off Highway 69, just north of the Hungry Bear Restaurant.

ALTERNATIVE ACCESS The French River Supply Post, east of Highway 69.

ALTERNATIVE ROUTE The route can be extended by continuing east along Georgian Bay and looping back to Wanapitei Bay by way of the Pickerel River.

OUTFITTERS
Grundy Lake Supply Post
Highway 69
Britt, ON, P0G 1A0
705-383-2251

White Squall Paddling Centre
53 Carling Bay Road
Nobel, ON, P0G 1G0
705-342-5324
www.whitesquall.com

Hartley Bay Marina
2870 Hartley Bay Road
R.R. 2
Alban, ON, P0M 1A0
705-857-2038
www.hartleybaymarina.com

FOR MORE INFORMATION
Ministry of Natural Resources
705-564-7823
www.mnr.gov.on.ca

French River Provincial Park
705-857-1630 (visitor center)
www.ontarioparks.com

MAPS The Ministry of Natural Resources has produced a canoe route map for the entire French River.

TOPOGRAPHIC MAPS
41 I/2, 41 H/14 & 41 H/15

GPS COORDINATES
46.035278, -80.759579

Philip Edward Island

4 to 5 days None •----• 70 km **Moderate skills are required due to navigation issues and possible high winds out on Georgian Bay.**

PHILIP EDWARD ISLAND is just south of Killarney Park and is another proposed extension of the park through the Living Legacy Program. It's a fantastic four-to-five-day route that has been rated by a number of leading canoe and kayak magazines and websites as one of the top 10 paddle destinations in North America.

The trip circumnavigates 50 kilometers of island shoreline, starting out from either the marina in the town of Killarney or a Chikanishing River access point. If you choose Killarney, be warned: it's a long, treacherous paddle out to the island. Chikanishing boat launch is a better bet, but make sure to pay for a parking permit at the George Lake Campground gatehouse first. From here, drive 3 kilometers west of the campground on Highway 637 and make a left on Chikanishing Road (just before the bridge).

You can paddle around the island in either direction, but the preferred way is counterclockwise due to the prevailing winds. The exposed southern shoreline is also the most scenic and many paddlers simply go to Beaverstone Bay and back. But the north shore is still well worth a visit. It has a protective channel, Collins Inlet, and it is fascinating for historians, as it seems everyone in Canadian history paddled through here.

It is possible to take a canoe on this route. Twenty years ago I explored Collins Inlet by canoe, but a kayak makes far more sense, and having just recently given kayaking a try, I had the urge to do a full-week trip around the island.

I'm glad no one was around to witness me loading up at the put-in. I looked like a complete dork. It took me three attempts to find room to stuff all my gear under the deck (my skirt was on backward), and I went for an unintentional swim while trying to enter the cockpit. Don't get me wrong, I wasn't going about it blind: over the three previous weekends I had completed a full introductory course in paddling a kayak. But this was still new to me, and I was a little nervous. For almost 30 years I had used a canoe to travel across the water. Loading up and pushing off from shore in an open boat was nothing out of the ordinary. But this just wasn't the same thing; it was darn embarrassing for a seasoned canoeist. And being such a canoehead, I still wore my regular uniform of plaid

Philip Edward Island

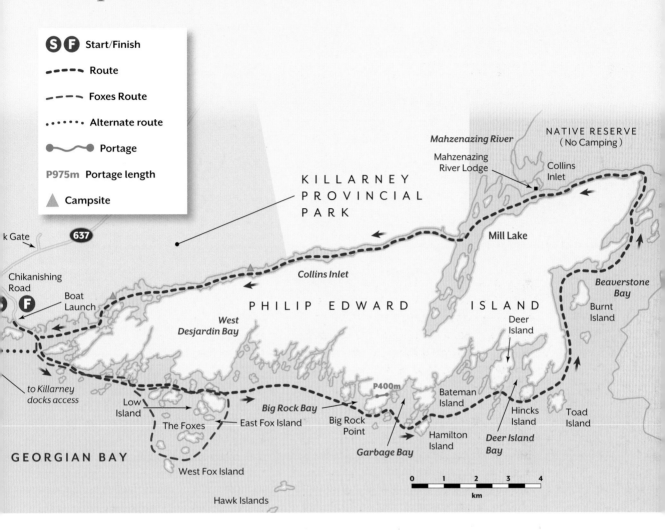

Legend:
- **S** **F** Start/Finish
- Route
- Foxes Route
- Alternate route
- ●━━● Portage
- P975m Portage length
- ▲ Campsite

KILLARNEY PROVINCIAL PARK

Mahzenazing River

Mahzenazing River Lodge

NATIVE RESERVE (No Camping)

Collins Inlet

Mill Lake

k Gate 637

Collins Inlet

Chikanishing Road

Boat Launch

F

PHILIP EDWARD ISLAND

Beaverstone Bay

Burnt Island

Deer Island

West Desjardin Bay

to Killarney docks access

Low Island

The Foxes   East Fox Island

Big Rock Bay

P400m

Bateman Island

Hincks Island   Toad Island

Big Rock Point

Deer Island Bay

GEORGIAN BAY

West Fox Island

Hamilton Island

Garbage Bay

Hawk Islands

0 1 2 3 4
km

shirt and baseball cap rather than get decked out in full Neoprene ensemble topped off with a bright white Tilley hat.

After a few minutes of practicing my kayak skills, I was ready for the big stuff and convinced myself to exit the protective cove. And there to greet me was a continual line of large surfing waves. The chop wasn't huge, but it was impressive enough that had I been in a canoe I would have definitely turned tail and returned to the put-in. It was surprising, but what actually encouraged me to move forward was the thrill of paddling into the vastness of Georgian Bay. There's a fine line between feeling thrilled and feeling anxious, even a little nauseous, about paddling in big water, but the more my double-bladed paddle propelled me through the troughs the more I liked being there.

I spent three days island-hopping from the western shore of Philip Edward Island to the opening of Beaverstone Bay, with my first night spent camped at the mouth of West Desjardin Bay and the second near Bateman

Island. The wind remained calm for the most part, and my nerves were shaken only once, while rounding Big Rock Point. The wind picked up slightly just before I started out toward the exposed point, and I considered making use of a rough 400-meter portage that cuts across from Big Rock Bay to Garbage Bay. The only problem with that idea, however, was that the water levels were extremely low at the time and many of the bays and inlets had become mudflats. Getting to the portage might have been a bit of an issue, so I took my chances and paddled around the point. The 20-minute paddle felt more like an hour, and the waves did grow larger the farther along I went, but I was never in any true danger. My third night was spent on gorgeous Hincks Island, between Deer Island Bay and the mouth of Beaverstone Bay. A black bear was just leaving when I arrived, and I briefly questioned camping there, but the spot was too nice to pass up, so I took the chance that the bear had only swum over for a quick fill of blueberries and was now happy on the mainland.

I stopped for a late lunch near the old lumber town of Collins Inlet, established at the mouth of the Mahzenazing River in 1868. Collins Inlet is still a well-traveled passageway, used now by powerboats and yachts, and it can get quite busy at times. But then again, I have a feeling this protective channel has always been busy. Explorers, Jesuits and voyageurs used it to escape the heavy winds of Georgian Bay, just as current boaters do today. And long before that, Native peoples used the route extensively. Today, ocher pictographs can still be seen as evidence of their time here. Located just to the west of the Collins Inlet site is a pictograph of a canoe with one of its occupants crowned with a cross, indicating a priest.

Just west of Collins Inlet a big slice of land has been taken out of the eastern end of Philip Edward Island and the result is Mill Lake. I camped my second-to-last night on its main shoreline. It wasn't supposed to be my second-to-last night, but bad weather was on the way and I wanted to make as much time as possible. I woke up to a slight drizzle of cold rain, which quickly turned into a downpour. By the time I packed up and headed out on the water, a stiff wind was funneling down the channel. What should have been a leisurely few days of exploring the most protected part of the trip ended up being an 11-hour ordeal of trying to escape the elements while staying as close to the put-in as possible.

I constantly maneuvered the kayak diagonally back and forth across the inlet, cut my corners sharp to lessen the distance I had to paddle and attempted to reduce the amount of times a gust of wind would catch my paddle blade and place strain on my wrists and arms.

The less-than-stunning view along the way didn't help matters. Not only were the sheets of rain dulling the landscape, but the scenery is less striking on the far side of Philip Edward Island, where the La Cloche hills and Manitoulin Island are no longer a backdrop. Mounds of pink granite abound, all sizes and shapes. I took a breather on the shelter side of a chunk of granite and marveled at the remarkably diverse species taking shelter in the fissures of the rock.

Squalls continued to chase one another all day, bringing more rain and more gusts of wind. I should have stopped to make camp long before reaching the western entrance to Collins Inlet; my clothes were soaked through and I was beginning to get a chill. But even though my body refused to cooperate at times, my mind remained focused on making more distance in case the weather became even worse the following day.

It was 9:30 p.m. when I pulled up on shore. At this point I had only enough energy to put a tarp up and light a campfire. I lay down on the hard rock, snuggled inside my sleeping bag and fell asleep beside the fire.

There I was, camped along Collins Inlet, once a safe passageway for Native people, voyageurs and steamship captains. Tonight, it was a haven for one lonely kayaker, a kayaker who was finally content, away from danger and very thankful not to have brought a canoe.

FEE No fee is required at this time.

ALTERNATIVE ACCESS Killarney town docks, located at the end of Highway 637.

ALTERNATIVE ROUTE The route can be shortened by paddling out to the first cluster of islands southwest of Philip Edward Island and then back to the access point.

OUTFITTERS
Killarney Outfitters
Killarney, ON, P0M 2A0
705-287-2828 or 1-800-461-1117
www.killarneyoutfitters.com

Killarney Kanoes
Box 66, Stn. B
Sudbury, ON, P3E 4N3
705-287-2197 or 1-888-461-4446
www.killarneykanoes.com

FOR MORE INFORMATION
Killarney Provincial Park
705-287-2900 (information)
www.ontarioparks.com

Friends of Killarney
705-287-2800
www.friendsofkillarneypark.ca

TOPOGRAPHIC MAPS
41 I/3 & 41 H/14

GPS COORDINATES
45.994646, −81.414535

Bear Lake Loop

2 to 3 days   **5 portages**   **31 km**   **Some canoe-tripping skills are required.**

KILLARNEY PROVINCIAL PARK extended its northern boundary a few years back. Prior to the extension I volunteered to travel possible routes that could be added to the area. What I found was an absolute paradise.

My first outing was a solo trip, beginning at an unregulated, or unmaintained, government launch on the west end of Walker Lake. I was hoping to locate a series of portages that would lead me northeast to Lake Panache and then back to Walker. If the route existed it would definitely add a different dimension to paddling the north end of Killarney Park.

From Sudbury drive west on Highway 17 and then south on Highway 6, through the town of Espanola. Take a left on Queensway Avenue (Panache Lake Road) directly across from the Tim Hortons coffee shop. Panache Lake Road is gravel all the way and gets rougher the farther along you go, but it's still manageable for a two-wheel vehicle. Drive 9 kilometers to the first fork, where you will go right, toward Hannah Lake (follow the Mountain Cove Lodge sign). Then after another 10 kilometers a sign shows to go either left to Walker Lake or right to Hannah Lake. (If

your vehicle can't handle the rest of the road, then start your trip on Hannah Lake; there's a makeshift public launch at the north end.) If you go left to Walker, at the 23-kilometer mark you can either drive directly down to Walker Beach public launch or take a left just before and make use of Mountain Cove Lodge. The owner of Mountain Cove Lodge has been there for over 30 years, and not only did he drive me and my gear down to the Walker Beach launch, he also gave me a tour of his main cabin—a historical gem left over from the logging era. He's a great guy and really deserves the business. You can choose to put in nearer to Mountain Cove Lodge on Lake Panache, but I prefer starting on Walker Lake to avoid portaging 150 meters around a dam between the two lakes.

The conditions weren't ideal when I headed out across Walker. The wind from the east made for some difficult solo paddling and was a sure sign that rain was on the way. By the time I reached the southeast of Walker Lake to Little Bear Lake I was overwhelmed with it all. Paddling solo into the wind can be extremely difficult. It's still doable, however, if you know how to tack into the wind. By pointing the bow

Bear Lake Loop

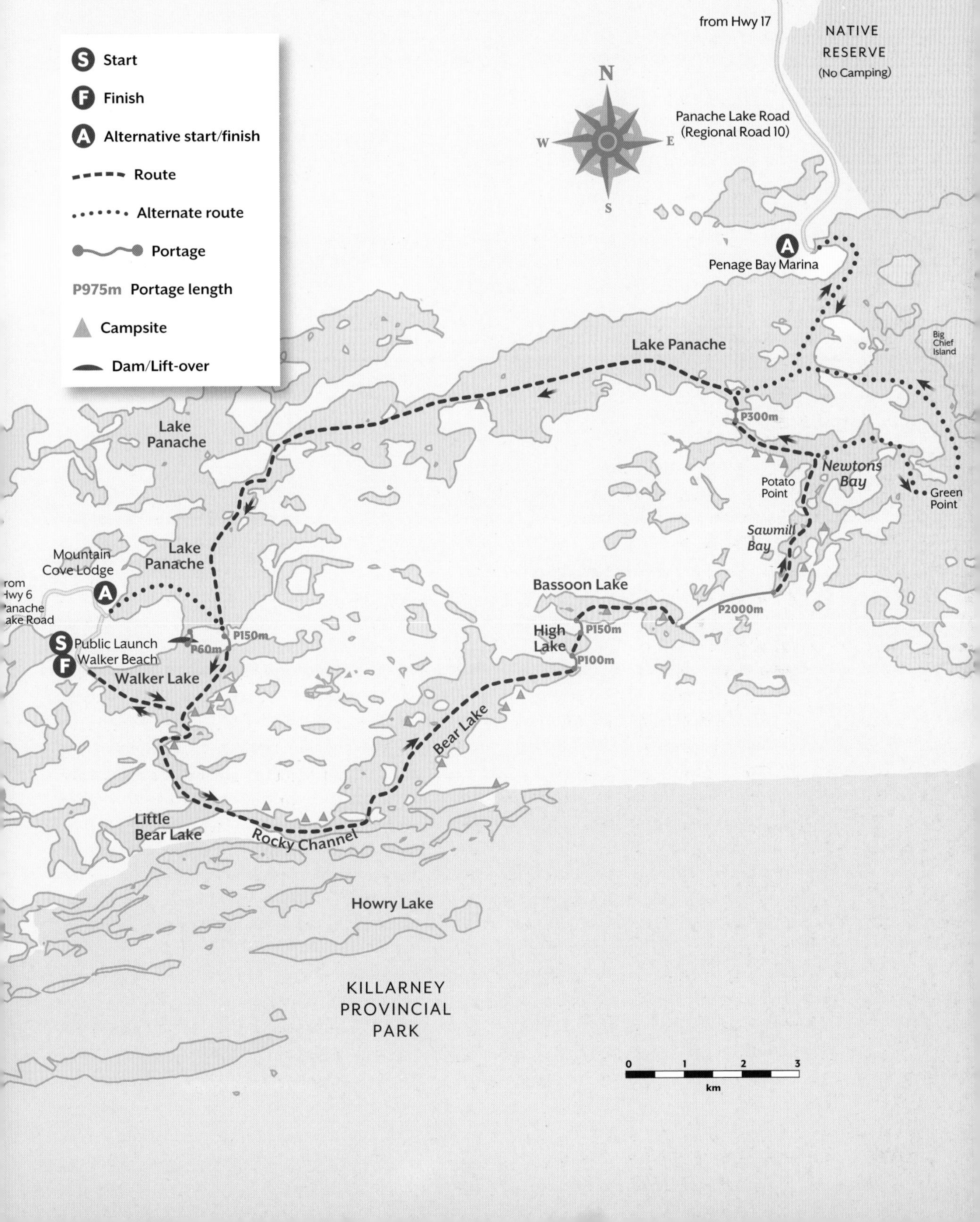

S Start

F Finish

A Alternative start/finish

- - - Route

· · · Alternate route

●—— Portage

P975m Portage length

▲ Campsite

—— Dam/Lift-over

N
W E
S

from Hwy 17

NATIVE RESERVE
(No Camping)

Panache Lake Road
(Regional Road 10)

Penage Bay Marina

Lake Panache

Big Chief Island

P300m

Newtons Bay

Potato Point

Green Point

Lake Panache

Sawmill Bay

Lake Panache

Lake Panache

P2000m

Mountain Cove Lodge

from Hwy 6
Panache Lake Road

A

Bassoon Lake

High Lake

P150m

P100m

S Public Launch
Walker Beach
F

P150m

P60m

Walker Lake

Bear Lake

Little Bear Lake

Rocky Channel

Howry Lake

KILLARNEY PROVINCIAL PARK

0 1 2 3
km

into the wind at a 45-degree angle I was able to propel the canoe forward, enough anyway to reach the east end of Rocky Channel.

I had a quick lunch on a small island along the western shore of Bear Lake. I should have kept to the eastern shore to make it easier to deal with the wind, but I insisted on keeping clear of the lodge owner on the large central island on Bear Lake. Prior to the trip I had informed him that I was planning on paddling the area to do research for a guidebook. In return, he made it perfectly clear to me that he didn't appreciate anyone, especially canoeists, writing guidebooks and making use of his lake unless they were associated with his lodge. I knew darn well that if we met out there, our points of view would clash. In his mind, he had invested a lot of money to make the area special for his paying customers. In my mind, this area was Crown land, soon to be an extension of Killarney Provincial Park, and that he had no right claiming it as "his" lake. Both outlooks are self-interested, I guess, but mine was strong enough to make me stand up in my canoe, drop my pants and moon the island as I drifted by.

When I reached the far northeast corner of Bear Lake the wind had died and with it the rain. I was making surprisingly good time, and there was still enough of the afternoon left for me to continue on to Bassoon Lake to check out the mythical portage to Lake Panache—a trail that the Bear Lake lodge owner had denied existed, which made me further believe it was there.

First there is a 100-meter portage from Bear Lake's northeastern bay to High Lake, located to the right of a small cascade and complete with one short but steep incline halfway along. And then, directly across on the opposite shore, is another short 150-meter portage (also with a short but steep incline halfway along) leading into Bassoon Lake.

It was just before 4:00 p.m. when I reached Bassoon. However, rather than stop and set up camp on the first island site, I continued on to the east end of the lake to begin my search for the historic portage. It's not that I was desperate to find the trail; I just didn't want to stop paddling. Throughout the day I had set a good rhythm for myself, I had outsmarted a disgruntled lodge owner and the weather had turned around completely. I was enjoying being out here alone, soaking it all in and being part of the raw, silent wilderness.

After half an hour hugging the eastern shoreline, I came across a new canoe padlocked to the same tree that a rotted cedar canvas canoe was chained to. No path led away from the boats, though. The creek at the far southeast end of the lake was so clogged with driftwood that it couldn't be considered a navigable route to Panache. And to the northeast corner, between two small islands, I discovered two rough paths leading into the bush, each marked with a single piece of flagging tape. I got out and checked the second trail, only to find out that it eventually met up with the first one. It was a route to somewhere for sure, but most likely just a snowmobile trail, not a portage. A good portion of the path went straight through bogs, and saplings had been cut a foot from the ground, indicating that the trail had been cleared in the winter on top of snow. I walked the path for a good 20 minutes but came to the realization that no recreational canoeist would enjoy using this route to Lake Panache, so I abandoned the search.

While walking back to my canoe I happened to flush two sandhill cranes that were being stocked by a black bear. I also caught a glimpse

of a small wolf (or possibly a coyote) trekking through a birch grove. A bit farther along, I came upon a stand of gigantic hemlock trees. They weren't big enough to be considered part of an old-growth forest, but the darn things were impressive all the same. So much so that I stopped to hug one of the largest in the group. I must confess it was an odd thing to do. I even looked around to see if anyone was watching before I gave a second one a squeeze. I wrapped my arms around the tree's wide trunk for several minutes before letting go and then finished my walk back to the canoe.

The next morning, over a strong cup of coffee and a stack of pancakes, I thought about my failed survey of the eastern shore and concluded there just had to be some type of portage to Panache leading from those two

canoes I had found; why else would they be left there? So I packed up my gear, paddled back over to the spot and examined the area once again. Sure enough, about 100 meters straight through a birch and poplar grove was a pile of logs placed across a small creek, and not far from that, to the left, a faint path that worked its way along the side of a large cattail marsh, eventually opening up to a more obvious portage. I had found it. Actually, the only portion of the trail that was hidden from view was the first 100 meters after the take-out on Bassoon. What remained was a rarely used but clear and flat 2,000-meter trail leading to the lower southwest corner of Lake Panache's Sawmill Bay. My perseverance had paid off, and I was able to continue the loop.

I kept to the western shoreline of Sawmill

NOVA CRAFT CANOE

Bay, named for the activities of the Fielding Logging Camp, which once worked out of the south end of the bay, and then went left, around Potato Point. My expected route was to the right, navigating all the way around Green Point, and then west on Panache, but I was hoping for a shortcut—a possible portage located somewhere along the north shore of Newton's Bay. If it existed the trail would allow

me to cut 10 kilometers off of my paddling on a very exposed stretch of lake.

My luck prevailed. About halfway along Newton's Bay I discovered an easy 300-meter bush trail leading from a small inlet to the southern shoreline of Lake Panache, directly in front of Flat Island.

From here I paddled west and then southwest on Panache for a full 12 kilometers. It had been a long day, but I decided to take full advantage of a rare calm on such a big body of water. By the time I reached the 150-meter portage, found in the small bay to the left of the Walker Lake dam (an alternative 60-meter portage exists directly to the left of the dam), it was getting dark. At 8:30 p.m. I pulled myself up on the first possible campsite on the east shore of Walker Lake, made peanut butter and jam sandwiches for dinner and then crawled into the tent for a well-deserved rest—ending one fantastic trip that now is marked on Killarney Provincial Park's canoe route map!

LONGEST PORTAGE 2,000 meters

FEE An interior camping permit must be purchased from Killarney Provincial Park.

ALTERNATIVE ACCESS Penage Bay Marina on Lake Panache or Mountain Cove Lodge on Lake Panache.

ALTERNATIVE ROUTE You can complete the loop by beginning at the Penage Bay Marina on Lake Panache.

OUTFITTERS
Killarney Outfitters
1076 Highway 637
Killarney, ON, POM 2A0
1-888-222-3410 or 705-287-2828
www.killarneyoutfitters.com

Mountain Cove Lodge
Summer Address:
Box 1270
Copper Cliff, ON, POM 1N0
705-682-4072
www.mountaincovelodge.com

FOR MORE INFORMATION
Killarney Provincial Park
960 Highway 637
Killarney, ON, POM 2A0
705-287-2900
www.ontarioparks.com

MAPS The Friends of Killarney has produced a good map for the park. Jeff's Map also has produced an interior route map.

TOPOGRAPHIC MAPS
42 J/3 & 42 J/4

GPS COORDINATES
46.210710, -81.529883

Great Mountain Lake

 2 to 3 days

 12 to 16 portages

●-----● 42 km

Some canoe-tripping skills are required.

I LOVE KILLARNEY'S NORTHERN range. The main reason is simple—there are fewer people. Paddlers usually keep to the areas south where white quartzite and crystal clear lakes dominate. The northern range has a subtle charm of its own, however. There's a sense of history here, not to mention lots of fish to catch. The lakes near the La Cloche mountain range are beautiful to look at, but they are also devoid of life. Quartzite isn't a good buffer for acid rain, which is caused by the pollution created in nearby Sudbury. That's why the lakes that are surrounded by white quartz are always turquoise blue and have little plant life. The pink granite, however, is able to protect the water quality and, consequently, allows aquatic plants (and fish) to thrive.

The northern portion of the park is also the better way through which to reach one of the best lakes in Killarney—Great Mountain Lake. Not many have viewed it or camped on it, likely because to reach it from the main entrance from the south, where most paddlers begin their trips, you have an intense 3-kilometer uphill portage. It's not pleasant. However, if you access the lake from the north it's a far easier journey.

To begin your trip you can use two main access areas on Lake Panache: Penage Bay Marina or Mountain Cove Lodge. The first option is quicker and easier to access by car. However, you'll have to paddle a good chunk of Lake Panache to reach Mountain Cove at the far southwestern end. The Penage Bay Marina is reached by turning off Highway 17 onto Regional Road 55 and then turning right onto Panache Lake Road (Regional Road 10). Travel 14 kilometers to the access point at Penage Bay Marina. To reach Mountain Cove Lodge, turn off Highway 17 onto Highway 6, turn left onto Queensway Avenue (which will turn into Panache Lake Road) and drive 9 kilometers east until you reach a fork. There will be a sign indicating to go to the right of the fork to Mountain Cove Lodge. You can make use of a rustic public launch on Walker Lake, but it's not maintained and probably not the best place to park your vehicle. I prefer using the lodge to store my vehicle and either putting in at Lake Panache or having the lodge owner drive me down to the public launch on Walker.

From the Mountain Cove Lodge put-in you must portage around a dam at the

Great Mountain Lake

from Hwy 17

NATIVE
RESERVE
(No Camping)

Panache Lake Road
(Regional Road 10)

S Start

F Finish

A Alternative start/finish

- - - - Route

· · · · · Alternate route

– – – Trail

●⌒⌒⌒● Portage

P975m Portage length

▲ Campsite

▬ Dam/Lift-over

Penage Bay
Marina **A**

Lake
Panache

Lake
Panache

Lake
Panache

from
Hwy 6
Panache
Lake Road

Mountain
Cove Lodge

S

F

A

P150m

P60m

Walker Lake

Bear
Lake

Little Mink
Lake

P285m

P585m

Goose
Lake

Round Otter
Lake

P100m

P285m

Fish Lake

P440m

Little
Bear Lake

Rocky Channel

Great
Mountain
Lake

P155m

Gail
Lake

Little
Mountain
Lake

P55m

KILLARNEY
PROVINCIAL
PARK

0   1   2   3
km

Access
to Silhouette Trail

southwestern end of Lake Panache to reach Walker Lake. There's a 150-meter trail found in the small bay to the left of the dam or an alternative 60-meter portage directly to the left of the dam.

From Walker Lake you will have a good long paddle through Little Bear and Bear lakes before you have to get out of your canoe again. At the southeastern end of Bear Lake a narrow channel takes you to a portage (285 m) leading into Goose Lake, a shallow body of water that's covered in lily pads. If the water levels are up then the next portage—585 meters alongside the creek that exits Goose Lake to the east—becomes just a couple of lifts over beaver dams. Just make sure to go right where the creek forks farther along. You want to go to Round Otter Lake, not Little Mink Lake.

Round Otter Lake is small (and round), but it's a great place to cast a line for bass or pike before you head into Fish Lake—which is an even better place to try to catch a shore lunch. Two back-to-back portages (100 m and 285 m) take you in and out of a small, unnamed pond before you reach Fish Lake.

Fish Lake marks the end of the northern pink granite. The moment you finish the last portage—an easy 440 meters marked to the right of an old cabin on the east end of Fish Lake—the quartzite La Cloche mountain range can be seen bordering Great Mountain Lake.

Fishing isn't allowed on Great Mountain Lake because of the acid rain, but there are plenty of other things to do. A short 55-meter portage will take you into Little Mountain

Lake where you can connect to the La Cloche Silhouette Trail for a hike along the northern mountain range. There's also Gail Lake, which is reached by a short but very steep 155-meter portage. Gail has one campsite, which means if you're lucky enough to reserve it then you get the lake to yourself. It's a perfect place to relax, swim and pick fresh blueberries.

The last time I was on Gail Lake my trip turned sour when I had to deal with a bunch of canned food some idiot canoeist had left behind. They had placed tins of spaghetti sauce, creamed corn and evaporated milk under a medium-sized boulder close to the campfire ring. I'm guessing they were novice paddlers who didn't realize how silly (and illegal) it is to bring canned food into Killarney's interior and how placing what remained under a boulder would do little to dissuade a bear from coming onto the campsite for a free meal. I also found human feces directly in the middle of one of the tent rings. Who would do such a thing?

It seems there's a self-interested attitude going on out in the woods. I see fewer people leaving behind firewood for the next person; trashed campsites and graffitied rock cliffs seem to be commonplace; and a lot of paddlers don't even bother saying hello while passing you on a portage. A few years back I wrote an article for a magazine about the hermits of the north. I interviewed three individuals who decided to escape society and live alone in the wilderness. When I asked them what would cause the demise of the human species on this planet, each answered the same: self-interest. It wasn't nuclear holocaust or a zombie apocalypse, it was people not thinking of anyone except themselves.

My mood definitely improved on my paddle back to the access point the next day. I met a youth camp portaging out of Fish Lake. They were an enthusiastic and ethical bunch who stopped to chat and even helped carry my gear. What great paddlers to meet on the trail! They left singing camp songs and generally having a good time—definitely no self-interest plagued this group.

LONGEST PORTAGE 585 meters

FEE An interior camping permit must be purchased from Killarney Provincial Park.

ALTERNATIVE ACCESS Penage Bay Marina on Lake Panache.

ALTERNATIVE ROUTE Paddle west across Panache Lake from Penage Bay Marina to the dam that leads into Walker Lake.

OUTFITTERS
Killarney Outfitters
1076 Highway 637
Killarney, ON, P0M 2A0
1-888-222-3410 or 705-287-2828
www.killarneyoutfitters.com

Mountain Cove Lodge
Summer Address:
Box 1270
Copper Cliff, ON, P0M 1N0
705-682-4072
www.mountaincovelodge.com

FOR MORE INFORMATION
Killarney Provincial Park
960 Highway 637
Killarney, ON, P0M 2A0
705-287-2900
www.ontarioparks.com

MAPS The Friends of Killarney has produced a good map for the park. Jeff's Map also has produced an interior route map.

TOPOGRAPHIC MAPS
42 J/3, 42 J/4 & 42 J/6

GPS COORDINATES
46.210710, -81.529883

McGregor Bay

 4 days    16 portages   ●----● 61 km   **This is a moderate route. Good canoe-tripping skills are required, especially to deal with potentially high winds on McGregor Bay.**

KILLARNEY'S PHILIP EDWARD Island, located east of the town of Killarney, is a popular paddle destination. The area to the west of the town isn't, and I have no idea why. It offers the same amazing open-water paddling, as well as perfect places to pitch a tent on Crown land that is free of camping permits. Killarney Provincial Park is incredibly beautiful—a majestic landscape of quartzite mountains and aquamarine-colored water. It's also one of my all-time favorite places to visit.

The water surrounding the town of Killarney is more suitable for a kayak. That's not to say you can't paddle it in a canoe; you just have to keep a closer eye on the wind and waves. Georgian Bay and Lake Huron are the backdrop, and the enlarged lakes are more like inland seas.

The route starts at the town's boat launch and heads west, exiting the channel and out into Killarney Bay. You may have to dodge a few fancy yachts on your way out of Killarney harbor. Next is a recommended portage (or two) to get from Killarney Bay to Frazer Bay. You can paddle southwest and go around the peninsula that separates the bays, but it's not really worth it. The portage route is far easier, and you have two choices. Directly across Killarney Bay is Rat Portage, located in Portage Cove and made up of 40-meter and 150-meter back-to-back trails. If you prefer to portage just once, take a 600-meter snowmobile trail located farther north along Killarney Bay. It's a swampy trail that gets little use in the summer. Rat Portage is an easier route, but paddling up to the more northern end means you're less exposed to the wind and safer. It also allows you to catch a glimpse of Indian Head Rock, a quartzite cliff face that's been sculptured by wind and time to look like a person's profile.

The waters of Georgian Bay and Lake Huron have an addictive quality. The sheer size of the waves, the rocks and the sheer expanse of the lakes keeps you spellbound. However, the waters can get rough. If the winds make navigation across Frazer Bay too difficult, there's a 940-meter portage marked on the north shore that heads directly overland to Baie Fine.

I usually spend the first night along the southern shore of Baie Fine. A number of Crown land campsites are set up here, and most yachts seem to anchor a good distance

McGregor Bay

Legend:
- **S** Start
- **F** Finish
- - - - Route
- ····· Alternate route
- ●‿● Portage
- **P975m** Portage length
- ▲ Campsite

Nellie Lake

Carmichael Lake

Faux Lake

Helen Lake

P2425m

P60m

Low Lake

P25m

P55m

North Channel

KILLARNEY PROVINCIAL PARK

West Sampson Island

East and West Channel

East Sampson Island

Middle Sampson Island

McGregor Bay

Baie Fine

P15m
P20m
P75m

McGregor Point

Frazer Point

P940m

Cloche Mountains

P600m

Killarney Bay

P150m
P40m

Rat Portage

Portage Cove

Killarney

Frazer Bay

S F

N
W · E
S

0 1 2 3
km

Badgeley Point

George Island

from the shore. Be warned: at times this is a busy place for boats, but the area is so expansive with so many bays and inlets that they don't necessarily take away from it all. The vessels here aren't pesky speedboats or Jet Skis. They're usually big, fancy sailboats that seemingly blend in with the stunning scenery.

On the second day take a series of short portages that link Baie Fine with McGregor Bay (75 m, 20 m and 15 m). Again, though the trails aren't used much, the passage through is doable. McGregor Bay is just as scenic as the other inlets—even more picturesque, actually. A good day can be spent floating freely, hopefully in a moderate chop with a slight breeze behind you the entire way, to your next stop: the entrance to Killarney Provincial Park's western border.

Once you hit the East and West Channel, you have some choices. You can loop back to McGregor Bay by heading west on the East and West Channel, using any of the smaller channels that split up the Sampson Islands to return south. I prefer taking a couple days and extending my trip by portaging into Killarney Provincial Park's Nellie Lake and then looping back. This second option is a tough route but definitely worth it. After all, this is the same area that once inspired members of the Group of Seven to capture Canada's iconic wilderness on canvas.

A short, 55-meter portage into a beaver pond marks the entrance to Killarney Provincial Park. Last time I had a wasp welcome me on the first portage. Wasps are my nemeses. Each year I get stung once or twice, and each

time I seem to swell up more. I took a couple of allergy pills, kept my EpiPen handy just in case things got out of hand and continued on the portage. When I arrived at the pond, it was totally choked with white lily plants that had grown to near-mythical proportions. I've never seen this floating aquatic plant grow so large. From the pond, another portage (25 m) leads you into Low Lake. Locating the portage can be challenging. It is to the right of a small creek, but last time there was no sign of an opening through the lily pads. I guessed at a narrow inlet on the northeast corner and managed to find the take-out. The creek's water levels were high enough for me to paddle over a couple of logjams that probably require a lift-over most summers.

From Low Lake, a short but steep 60-meter portage will take you into the beautiful Helen Lake. Helen's scenery is like that of most lakes in Killarney: turquoise water surrounded by jagged quartzite cliffs—an absolutely stunning combination. Camping here for a night is a great way to experience the outstanding landscape Killarney has to offer.

You may choose to continue on to Nellie Lake, which in my opinion is the most scenic lake in the park. Be warned, however: you have to carry across one of the toughest portages in Killarney. The trail is 2,425 meters and goes uphill most of the way. Thankfully, when I was there the small pond along the first section had enough water to paddle for a bit, which cut off about 400 meters.

On Nellie Lake I met two park wardens, who happened to be brothers, and invited them for tea. They joined me just after an early evening storm had moved in. I enjoyed their company and their stories of paddling and maintaining Killarney's interior. It felt good having the park staff pay me a friendly visit, and obviously the brothers were enjoying their summer jobs in the park. Why wouldn't they? Killarney is thought to be Ontario Parks' crown jewel. The scenery can't be matched and this northwest corner is one of my favorite places to paddle in all the province—a chunk of wilderness I find myself returning to time and time again.

LONGEST PORTAGE 2,425 meters

FEE An interior camping permit must be purchased from Killarney Provincial Park.

ALTERNATIVE ACCESS None

ALTERNATIVE ROUTE Instead of venturing into Killarney, you can loop back to McGregor Bay by heading west on the East and West Channel and using any of the smaller channels that split up the Sampson Islands to return south.

OUTFITTERS
Killarney Outfitters
1076 Highway 637
Killarney, ON, P0M 2A0
1-888-222-3410 or 705-287-2828
www.killarneyoutfitters.com

FOR MORE INFORMATION
Killarney Provincial Park
960 Highway 637
Killarney, ON, P0M 2A0
705-287-2900
www.ontarioparks.com

MAP The Friends of Killarney has produced a good map for the park. Jeff's Map also has produced an interior route map of Killarney Provincial Park.

TOPOGRAPHIC MAPS
41 G/13 & 42 J/4

GPS COORDINATES
45.971913, -81.511497

Kirkpatrick/Blue Lake Loop

⏱ **4 to 5 days**   🛶 **14 portages**   ●----● **36 km**   **Moderate to advanced due to low maintenance done on the portages and the lack of obvious campsites.**

I'VE ALWAYS NOTICED that if the guides at a fishing lodge are the same guides year after year, then the lodge is guaranteed to be bounded by some amazing scenery. That was my first clue that the Blue Lake region, set in the midst of the Algoma Highlands' Penokean Hills, was a special place. The senior guide of Blue Fox Lodge, Peter Roberts, was an environmental engineer from Ottawa who took his holidays to labor here since his first visit some 20 years ago. The other two guides, Chris Moose and Brien Konopka, came to work at the camp the previous year, taking it on as a summer job between post-secondary school (Chris was actually one of my students at Sir Sandford Fleming College where I teach part time), and returned immediately after school was out. Even the chef, Evan Williams, who Dr. Morgan, the lodge owner, picked up hitchhiking at the age of 14, couldn't resist the invitation to spend time cooking at the camp and has done so for the last dozen years. And then there was Jay Mothersill, owner of Paddle Shack in Muskoka and one of the canoeists who were joining me on the canoe trip in the Blue Lake region (and also a past student of mine from the college). Jay was returning to

the area after a seven-year hiatus from guiding there himself. All of them were in absolute awe of the place, and so would the rest of us be by the end of our trip there.

The Penokean Hills and its countless turquoise-colored lakes are sprawled out north of Elliot Lake, across one of the most rugged landscapes in Ontario. Blue Fox Camp, situated at the very bottom end, on the south shore of Kirkpatrick Lake (known locally as Blue Lake), is the centerpiece, and acts as a perfect starting and ending point for exploring the area. My original intent was to access the chain of lakes on Toodee Lake, at the northwest corner of the Blue Lake region, using Seymour Road from Highway 129. That was the maintained access point when there was still a canoe route established. But in 1981, the paddle loop was no longer maintained or promoted by the Ministry of Natural Resources. There was also an option given to me by William (Sandy) Millroy, a MNR employee who first informed me of the Blue Lake paradise: a new logging road that came close to the northeast end of Duval Lake by veering off an older logging road that arched across the top of the region. It wasn't in the

Kirkpatrick/Blue Lake Loop

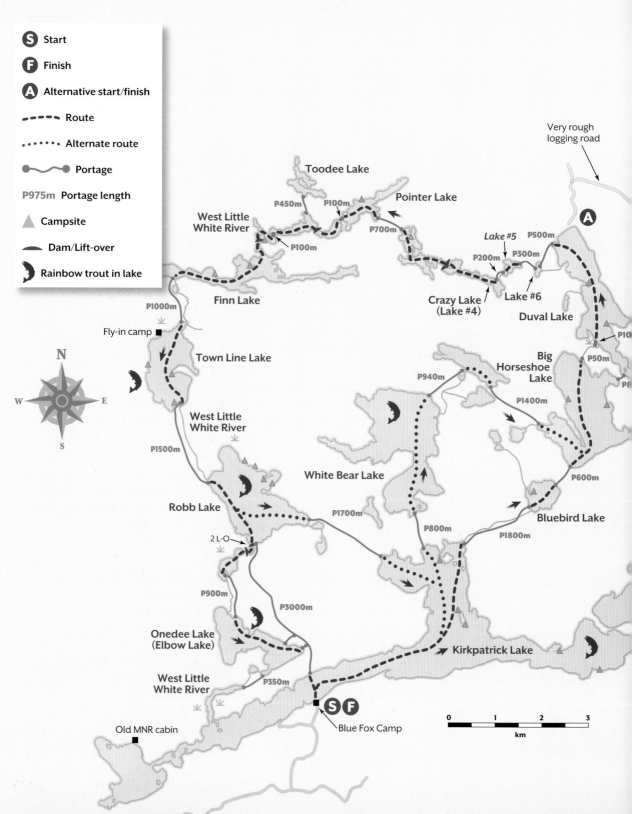

Legend:
- **S** Start
- **F** Finish
- **A** Alternative start/finish
- ----- Route
- ••••• Alternate route
- ⬤〜⬤ Portage
- **P975m** Portage length
- ▲ Campsite
- ⌒ Dam/Lift-over
- 🌙 Rainbow trout in lake

Very rough logging road

Toodee Lake

P450m

P100m

Pointer Lake

West Little White River

P100m

P700m

Lake #5

P500m

A

P200m

P300m

Lake #6

Finn Lake

Crazy Lake (Lake #4)

Duval Lake

P100

P1000m

P50m

Fly-in camp

Town Line Lake

Big Horseshoe Lake

P8

N

P940m

W — E

S

West Little White River

White Bear Lake

P1400m

P1500m

P600m

Robb Lake

P1700m

Bluebird Lake

2 L-O

P800m

P1800m

P900m

P3000m

Onedee Lake (Elbow Lake)

Kirkpatrick Lake

West Little White River

P350m

S **F**

Blue Fox Camp

Old MNR cabin

0   1   2   3
km

best of shape either. So we opted for flying in and out of Blue Fox Camp by bush plane from Timber Wolf Air in Blind River. Not only was it the ethical choice, it was also the easiest and the cheapest way in. At a cost of $700 for the flight in and out, which was split up among the four of us going (Jay Mothersill and his business partner at Paddle Shack, Jeff Dupuis, and Ashley McBride and myself), you couldn't go wrong.

While the pilot taxied the plane up to the docks of Blue Fox Camp, we could see Peter and Moose waiting with canoes and packs. They were just as eager to explore the area north as we were. Going clockwise or counterclockwise was the only discussion we had before paddling off from the lodge. The old route documentation had the trip going clockwise, but Peter, who had traveled the route before, suggested counterclockwise—a decision that would later prove very advantageous. Kirkpatrick Lake, which prior to the logging days was split into two separate lakes (the separation point being just west of the lodge) is close to 20 kilometers long, so the first objective was to paddle a good distance to the northeast corner of the lake's central bay to locate the first portage. It took longer than normal, not because of rough water or poor weather; conditions were perfect, actually. It was that we took way too much time checking out the scenery of this place. What a gem of a lake, circled by high cliff faces and equipped with perfect island campsites. The whole time we paddled across Kirkpatrick Lake I wondered why we were so eager to leave it. A paddler could easily stay here for a week and explore from end to end, even using the lodge as a base camp. A quick glance at the map also showed countless smaller lakes to the east, west and south of Kirkpatrick, all full of brook

trout and an idyllic wilderness setting, that could provide numerous day trips from the lodge or three-to-four-day paddling ventures.

The idea of finding even more remoteness north of Kirkpatrick was what made us continue on. The first portage, measuring 1,800 meters, was surprisingly marked with a brand-new government portage sign, thanks to Sandy at the MNR who had led a group of Junior Rangers through to recut a good portion of the route the previous year. The trail wasn't perfect by any means. The last part in particular was quite rough. The old canoe route pamphlet had a beaver pond marked at the last quarter, which had since dried up, and we were forced to maneuver through a stand of young birch and knee-high boulders. However, if Sandy's group hadn't done work before, it would have been a frustrating walk. Experiencing the beauty of Bluebird Lake was worth it though. The water was a rich turquoise, full of brook trout, and a nice campsite was set up on the western point. It was still early, however, and our group made the decision to carry over to Big Horseshoe Lake before making camp. The portage (600 m) over to Big Horseshoe began in the northeast corner of Bluebird and was a good carry except maybe for the dramatic drop near the end (it was steep enough that canoes were lowered down rather then carried). Ashley caught a lake trout five minutes into the paddle across Big Horseshoe Lake. I then caught one and so did Jay. We were all a little surprised that we hooked the trout in less than 2 feet of water and an arm's length from shore. It was the last week in May, but weather conditions made it seem like it was the first week. The birch leaves had just opened up, blackflies were out but not yet biting, and it got to -1 that night where we camped on the west shore on Big Horseshoe Lake.

Day two was a long one. It began early, leaving Big Horseshoe Lake and into Duval Lake by two routes. Peter and Chris chose a newer trail (80 m) located at the end of the northeast bay. The rest of us chose the way the old route pamphlet suggested, with two short portages (50 m and 100 m) along a creek flushing out of the northeast corner of Big Horseshoe Lake. Peter and Chris found the 80-meter trail easy, but complained about the last bit going through a mucky boot-sucking marsh. Our group found our choice to be a breeze. The first trail wasn't necessary since high water made it possible for us to paddle straight through, and the second carry was a cakewalk. Duval Lake was just as nice as Big Horseshoe Lake. We did, however, see two motor boats with the occupants fishing and ATVs parked at the north end of the lake. I'm guessing they used the logging road access to reach the lake, but looking at the mud splattered on their ATVs, it was a good assumption that the road wasn't the best choice to reach Duval.

After Duval we saw no one else, for good reason of course. The route that exited the lake was confusing to follow most of the time. In fact, if it wasn't for the Junior Rangers marking the first portage leaving Duval with a bright yellow sign, we'd still be there looking for it. The 500-meter trail started at the far northwest corner of Duval, far away from the creek that linked the lake to a chain of small ponds we were to follow for the rest of the day. It made sense why the trail started here once we started walking it. This was the flattest part of the rolling landscape. And after a brief walk along an old logging road, cutting through a dense stand of hardwoods, the trail split, and we went right to continue along the creek. After crisscrossing the shallow stream in several places, the portage ended where a stand of old-growth red pine crowded the shoreline of what's labeled as Lake #6.

The next portage (300 m), which began pretty much on the opposite side of Lake #6, was even more confusing. It started off direct, going up a moderate slope. But then the trail disappeared in a patch of trees and swamp, split between a massive clear-cut. I was furious with this. When I worked in the north in the early 1980s as a forest technician we would always, by law, leave a minimum of 60–200 meters' space between the cutting and the portage. Not here. When I did eventually locate the remainder of the trail we were following, the foresters had left less than 5 meters. And people ask me why I continue to promote canoe routes. This is why. If you don't, they simply disappear by the over-abuse of other users. We lost the portage one more time before reaching Lake #5. The old route information had a small pond that needed to be paddled across before reaching the put-in of the most northeasterly bay. However, the pond was a grassy marsh that we had to wade across, then carrying over a mound of granite covered in a bunch of downed jack pine, looking like a gigantic game of pick-up-sticks.

Lunch was had after we bushwhacked through the remaining 60 meters of muck, sedge grass and jack pine blow-downs. The next portage was no different than the previous ones. It only measured 200 meters, and it was in relatively good condition once we were on it. The problem was getting to it. The creek and marshy area before the take-out had dried up, and it was a good boot-sucking trek of about 60 meters before we could reach dry ground and begin carrying without sinking past our knees in swamp ooze. Once the ordeal was over, however, we enjoyed a

peaceful paddle down Crazy Lake (Lake #4). This was one of our favorite lakes en route. It was an intimate and seemingly remote body of water surrounded by a mixture of red, white and jack pine rooted on mounds of granite. It was also a haven for brook trout. But for some odd reason we caught nothing here. The fish stocking list had the lake listed as a brook trout fishery but not one of us had a single strike. It had to be either too late in the day for them to bite or the lake somehow received too much winter fishing pressure from snow machines. Whichever the reason, it didn't seem to matter to us. We enjoyed being alone here and took our time to explore every bay and inlet.

A beaver dam separated the lake into two sections halfway along and we did a quick lift-over, Ashley and I using a pull-over on the extreme north (right) end and the others using an easier section near mid-lake. It was an easy bit to navigate. However, getting to the portage (700 m) to carry over to the next lake was not. First, we had to guess where the

was here we camped for our second night out, pitching our tent on a perfect outcrop of rock adjacent to the put-in of the last portage. The site hadn't seen much use for quite some time, but it was a perfect spot to end the day. And with the prospect of catching a brook trout being questionable, we decided to go ridge hiking instead, clambering up a knob of rock between Pointer and Spot lakes to the northeast. From the ridgetop we could view the entire surrounding landscape. All of us stayed up top until the sun completely set, making promises to come back and explore the lakes and rivers we could see beyond.

During morning coffee of day three, a group decision was made to split up for the rest of the trip. Peter and Chris were rushed to get back to the lodge since they had customers flying in soon. We (Jay, Jeff, Ashley and I), on the other hand, were in no hurry to return. So it was decided that after breakfast, Peter and Chris would leave us behind and finish on their own that day, and on the way back would check out two alternative routes back to Kirkpatrick Lake. The rest of us would keep to the old canoe route pamphlet and take two or three more days to explore.

A 100-meter portage took us out of Pointer Lake at the southwest corner. It was to the right of a bay clogged with half-submerged logs and then ended by going down a steep grade to a grassy bay. Then, shortly after, was a quick and painless lift-over on a miniature beaver dam.

To the right of the lift-over, in a small bay, we took note of a portage sign indicating where the original route came down from Toodee Lake. As mentioned earlier, this road is extremely rough and not worth the effort.

Another 100-meter portage was needed not too far along and marked to the left of where

take-out actually was. The old route information recorded a "vast expanse of grass" to paddle through at the far end of the lake's northwestern inlet. What we saw at the far corner of the lake was a dried-up section of swamp, forcing us to drag the boats and gear to the edge of the forest and hope the portage started somewhere nearby; it did. Then, not far along the trail—where the canoe route pamphlet stated that the trail went through two grassy areas—we had to paddle across an actual mini-pond and skirt the edges of another stagnant flooded area. Things had obviously changed here since the 1980s.

After the unscheduled pond-hopping, however, the trail was simple to follow, leading us down through a stand of mature red pine and then to the shores of Pointer Lake. It the West Little White River narrows. Then the waterway takes a dramatic turn to the south, where another beaver dam, much more significant than the previous one, needed to be lifted over before entering Finn Lake. It was here, while Ashley and I stood knee-deep in the stagnant water at the beaver dam before pushing our canoe over the pile of sticks and mud, that I witnessed over 40 leeches swimming around our feet. Honest! It was the most unusual leech encounter I have ever seen. And they weren't all the same species; some had red dots while others were green and as long as a snake. Yikes! At least we were able to catch and try a few for live bait for the trout on Finn Lake.

Finn Lake was incredibly scenic, but totally devoid of obvious campsites. There were a couple of possible spots to the left and right of the bay we exited after the beaver dam lift-over. But it seemed odd that a lake so idyllic had no place to make camp on. The only saving grace was that it was only noon when we paddled the lake, and we had a good distance to cover still before calling it a day.

The 1,000-meter portage out of Finn, located at the far western bay and heading south toward Town Line Lake, was right of where the river flushed out of the lake and where logging debris cluttered the forest. At the take-out were lift-overs of log booms, tramways and flumes; about three-quarters of the way along, three cabins and a storage shed stood half-decayed in the woods. Jay even stepped on a crosscut saw while wading his canoe into the lake at the put-in.

Located at the far northwest corner of Town Line Lake was a fly-in fishing camp. No one was using it, but they should have been. The lake is populated with lake trout, brook trout and rainbow trout, with the rainbow trout rising everywhere along the shoreline for emerging mayflies. Our group took some quality time on the lake casting for all three species of trout and felt sorry for poor Peter and Chris who had probably raced across this lake earlier in the day without once wetting a line.

It was 4:30 p.m. by the time we reached the southeastern corner of the lake, where the next portage waited for us to reach Robb Lake. It measured 1,500 meters but felt more like over 2,000 meters. We should have waited until the next day to carry over because we didn't complete it until just before 8:00 p.m. It wasn't just the length that slowed us down. We first had trouble finding the starting point (we eventually located the path in a clearing, behind an old decayed cabin and to the right of the creek that flushes out of Town Line Lake). Near the finish, the trail was even more confusing to locate at times as it disappeared for a bit in a grove of young birch trees. A few downed trees also blocked our way halfway along. The problem was, we couldn't find a decent place to camp on Town Line and thought Robb Lake would be better. It really wasn't, and we resorted to pitching our camp on top of a mound of rock along the eastern shoreline. Don't get me wrong, both lakes were scenic enough, but campsites were not established on either. It didn't matter much where we camped that night, however. Our surroundings were idyllic, the sunset was spectacular and fish were caught right from shore. You can't get any better than that.

We figured our last day en route would be the easiest. All we had to do was paddle a section of West Little White River, portage through a few small lakes to re-enter Kirkpatrick Lake and then relax back at the lodge with a sauna, hot shower and fancy meal provided by the camp chef. It was, however, the only section of the route that the Junior Rangers hadn't maintained the previous year, meaning it hadn't been cleared since 1981. But our other options seemed worse: a 1,700-meter snowmobile trail leading out of Robb Lake's southeast bay to the central bay of Kirkpatrick or a direct, but very long 3,000-meter snowmobile trail from Robb's southwest bay, beginning left of the West Little White River, and ending on the north shore of Kirkpatrick, directly across from the lodge.

We began the day early, paddling to where the West Little White River flushes out of Robb Lake, over an old and half-decayed logging dam, before 9:00 a.m. To the left of the small river we noticed the 3,000-meter trail leading directly to Kirkpatrick and wondered if we should just haul everything over that way. But we all wanted to keep to the original route and went over to the right side of the river to look for the first of two consecutive marked lift-overs on our old map. There were none. Just thick bush. So we just balanced over the decrepit dam and then flushed our canoes down the remaining shallow gravel rapids. It seemed easy enough and we continued on, thinking we'd be at Kirkpatrick by noon (we arrived after 7:00 p.m).

A small lake/pond was next, and it was here we spotted our first moose of the trip. Jeff and Jay were ahead of us at the time, and Ash and I noticed them giving the well-recognized sign for moose ahead—hands placed on top of your head with fingers spread out—and we snuck up with video camera put on "record."

The cow moose was feeding in the far end of the pond, and at first we thought it would be impossible to sneak up on her before she spotted us. But we did. We snuck up too close, actually. A stiff wind blew us right to her.

The cow looked up at us drifting only two canoe lengths away, and the sight of us snapping photos and shooting video must have been nightmarish for the poor creature. She turned and ran, stopped to take a pee (moose do that when they are startled) and then, surprisingly, turned around and ran directly at us. We managed to escape into another back bay and let the cow moose return to its foraging.

With all the moose action, we ended up being a tad confused as to our exact whereabouts on the pond and blindly started looking (in the wrong bay) for the old 900-meter portage that would take us farther along the route. Two full hours later our group was still wandering through thick bush and swamp ooze looking for a blaze or faint path through the woods, finding nothing except for a very perturbed beaver who I nearly stepped on while trudging through a thick patch of sedge. We scared the daylights out of each other.

Actually it was only Jeff, Jay and I who got lost. Ash stayed back with the canoes, munched on GORP (Good Old Raisins and Peanuts) and had a snooze. He insisted we were in the wrong bay and decided it would be foolish to look for the portage from where we were. We mocked him—that is until after the two hours of searching we had found nothing. When we backtracked to the other bay, we found a big blaze on a massive white pine tree, indicating the beginning of the portage.

Even though we eventually found the proper trail, it still wasn't a perfect portage. I walked it for a while and noticed a few sections were faint and a number of trees had fallen across. It was doable, we figured, but the group thought that since the first half seemed to follow the left bank of the shallow river, it might be wise to just paddle, pole and wade down as far as we could get. So we did and ended up losing the trail completely and dragging the entire stretch of the rock-bound river to where it enters Onedee Lake.

At the far left bay of Onedee Lake (Elbow Lake on some older maps) our map showed one last portage of 350 meters marked to the left of the river before entering Kirkpatrick Lake. However, we were quite concerned about its condition and decided to take Jay's advice for locating a trail he knew of along Onedee's northeast shoreline that linked up with the last quarter of the 3,000-meter snowmobile trail leading to Kirkpatrick Lake.

None of us will ever know if the 350-meter trail was doable or not. But we do know that Jay's "shortcut" was a very long "shortcut." It took us an hour and felt like a kilometer and a half. We did, however, find a path that linked to the snowmobile trail; two paths, actually. The first was new and freshly marked with orange flagging tape. It was also flat but meant a much longer time spent carrying canoes and gear. The second was the one that Jay remembered from when he guided here — but he forgot how steep the first section was (even a goat would find it a challenge!).

A cold rain had also soaked us through on the way across the trail, and we were already chilled from walking down the river. Good news was that we could see Blue Fox Lodge directly across the lake. What a sweet sight, smoke coming out of the main lodge's chimney and the chime of the dinner bell echoing across the lake.

A 10-minute paddle, and our canoes were beached, and suddenly it was all over. No packs to be readied, no rapids to wade, no wind to struggle against, no painful portage to carry over. After relishing in the comforts of the lodge, we quickly grew eager to get back home ... and plan our next adventure north.

LONGEST PORTAGE 1,500 meters

FEE The route travels through an unmanaged and newly proposed provincial park and a fee structure is not yet in place.

ALTERNATIVE ACCESS Toodee Lake, at the northwest corner of the Blue Lake region, was the original access point when this route was maintained prior to 1891. It was reached by using Seymour Road from Highway 129. It's a very rough road, however, and not recommended. Also, a new logging road that comes close to the northeast end of Duval Lake is possible. It veers off an older logging road to the east of the route and that arches across the top of the region at the 20-kilometer mark.

ALTERNATIVE ROUTE Kirkpatrick Lake is an excellent place to paddle due to its sheer size and elongated shape. A number of smaller lakes to the south and west of Kirkpatrick offer exceptional shorter outings (contact Blue Fox Camp for details on these side trips).

OUTFITTERS
Blue Fox Camp
Kirkpatrick Lake
Iron Bridge, ON, P0R 1H0
519-265-7756

Louie's Outposts / Timber Wolf Air
Box 444
Blind River, ON, P0R 1B0
1-877-292-1051
www.louiesoutpost-timberwolfair.com

FOR MORE INFORMATION
Mississagi Provincial Park
705-848-2806 (June to September)
705-865-2021 (October to May)
www.ontarioparks.com

TOPOGRAPHIC MAPS 41 J/11

GPS COORDINATES
46.647953, -83.130115

Mississagi River

 6 to 8 days    26 portages   ●━━━━● 177 km   Moderate whitewater and wilderness-tripping skills are needed.

MY WIFE, ALANA, and I have always wanted to paddle the Mississagi River. What kept us from organizing a trip, however, was the reality of the lengthy car shuttle needed to travel the best portion, between Biscotasing and Aubrey Falls—most of this 177-kilometer stretch being under the protection of a Provincial Waterway Park. Then, while browsing the shelves of a used bookstore, I happened upon a copy of Grey Owl's *Tales of an Empty Cabin*, which includes a detailed description of canoeing the Mississagi.

For this is no ordinary stream, but a very King among rivers ... the Grand Discharge of Waters of the Indians, pouring its furious way between rock-bound shores, sweeping a path for twice a hundred miles through forest lands, levying tribute, in all its branches, from four thousand square miles of territory, untamed, defiant and relentless, arrogantly imposing its name on all surrounding country; so that a man may travel many a day by canoe and portage through an intricate network of stream and lake and forest, among a rich infinite variety of scenery and still be within Mississagi's far-flung principality ...

How can any canoeists read such an elaborate account and not want to see it for themselves? In a week, my wife and I were packed and driving north to the Mississagi.

To deal with the long two-and-a-half-hour car shuttle, Alana and I had Missinaibi Headwaters meet us at the parking lot for the Aubrey Falls Hiking Trail, which is marked by a provincial park sign on the right side of Highway 129, 108 kilometers north of Thessalon. We left our vehicle behind and allowed the outfitters to drive us to the access point. It would have been cheaper to have a local outfitter drive up to the access point with us and then shuttle our truck back to the parking lot, but with most of the drive being on a gravel logging road, it seemed a better choice to have Missinaibi Headwaters worry about the wear and tear on their own vehicle.

From the parking lot we headed north on Highway 129 for a good hour, and then turned right onto Highway 667. Once past a small hamlet called Sultan, we turned off onto the Sultan Industrial Road (owned by E.B. Eddy) and, rather than driving all the way to Biscotasing, we saved a day of lake paddling by accessing the river just south

Mississagi River

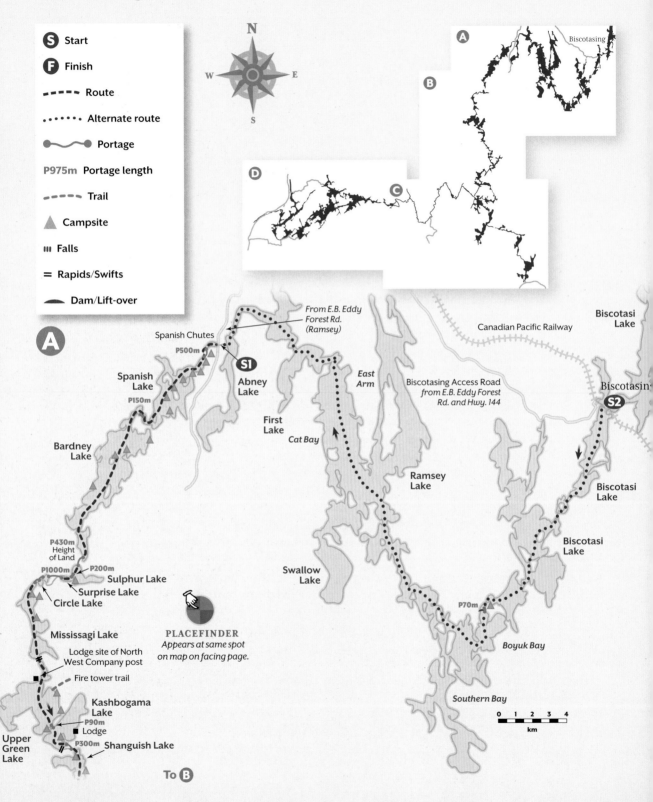

Legend:

- **S** Start
- **F** Finish
- - - - - Route
- · · · · · Alternate route
- ⬤〰️⬤ Portage
- **P975m** Portage length
- - - - Trail
- 🔺 Campsite
- ‖‖ Falls
- = Rapids/Swifts
- ⬛ Dam/Lift-over

Biscotasing

Canadian Pacific Railway

Biscotasi Lake

From E.B. Eddy Forest Rd. (Ramsey)

Spanish Chutes

P500m

Spanish Lake

P150m

Bardney Lake

Abney Lake

S1

First Lake

Cat Bay

East Arm

Biscotasing Access Road
from E.B. Eddy Forest Rd. and Hwy. 144

Biscotasin

S2

Biscotasi Lake

Ramsey Lake

Biscotasi Lake

P430m
Height of Land

P1000m P200m

Sulphur Lake

Surprise Lake
Circle Lake

Mississagi Lake

Lodge site of North West Company post

Fire tower trail

Swallow Lake

P70m

Boyuk Bay

PLACEFINDER
Appears at same spot on map on facing page.

Kashbogama Lake

P90m

■ Lodge

Upper Green Lake

P300m Shanguish Lake

Southern Bay

0 1 2 3 4
km

To **B**

A

B

D

C

A

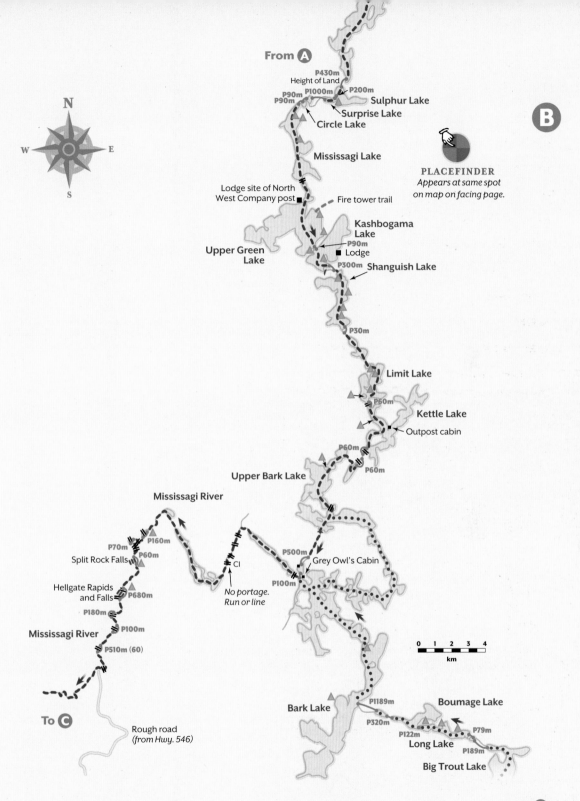

From (A)

P430m
Height of Land
P1000m — P200m
P90m
P90m — Sulphur Lake
Surprise Lake
Circle Lake

(B)

Mississagi Lake

PLACEFINDER
*Appears at same spot
on map on facing page.*

Lodge site of North
West Company post
Fire tower trail

Kashbogama
Lake
P90m
Lodge
Upper Green
Lake
P300m — Shanguish Lake

P30m

Limit Lake

P60m
Kettle Lake
Outpost cabin

P60m
Upper Bark Lake
P60m

Mississagi River

P70m — P160m
Split Rock Falls
P60m
Cl
No portage.
Run or line

Hellgate Rapids
and Falls — P680m

P180m

Mississagi River
P100m

P510m (60)

P500m
Grey Owl's Cabin

P100m

To (C)

Rough road
(from Hwy. 546)

Bark Lake

P1189m
Boumage Lake

P320m
P79m
P122m
Long Lake
P189m

Big Trout Lake

0 1 2 3 4
km

From (C)

Mississagi River (continued)

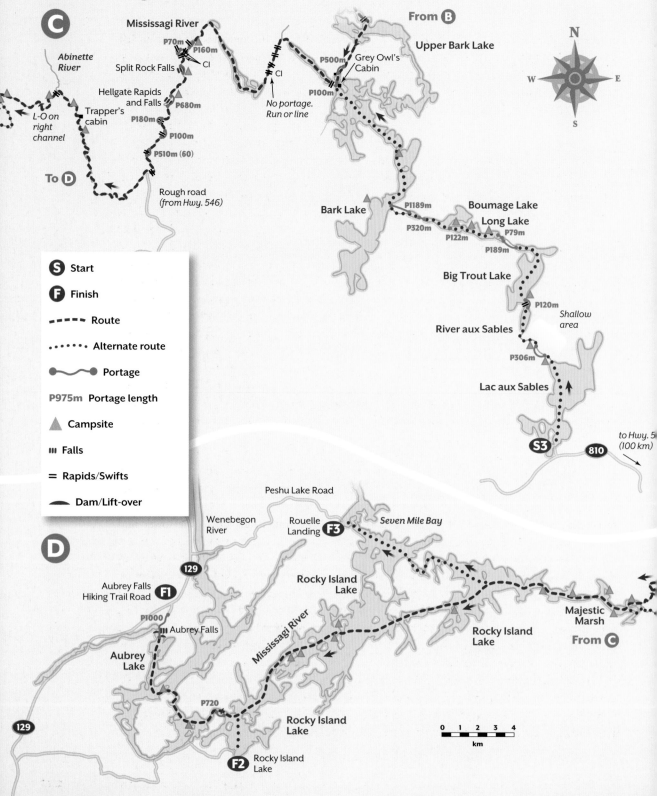

C

Mississagi River

Abinette River

P70m
P160m
CI
Split Rock Falls
Hellgate Rapids and Falls
P680m
Trapper's cabin
P180m
P100m
L-O on right channel
P510m (60)

CI
No portage. Run or line

P500m
Grey Owl's Cabin
P100m

From B

Upper Bark Lake

To D

Rough road (from Hwy. 546)

N
W   E
S

Bark Lake

P1189m   **Boumage Lake**
P320m   **Long Lake**
P122m   P79m
           P189m

Big Trout Lake

P120m   *Shallow area*

River aux Sables

P306m

Lac aux Sables

S3   **810**   *to Hwy. 5 (100 km)*

Legend

S Start
F Finish
- - - - Route
· · · · Alternate route
●〜● Portage
P975m Portage length
▲ Campsite
⫼ Falls
= Rapids/Swifts
▬ Dam/Lift-over

D

Peshu Lake Road

Wenebegon River

Rouelle Landing **F3**   *Seven Mile Bay*

129

Aubrey Falls
Hiking Trail Road **F1**

Rocky Island Lake

Mississagi River

Rocky Island Lake

Majestic Marsh

From C

P1000
⫼ Aubrey Falls

Aubrey Lake

P720

Rocky Island Lake

129

F2 Rocky Island Lake

0 1 2 3 4
km

of Ramsey, putting in at the Spanish Chutes. Take note, however, that the drive along the E.B. Eddy Road is confusing, not to mention dangerous (logging trucks don't take kindly to canoeists hogging their road), and again, it was well worth the money to have Missinaibi Headwaters deal with it all.

From Spanish Chutes the route heads upstream on the Spanish River. The first portage (500 m) is on the left, partway up a small swift. Numerous islands and rock outcrops on Spanish Lake and on Bardney Lake (connected at the southwestern end of Spanish Lake by a 150-meter portage to the left of Bardney Creek Dam) make for excellent campsites. Alana and I decided to continue on, though, taking the steep 430-meter Height of Land portage to Sulphur Lake before stopping for the day. We signed the register at the put-in, adding to only a dozen other canoeists who had traveled the route before us, and then paddled across to the take-out of the next portage (200 m) to set up camp.

Our first day was an eventful one. By 6:30 p.m. we had dodged insane truck drivers on the 80-kilometer E.B. Eddy Road, hauled ourselves over from one watershed to the next and then made camp on one of the most remote lakes we had been to in years. Along the way we spotted a total of three bald eagles, a family of curious otters, a solitary moose, the back end of a very shy lynx and a giant northern pike as it devoured a baby loon only a few meters away from the bow of our canoe. It was obvious to us now that the rich rewards of this isolated river far outweighed the hassles of any lengthy car shuttle.

The next morning was spent paddling a chain of mucky ponds (Surprise Lake and Circle Lake) connected by three portages (a 1,000-m trail, cursed with five steep inclines

toward the put-in, and two soggy 90-m lift-overs). It was an easy paddle down Mississagi Lake, however, and near the middle of the lake, Alana and I even stepped out of the canoe and onto a sandbar to soak our aching feet — that is, until I noticed a monster leech attached to my big toe.

Mississagi Lake is made up of three sections joined together by a series of shallow narrows. At the south end of the lake, the slow-moving current squeezes its way through another rock-strewn channel that eventually empties out into Upper Green Lake. A modern lodge stands at the entranceway, built in the same location as was the North West Company's post. (The post was constructed in the late 1700s by Montreal traders; the HBC took over the site in 1821.) The fur traders decided on the Upper Green Lake location to accommodate the Natives who had used the river as a travel corridor since prehistoric times. The post was abandoned in 1892, however, when it became easier to ship furs out by rail at Biscotasing.

The route heads southeast now, across a large bay. There's a fire tower on the left-hand shore, perched high above a stand of stout pine. Alana and I went to stop for lunch where the trail heads up to the tower and came across our first group of canoeists — a youth camp from Algonquin who make this spot an annual pilgrimage. They invited us to join them in climbing the tower but we immediately declined, claiming that we had to be on our way before the wind picked up out on the lake. High winds are a problem on Upper Green Lake. In fact, well-known artist and canoeist Tom Thomson and friend W.S. Broadhead, out on a two-month sketching trip down the Mississagi River, swamped their canoe here during a thunderstorm. But the danger of heavy winds seemed a poor excuse for Alana and me, since there wasn't even a slight breeze blowing across the lake. The truth of the matter was that we were both squeamish about scrambling up a dilapidated fire tower in the middle of nowhere with a group of overenthusiastic youths.

The portage connecting the southeast bay of Upper Green Lake and Kashbogama Lake is an easy 90 meters, marked to the left of a short rapid (look for the old telegraph wire embedded in the giant pine near the put-in). Shanguish Lake is next, with the 300-meter portage beginning at the end of the bay northeast of the rapids themselves. Then a quick 30-meter portage to the upper end of Limit Lake soon follows, just before a logging bridge crosses the river. Make sure that you do not follow the road here. The trail is directly to the left of the rapid.

Alana and I ended our second day on Limit Lake. We first looked for a site on the north end, but the two designated sites were littered with empty beer bottles (the offenders must have come in on the logging road). So we continued down the lake, getting lost more than once trying to find the way to the southwest bay, and then set up camp on the island just before the 60-meter portage leading into Kettle Lake. It was a typical bush site, furnished with a makeshift fire ring, a table made from pieces of driftwood and a wooden tent frame under which Alana pitched our own tent. We cooked our diner on a slab of rock on the island's north end where the wind was stronger and the bugs were less fierce. The feast consisted of pita bread and tabbouli mixed in a hot spicy salsa sauce, washed down with white wine.

In the morning we had our coffee and pancakes on the same slab of rock, enjoying the warming air. Then we carried over to Kettle Lake. We kept to the right shore, staying between the large island and the shore until we met up with the river once again to the southwest. To enter Upper Bark Lake we first made use of two quick, 60-meter portages to avoid a double set of rapids; the first is marked to the right and the second to the left, at the end of a small bay directly across from first portage. Not far downstream the river twists to the right and eventually empties out into Upper Bark Lake.

We now headed southwest until the river curved to the left. There, it flushes down a shallow swift and then out into the lower section of Upper Bark Lake. The regular route continues east from here and then eventually snakes its way back to the west. It's a scenic tour of Bark Lake—what Grey Owl describes as "a large body of water, beautiful with its islands, inlets and broken, heavily timbered shores." The paddle takes up most of the day, however, and most canoeists make use of a shortcut by continuing southwest down a shallow narrows (the entrance marked by a dilapidated beaver dam). A rough 500-meter portage leads from there to a small unnamed lake, followed by a 100-meter portage to Bark Lake.

At the put-in of the last portage, a group of cabins mark the site of what was the headquarters for the Mississagi Forest Reserve. Grey Owl signed the inside wall of the main log cabin during his stay in 1914, but the cabin is now private and remains locked. On the outside walls, however, other canoeists have left their mark throughout the years: R. Josgauthier (1948), Ray Dickie (1954) and Bisco Ned (1991), to name just a few.

The Mississagi River flows west from here, beginning with a small swift. But it's not until the river twists to the south—about an hour's paddle downstream—that the rapids begin in earnest. Four sets follow in quick succession, all easy runs except maybe the last, which you may want to line your canoe down. The banks then widen out and the river heads northwest, squeezing its way through a cluster of small islands (be sure to stay left to avoid dead-end inlets).

This is where Alana and I should have made camp for our third night out. But we figured the next stretch of fast water, where the river changes course to the southwest again, would provide better campsites, and it was well after 5:00 p.m. when we reached the next set of rapids. The 160-meter portage, marked to the left of the 6-foot drop, had an adequate campsite near the put-in, but a fresh pile of bear dung directly beside the fire ring forced us to continue even farther downstream.

It seemed that around every bend in the river there was another rapid—but no campsites. We scouted four main sets and were able to run them all except for the second. Each rapid did come with a short portage (60–160 m) marked along the left bank.

Then came Split Rock Falls. It was 7:30 p.m. by the time we reached this narrow gorge and, even though the run looked simple enough, we figured it was too late in the day to trust our judgment. So we made use of the 60-meter portage to the left and jumped with joy when we found a pristine campsite looking over the scenic drop.

Alana and I slept in the next morning and didn't reach Hellgate Rapids and Falls until mid-morning. The cataract is an incredible spot. After we carried the canoe and packs over the rather strenuous 680-meter portage located on the left bank, we backtracked and

took the side trail leading to the main drop. Here, while Alana picked a fresh crop of blueberries almost the size of ping-pong balls, I clambered down the moss-covered rocks and snapped half a roll of film.

The strong current remains for at least another two hours downstream, giving you three rapids that require portages (180 m to the right, 100 m to the left and 510 m also to the left). Take note, however, that the last rapid is made up of three main drops; Alana and I had to carry around the first set only and reduced the 510-meter portage to a mere 60 meters.

One final swift remains, just before where an access road comes in from Highway 546 (the road is a rough one and is not recommended). Then the river quickly changes character, meandering through a seemingly endless swampy maze interrupted only by

clumps of granite topped with stunted spruce and scraggly jack pine. It's a great place for wildlife—moose, otter, osprey and the occasional bald eagle frequent the area—but it's also a breeding ground for mosquitoes and blackflies, and maneuvering your canoe through the constant twists and turns in the river can become irritable work.

After two hours of paddling through the labyrinth, Alana and I met up with a lone trapper who owned the only cabin on this stretch of the river. He had been working on an addition to his cabin for two months and was now taking his powerboat upstream to the Highway 546 access road to meet his wife for a weekend vacation. The man was kind enough, but he had a bad habit of reminding us how quick his boat was compared to our canoe. Once he informed us that it would only take 20 minutes to reach the road (a distance that took us over two hours), Alana, disgruntled, pushed us away with her paddle, wished him and his wife a good holiday, and then silently prayed he would shear a pin while making his way upstream.

Not far from the cabin, just a half hour beyond where the Abinette River empties into the Mississagi, the river forks; to the left is a giant logjam and to the right is a small boulder-strewn rapid. It's possible to portage around the logjam to the left (no trail), but Alana and I found it much easier to lift over and then line down the left side of the small rapid.

Farther along, where another massive pile of rotten logs clog the route, the river splits again. The main channel is to the left. Alana and I, however, followed a smaller channel to the right, just past the logjam. We lined to the right of another small rapid and then snaked our way through a vast field of swamp grass.

It was an unplanned shortcut, but we figured the side route saved us over 40 minutes of paddling by the time we reached Majestic Marsh—one of the most productive wetland areas in the province.

There are birds by the thousands here: geese, ducks, sandpipers. Where the two channels meet, Alana and I were lucky enough to spot another bald eagle soaring overhead and heard about half-a-dozen sandhill cranes making a ruckus, the sound a lot like a car engine trying to turn over on a cold winter morning. But places to camp are few and far between, with the odd knob of rock providing space for only one or two tents. Having learned our lesson from the previous day, however, Alana and I grabbed the first site we came to—a clearing among a patch of spruce. We paddled too far that day. Actually, we had paddled too far every day. So a quick supper was prepared, the tent went up, and we crawled into our sleeping bags well before dusk.

The next morning we were up extra early, eager to reach the expanse of Rocky Island Lake before the wind picked up. The water level was down when we reached the entrance to the lake, revealing hundreds of stumps left behind by the construction of the hydro dams downstream. The shoreline also seemed bare, almost desert-like. It seemed somewhat less than poetic when Alana chanced upon a First Nations crematorium that had been exposed after the water level had reached a record low.

Alana and I had planned to take out below Aubrey Falls, but it is possible to end your trip on Rocky Island Lake by paddling up the north channel, just beyond the large central island, to Seven Mile Bay. The take-out is called Rouelle Landing and is located at the end of the Peshu Lake Road. You can also paddle west to another access road located at the southerly end of the last bay. Both access roads (especially the Peshu Lake Road) can be hard on your vehicle, however, and we figured the extra day spent paddling to Aubrey Falls was worth it.

The morning remained calm and we crossed the middle section of Rocky Island Lake with a great sense of relief. This is a notorious stretch of water where canoeists can easily find themselves windbound for days. Upon reaching the far western narrows, we spotted a colony of tents nestled on top of a small island. Other than the mad trapper we had met the day before, this was the first group Alana and I had come across in days, so we gave them a cheerful hello.

The cluster of islands provided a number of places to camp. But Alana and I decided to take the 720-meter portage leading into Aubrey Lake, marked to the left of the hydro-electric dam. We made camp on a small island and, finally feeling somewhat secluded, enjoyed a quick skinny dip from a beach in the back bay.

From our campsite on Aubrey Lake it was only a two-hour paddle to Aubrey Falls. Here, a 1,000-meter portage, marked between two massive hydro dams, leads back to the parking lot near Highway 129. The portage first heads up a gravel road to the top of the power dam. Then a trail leads down beside the steep slab of concrete, crosses a rocky gorge and then continues up the opposite side to a viewing area of the falls. It then continues on, over a footbridge and up a gravel path, to the parking lot. Before crossing the footbridge, however, Alana and I took a break to view the 100-foot falls. It was impressive, but compared little to what Grey Owl would have witnessed during his travels. Obviously the Mississagi is no longer "untamed, defiant and relentless."

LONGEST PORTAGE 1,000 meters

FEE Apart from the possible shuttle service, no fee is required.

ALTERNATIVE ACCESS There are a number of options to begin your trip. The town docks in Biscotasing, Lac aux Sables along Road 810 (north of Highway 553), and Rouelle Landing reached by a rough road from Highway 129.

ALTERNATIVE ROUTE A 2-day extension can be added from the town of Biscotasing, crossing Biscotasing, Ramsay and First Lake before arriving at the Spanish Chute access. Or, to shorten your trip, you can paddle up from Highway 553 at Lac aux Sables to the south end of Bark Lake by using a series of short portages.

OUTFITTERS
Missinaibi Headwaters Outfitters
Box 1148
Chapleau, ON, P0M 1K0
855-226-6366
www.missinaibi.com

Kegos Camp
R.R. 3
Thessalon, ON, P0R 1L0
1-888-698-3889
www.kegos.com

FOR MORE INFORMATION
Ministry of Natural Resources
705-864-1710
www.mnr.gov.on.ca

MAPS The Ministry of Natural Resources has produced a canoe pamphlet titled *Mississagi Canoe Route: Mississagi Provincial Waterway Park.*

TOPOGRAPHIC MAPS 41 O/8, 41 O/1, 41 J/15 & 41 O/2 Provincial Series: Scale 1:100,000 Biscotasing 41 O/SE, Bark Lake 41 J/NE & Wakomata Lake 41 JN/W

GPS COORDINATES
47.325201, –82.389461

Spanish River

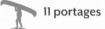

🕑 5 to 6 days   11 portages   ●- - - -● 142 km

Moderate experience in running whitewater (not all sections of whitewater can be portaged).

I was mid-June and my wife-to-be and I were in the midst of organizing our upcoming wedding. After dealing with stress-filled days of ordering flowers, booking a dance hall and mailing out invitations, we decided to escape the premarriage madness and head north for a quick and easy canoe trip. We were in the mood for an adventurous river route with good road access, few portages, moderate level whitewater and long stretches of unblemished wildlands. With little time to plan, we also needed a route as close to our home in Peterborough as possible. We gave the Ontario road map a quick glance-over and concluded that the Spanish River met our criteria perfectly.

For 142 kilometers the east branch of the Spanish River, beginning at Duke Lake and ending at Agnew Lake, flows through a diverse landscape. One minute you're floating across calm waters, sighting moose and beaver, and the next you're bumping and scraping over sunken gravel bars, riding down chutes, ferrying into powerful eddies and shooting along strong, deep channels between massive boulders. It's an incredible joyride.

A car shuttle must be organized before you head down the river. Agnew Lake Lodge or Stewart's General Store is probably your best bet. The roadway into the lodge is situated just west of Webbwood. Turn right off Highway 17 onto Agnew Lake Lodge Road. The camp is 11 kilometers in from the highway.

For a moderate fee, a driver will drive with you and your vehicle back to Highway 17, then north on Highway 144 until eventually, to the left, you reach a 1.5-kilometer long gravel road leading to the northern tip of Duke Lake. Believe me, paying for the shuttle and having your vehicle waiting for you at the end of the trip is far better than driving all the way back to the put-in after spending five days on the river.

The first day and a half of paddling is spent traveling south through a series of 10 lakes, numbered in descending order. Each lake is linked by navigable swifts.

The first major whitewater requiring some attention is Scenic Rapids, between First Lake and Expanse Lake. Supposedly there is a lengthy portage beginning at the south end of First Lake, on the west bank. However, Alana and I saw no sign of the trail on our way through and decided it would be best to

simply maneuver carefully down the narrow channel.

What we found dangerous about Scenic Rapids is that it is a very deceptive run. You start off navigating down mere riffles, so mild that it seems inconceivable that dangerous water looms ahead. Luckily, we exited the canoe three-quarters of the way down, just before a bend in the river. As we cautiously lined the canoe around the corner, Alana and I beheld three abandoned vessels (a motorboat, an aluminum canoe and a kayak) wedged into a pile of rocks midstream. We later met the two owners of the canoe downstream, waiting patiently alongside the CPR line to catch a ride on a passing train.

Expanse Lake is a long stretch of open water, and depending on the direction of the wind, it can be either a painstaking paddle or a pleasant sail to get across to the southern end of the lake.

The river speeds up once again at the base of Expanse Lake, starting with a moderate chute, and continues for almost 2 kilometers, gushing over rock ledges and gravel bars right up to the forks where the east branch meets up with the west.

A large island, almost completely covered in thick brush, splits the river midstream. It's best to keep to the right here and paddle between the narrow slice of land and the right-hand shoreline, where the railway track runs along at the top of the steep bank. A 4-kilometer stretch of slow and deep water follows a large swift that must be run shortly after the fork.

The next obstacle is a double set of rapids, one over 2 kilometers apart from the other. Both runs have portages (200 m each) marked to the right. Experienced canoeists usually opt to portage only around the first chute of the first set of rapids and will run the remaining whitewater.

From the preceding rapids to Spanish Lake the river is constantly changing in character, from almost non-existent current to

Spanish River

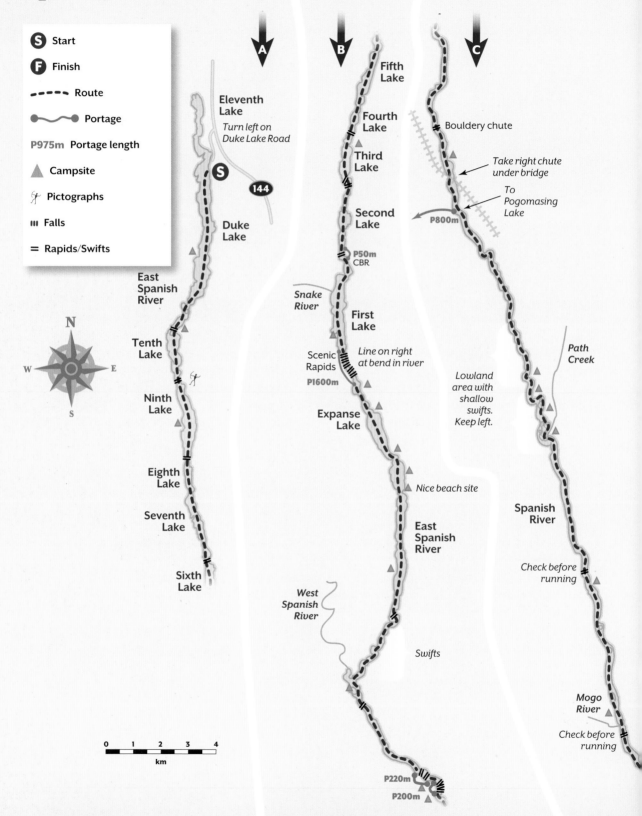

Legend:

- **S** Start
- **F** Finish
- - - - Route
- ●~~~● Portage
- **P975m** Portage length
- ▲ Campsite
- Pictographs
- ⫿⫿⫿ Falls
- = Rapids/Swifts

Eleventh Lake
Turn left on Duke Lake Road

S

144

Duke Lake

East Spanish River

Tenth Lake

Ninth Lake

Eighth Lake

Seventh Lake

Sixth Lake

N
W E
S

0 1 2 3 4 km

Fifth Lake

Fourth Lake

Third Lake

Second Lake

P50m CBR

Snake River

First Lake

Line on right at bend in river

Scenic Rapids
P1600m

Expanse Lake

Nice beach site

East Spanish River

West Spanish River

Swifts

P220m
P200m

Bouldery chute

Take right chute under bridge

To Pogomasing Lake

P800m

Lowland area with shallow swifts. Keep left.

Path Creek

Spanish River

Check before running

Mogo River

Check before running

A   B   C

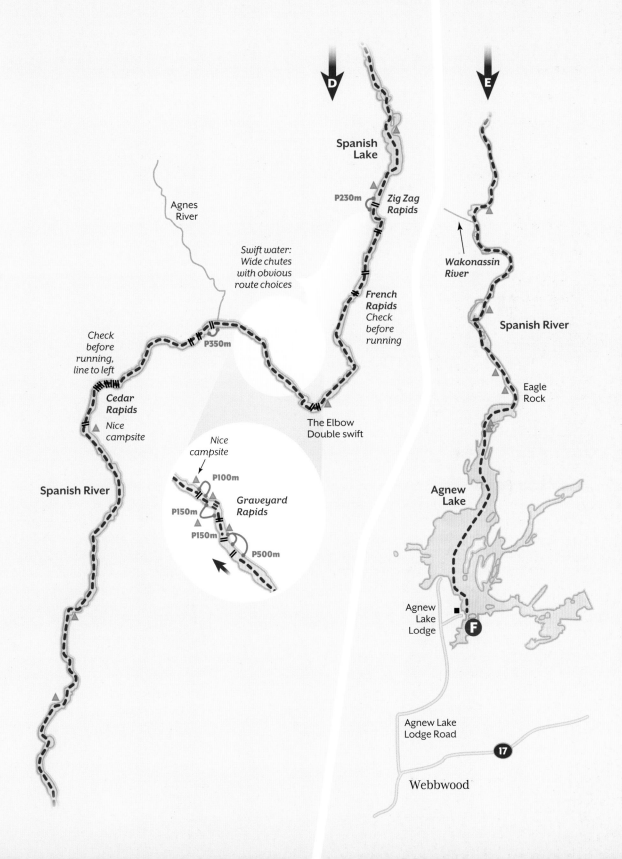

D

Spanish
Lake

Agnes
River

P230m Zig Zag
Rapids

*Swift water:
Wide chutes
with obvious
route choices*

*French
Rapids
Check
before
running*

*Check
before
running,
line to left*

P350m

**Cedar
Rapids** *Nice
campsite*

*Nice
campsite*

P100m

P150m **Graveyard
Rapids**

P150m

P500m

The Elbow
Double swift

Spanish River

E

Wakonassin
River

Spanish River

Eagle
Rock

**Agnew
Lake**

Agnew
Lake
Lodge

F

Agnew Lake
Lodge Road

17

Webbwood

narrow swaths cut through islands of reeds, to ripples of water gliding over gravel lumps, and miniature rapids gushing between high canyon walls.

There are four noteworthy sets of whitewater before Spanish Lake. The first is a bouldery chute that comes shortly after the place where the railway joins the river once again. The second is just downstream, where the river flows under the railway bridge by way of two channels. (As the left channel is too shallow and requires a lift-over, it's best to stay to the right.) The third area is a long stretch of swift water below the ghost town of Pogamasing (Ojibwa for "where water flows over gravel"). The river spreads out over an expanse of sand and gravel bars caused by the Wisconsin Glacier, right up until it spews out into Spanish Lake. Running the rapids is the easy part. Finding the proper channel, however, is quite a challenge, especially just before and after Path Creek. When in doubt, keep to the left of the river. The last section that demands a bit of caution is a rock ledge just after Mogo River. The rapids here may be a little tricky, especially during high water levels.

As the growing river surges sweetly on from Spanish Lake to the Elbow, most sections are simple runs, with wide chutes and obvious route choices. The Zig Zag Rapids, a short paddle down from Spanish Lake, should be treated with some respect. A 230-meter portage is marked to the right, but you may opt to line the canoe instead.

The most serious whitewater on the Spanish, the Graveyard Rapids, is just ahead, about 2 kilometers from the Elbow. Here the river valley grows more canyon-like, constricting the current and quickening its pace. A double set of rapids before the main drop can and should be portaged to the right. However,

experienced whitewater fanatics can choose to run the first set (watch out for the big, jagged rock midstream) and shorten the 500-meter portage to a mere 150 meters.

After running, lining through or portaging around a short swift between these double rapids and the Graveyard, keep a watchful eye open for the 150-meter portage to the left, which avoids a dangerous falls. Then you must lift over or portage (100 m) around the next drop along the right-hand shoreline.

Farther downstream, vigor renewed, the water cuts a deep bed where the river is pinched narrowly between another section of rock. Here, opposite the mouth of the Agnes River, a 350-meter portage (marked on the left) avoids a short section of whitewater. Two more shallow rapids follow, and these can be easily run or waded.

Cedar Rapids concludes the Graveyard series. There is no noticeable portage, and even though the section can be lined along the left bank, it is usually runnable if you carefully check it over beforehand.

After Alana and I cautiously lined or portaged the majority of foam and froth upstream, we decided to test our whitewater skills on Cedar Rapids. At the foot of the rapid the current was pulsing under the canoe as we zipped up our life jackets and pressed our knees firmly against the gunwales. Once into the rush of water we were back-paddling vigorously and began shouting our strategy back and forth.

The standing waves played with our boat as we slid downstream, and we braced our paddles on opposite sides to act as outriggers. Then, in the thick of it all, I caught a glimpse of only half a canoe wedged into a pile of dead trees pushed up on shore by the spring flood. A lump formed in my throat.

But after that 20-second ordeal was over, I suddenly realized how good the boat felt as it responded to our strokes so smoothly, through to the last stretch. Ceremoniously we yelped out a "Yahoo!" and spun our paddles above our heads and then continued on downstream, relishing every bit of our magnificent teamwork.

As the river twists around a bend, the rapids diminish, leaving only erratic sets of swifts and ripples driving your canoe toward Agnew Lake.

The only significant rock face is Eagle Rock, at the entrance into Agnew Lake. The granite cliff was believed by the Ojibwa people to be the place where the spiritual messenger of earth and sky, shaped in the form of an eagle, could be found.

I strongly suggest you spend your last night on the river and not at Agnew Lake. The man made lake was created in 1920 by Inco's Big Eddy hydroelectric plant, and with its eroded banks and flattened landscape, has to be one of the biggest disappointments of the entire route.

Alana and I camped along Agnew's eastern shoreline. We awoke early the next morning and while paddling south down Agnew Lake toward Agnew Lake Lodge, we reminisced about evenings we enjoyed by the dim light of a campfire, going over and over our wedding list, wondering how we could ever gather enough money to wine and dine all of our uncles, aunts, cousins, nieces and nephews.

Four months later, with camp mugs instead of wine glasses placed at the dinner tables, a miniature canoe used as a cake topping, and even guests arriving in animal costumes, our trip down the aisle together went as smoothly as our voyage down the Spanish.

LONGEST PORTAGE 500 meters

FEE Spanish River is now an operating park and camping permits are required.

ALTERNATIVE ACCESS Regular train service from Sudbury will take you to the town of Biscotasing to paddle the West Branch of the Spanish River. Another possibility is to take the train—the "Bud Car"—from Sudbury to Pogomasing.

ALTERNATIVE ROUTE Rather than paddle the series of lakes on the East Branch, take the train to Biscotasing and paddle the swift water on the West Branch. You can also shorten your trip to 3 days by organizing a car shuttle to the Elbow through Spanish River Outfitters (Fox Lake Lodge).

OUTFITTERS
Missinaibi Headwaters Outfitters
Box 1148
Chapleau, ON, P0M 1K0
855-226-6366
www.missinaibi.com

Spanish River Outfitters
Box 390
Levack, ON, P0M 2C0
705-965-2701
www.foxlakelodge.com

FOR MORE INFORMATION
Ministry of Natural Resources
Gogama District Office
705-894-2000
www.mnr.gov.on.ca

MAPS The Ministry of Natural Resources has produced a canoe route guide: *The Spanish River Route.* Chrismar has also produced an excellent canoe route map: Spanish River.

TOPOGRAPHIC MAPS
41 P/4, 41 P/5, 41 I/5, 41 I/12 & 41 I/13

GPS COORDINATES
47.387532, –81.850444

Biscotasing Lake to Sheahan

🕐 7 to 10 days   🛶 18 portages   ●----● 92 km   **Portages are not maintained. Moderate whitewater skills are needed if the West Spanish River is added.**

ALL VETERAN PADDLERS know that plans don't always work out the way they should. Take my Biscotasing trip, for example. It was always a dream of mine to paddle down the West Spanish River from Biscotasing Lake and then loop back by a series of lakes and portages from Pogamasing Lake to Biscotasing.

Who knew that the first week in June would see water levels the lowest in Ontario's history, making the mighty Spanish River a mere trickle of water gushing over a jumble of rock? Who knew my canoe partner would cancel on me two days before the trip? Who knew I'd be robbed of a good portion of my camp gear while staying at a campground on the way north?

I heard about the low water levels just prior to my trip, but didn't put much thought into changing or altering the route. It wasn't until I reached the Watershed Truck Stop at the crossroads for Highway 144 and Sultan Industrial Road that I was reminded about how serious the low water situation was. While filling up for gas, I happened to meet an old student of mine I had taught at the college where I teach part time. He was working as a Fish and Wildlife Technician in the district and informed me that the Spanish wasn't just low—it was absolutely unnavigable!

That got me thinking—I'd better ponder over an alternative. But still, while I drove the bumpy washboard Sultan Industrial Road, with the topographic maps spread out on the passenger seat beside me, nothing solid came to mind. I still had a lot of time to think, though. At the 30-kilometer mark along Sultan Road, I went left for another 10 kilometers and then left again for another even bumpier 30 kilometers. But even when I finished the drive and went to pay for parking at the historic Biscotasing general store (through town and across the train tracks), the same place the famed Grey Owl, Archie Belaney, allegedly threw knives at the passing trains after a bout of heavy drinking, I hadn't a clue where I planned to paddle.

I shared a beer with the owner of the store, Gord, and a former park warden, Cort, who was visiting a local camp for a stag. They were great company, but my social visit with them meant I was delayed heading out. It was 7:00 p.m. before I decided to just paddle down the west side of Biscotasing Lake and see where the wind would take me. Why not? My canoe trips are usually way too organized anyway. Maybe thinking outside the box would be good for once.

From the local dock, I paddled under the railway bridge and headed southwest on Biscotasing to search out a campsite for the night, which I found on a small island among a cluster of smaller islands. I rose early, sipped some herbal tea and looked over the topographic maps one more time before paddling off. A solid two-hour paddle during the calm of the morning got me to the take-out for the Indian Lake portage at the very far southwest corner of Biscotasing Lake. I kept to the left shoreline most of the way, except for choosing the more immediate route titled Straight Narrows, rather than the Crooked Narrows route. I also took a less exposed route where the lake opens up to the west by portaging 20 meters over a strip of sand connecting the mainland to an island hugging the eastern shore. And a stopover was had at the narrows before the last expansive bay (O'Neil Bay), a constricted piece of shoreline labeled "Wayne's World." And there to meet me were Wayne and Jenny (Virginia) Farrows. The couple were from Kitchener, Ontario, but had base camped on Biscotasing Lake since the 1960s. Hearing their passionate stories about the area inspired me to continue on.

The portage, measuring approximately 250 meters and linking Biscotasing to Indian Lake, was memorable. It comes complete with a rail line and rail cart to haul boats across. The cart was gone, and I assumed it was on the opposite side. So I carried my pack and my dog Ellie carried hers. To greet us at the other side was a group of anglers from nearby Sudbury. They were making use of the rail cart to haul their

boats back to Biscotasing Lake. And as a favor they hauled my canoe over to Indian Lake while bringing the cart back for their second load. It was a comical act and a bonus for sure.

I spent the day paddling slowly along the western shoreline. Indian Lake is dam controlled, which made the levels worse. Levels had to be at least 4–5 feet but looked like 5 or even 6 feet lower than normal.

The top of Indian Lake had a cluster of islands with campsites but it was too early to camp when I passed by. The one I did choose later in the day was located close to the entrance to Metagama Bay. The humid weather during the day had persisted after sundown and that usually means a nasty storm is on the way. And one did arrive, just after 10:00 p.m. I was in the tent, just about to call it a night, when I heard the chilling sound of a curtain of wind and rain rushing across the lake. I've heard this before and it's scary as hell. It sounds something like a freight train heard in the distance. And when it hits, it's nasty.

I scurried out of the tent to secure camp. First was the canoe. I had already tied it up against the shoreline but the winds were rubbing it hard against the granite. I unknotted the boat, pulled it farther back and retied the bow rope onto a stout pine. Next was the rain tarp. I had set it up earlier in the evening, expecting rain. But now it was flipping wildly in the wind and if I didn't quickly pull it down and store it, not much of it would survive by the end of the storm. I then unpegged the tent and dragged it deeper into the woods. Poor Ellie was still inside, curled up in the corner and wondering what was going on. Once the cold front settled in, the storm calmed enough for me (and Ellie) to finally get some sleep.

Biscotasing Lake to Sheahan

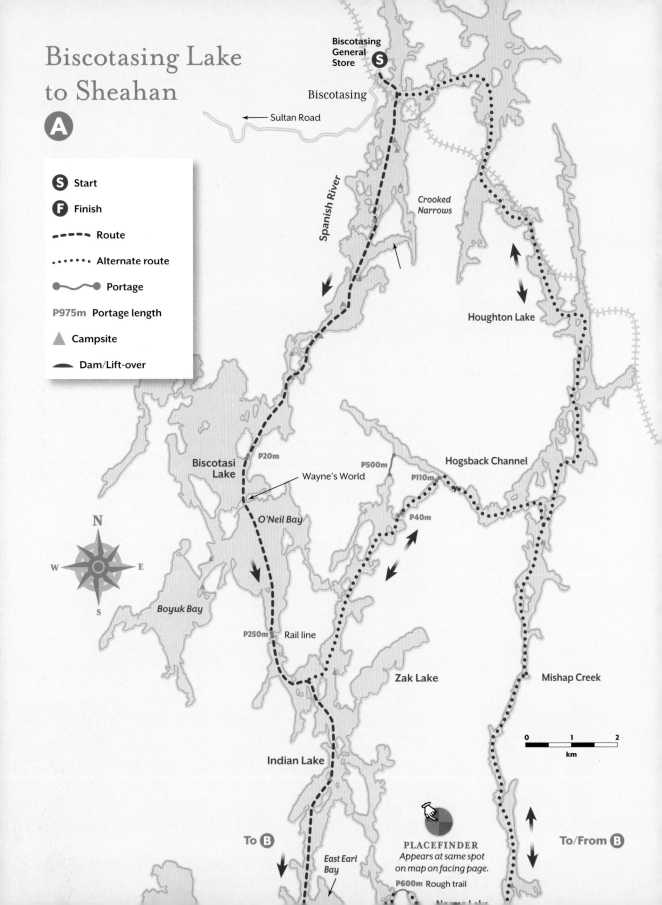

A

Biscotasing General Store **S**

Biscotasing

→ Sultan Road

Spanish River

Crooked Narrows

Houghton Lake

Legend

S Start
F Finish
- - - - Route
• • • • Alternate route
●〜● Portage
P975m Portage length
▲ Campsite
⬭ Dam/Lift-over

Biscotasi Lake

P20m

Wayne's World

O'Neil Bay

P500m

P110m

Hogsback Channel

P40m

N
W · E
S

Boyuk Bay

P250m   Rail line

Zak Lake

Mishap Creek

Indian Lake

To **B**

East Earl Bay

0   1   2
km

PLACEFINDER
Appears at same spot on map on facing page.

To/From **B**

P600m Rough trail

Nemo Lake

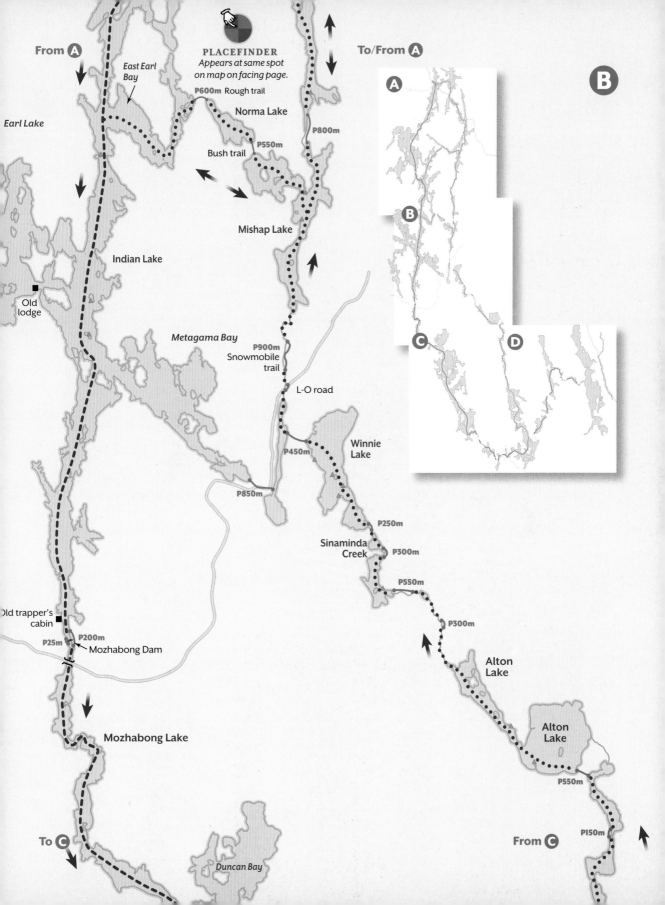

From **A**

East Earl Bay

Earl Lake

P600m Rough trail

Norma Lake

P550m

Bush trail

Mishap Lake

Indian Lake

■ Old lodge

Metagama Bay

P900m Snowmobile trail

L-O road

P450m

P850m

Winnie Lake

P250m

Sinaminda Creek

P300m

P550m

P300m

Alton Lake

Old trapper's cabin ■

P25m **P200m** Mozhabong Dam

To **C**

Mozhabong Lake

Duncan Bay

Alton Lake

P550m

From **C**

P150m

PLACEFINDER
Appears at same spot on map on facing page.

To/From **A**

B

A

B

C **D**

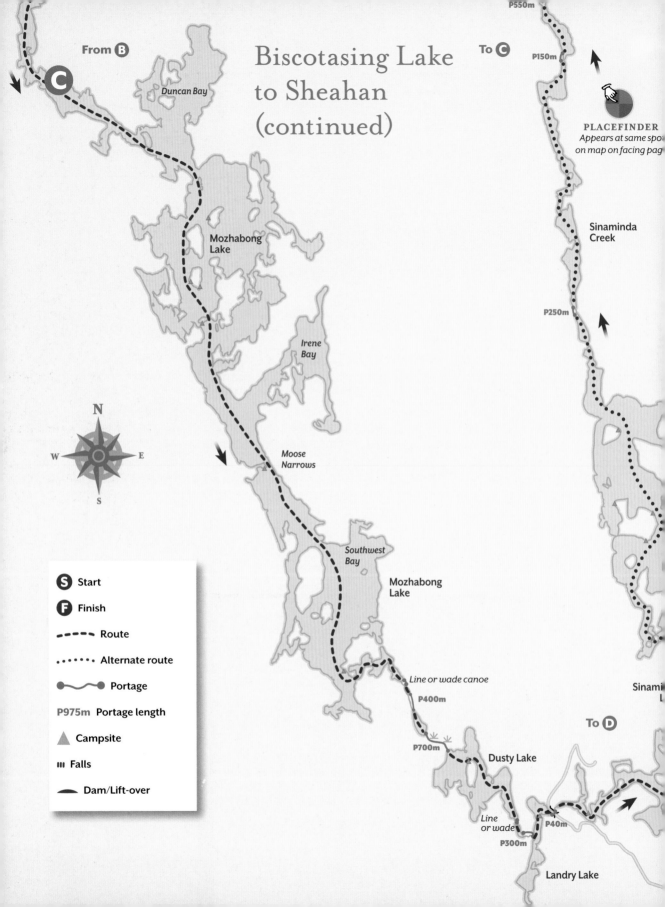

From **B**

Duncan Bay

Biscotasing Lake
to Sheahan
(continued)

To **C**

P550m

P150m

PLACEFINDER
*Appears at same spo[t]
on map on facing pag[e]*

Sinaminda
Creek

Mozhabong
Lake

P250m

Irene
Bay

N
W — E
S

Moose
Narrows

Southwest
Bay

Mozhabong
Lake

S Start

F Finish

- - - - Route

· · · · · · Alternate route

●–––● Portage

P975m Portage length

▲ Campsite

▥ Falls

▬ Dam/Lift-over

Sinami[nda]
L[ake]

Line or wade canoe

P400m

To **D**

P700m

Dusty Lake

P40m

*Line
or wade*

P300m

Landry Lake

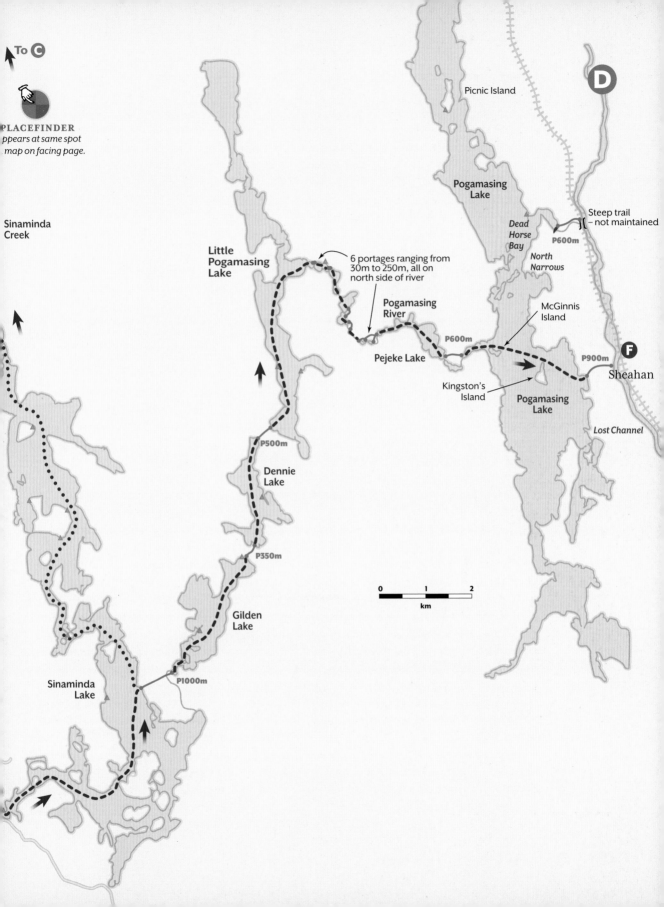

To **C**

PLACEFINDER
ppears at same spot
map on facing page.

D

Picnic Island

Pogamasing Lake

Dead Horse Bay

Steep trail – not maintained

P600m

North Narrows

Sinaminda Creek

Little Pogamasing Lake

6 portages ranging from 30m to 250m, all on north side of river

Pogamasing River

McGinnis Island

P600m

Pejeke Lake

P900m

F

Sheahan

Kingston's Island

Pogamasing Lake

Lost Channel

P500m

Dennie Lake

0   1   2
km

P350m

Gilden Lake

P1000m

Sinaminda Lake

It was after 8:00 a.m. when I crawled out of the tent. There was no need to get up earlier. The rain had continued all night, and since I took the tarp down when the storm hit, I didn't have the driest conditions ready and at hand to prepare breakfast. The relaxed pace in the morning, however, gave me time to once again glance over the topographic maps and try to figure out where I was going to paddle. I made the decision to at least visit Mozhabong Lake. But before that I wanted to backtrack on Indian just a bit and check out what was left of the lodge once built for the visit by the Prince of Wales in 1939. Rumour has it that when the Prince arrived in Biscotasing and stepped off the train, the blackflies were so bad he simply stepped back on the train and continued on. The locals were so angry that they went and burnt the lodge to the ground and all that remains now is the stone fireplace. After visiting the site of the historic lodge, I decided to paddle to the far eastern end of the bay to see if a portage was available to link Indian Lake with Ramsey Lake.

I was on the water paddling down Indian Lake by 7:30 a.m. and by 11:30 a.m. I found myself near the dam at the far southern end. Along the right shoreline, a few hundred meters before the dam, was the remains of an old cabin rumored to have been used by Grey Owl when he was actually the forest ranger Archie Belaney. Whether he used it or not, it makes sense that the rangers would have used it. Rather than paddling up the West Spanish River to get to Biscotasing, they would have used the same series of lakes and portages I was retracing.

The portage around the dam had two takeouts on the left. I took the second, but with low water levels, it wasn't easy to reach. I also noticed a short (25 m) but steep portage to

the right of the dam but water levels made it impossible to get close enough to it. The portage I took measured about 200 meters and, oddly enough, it felt good to do the carry. Ellie and I needed to stretch our legs.

From the dam to Mozhabong Lake was a tedious paddle. The waterway changed little in character for over 5 kilometers. It was made up of a weedy channel, twisting its way past deadheads and dried-up bays and inlets. The previous distress of the drought and past effects of the dam made the landscape quite mundane. It did look promising at first. Ten minutes up the waterway I spotted an eagle soaring above where a logging bridge crosses over. After that, however, even a single chickadee didn't show itself. It took close to two hours of paddling to reach where an elongated bay opens up into Mozhabong's top end.

Witnessing Mozhabong Lake was well worth the uninteresting paddle up the weedy channel that led me there. The water is turquoise in color, rock ledges border the shoreline and stands of old-growth red and white pine dominate the backdrop. It's no wonder it was made into a Conservation Reserve.

I counted four camps on the lake, one of which was being newly renovated. But no one was home and I had the lake all to myself. It took me another couple of hours to paddle around and find a suitable campsite. Similar to Indian Lake, most campsites were located on islands but were also trashed. Mozhabong Lake sites were worse than Indian, however.

The next morning, after squeezing through a section of Mozhabong Lake called Moose Narrows, a rocky point presented itself for another chance to take a break. I pulled up on a mini-beach on the back end of the rock and built a small fire for poor Ellie. And before I knew it we both dozed off and woke

over an hour later. Our nap only left enough time to paddle to the end of Mozhabong's Southwest Bay and portage into the next lake (Dusty Lake) before looking for another place to pitch a tent for the night. Oddly enough, I was looking forward to carrying the pack and canoe. I hadn't portaged much on the trip so far and paddling solo can become a bit mind-numbing at times. I still had some paddling to do before the portaging began, however. A good chunk of Southwest Bay had to be crossed until I reached an inlet along the far eastern shore, about half a kilometer before the end of the lake. The channel soon twisted to the right, and I came to where a creek flushes into Mozhabong.

I was now following valuable and detailed route information given to me by "The Summer School Brotherhood" made up of Jamie Dietrich, Mark Keating, George Luck, Mike deMunnik and Rob Coulas. Low water levels really became a problem here, and in retrospect I should have turned around at

this point and headed back the way I came. But my stubborn character forced me to push on, and I waded through a trickle of water and lifted over a pile of exposed rocks constricting the shoreline of the creek prior to a mud-filled pond. This section most likely is easily navigable by canoe but at this point there wasn't even enough water for a duck to have a bath in.

To reach the take-out of the first real portage, I had to resort to stepping out of the canoe and dragging it. To make matters worse, the creek bed wasn't too solid at this point. The portage itself wasn't too bad, however, measuring 400 meters and following a ridge line down to another pond. Next was a 700-meter portage leading to Dusty Lake and beginning to the right of a large swampy area. A knob of rock marked the halfway point of the trail and was the only place that had any solid ground to step on. At least the low water was helping me here. I can imagine this portage can be a boot-sucking nightmare after heavy rains.

Dusty Lake is where I camped. I found two island campsites, one small and one large. The large island wasn't in pristine condition so I settled on the small island site. The only downfall was a beaver visiting us around midnight to finish felling a poplar tree near my tent. Ellie heard the animal first but didn't bark (she's never barked); she nudged me with her nose. I crawled out of the tent and spooked the beaver back into the lake, feeling a little guilty about it.

Low water levels just kept getting worse out of Dusty Lake. In the morning I had to wade up an almost dried-up creek bed and pole the canoe up a weedy channel to a 300-meter portage into Landry Lake. From here I went north and downstream, lifting over on the right (40 m) of an old bridge. The channel flushed out into Sinaminda Lake. This is one large lake but made up of many bays and inlets, all now extremely shallow, with countless exposed tree stumps. It was an incredibly difficult place to navigate through at first, and I ended up asking some anglers in a motorboat for directions. They were the first people I'd seen in three days. The boat buzzed up behind me and I was a little shocked seeing them, as they were to see me. The occupants had come in from a dirt road and launched at the Sinaminda dam. They said it was a tough route but second-guessed it when I told them how I got into the lake. We shared the common angler hello, "Catch anything?" and discovered I was having better luck fishing than they were.

After they pointed out where the portage leading out of the lake was, I shared a beer with them. After guzzling it down, I packed the can in the top of my pack. The anglers all gave me a puzzled look and one finally asked, "You gonna carry that out with ya?" I kept my response simple; I didn't want them to think I was some purist trying to teach them a lesson. "Might as well," I said. "It doesn't seem right to leave it out here." My candor seemed to work wonders with them. The group gulped down their beers and stored them away as well.

A fellow paddler, Erhard Kraus, had sent me documentation of a route looping back to Biscotasing by exiting the north end of Sinaminda Lake and following a series of small lakes and Mishap Creek (how ironic). However, I figured the low water levels would definitely make his route impassable. I seriously have never witnessed levels so low. This meant that I either turn tail or continue on to the Spanish River and take the train back to Biscotasing. The train was obviously the best choice. Problem was, since I never intended taking the train back, I didn't know the schedule. The decision was to paddle to Pogamasing Lake and then turn back the same way I came. A silly idea, but I had lots of time and lots of food. And I was in no hurry to leave this wild place.

Portage-wise, the route improved after Sinaminda Lake. There are two trails on the eastern shore that link the lake with Gilden Lake. The original portage hadn't been used for quite a while due to a number of trees blown down and blocking the route. But a newer trail, located just north of the older one, wasn't a bad carry, even though it measured 1,000 meters.

A couple of overturned boats pulled up on the shoreline helped me locate the next portage on the opposite side of Gilden Lake. The portage, leading to Dennie Lake, measured 350 meters and, again, wasn't a bad carry.

I stopped to fish on Dennie Lake for a half hour or so. It holds brook trout, and I was lucky enough to catch a few on a small spinner. Dennie Lake also had a fair campsite on the island to the southeast corner, but I decided to go over one more portage—another good carry measuring 550 meters—to Little Pogamasing Lake. The campsite was set not too far up the west shoreline and it was here again, after igniting a campfire and boiling water for tea, I folded out the maps to decide my next move. The decision was to either turn tail here in the morning or continue on to Pogamasing Lake and the Spanish River to catch the train back to Biscotasing at Sheahan (a makeshift train stop that serves canoeists paddling the Spanish River and camp owners on Pogamasing). After my second cup of tea I settled on doing a combination of the two; I'd spend half a day paddling and portaging into Pogamasing to check out an island in mid-lake (Kingston's Island) that was the site of an old Hudson Bay post (1869–1885) and walk through the scattered stands of old-growth pine left over from the logging that happened in the area in the late 1800s.

After that I'd begin retracing my route back to Biscotasing Lake.

Keeping to the character of the trip, I couldn't reach Pogamasing Lake the next day due to low water levels in Pogamasing River. I started paddling the stream that links the two lakes but was continually blocked by either a mud bath or a garden of rock. It's a small creek and it's probably quite low in the summer—but still doable. With the drought conditions, however, it would have been foolish to try it. Thankful I didn't need to catch a train along the Spanish River, I turned around and went back to Little Pogamasing. By mid-morning, I was passing my previous campsite and beginning to retrace my route back to Biscotasing.

The winds were in my favor the entire week back, and I even got to my vehicle a couple of days early. And I ended my trip as I started it, by sharing a beer with the owner of the Biscotasing general store. He asked me where I went. My response was simple: "Not where I planned to go but certainly where I'd go back to." The store owner's reply was even simpler: "Sounds like a normal canoe trip to me."

LONGEST PORTAGE 1,000 meters

FEE No fee is required at this time.

ALTERNATIVE ACCESS It's possible to begin at Sheahan and paddle to Biscotasing Lake.

ALTERNATIVE ROUTE Hogsback Channel can be used to loop back to Biscotasing. Also, by linking up a series of unmaintained portages along Mishap Creek and Sinaminda Creek, an alternative route can be used to loop back to Biscotasing from Sinaminda Lake.

OUTFITTERS
Spanish River Outfitters
Box 390
Levack, ON, P0M 2C0
705-965-2701
www.foxlakelodge.com

VIA Rail will also drop you off or pick you up at other points along the river if you arrange it in advance. See www.viarail.ca or call 1-888-842-7245 (Montreal) or 705-673-1138 (Sudbury).

FOR MORE INFORMATION
Ministry of Natural Resources
705-894-2000
www.mnr.gov.on.ca

Mississagi Provincial Park
705-865-2021
www.ontarioparks.com

TOPOGRAPHIC MAPS
41 O/1, 41 O/8, 41 J/16, 41 P/4 & 41 P/5

GPS COORDINATES
47.299775, -82.100038

Lac aux Sables: Bark Lake Loop

🕐 4 to 5 days    13 portages   ●–––● 80 km   **This is an unmaintained route. Low water levels can also alter some areas and make travel difficult.**

Y WIFE AND I first viewed Bark Lake while paddling down the Mississagi River in 1996. It was a quick glimpse. We paddled across the extreme north end while visiting the cabin once used by Archie Belaney—later known as Grey Owl. But it was enough to make us want to return and explore all that we had missed before. However, rather than revisit the 177-kilometer river route, which required an extremely costly car shuttle and at least eight days of paddling, Alana and I decided to try a shortcut—a little-known circle route, accessed from Lac aux Sables, south of Bark Lake.

The launch area is located 83 kilometers north of the town of Massey, just beyond where Highway 553 and the 810 ends. It's a rough ride most of the way, with the worst section being the last 7 kilometers, past Ritchie Falls Resort. And since both Alana and our canoe dog, Bailey, suffered numerous bouts of car sickness on the way in, it was quite late by the time we pushed off from the access point.

Our tardy departure ended up being a positive thing. Originally we had planned to paddle the full length of Lac aux Sables and then make camp on the first possible

campsite along the River aux Sables. However, by 5:00 p.m. we found ourselves only at the entrance to the northwest bay of the lake, still a half-hour's paddle from the river mouth, and decided to make camp on a small rock outcrop.

Seconds after setting up the tent, a massive thunderstorm struck, probably brought on by the intense heat of the day. With it came large hail and turbulent winds, strong enough to snap two of the four nylon ropes holding down our tarp. It was a frightening experience, especially for poor Bailey, who has a terrible phobia of such extreme weather disturbances. It wasn't until Alana and I began paddling up the river the next morning, however, that we realized the brunt of the storm had actually missed us. Not far upstream a wind-burst had toppled over a couple-dozen trees, with the worst area affected being the campsite we had initially planned on occupying. (The toilet seat from the outhouse had actually been catapulted across the river.)

On a positive note, the heavy rains did manage to raise the water level enough to keep our feet dry for a little while. It wasn't until just before the place where a new logging

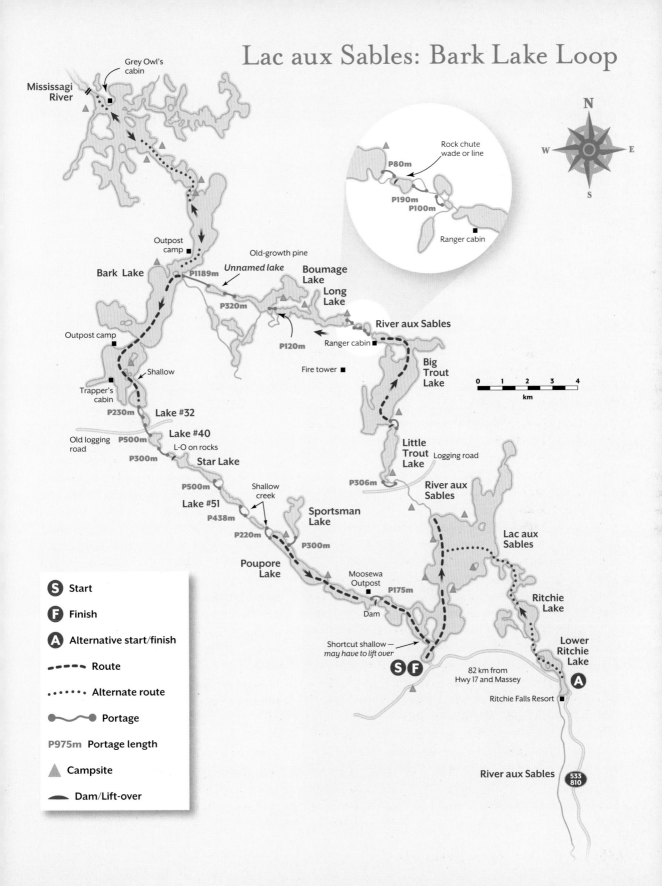

Lac aux Sables: Bark Lake Loop

Grey Owl's cabin

Mississagi River

Rock chute wade or line

P80m

P190m

P100m

Ranger cabin

N
W   E
S

Outpost camp

Old-growth pine

Unnamed lake

Boumage Lake

Long Lake

P1189m

Bark Lake

P320m

River aux Sables

P120m

Ranger cabin

Big Trout Lake

Outpost camp

Fire tower

Shallow

Trapper's cabin

P230m

Lake #32

Little Trout Lake

Logging road

Lake #40

Old logging road

P500m

L-O on rocks

P300m

Star Lake

P306m

River aux Sables

P500m

Shallow creek

Lake #51

Sportsman Lake

Lac aux Sables

P438m

P220m

P300m

Poupore Lake

Moosewa Outpost

P175m

Ritchie Lake

Dam

Lower Ritchie Lake

Shortcut shallow — may have to lift over

S **F**

82 km from Hwy 17 and Massey

A

Ritchie Falls Resort

River aux Sables

533 810

0 1 2 3 4
km

Legend

S Start

F Finish

A Alternative start/finish

- - - - **Route**

.... **Alternate route**

⬤—⬤ **Portage**

P975m Portage length

▲ **Campsite**

▬ **Dam/Lift-over**

road crossed River aux Sables that we had to finally get out and wade.

Not far past the bridge we also had to portage. However, the 306-meter trail, found to the left of a former log sluice, was an easy walk—especially since most of its length was along a well-maintained ATV trail.

Not long after the portage, where the river turns sharply to the right, we entered Little Trout Lake and then, eventually, Big Trout Lake by way of a 120-meter portage to the right of an old dam.

Both lakes are incredibly scenic, with a mixture of sand beaches and rock outcrops making up most of the shoreline. We held off choosing a lunch spot, though, until we linked back up with River aux Sables. The entrance, located at the far northwestern inlet of Big Trout Lake, is to the right of an abandoned shack, once used during the 1950s by forest rangers operating the neighboring fire tower.

Wading was necessary almost immediately once we were back on the river, and this section proved far more challenging than the lower half. The gravel base had now been replaced by mud, lined with marsh grass and teeming with leeches.

Portaging also became an ordeal. The first trail—a faint 100-meter path to the left of a large beaver dam—was the easiest. Surprisingly, though, it wasn't even marked on our route map. The second portage was much more tedious. It was a short distance (190 m) and the path itself was an easy walk. But finding the take-out was a real problem. We eventually found it to the extreme left of where the river flushes into a shallow marsh, marked only by a rusty beer can, mounted on a stick. Finding the third portage—an 80-meter trail leading directly into Long Lake—was less of an issue. The dilemma here was that Alana and I had to push the canoe through an almost stagnant pond and then wade waist-deep up a rock-lined chute before actually reaching the trailhead.

After dealing with the obstacles on River aux Sables, Alana and I chose to take on only one more portage—a 120-meter trail that connects Long Lake and Boumage Lake—before making camp. Once on Boumage, however, a small forest fire burning on the east shore forced us to change our plans. The fire was probably brought on by the hot weather. Or maybe even ignited by a lightning strike the night before. Whichever the reason, we knew it wasn't wise to camp there. To play it safe we chose to continue on, all the way to Bark Lake. It was a much larger body of water and even had a couple of outpost camps equipped with radiophones if the fire happened to get out of hand.

Of course, that meant we had two more portages to endure. The first, located at the end of Boumage Lake's western inlet and leading into a small, unnamed lake, wasn't too bad. Both the put-in and take-out had a soggy bog to wade through. But the distance was only 320 meters. The second portage, however, was a long 1,189 meters. And to make matters worse, the recent storm had also forced trees down across the trail. And these weren't ordinary trees—they were massive, 300-year-old pine.

The pine, left over from the historic 1948 Mississagi fire, which burned over 2,590 square kilometers of forest, represented one of the most impressive stands of old growth in the province. They also presented a major obstacle for Alana and me. It was a stressful time, to say the least, trudging through a tinder-dry forest, knowing a small fire was burning close by.

It wasn't until we caught a glimpse of a government spotter plane flying low overhead, followed soon after by a MNR helicopter, that we eased up a bit. In retrospect, apart from climbing up and over a few giant pine, wading through a mud-filled bog near the take-out and then getting lost for a few minutes at a fork in the trail (make sure to go right where the portage splits closer to the put-in), pushing ourselves all the way to Bark Lake was well worth the effort. Alana and I found a spectacular beach site a couple of kilometers north

of the portage and, since we were now ahead of schedule, made the decision to spend two full nights here.

We awoke in good humor, knowing all we had to do on day three was paddle a couple of hours farther north on Bark Lake to pay homage to Grey Owl's cabin. The site, situated directly where the Mississagi River flushes out of the northwest end of Bark Lake, had changed little since our time here five years before. The cluster of buildings was still privately owned and had just received a fresh coat of paint. The main log structure, noted for housing Archie Belaney (Grey Owl) and senior ranger William Draper in 1914, as well as the painter Tom Thomson and friend W.S. Broadhead on a two-month sketching trip in 1912, was also in relatively good condition.

I was quite surprised that it was still standing. The main cabin was built in 1908 to serve as a base for the Mississagi Forest Reserve (and also later used as a Junior Ranger Camp before being sold off in the late 1970s). But the wood used was even older. The Forestry Department made use of the lumber left over from the Hudson Bay post that was abandoned on Upper Green Lake in 1892.

Revisiting the historical site was definitely a highlight. But what really made the day was our leisurely paddle back. We stopped for lunch and a swim on one of the many islands scattered across the top end of the lake and then spent the rest of the afternoon fishing for monster pike along the heavily timbered shoreline. We even spent some time chatting with a local trapper and his wife who were out trolling for lake trout.

The couple was amazed at how well my wife and I paddled together. I guess it's true that matching up with a perfect canoe partner is next to impossible. And it's especially true that spouses usually don't mix well in a boat. But I had to agree that Alana and I were a good team while out on a trip. It's not perfect, mind you. There have been times in mid-rapid when I've yelled left and Alana went right, and yes, I've disappeared to collect more firewood just as camp dishes were about to be washed. But for the most part we communicate well in stressful circumstances and share camp duties equally.

Of course, to realize how well our relationship in a canoe works, we've both had to endure one or two disastrous trips with other less compatible partners. As a rule we've now learned not to share a canoe with those whose most important item is their beer supply. We also stay clear from individuals who have a tendency to discuss only religion and politics around the evening fire, or, even worse, constantly brag about how fit they are but continue to choose to carry the lightest load across the portage.

The trapper and his wife also seemed a well-suited pair. They were both from the Toronto area but preferred to spend most of their time together out at their cabin, located at the far south end of Bark Lake. They knew the area well, except for the route Alana and I had planned on taking back to Lac aux Sables—which seemed odd, since it began not far from their cabin.

Feeling a little uneasy about what lay ahead of us, Alana and I were packed up by 6:00 a.m. the next morning. By 8:00 a.m. we had reached the far end of Bark Lake, keeping to the left-hand shoreline all the way until a narrow inlet led us into the most southerly bay.

On the way down the lake, the landscape seemed less dramatic. The large pines were replaced by second growth, and some sections of forest had been recently clear-cut. Wildlife sighting still remained good, however. We spotted an osprey, a golden eagle and a nesting pair of bald eagles sharing the same thermal of hot air and counted 14 loons gathered between a large island and the southern inlet.

The paddle across Bark Lake went smoothly, especially considering it is such a large piece of water. And it wasn't until Alana and I turned left at the end of a cluster of islands, entering a weedy bay to begin searching for the first portage, that we felt anxious again about our chosen way back to Lac aux Sables. There was no doubt that the route had been used before, maybe even recently. But we had little to go on. No trip notes or updated government maps existed for this section. And the tension built up until Alana took note of another beer can mounted on a stick, approximately 30 meters to the right of where a small creek entered the bay.

Once we located the concealed portage the rest was easy. The 230-meter trail went up a moderate slope and then across a floating bog to reach the north end of Lake #32—an almost stagnant pond that Alana and I decided to nickname Mud Lake.

The next portage, almost directly across the pond, was easier to locate. The 500-meter trail wasn't as direct, however. Halfway along, an old logging road crossed our path. The portage started up again less than 20 meters to the left. Of course, we went right.

We eventually retraced our steps and found our way to the put-in on Lake #40. It was here that we almost lost poor Bailey. The dog fell into a pool of muck and then sank like a rock, weighed down by her pack full of kibble. Alana and I were too busy trying to find a way out of the swamp ooze ourselves to notice Bailey's predicament at first. We could hear

her whimper. But our dog always whines on portages. It wasn't until I turned around to call her into the canoe that I noticed that only the dog's head was poking out from the slime. I had to reach down into the mud, grab her collar and then yank her free. Lake #40 was then renamed Mud Dog Lake.

The next portage—a 300-meter trail that leads into Star Lake—was the most difficult en route. Locating the take-out wasn't a problem. We simply had to paddle across from the previous portage, make our way down a rock-lined creek and then pull out on the right shore once we ran out of water. However, getting the canoe and gear unloaded and then carried across the slippery boulders just before the take-out was another story. Even after completing the portage (be sure to go right another 50 m when the trail meets back up with the creek), we still had another stack of boulders to lift over before we could enter the main lake itself.

Star Lake is divided into two sections, making it somewhat larger than the first two ponds we had paddled across. But the water level was still as low and the quality just as poor. It did improve somewhat as we approached the next portage, located at the end of the second half of the lake, but not enough to trust filling our water bottles.

Maybe we were being somewhat phobic. After all, a local trapper, Ron Thatcher, had built his main cabin at the portage some years ago. But then again, some locals in the town of Massey had told us that Ron never did drink much water.

We easily spotted the beginning of the 500-meter trail leading into Lake #51 (which Alana and I were calling Thatcher Lake). There were two aluminum boats, owned by Moosewa Outpost on Poupore Lake, pulled up on shore there. But nothing much remained of Ron's cabin, just some debris stacked up in the center of a makeshift campsite. (We later found out that it had burned down three years before.)

We used the campsite as a lunch spot before moving on and then spent the rest of the afternoon taking on a couple more portages. The first, measuring 438 meters, was to the right of where a creek empties out of Lake #51. (This time the take-out was marked with a beaver skull tied to a tree rather than a beer can mounted on a stick.) Then, after paddling 20 minutes down a widening in the creek, we began the second portage that led into Poupore Lake. The 220-meter trail, also marked on the right, was the best yet. Moosewa Outpost, situated at the far end of the lake, had obviously kept it clear for their moose-hunting clients. We later discovered that it was the owner, Jamie Budge, who had cleared most of the portages along our entire route. He definitely got on our Christmas card list that year.

Alana and I decided to end our day on Poupore Lake rather than camp on the familiar Lac aux Sables, linked to Poupore by an easy 175-meter portage found between Moosewa Lodge and an old dam.

Poupore was a scenic lake but lacked adequate campsites. The first place we checked out was a slab of rock on the left-hand shore, near where a bush trail leads into Sportsman Lake. The fire ring was filled with broken liquor bottles, though, so we moved on down the lake and chose a small island, using a patch of moss a little larger than a doormat to set up our tent.

It wasn't the best campsite we've ever stayed at. But it represented what we liked about the route we had just taken on, as well as all the other trips Alana and I had shared that season. Each one was set outside a manicured park, in a place where portage signs and designated campsites were definitely not the norm. It was frustrating at first, finding ourselves constantly lost and having to stop for the night at some inhospitable bush site. But by midsummer we had grown used to it. Actually we craved it, preferring to guess our way through a grown-over portage, knowing that each one would take us deeper into the wilderness. And, when setting up camp at a place where few had stayed before, we both felt we had actually earned the right to be there.

LONGEST PORTAGE 1,189 meters

FEE No fee is required at this time.

ALTERNATIVE ACCESS Lower Ritchie Lake Dam, 76 kilometers north on Highway 553/810.

ALTERNATIVE ROUTE To avoid driving the last bit of rough road between Ritchie Falls Resort and Lac aux Sables, it is possible to paddle

north from Lower Ritchie Lake Dam to reach Lac aux Sables. In low water it may be best to paddle to Bark Lake and back by way of River aux Sables and avoid the ponds altogether. In high water conditions it is also quite possible to paddle the entire loop clockwise, which would allow you to paddle downstream on River aux Sables.

OUTFITTERS
Ritchie Falls Resort
Box 5259
Espanola, ON, P5E 1S3
705-965-2490 (after 1 ring and tone sound, dial 036)
www.ritchiefallsresort.com

TOPOGRAPHIC MAPS 41 J/9 & 41 J/16

GPS COORDINATES
46.752096, -82.338164

Ranger Lake Loop

🕐 4 to 5 days   12 portages   ●----● 104 km   **Portages are not maintained and low water levels can make travel difficult along the Nushatogaini River.**

T HE MAIN REASON I took on Algoma's Ranger Lake Loop is that it was here, at the age of 12, that I first paddled a canoe. It wasn't an actual canoe trip. My father and I were staying at Megisan Lake Lodge—located halfway along the 104-kilometer canoe circuit—and spent a good part of the week trolling the main lake without much luck. The second-last day, my dad and I decided to borrow one of the lodge's beat-up aluminum canoes and portage into a neighboring lake to try for speckled trout. It was then that I began my love affair with the canoe. And now, 25 years later, it was time to return.

Things had obviously changed since then. The Ministry of Natural Resources stopped maintaining the route leading in and out of Megisan Lake in 1988. And even though Ontario Parks made the Ranger Lake Loop part of the newly designated Algoma Headwaters Provincial Park in 1999, no one in the government seemed to know much about it. In fact, my research showed that it was one of the most "lost" routes in the province. So it was only fitting that I asked the new park planners, Nancy Scott and Bob Knudsen, to tag along on my exploratory trip.

Also accompanying me were Kip Spidell and Andy Baxter.

We all had wanted to paddle the entire route, beginning at Ranger Lake and then looping around by traveling upstream on the West Aubinadong River and then downstream on the Nushatogaini River. This would take 10 days to complete, though, and we had only five. So we cheated by beginning at the Gong Lake access point—eliminating two long days of lake travel—and then omitted the Nushatogaini River altogether by being flown out of Megisan Lake and brought back to Gong. The leisurely pace would allow time for Kip, Andy and I to film, and Nancy and Bob to complete their recreational inventory.

Andy, Kip and I, all from the Toronto area, met Nancy and Bob, both from Sault Ste. Marie, at Gong Lake (known locally as Bell Lake) at 4:30 p.m. We had planned to convene as early as 2:30 p.m. but we got a little lost along the network of logging roads on the way to the access point. The directions were simple enough—turn left off Highway 129 onto Ranger Lake Road (No. 556), drive 12 kilometers before turning right onto Domtar Road, drive another 30 kilometers along a rough road and just

Ranger Lake Loop

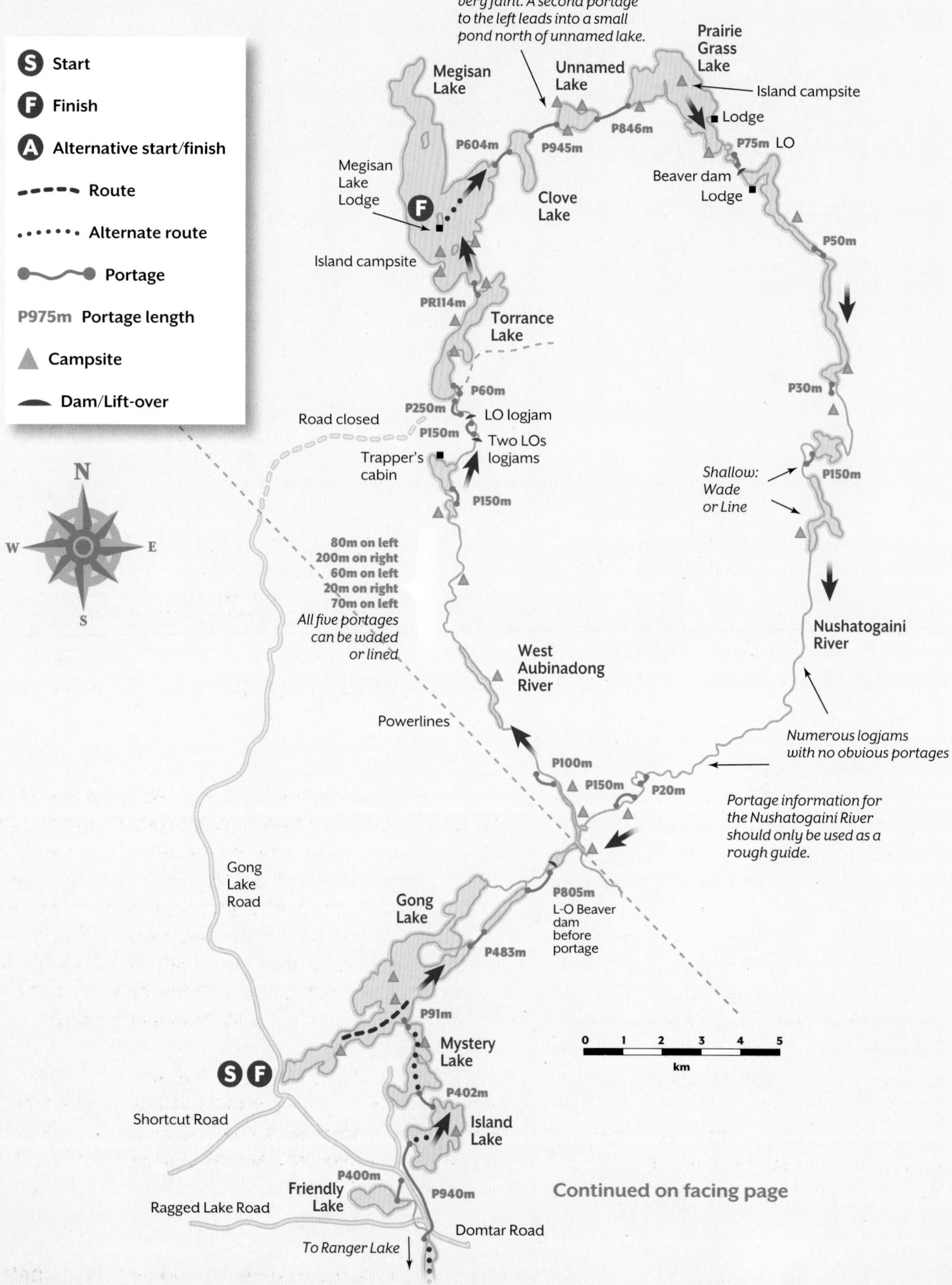

Continued on facing page

Legend:

- **S** Start
- **F** Finish
- **A** Alternative start/finish
- - - - - Route
- ••••• Alternate route
- •—•—• Portage
- **P975m** Portage length
- ▲ Campsite
- — Dam/Lift-over

Note: Take-out for portage is very faint. A second portage to the left leads into a small pond north of unnamed lake.

Megisan Lake

Unnamed Lake

Prairie Grass Lake

Island campsite

Lodge

P604m

P945m

P846m

P75m LO

Megisan Lake Lodge

Clove Lake

Beaver dam Lodge

F

P50m

Island campsite

PR114m

Torrance Lake

P30m

Road closed

P250m

P60m

LO logjam

Shallow: Wade or Line

P150m

P150m

Two LOs logjams

Trapper's cabin

P150m

80m on left
200m on right
60m on left
20m on right
70m on left
All five portages can be waded or lined

Nushatogaini River

West Aubinadong River

Powerlines

Numerous logjams with no obvious portages

P100m

P150m

P20m

Portage information for the Nushatogaini River should only be used as a rough guide.

Gong Lake Road

Gong Lake

P805m

L-O Beaver dam before portage

P483m

0 1 2 3 4 5
km

P91m

Mystery Lake

S **F**

P402m

Island Lake

Shortcut Road

P400m

Friendly Lake

P940m

Ragged Lake Road

Domtar Road

To Ranger Lake

N
W   E
S

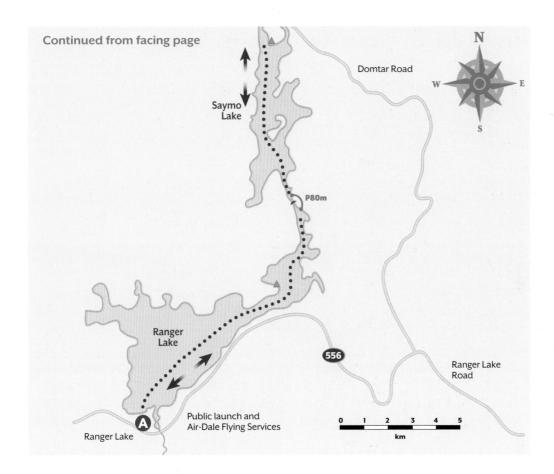

Continued from facing page

Domtar Road

Saymo
Lake

P80m

Ranger
Lake

556

Ranger Lake
Road

Public launch and
Air-Dale Flying Services

Ranger Lake

0   1   2   3   4   5
km

past Shortcut Road turn right again on a short access road leading down to Gong Lake.

Somewhere between the bridges crossing the East and West Aubinadong rivers we went right when we should have stayed left and then veered left when we should have stayed right just beyond Saymo Lake. It was 8:00 p.m. by the time we had packed up the canoes and paddled halfway down Gong Lake to make camp. It was well past 9:00 a.m. the next morning when we crawled out of the tents to continue on the trip.

The first portage (483 m) was located at the far end of the northeast bay of Gong Lake. Surprisingly, it was an easy carry, something

our group didn't quite expect since we were told that the route was no longer maintained.

The next portage—a long 805 meters—made Kip's day, however. The trail wasn't groomed at all. Even before the take-out, we had to lift over a giant beaver dam and then choose to either bushwhack an extra 200 meters to the right of a beaver meadow or push directly through a deep patch of swamp ooze.

A couple more beaver dams had to be lifted over not far past the put-in, and Gong Creek remained shallow right up to where it passed under a hydro line and then met up with the West Aubinadong River.

Here we went left, paddling up to the confluence of the West Aubinadong and Nushatogaini rivers. And after a quick lunch at a bush site north of the river junction, we continued up the West Aubinadong by heading left again.

We paddled 4 kilometers upriver before calling it a day, having to deal with only a couple more beaver dams, a few shallow sections that needed to be waded and one more brushed-over portage (100 m and marked to the left).

Our campsite was directly across from an old clear-cut. It wasn't the best of sites, especially as it was overlooking the thin line of mature trees left behind to screen out the planted crop of monoculture jack pine.

Places like this make me wonder what's really left of our wilderness areas. In 1984, after graduating from Sault College as a

forest technician, I spent two years working at both cutting trees down and replanting them. During that time, I strongly believed in the philosophy of sustainable yield—a scientific and modern approach to clear-cutting. It's something I still believe in. The problem is that somehow we managed to get ahead of ourselves. Lumber companies became greedy; technologically advanced mills increased the output but closed small milltowns; replanting same-species forests and advanced forest-fire fighting skills took away diversity; logging roads helped destroy remote areas; and, most of all, society's consumption rates continue to increase dramatically.

By planting over the clear-cut across from our campsite, forest managers may be able to produce lumber—all of the same vintage and size—in less than 60 years. But it will never

NORTHERN ONTARIO | **RANGER LAKE LOOP**

bring back the old-growth forest that once dominated this landscape.

Even having the 112,390-acre park protect what's left is a bit of a fallacy. In reality, it only protects the remaining old growth the way a museum protects a valuable artifact—the forest becomes an object to sit back and admire, merely helping us to recall what we once had.

Our third day out, the longest en route and certainly the most remote, helped erase negative feelings left over from camping near the old clear-cut. It took us 10 hours to travel 9 kilometers. Filming the route didn't help quicken our pace, but it was actually the lack of water and a surplus of beaver dams that took up most of the day. There were also more indistinct portages to deal with. The first five (70 m on the left, 20 on the right, 60 on the left, 200 on the right and 80 on the left), all avoiding small rapids, were clumped together where the river narrows for a 2-kilometer stretch just north of the clear-cut.

Another 150-meter portage was on the right, between two lake-like sections of the river. The trail, however, avoided only a shallow stretch that was much easier to wade up than to portage along. In fact, having become more used to walking our canoes upriver than paddling them, we had pushed our way up the entire section before noticing there was even a portage to use.

Shortly after, the river opened up again and we took time out to explore a small cabin north of the outlet. (The shack site was leased to trapper Garry Boissienau, who had recently buried his dog Barney behind the cabin and adorned the gravesite with a big white cross and a bouquet of plastic flowers.)

Another 20 minutes of paddling brought us to the worst set of portages yet. The first, a 150-meter trail to the left of a rock-strewn rapid, could be reached only by lifting over two logjams ahead of the take-out. The second, a 250-meter trail also found to the left, had a number of trees down across the take-out. It took us a few minutes to first locate the portage, and then a good half-hour's work with hatchets and saws to clear a path wide enough to fit the canoes and packs through.

This was a perfect time and place for an injury to occur. We were carrying over a hard-to-follow portage late in the day, with everyone beyond exhaustion. What amazed me, however, was how well we all worked together to make it through relatively unharmed. Kip did manage to twist his ankle on a tree root and Bob smacked his head quite hard on a low branch. But we all made it to the end without any serious damage.

The last portage of the day was a quick 60 meters leading into Torrance Lake. This time the take-out was clearly marked to the right. But most of the trail itself was so bushed over that we chose to lift up and over the miniature falls it avoided instead.

Torrance Lake Road access, now unmaintained and soon to be removed by the ministry to control entry to this remote area, was to the left of the cascade. We thought of staying the night here—among the beer cans, fish guts and toilet-paper mounds—but decided to push on and hope for something better. It was a good call. Halfway down Torrance Lake we found a prime campsite, where inadvertently we were forced to stay for an extra night because Kip took violently ill. We never did properly diagnose him but figured it was a combination of dehydration, sunstroke and a few too many infectious mosquito bites.

TOP 60 CANOE ROUTES OF ONTARIO   259

The event messed up our plan to reach Prairie Grass Lake by day five. But none of us seemed to mind taking the time off. Most of the day was spent loafing around, drinking continuous pots of coffee and munching on treats. (Kip kept to herbal tea and plain white rice.) To deal with the issue of meeting Air-Dale on Prairie Grass Lake we simply had Bob call up the air service by way of satellite phone (most government workers now carry communication devices while in the interior). Now we just had to get ourselves to Megisan Lake Lodge by late afternoon the next day for pickup.

After seeing how easy it was for Bob to make contact with the outside world, the rest of the group pleaded with him to also use the phone. Everyone chose to call home. Except for me. I decided to dial up my father. Yes, I would have loved to speak with my wife. But I knew Alana would understand how special it would be to reminisce with my dad while on one of the same lakes we had paddled 25 years ago.

The conversation only lasted a couple of minutes before I lost my connection. Which was fine since my father isn't much of a talker. He asked how the fishing was. I answered, "Not bad," even though we'd been too busy to throw a line in yet. He asked how the weather was. I replied, "Not bad," even though it was pouring down rain and only 10 degrees at the time. Then he wished me luck, told me to be careful and handed the phone over to my mother.

I had mixed feelings about using the phone after that. It wasn't the short conversation I had with my father that bothered me. That's just the way he's always been. It was the idea of having a phone along on a wilderness trip in the first place. In one way, it was a great emergency device. But it also meant we hadn't really got away from it all.

Since Kip was still feeling a little nauseous the next morning, we were slow to start. And by the time we completed the 114-meter portage leading to the south end of Megisan, marked to the right of where the creek flushes into Torrance (you may consider just walking up the shallow stream rather than taking the portage), strong winds had built up from the north.

Megisan Lake, the largest lake en route, was a mess. The steady gale had formed massive whitecaps that smacked hard against our hulls, and minutes later we found ourselves windbound on a miniature island in the southwest corner of the lake.

Bob unpacked the satellite phone once again to announce our change of plans to the pilot, only to discover that due to the high winds the pilot couldn't even take off from the air base anyway. So again we relaxed around camp, cooking up double helpings of lunch and dinner.

Kip and I also used the time to film. First, we walked back behind our site to record the 200- to 300-year-old white pine. Then, with a bit of artistic license, we created a make-believe scene where I ran low on food and had to resort to eating prunes and GORP (Good Old Raisins and Peanuts). Little did we know that the fictional event would soon become reality.

The wind continued to blow the next day and our pilot still couldn't take off from his home base (this was the same cold front, by the way, that formed three tornadoes that touched down in central Ontario).

Bob attempted to order in a ministry helicopter but found out the pilot had just been grounded the day before.

We then made a run for Megisan Lake Lodge, situated on the center island. The camp was unoccupied and had limited supplies, just a few rusted cans of stew that looked as if they had been there since my father and I visited in 1978.

At 7:00 p.m. the winds finally died and Bob made another call to Air-Dale to arrange pickup as early as possible the next morning. The group then made themselves comfortable in the main lodge, cooking up a combination of vegetable soup mix, onion and instant potatoes (we called it Megisan Mash).

By 9:00 p.m. we were all bedded down. Kip and I chose the floor beside the woodstove. Nancy and Bob slept under separate dining tables to avoid being pooped on by the dozens of bats hanging from the ceiling. And Andy unrolled his foam pad directly on top of the pool table.

We awoke abruptly to the sound of a float-plane flying low overhead. Our morning pickup was an hour early, and our group had to scramble to gather up our gear before the pilot taxied up to the dock.

We then drew straws for the first flight out. Bob and I won, which was a bittersweet victory since we ended up having to change two flat tires on our vehicles while the plane returned for the second load.

In all, though, it was well worth the hassles. Not only did I travel through some of the most scenic country the province has to offer, I had lived out a boyhood dream, and along the way reaffirmed my love affair with the canoe.

LONGEST PORTAGE 805 meters

FEE No fee is required at this time.

ALTERNATIVE ACCESS Get to Megisan Lake by floatplane or Ranger Lake by way of Ranger Lake Road (No. 556). Parking is available at Ranger Lake Lodge and Air-Dale Flying Services on Ranger Lake.

ALTERNATIVE ROUTE Paddling the route described in reverse would obviously be a better option: have Air-Dale fly you into Megisan Lake from Gong Lake or their home base on Ranger Lake. The entire Ranger Lake Loop can also be completed in 8 to 10 days from Ranger Lake or 6 to 7 days from Gong Lake. The route through Ranger Lake, Saymo Lake, Island Lake, Mystery Lake (South Anvil Lake) and Gong Lake is kept in fairly good condition by local use. The owners of the outpost camps on Megisan Lake and Prairie Grass Lake also keep the portages between the two lakes (600 m from Megisan Lake to Clove Lake, 950 m to a small unnamed lake and 850 m out to Prairie Grass Lake) clear of major obstructions.

However, the remaining route, down the Nushatogaini River from Prairie Grass to the West Aubinadong River, is quite rough. I was unable to explore this section because of unusually low water levels during the 2001 season. An old map I obtained from an area trapper does indicate a short portage and quick lift-over leading out of Prairie Grass Lake and nine portages, as well as numerous lift-overs on the Nushatogaini River itself. I've been told by some fellow canoeists who paddled the route a year before that it's no more difficult than the West Aubinadong.

OUTFITTERS
Air-Dale Flying Services /
Ontario Wilderness Vacations
Box 1194
Wawa, ON, P0S 1K0
705-889-2100
www.ontariowilderness.com

Ranger Lake Lodge
Box 175
Searchmont, ON, P0S 1J0
705-841-2553
www.rangerlakelodge.com

FOR MORE INFORMATION
Ministry of Natural Resources
705-949-1231
www.mnr.gov.on.ca

TOPOGRAPHIC MAPS
41 J/13, 41 O/3, 41 O/4, 41 O/5 & 41 O/6

GPS COORDINATES
47.057206, –83.573553

Lake Superior

🕐 4 to 5 days (3 days in good weather)　　None　　●----● 20 km　　Canoeists must be experienced in paddling rough water and prepared to spend two days being windbound.

I'LL NEVER FORGET the first time my trip buddy John and I experienced the magical powers of Lake Superior. We were paddling out of the mouth of the White River with some colleagues, all of us feeling the ill effects of a can of toxic oysters I had packed, and as we leaned over to retch into the water, John and I observed flat-bottomed clouds drifting across from the west. Wind patches soon appeared on the once-smooth surface and swells quickly began to lift and deepen. Then swirling wind flicked ice-cold water off the crests of the waves and into our now flimsy-seeming canoe. Within minutes the lake shifted from a gentle undulation to a jostling of bottomless swells and tumbling breakers.

After witnessing such a drastic change of conditions, it is easy to feel some understanding of the Ojibwa belief that Superior is a major spiritual center, an enchanted place regarded with deep veneration, where one must give homage in order to travel without peril.

So, on a return trip, this time joining John's daughter Kerry and friend Grace, visiting from New York, to paddle Lake Superior

Provincial Park's coastline, we ceremoniously tossed an offering of tobacco into the lake before heading up the coast. We felt somewhat skeptical at first, even joking about how we resorted to using a cheap cigar we had purchased at a roadside cafe. But when we were done and headed out on Superior, it was as if the unrehearsed ceremony had rewarded us with a sort of calm assurance, a sense that we had done something right.

Originally we had planned to paddle the park's remote Sand River. Once we arrived, however, we quickly discovered the effects of a three-week dry spell. The river had been transformed from a rushing waterway into a dried-up boulder garden.

Disappointed, we somberly chose to cancel the river trip and began making the necessary arrangements for traveling up the coast. By noon we had paid for an interior camping permit at the Agawa Bay gatehouse, shuttled a second vehicle down the 12-kilometer bush road to Gargantua Bay and then parked along the west side of Highway 17 to unpack our gear at the Coldwater–June Creek access point.

The first day out we took advantage of an unusually calm Lake Superior and paddled

Lake Superior

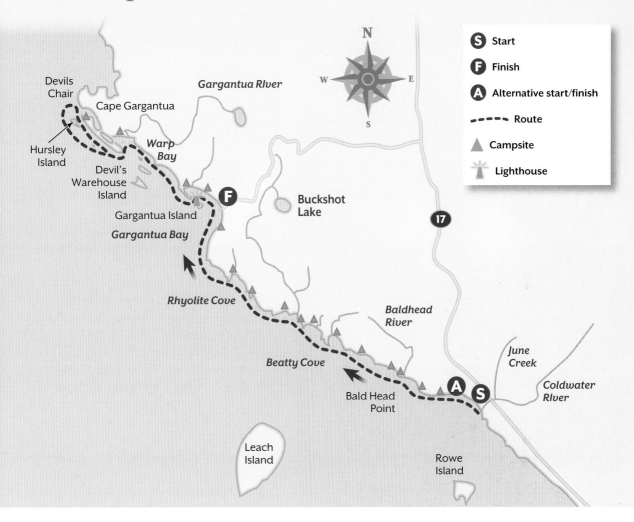

close to the heaped boulders and steep, jagged cliffs of Bald Head Point, taking time out to collect multicolored rocks, identifying various species of raptors hunting flocks of shorebirds and snapping photos of ancient Arctic plants rooted in inhospitable knobs of granite. We had an extended lunch stop on the cobble terrace at the mouth of the Baldhead River, where the Group of Seven's Lawren Harris once depicted the rugged shore of Superior on canvas, and then paddled up to the twin falls for a refreshing swim.

It was only 3:00 p.m. when we pitched our tents at the designated campsite in Beatty Cove, a crescent of sheltered water screened from the expanse of the lake by a 70-meter-long raised beach. Enjoying the hot sun beaming down on the sandy shore and the slight breeze that was keeping the bugs at bay, we no longer felt disheartened about abandoning the river trip. Life out on Superior was far better than dragging a canoe down a dried-up riverbed.

The calm persisted the next day, with only

the one-billion-year-old volcanic rocks meet. This gap of time represents one of the most extensive periods of erosion along the coast.

After our shoreline excursion the group decided to call it a day and we paddled around to the campsites in Gargantua Bay. At the entrance to the protective inlet, however, Kerry and Grace suddenly steered their canoe back toward shore. At first, John and I figured they had gone inland for a pee stop. But after waiting out in the swells for nearly half an hour we decided to check things out. One hundred meters away we could see Grace bent over and vomiting onto a slab of rock.

I was worried that it might be food poisoning and said so. "Well, we all ate the same thing at that grease pit up the highway," John replied. "I guess we'll all know in the next 24 hours."

For Grace's comfort we decided it would be best to paddle to my truck, which we had shuttled to the end of Gargantua Road, and have Kerry drive her to the hospital in Wawa. In the meantime, John and I set up camp on the beach near the parking area and waited.

By 10:00 p.m. we were sitting on the beach still waiting. Sundown brought a sharp change in the weather. The temperature plummeted and we could hear a line of rain squalls approaching from the west. As we ducked for cover the wind fell off, though the rain began falling hard against the parched soil. John and I lay beside each other inside the tent, silently spending the time counting the seconds between flashes of lightning and the echoing thunder, and consciously keeping tabs on our bodies for the initial symptoms of food poisoning—headache, nausea, severe stomach cramps.

By morning the storm had gone and so had our worries about the highway diner's

a slight breeze barely ruffling the surface of the lake. We continued north, enjoying brunch on a small island, mop-topped with stunted timber, and then spent two full hours investigating the reddish rock mass north of Rhyolite Cove. The bizarre geological structure marks the place where the two-and-a-half-billion-year-old granite rocks and food. To celebrate, John and I pumped up the camp stove and cooked a stack of buttermilk pancakes, spiced with cinnamon.

An hour later, still working on my second helping of flapjacks, I saw Kerry and Grace wandering back up to the campsite. I quickly leapt to my feet, ran down the beach to meet them and, gasping for breath, asked, "Well, was it food poisoning?"

"Worse," Kerry replied. "Try a hernia an hour away from peritonitis setting in." We all just stood there dumbfounded.

So, choosing to recover from her operation on the sandy shores of Lake Superior rather than in a hotel room in Wawa, Grace stayed back at camp while we took turns day tripping up the coast. The first day we explored Gargantua Harbour itself, rummaging through the ruins of the once-thriving fishing village that dates back to 1871. The place is deserted now, with only two rustic shacks remaining. Just out from the deteriorated docks, the barely submerged skeletal remains of the 150-foot wooden tug *Columbus* can be seen. In 1909 the ship caught fire at the docks and was pulled out to the harbor and left to sink there.

On the island at the mouth of Gargantua Harbour lies yet another historical gem—the charred ruins of the Miron Lighthouse. The structure was built in 1889 and was tended by three generations of the Miron family. The light was dismantled in 1948, and now a solar-powered automatic beacon has taken its place upon the bleak rock.

On the second day, with Superior still surprisingly calm, John and I paddled up to the mouth of the Gargantua River. We spent the first part of the morning paddling upstream, following woodland caribou tracks along the beach and chatting with a group of fish and wildlife specialists who were working in the area. We were amazed to learn that they had heard stories of Grace's ordeal back at their home base in Wawa. We then traveled north to have lunch near the Devil's Chair (a sacred place believed by the Ojibwa to be where the Great Spirit Nanabozho rested after jumping over the lake). Then on our way back to the campsite, we took time out to visit Devil's Warehouse Island to search for the sites where ocher might have been mined. On the east side of the island we found an incredible dome-shaped cave, probably used hundreds of years ago as a shelter by shamans while visiting Devil's Warehouse to gather the red-colored rock used to paint the pictographs at Agawa Rock.

These islands were not originally named after the Devil. This place, revered by the Ojibwa as the altar inside their cathedral, was renamed by Christian missionaries who saw their own Satan in the Great Spirit of the Native peoples. Even the voyageurs named Gargantua Bay itself after seeing a similarity between the antics of Nanabozho and the hero in the satirical romance *Gargantua and Pantagruel*, written by Rabelais in 1552.

John and I returned late in the day to find that Grace and Kerry had taken the time to pack in fresh groceries, and for our last night's dinner on Superior we gorged ourselves on milk, vegetables and beer. Kerry even opened a can of oysters. Poor Grace, keeping to her strict diet, slurped her soup as we feasted. We finished our dessert of strawberries and cognac (Grace had applesauce), and feeling somewhat guilty about our gluttony, we treated our hernia victim by chauffeuring her by canoe to the north end of the harbor, where the Coastal Hiking Trail leads to a prominent lookout point.

John, Kerry and I helped Grace hobble up to the ridgetop, and from the slab of rock we watched as the sun set, illuminating this wild place with its reddish glow. We stood in awe of the expanse of it all, questioning how a landscape so beautiful could be mistaken by the black-robed Jesuits as a home for the Devil. To us, Gargantua Harbour had become a place of benediction.

We stood there on that ridge until the stars came out, not saying anything, but everyone was quite conscious that if we had chosen to venture down the remote Sand River rather than being lured out into the calm of Lake Superior, our canoe trip to Northern Ontario would have ended as a tragedy.

FEE You must purchase a provincial park interior camping permit at the Agawa Bay or Old Woman Bay campground gatehouse before heading out onto Lake Superior.

ALTERNATIVE ACCESS Depart from the parking area for the Orphan Lake Trail, located a short distance north of the Coldwater–June Creek access point on the west side of Highway 17.

ALTERNATIVE ROUTE The trip can be extended by continuing north along the Lake Superior coastline to Cape Gargantua, making camp at Indian Harbour and then returning south to the parking area at Gargantua Harbour.

OUTFITTERS
Naturally Superior Adventurers
R.R. 1 Lake Superior
Wawa, ON, P0S 1K0
1-800-203-9092 or 705-856-2939
www.naturallysuperior.com

FOR MORE INFORMATION
Lake Superior Provincial Park
705-856-2284
www.ontarioparks.com

MAPS The Ministry of Natural Resources Lake Superior Provincial Park coastline map.

TOPOGRAPHIC MAPS
41 N/7, 41 N/11 & 41 N/10

GPS COORDINATES
47.468911, –84.788632

Old Woman Lake

 2 to 4 days    14 portages   ●----● 22 km   Due to some rugged portages, moderate canoeing skills are required.

M Y FIRST TIME visiting Old Woman Lake was back in the mid-1990s when my wife and I took the Bush family from Madison, Wisconsin, there. Darren Bush is the owner of Rutabaga, a very large outdoor store in the United States, and the organizer of Canoecopia (a paddle sport show that somewhat resembles a Star Trek convention for canoeists), where I have spoken for a number of years. Originally we were to paddle along the Lake Superior coastline. However, strong winds and big waves, something quite normal on Superior, caused us to alter our route. We chose Old Woman Lake, accessed then from Mijinemungshing Lake (Miji for short). Miji Lake itself is the largest inland lake in the park and an incredible body of water to paddle, full of bays and inlets complete with prime campsites. Problem is, low water levels can be an issue where Miji Lake's southeastern inlet joins up with Wabigoon Lake. An old logging dam, originally built in the 1920s, has slowly deteriorated along the Anjigami River and the park staff are now suggesting an alternative route from Gamitagama Lake.

Miji to Old Woman still may be possible in high water levels. Just check with the park staff prior to your trip. It's also far easier than accessing from Gamitagama Lake. The route links up with Wabigoon, Mirimoki and Piquer lakes. Mirimoki is connected to Piquer Lake by way of a 1,350-meter portage to a small pond and then a 350-meter portage. Piquer Lake connects with Old Woman Lake with a 130-meter portage.

Again, the route isn't too difficult. The longest portage does have a good steep incline and the two shorter trails had a few wet spots to trudge through, including a small creek—but overall it was a good trip when I completed it with the Bush family. That was back in 2004, however, and even then the paddle through Miji Lake's southeastern inlet to Wabigoon Lake was an ordeal. It became muddier and less navigable by canoe the closer we got to the take-out for the first portage.

The year I came back to visit Old Woman Lake there was a drought. So I obviously chose Gamitagama Lake rather than Miji Lake to begin the trip. It also ended up being a solo trip, for good reason. The Gamitagama Lake route is rumored to be a very tough trip, especially the steep portage that leads you

Old Woman Lake

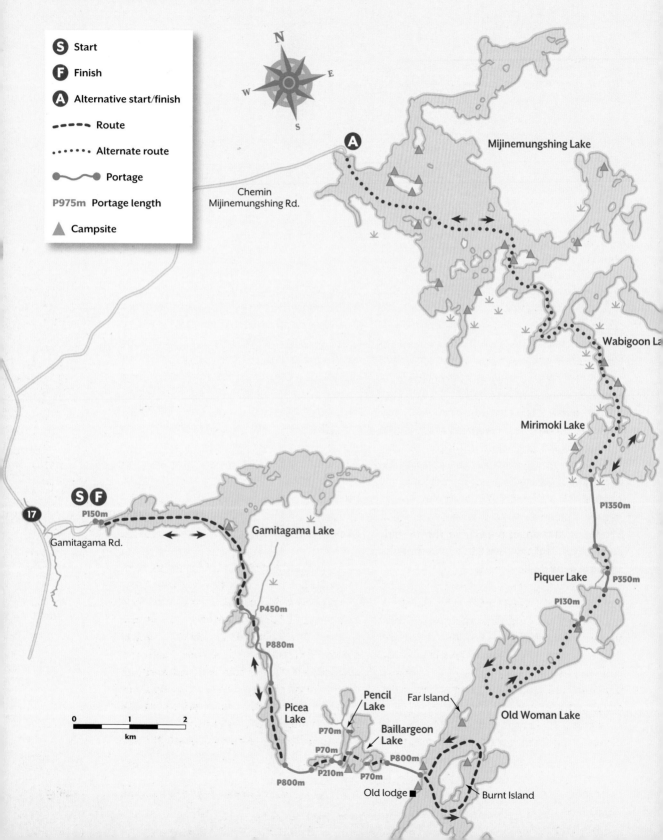

Legend:

- **S** Start
- **F** Finish
- **A** Alternative start/finish
- – – – Route
- ··········· Alternate route
- ●━━━● Portage
- **P975m** Portage length
- ▲ Campsite

Mijinemungshing Lake

Chemin Mijinemungshing Rd.

Wabigoon La

Mirimoki Lake

P1350m

Piquer Lake

P350m

P130m

S F

P150m

Gamitagama Rd.

Gamitagama Lake

P450m

P880m

Picea Lake

Pencil Lake

P70m

Far Island

Baillargeon Lake

Old Woman Lake

P70m

P70m

P800m

P210m

P70m

P800m

Old lodge

Burnt Island

0 1 2
km

17

down into Old Woman Lake; no matter how hard I tried, I couldn't convince any of my friends to go with me and see if the rumors were true.

The Gamitagama Lake access is off Highway 17, 5 kilometers south of the Miji Lake road and 10 kilometers north of Gargantua Road. The access road isn't marked; it's also a rough road and parking is limited at the end. You also have a 150-meter portage to do between the parking lot and Gamitagama Lake. There's a steep incline, and the trail's grade is a good indication of what's to come on the other portages en route.

The parking lot was small and I was the only one parking there. Not sure why. Gamitagama Lake is a pristine lake shouldered by thick brush and granite ridges, the water slightly tannin in color. I counted three campsites, the third being on a prominent island, before I headed south down a channel halfway down the lake to reach the next portage.

I took on the first and second portages before stopping for the night. The route from Gamitagama Lake could be completed in one full day, but I started out late and figured the single campsite on Picea Lake would be best. The first portage was a 450-meter portage, a crossing of a small pond, and the second portage (measuring a long 880 m) continually crisscrossed a shallow creek.

Waiting for me on day two were five portages leading to Old Woman Lake. The first was an 800-meter trail leading out of the southern end of Picea Lake, adjacent to my first night campsite, and into an unnamed pond. A good upward slope began almost immediately from the take-out and rose again closer to the put-in.

The next portage measured only 210 meters and brought me to another unnamed

pond (properly titled Pencil Lake for its elongated shape). A creek to the northeast joins this lake to the larger Baillargeon Lake and it may be navigable in better water conditions. However, I ended up taking a short but rough portage (70 m) to Baillargeon Lake. This was a scenic and remote spot and was well worth all the difficulty I had endured on the route so far.

Another short but rough portage (70 m), located at the southeast corner of Baillargeon Lake, led me to yet another small pond

where the final portage to Old Woman Lake began. The distance of the last trail was a solid 800 meters and the terrain was very, very rugged; especially the last quarter where the trail made its way down an incredibly sharp drop. Worse than portaging my gear down the abrupt ending was the thought of having to go back uphill the same way on my return!

I was worn out by the time I reached the familiar Old Woman Lake and I couldn't help but wonder how bad the Miji route would have been. Ten minutes later I got my answer. I spotted a red canoe approaching from the north end of the lake. The occupants were a young couple who floated over to ask how I had got to the lake. They were desperate not to return the way they came due to low water and boot-sucking mud at the base of Miji. I shared the route I had taken in with them, and we made plans on paddling and

portaging out together to Gamitagama Lake, where I would drive them back to their vehicle parked at Miji.

Old Woman Lake was just as scenic as I remembered it. I especially enjoyed revisiting the old lodge nestled in the woods on a small peninsula across from Burnt Island. It was built in 1950 by Vice President Cyrus Osborn of General Motors (Detroit) for executives. In 1971 the government cancelled the lease the cabin was on, and it's now used by park rangers and canoeists. There's not much to the outside structure, just rough sawed logs with a metal roof. Inside, however, there's an impressive fireplace mantel acting as the focal point on the main floor. Close to the fireplace is a mini-kitchen area and to the left is a staircase leading up to a loft overlooking the main room below. I found it in good shape and since it was pouring rain outside, I made the decision to sleep there that night, placing my solo tent in the middle of the floor to protect me from the dozens of mice running around the place during the night. There was also a log book on top of the fireplace mantel and my evening entertainment was reading the entries of all the canoeists, anglers and winter trekkers who had visited the lodge. I even found my past entry when I came here with the Bush family.

The next day I spent fishing, catching both brook trout and lake trout along the western shoreline of Old Woman Lake. I even portaged into Piquer Lake (130 m) from the top end of Old Woman Lake and caught a few brook trout. Weather had improved during the day as well and I decided against staying in the cabin for a second night and camped on a fantastic site on the northeastern tip of Burnt Island, directly across from the young couple I had planned on paddling out with the following morning.

My last day started early. I wanted to get to the parking lot by late afternoon to start the long drive home, so I paddled over to the other canoeists' campsite and after sharing a cup of coffee, we left the lake together to go back to Gamitagama Lake.

On our way out, the rain came back and the air was damp and heavy, and a thick blanket of fog covered the mountainous landscape around us. I wasn't too quick to leave the confines of Old Woman Lake, not only because I knew I'd miss the incredible scenery surrounding the lake, but also because I dreaded humping back up that long portage leading out of the lake. The portage, itself, was easier for me than the couple traveling with me, only because I'd endured it already. There's something to be said about that. Having completed a nasty portage once always makes the next trip over much easier. It also helps you convince yourself to come back and try a difficult route such as this again—something I plan on doing soon. Trust me. Old Woman Lake is worth it!

LONGEST PORTAGE 880 meters

FEE An interior permit must first be purchased at Lake Superior Provincial Park's Agawa Bay Campground.

ALTERNATIVE ACCESS
Mijinemungshing Lake, accessed by the Chemin Mijinemungshing Road east off Highway 17, can be used. A chain of lakes to the south will lead to Old Woman Lake. This is the original way to Old Woman but due to low water levels at the south end of Mijinemungshing Lake, it is no longer recommended by park staff.

ALTERNATIVE ROUTE
The Mijinemungshing Lake route links up with Wabigoon, Mirimoki and Piquer lakes. Mirimoki is connected to Piquer Lake by way of a 1350-meter portage to a small pond and then a 350-meter portage. Piquer Lake connects with Old Woman Lake with a 130-meter portage.

OUTFITTERS
Naturally Superior Adventures
R.R. 1 Lake Superior
Wawa, ON, P0S 1K0
1-800-203-9092 or 705-856-2989
www.naturallysuperior.com

FOR MORE INFORMATION
Lake Superior Provincial Park
705-856-2284
www.ontarioparks.com

MAPS Lake Superior Provincial Park has produced a canoe route pamphlet describing this and other canoe routes in the park.

TOPOGRAPHIC MAPS
41 N/10 & 41 N/11

GPS COORDINATES
47.658571, -84.794651

White River

🕐 5 to 7 days (count on at least one day windbound on Lake Superior) | 20 portages | ●----● 82 km | Moderate whitewater skills and an awareness of the dangers of river currents. High winds on Lake Superior.

IT WAS THE simple idea of paddling down-river to the legendary waters of Lake Superior—the world's largest freshwater inland sea—that first interested me in canoeing the White River. But the moment my topographic maps came in the mail and I unrolled them out on the kitchen table to catch the first glimpse of the snakelike strip of blue running across the paper, with its dark brown contour lines indicating the countless rapids and falls along the way, I knew the White would become one of the toughest, most dangerous and magnificent canoe trips of my life.

Considering the river's rugged terrain and seemingly remote setting, I opted out of a solo excursion and asked a few friends I knew from the college I lecture at during the winter months to tag along. Al McPherson and Neil Steffler, both instructors in the Parks and Recreation Department, partnered up in one canoe. And joining me in my canoe was John Buck, the now-retired associate dean, who, with his gray beard and weathered Tilley hat pulled down past his ears, reminded me more of a present-day version of Canada's canoe guru Bill Mason than a college administrator.

The route begins at White Lake Provincial Park, which is located along the Trans-Canada Highway (Highway 17), 35 kilometers west of the town of White Lake and 72 kilometers east of Marathon.

The park staff will register you for traveling through White Lake Provincial Park and then tell you how to obtain a permit for Pukaskwa National Park. They will also help you organize a car shuttle to the national park's visitor center parking lot in Hattie Cove. You can register at either the main gate or the registration booth down at the provincial park's launching site.

The Native people call the lake Natamasagami, meaning "first lake from Lake Superior." It was the European voyageurs and traders who, having to constantly battle the white-capped waves whipped up on the northern end of the lake by heavy winds, gave it its present name. The section of the lake you will be traveling on is quite sheltered, however.

Travel in a southwesterly direction and you will eventually paddle under a railway trestle and then to the Ministry of Natural Resources dam. This is where water levels are controlled, allowing the White River to be accessible

throughout the entire paddling season.

The first portage en route is right of the dam (240 m). During the summer season, you can usually shorten the portage to 65 meters by lifting your gear and canoe up and over on the right of the metal structure and then navigating the swift water down below.

Shortly after the dam, a series of rapids mark where the river begins to drop down off the Canadian Shield. These rapids can be bypassed by four portages. The first, a long 575 meters, is marked to the left. Along the path, however, you will notice a trail breaking off the main portage and working its way back to the river. This is where experienced whitewater canoeists have shortened the carry by navigating some of the runnable sections between the two major drops.

Along the entire route you'll notice a number of side trails on the portages. To keep

it simple I have decided to only include the main portages en route, leaving you to judge your own experience level while scouting out each run.

Downstream there is a 225-meter portage to the right, followed soon after by a 405-meter portage with a steep take-out just before a sharp bend in the river, and then a 95-meter portage also to the right.

For 4 kilometers the river slows down and is free of any portages. If you check the older maps, however, a path is marked around the first bend. The strange thing is that not even the slightest ripple exists here, let alone a major rapid. Instead, the river is calm and incredibly deep. It's been said that the portage was cleared by traveling Ojibwa years ago. They called it the land of Misshepezhieu and chose to portage around this section of the river because they believed it was home to

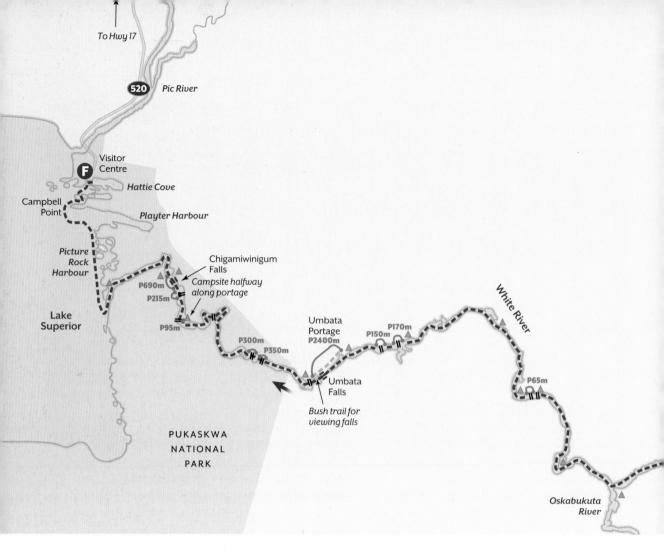

To Hwy 17

520 Pic River

Visitor Centre
F

Hattie Cove

Campbell Point

Playter Harbour

Picture Rock Harbour

Chigamiwinigum Falls

P690m

Campsite halfway along portage

P215m

P95m

Lake Superior

P300m

P350m

Umbata Portage P2400m

P150m P170m

White River

Umbata Falls

Bush trail for viewing falls

P65m

PUKASKWA NATIONAL PARK

Oskabukuta River

a dragon-like monster who dwelled at the bottom of the river, waiting to overturn canoeists who paddled by. To ensure yourself safe passage it might be wise to toss a bundle of sacrificial tobacco over the gunwales to appease the mythical creature.

Our party, laden with superstition, quickened the pace through the site and made camp farther downstream at the end of an 80-meter portage marked on the left of a stunted rapid. The site would have been perfect for our first night on the river if not for a noisy skidder, busy dragging spruce and jack pine logs through the bush close by our tents. Florescent flagging tape, wrapped around a

line of cedar trees, had also been left by mine claimers in search of the Hemlo gold motherlode.

Both the logging and mining companies had legal permits for their work in the area, but the drone of machinery and swaths of surveying tape, plus the rumor we heard before heading out on the river that Ontario Hydro plans to develop three dams along the river's length, quickly dissolved any notions we had of enjoying a wilderness experience the first day out on the river.

Early the next morning, before the loggers started up their chainsaws, we packed up and escaped downriver, where the low-lying

White River

Legend:
- **S** Start
- **F** Finish
- ----- Route
- ●—● Portage
- **P975m** Portage length
- ▲ Campsite
- ⫴ Falls
- = Rapids/Swifts
- ◣ Dam/Lift-over

Map labels: WHITE LAKE PROVINCIAL PARK, White Lake, Giles Bay, White River Dam, P65m, P225m, P405m, P95m, P480m, P95m, Pickerel Bay, P80m, P630m Chicagonce Portage (Angler Falls), P70m, P75m, P600m, SW, White River, P580m

Scale: 0 1 2 3 4 km

banks of cedar, poplar and birch are replaced by steep knolls topped with pinhead-shaped spruce. Here, the river takes another dramatic tumble off the Shield at Angler Falls.

John and I could hear the low, unmistakable roar of the waterfalls seconds before we nosed our canoe around a bend in the river. The banks quickly closed in and a small swift was formed ahead of the brink of the cascade, where the entire river flushed through and left only a fine mist floating skyward.

For a brief second, John and I pondered the idea of lining the canoe through the swift to cut some length off the 630-meter portage running along the left bank. As we caught sight of a wooden cross, erected years ago by the partner of a kayaker who drowned at this spot, we quickly made our decision and beached the canoe right at the marked take-out point.

Before carrying over the portage, we took a close look at the cross, which read, "Jerry Cesar / Born 11-26-40 / Drowned here 5-17-75 / Always at home in the bush / Now at home in Heaven / He believed in Jesus Christ."

From the steep put-in at the base of Angler Falls, you must navigate a quick swift before unloading your canoe once again, to portage a total of 600 meters along the left bank.

After a brief paddle, two short portages (70 m and 75 m) are marked on the right. The first avoids a runnable swift. The second, however, must be used to work around a maze of ledge rock and bellowing whitewater.

The next obstacle, a stunted falls, has a 580-meter portage to the right with an excellent sandy campsite at the put-in.

It was here that our uneventful voyage down the White took a turn for the worse. Clear skies quickly blackened without

warning and torrential rain soaked us to the skin. Feeling miserable from the surprise downpour, we decided to erect camp on the sandy point at the end of the portage, and to help boost our morale, I opened a can of oysters to snack on before dinner. Little did we know that each slimy marine mollusk we swallowed was toxic. Neil was the first to feel the ill effects of severe food poisoning, and as the trip progressed, so did the group's acute gastrointestinal condition. To make matters worse, the rain continued throughout the next few days, soaking every roll of toilet paper we had, except for one. By working together as a team, however, we pulled through the hellish ordeal and we were even able to enjoy the rest of the trip.

Between the last set of rapids and Umbata Falls (about 25 km) the course of the river is somewhat uneventful except for a few swifts before and after where the Oskabukuta River meets up with the White, and two sets of rapids just ahead of the falls. Both sets have portages (170 m and 150 m) marked to the right that make use of the Umbata Road.

Umbata Falls is awe-inspiring. We could hear the muted rumble of water plunging downhill from over a mile away. As you approach the monstrous cascade, the current seems to slacken, as though the water was resting up before it gathered force and then leaped down into the gorge below. Our group found ourselves inching our canoes along the north side of the river well before the take-out.

Take note that 2010 marked the completion of the "run-of-the-river" dam project at

Umbata Falls by the Ojibwa of Pic River First Nations. It's profiled as a 'free-flowing" system and that the falls and gorge were left "relatively" untouched. However, much of the water is still diverted, so expect a dramatic change in the view you get compared to what other paddlers were lucky enough to experience in the past. The Umbata Falls portage, measuring 2,400 meters starts at a very steep embankment and then follows alongside the Umbata Road. Near its end, the road comes close to a hydro line and heads back to the river. The put-in is just downstream from where a bridge crosses the White River. A trail was established after the completion of the dam from the base of the portage for paddlers to view the 100-meter falls.

Pukaskwa National Park is just below Umbata Falls, and it seemed that the moment we passed the government sign indicating the border of the federal park, wildlife became more abundant: curious gray jays perched themselves on tops of spruce trees to watch us drift by, sandpipers fluttered from rock to rock along the banks, a bald eagle soared overhead and a moose made an appearance.

The landscape grows more rugged here, and as the high rocky banks thick with coniferous forest closed in, it seemed each turn in the river revealed another cascade.

A total of five falls can be counted in Pukaskwa before the White drains into Lake Superior. The first three are avoided by portages on the right bank (350 m, 300 m and 95 m). Each of these portages is extremely steep and rugged, with piles of driftwood cluttering up every put-in.

The two final sets of falls are portaged on the left bank (215 m and 690 m), where the Pukaskwa Coastal Hiking Trail runs parallel to the river. Be aware that at the take-out of the last portage there are three trails branching out in different directions. The portage (named Chigamiwinigum Portage) heads directly up the hill, but it's worth your while to take time out to follow the hiking trail to the right. The path leads to a footbridge that crosses a deep-cut gorge in the river.

Less than an hour's paddle from Chigamiwinigum Portage, the White River drains into the expanse of Lake Superior.

When our group paddled out the mouth of the White, it seemed as if we had passed through a gateway into some type of dream world. The lake, notorious for its deadly wind and waves, was as smooth as a duck pond. The sky, however, was marked with an assortment of cloud formations: stratus, nimbostratus and cumulonimbus—all of which indicate an approaching thunderstorm. The paddle up along the coast to Hattie Cove takes approximately two hours, and we were forced to decide whether to take advantage of the calm before the storm or wait and hope that the lake would be smooth again the next day. Experience told us that the likelihood of having two calm days in a row out on Lake Superior was minimal so we voted to tempt our luck, and headed north.

For the first hour things went relatively well; we stuck close to shore, back behind the islands of Picture Rock Harbour. Then we reached the southern lip of Playter Harbour, where we were forced to cut across the width of the inlet to Campbell Point, a sheer wall of granite where beaching a canoe would be literally impossible. By looking at the topographic map, however, we figured that once we rounded the rocky point we would be safe among the islands of Pulpwood Harbour, just south of the entrance to Hattie Cove.

Ten minutes after breaking away from Picture Rock Harbour our canoes began fighting a slight choppiness—not much, but enough to give us a sense of our vulnerability. We began paddling harder. There were no lackadaisical strokes; we dug our paddle blades deep into the frigid waters for maximum effect. Campbell Point was really quite close, but to us, wrapped up in a state of near panic, it seemed to hang in the distance like a desert mirage.

By the time we rounded Campbell Point all our energy had been drawn, and we were forced to stop paddling between the rock cliff and the islands of Pulpwood Harbour. But as we drifted offshore, a thick fog dropped down—a reminder that the lake was still in full control of our destinies.

As the murky vapor cloaked everything around us, the group's whereabouts became dependent on my compass skills. Twenty minutes of paddling and a bearing of 56 degrees lead us to the sandy beach of Hattie Cove Campground, seconds before a fresh breeze blew in a major storm front that lasted three full days.

We were safe! Looking back to the perils of previous trips—a bear encounter on the Missinaibi River, almost swamping at the foot of Graveyard Rapids on the Spanish, weathering out hurricane winds under a collapsed tent on Algonquin's Big Trout Lake—I can say that paddling Lake Superior just ahead of an approaching storm was the only time I felt my life was in jeopardy. The idea of being tossed into the deadly cold water and then bashed against sheer rock was truly frightening. In retrospect I've come to realize that my good fortune was not that my skills as a canoeist got me to Hattie Cove, but rather that the spirits of this freshwater inland sea allowed me to survive that day.

LONGEST PORTAGE 2,240 meters

FEE An interior permit must be purchased for traveling through Pukaskwa National Park. To contact Pukaskwa National Park Service, phone 807-229-0801. Upon completion of your trip you must sign out at the park visitor center in Hattie Cove or at the registration booth at the mouth of the Pic River.

ALTERNATIVE ACCESS You can start from Negwazu Lake, located east of Highway 17, reached by way of a dirt road from Obatanga Provincial Park.

ALTERNATIVE ROUTE If you're interested in canoeing the entire river you can begin at Negwazu Lake. Highway 17 and the Canadian Pacific Railway (CPR) also cross the river at several points. For information on the CPR, contact VIA Rail at 1-800-361-1235. It's important to note, however, that water levels on the upper section of the river, before White Lake, can be extremely low, and at the present time it's poorly maintained by the Ministry of Natural Resources.

OUTFITTERS
Naturally Superior Adventurers
R.R. 1 Lake Superior
Wawa, ON, P0S 1K0
1-800-203-9092 or 705-856-2939
www.naturallysuperior.com

FOR MORE INFORMATION
Ontario Ministry of Natural Resources
705-856-2396
www.mnr.gov.on.ca

MAPS The Ministry of Natural Resources has produced a canoe route pamphlet covering the entire river: *White River Canoe Route.*

TOPOGRAPHIC MAPS
42 D/9 & 42 C/12

GPS COORDINATES
48.696192, -85.642015

Upper Missinaibi River

🕐 10 to 12 days   🛶 29 portages   ●--- ● 236 km   **Moderate to advanced experience running whitewater.**

D URING MY COLLEGE years in Sault Ste. Marie I spent many weekends chumming around with Jim Black, a fellow student. We were notorious for cutting class early on Friday and driving north to visit Jim's grandfather, who lived on the reserve just west of Wawa.

Much of our time was spent roaming the bush on foot, helping Jim's grandfather check his trapline. However, there were those special occasions when the grandfather would tie his old cedar-strip canoe on top of Jim's rusted-out pickup and take us somewhere for a paddle.

One memorable trip was on the Michipicoten River. We left the screaming gulls of Lake Superior behind and headed upstream, battling a continually changing current caused by a series of hydroelectric dams obstructing the Michipicoten's flow. It seemed that we spent more time portaging around cement structures and passing under humming hydro lines than soaking up the wilds of the waterway.

We made camp overnight on the river, and Jim's grandfather told us countless stories of his travels up the Michipicoten to visit the Missinaibi River, a place where he believed the land still remained wild and the spirits could still flow free.

The next morning, before we packed up and headed back down to Lake Superior, I made a promise to Jim's grandfather to return one day to paddle the river he spoke of the night before. And for 10 days in July, eight years later, I took a solo pilgrimage in search of the spirits of the Missinaibi.

It still is possible for a canoeist to travel right from Lake Superior by way of the Michipicoten River and then down the entire length of the Missinaibi and Moose Rivers to the salty waters of James Bay. However, most canoeists only have time to paddle either the upper section (236 km), from the town of Missanabie to Mattice, or the lower section (316 km), from Mattice to Moosonee.

I had an ongoing debate with my canoeing cronies before I left on my solo trip, on what was the best section of river to travel. Many canoeists said that they would choose to paddle the lower section so as to view the incredibly scenic Thunderhouse Falls and to be able to bless the bow of their canoe in the Arctic waters of James Bay. Other paddlers

Upper Missinaibi River

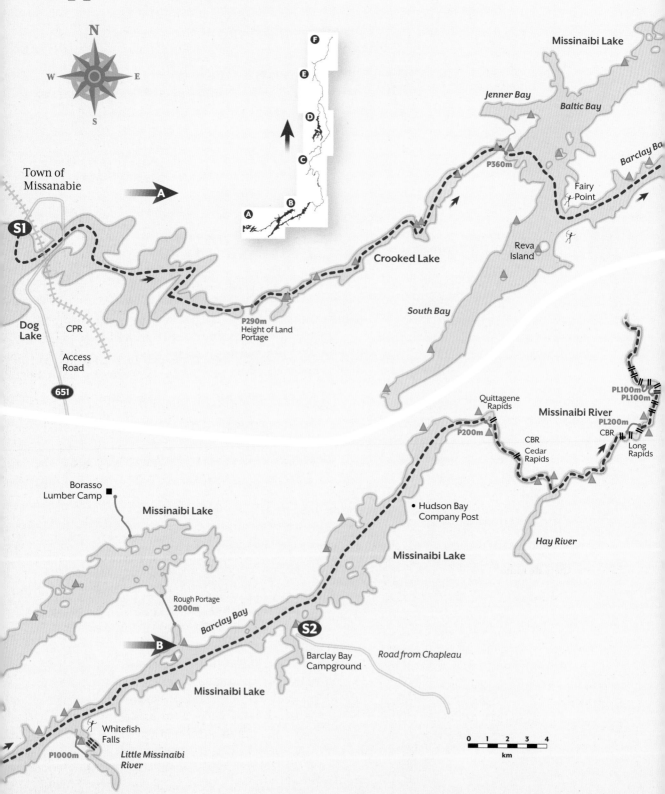

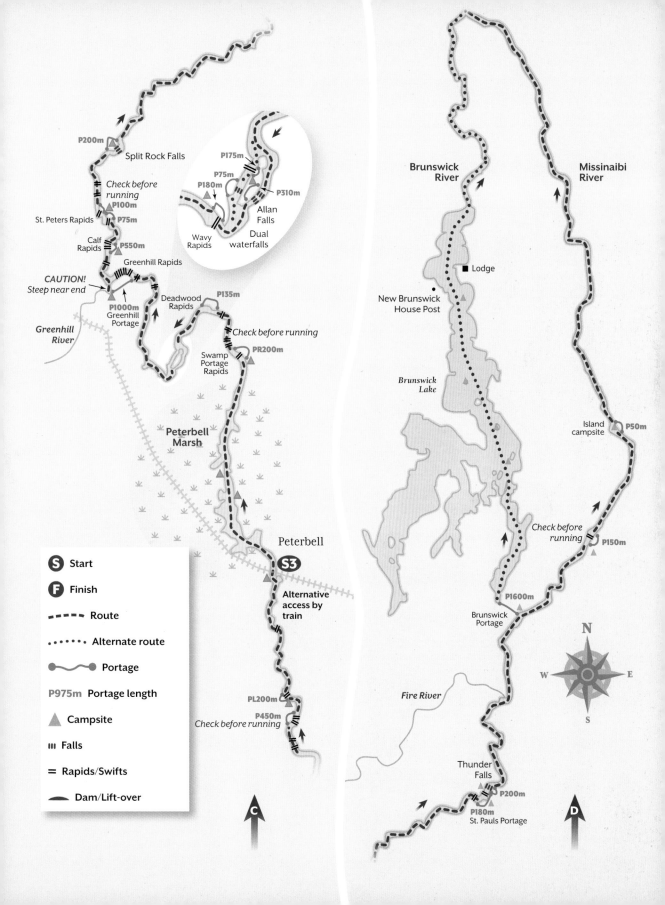

P200m
Split Rock Falls

Check before running

St. Peters Rapids
P100m
P75m

Calf Rapids
P550m

Greenhill Rapids

CAUTION!
Steep near end

P1000m
Greenhill Portage

Deadwood Rapids

P135m

Greenhill River

Check before running

Swamp Portage Rapids
PR200m

Peterbell Marsh

P175m
P75m
P180m
P310m
Allan Falls
Dual waterfalls
Wavy Rapids

Peterbell

S3

Alternative access by train

PL200m
P450m
Check before running

C

Legend

S Start

F Finish

- - - - Route

• • • • Alternate route

●—● Portage

P975m Portage length

▲ Campsite

||| Falls

= Rapids/Swifts

▬ Dam/Lift-over

Brunswick River

Missinaibi River

■ Lodge

New Brunswick House Post

Brunswick Lake

Island campsite
P50m

Check before running
P150m

P1600m
Brunswick Portage

Fire River

Thunder Falls
P200m
P180m
St. Pauls Portage

N
W **E**
S

D

Upper Missinaibi River (continued)

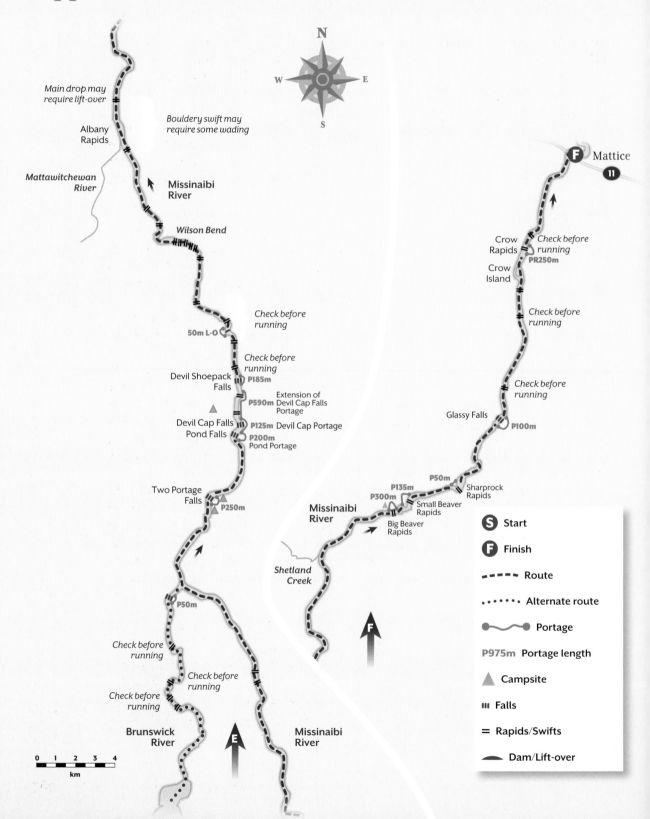

Main drop may require lift-over

Albany Rapids

Mattawitchewan River

Bouldery swift may require some wading

Missinaibi River

Wilson Bend

Check before running

50m L-O

Check before running

Devil Shoepack Falls   **P185m**

P590m   Extension of Devil Cap Falls Portage

Devil Cap Falls   **P125m** Devil Cap Portage
Pond Falls   **P200m**
                   Pond Portage

Two Portage Falls

P250m

Missinaibi River

Shetland Creek

P300m   **P135m**   **P50m**   Sharprock Rapids

Small Beaver Rapids

Big Beaver Rapids

Glassy Falls   **P100m**

Crow Rapids   *Check before running*
                    PR250m
Crow Island

Check before running

Check before running

F Mattice   **11**

Check before running
Check before running
Check before running

Brunswick River

Missinaibi River

E

F

0 1 2 3 4
km

Legend	
S	Start
F	Finish
- - - - -	Route
· · · · ·	Alternate route
●——●	Portage
P975m	Portage length
▲	Campsite
⊨⊨⊨	Falls
=	Rapids/Swifts
—	Dam/Lift-over

N W E S

preferred the upper section for its more technically challenging rapids.

It was the upper section I chose, and not out of a desire to playboat in whitewater, but for a more practical reason; the upper section of the Missinaibi happens to be far easier and cheaper to access than the lower.

Of course, like any other great river canoe route, the upper Missinaibi still requires a lengthy car shuttle. To allow more time spent paddling on the river, I opted to pay Missinaibi Outfitters to store my vehicle while I was on the river and then have it waiting for me at the take-out spot in the town of Mattice on my scheduled arrival date.

After considering the countless places to begin the trip on the upper Missinaibi, I found the best access point that met my needs was beside the hotel in the village of Missanabie. The hotel is on the far side of town, near Dog Lake. To reach the small hamlet, drive to the end of Highway 651, approximately 50 kilometers north of Highway 101.

I met Owen, the owner of Missinaibi Outfitters, at the put-in spot just before 9:00 a.m., after spending the night at Shoals Provincial Park along Highway 101. By 9:30 a.m. I had loaded up my canoe and handed over my truck keys to Owen, who, thinking that it would be wise to warn me of the increase in bear problems along the river, marked the whereabouts of two reports of nuisance bruins on my map before wishing me good luck and getting into my pickup.

Owen's warning did nothing to ease the bear phobia I had been plagued with ever since I heard a report on the radio of a bear attack in the same area only two days before. The 30-second news story told of a young geologist who, while crouching over to collect a soil sample, had been decapitated by a single blow of the bruin's paw. Apparently the predacious bear stalked the man, mistaking him for a moose calf—a dietary option for the bears when blueberry bushes become sterile from a late frost.

After waving a final goodbye to Owen I slipped into the canoe and headed east along Dog Lake, keeping an eye out for irritable bruins wandering the woods suffering from hunger cramps.

At the far eastern end of Dog Lake I portaged over a 290-meter path to Crooked Lake. Approximately three-quarters of the way along Crooked Lake, where the lake makes a sudden twist southeast, a number of good campsites can be found.

Paddling from Dog Lake to the far end of Crooked Lake was a long stretch for the first day out, making dinner my first priority.

Early the next morning I took a short paddle from my campsite over to the portage heading from Crooked Lake into Missinaibi Lake. At the end of the 360-meter well-worn trail, I signed the MNR registration book and headed out into the headwaters of the 245,000-acre provincial park.

Missinaibi Lake, its three main bays shaped like an elongated Y, stretches over 40 kilometers in length. It takes at least two days to reach the mouth of the Missinaibi River, to the northeast. A canoeist can spend an entire week exploring the lake. Visit Reva Island off South Bay to view the 350-year-old stands of white and red pine; fish for walleye at the base of Whitefish Falls; paddle upriver on the Little Missinaibi to explore the kettle formations decorated with unusual pictographs; or venture into the more isolated Baltic Bay to hike inland to the old Borasso lumber camp.

If your time is limited you may not have the opportunity to visit the lumber camps, the Little Missinaibi River or Reva Island. But Fairy Point should not be missed. This sheer granite cliff is adorned with over a hundred Native pictographs.

I made the hasty decision to put up for the night among fellow campers at the main campground at Barclay Bay. The next morning I was on the water bright and early, well before my neighbors attracted the local bear population with breakfast smells, and reached the sandy narrows at the far northeastern tip of Missinaibi Lake in time for brunch. I beached my canoe and set up my cookstove to fry up some bannock on the site of the historic Hudson Bay post. My break was short-lived after bear sighting number five. This time the bear was munching on a patch of clover less than a hundred meters from my beached canoe (I have a photo to prove it). I quickly leaped into my canoe, paddled through the last stretch of the grassy shallows and began heading downriver on the Missinaibi.

Shortly after where the waterway begins, the river makes a dramatic turn to the right. Here the first portage of the river section allows you to avoid running Quittagene Rapids. The 200-meter trail is marked along the right bank, just after a washed-out dam and bridge left behind from the logging era.

From Quittagene Rapids to Barrel Rapids, where I spent my first night camped on the river, the character of the Missinaibi is mixed. The slow-moving current, gurgling past cedar-lined banks and the marshy mouth of the Hay River, is interrupted by six sets of rapids and a number of swifts—all of which are runnable except possibly the fifth set, where the river rounds a bend. Two 100-meter portages, following in succession, can be found along the left bank.

By the time I reached Barrel Rapids, there

was just enough light in the day to scramble up the beginning of the muddy 200-meter portage along the left bank, pitch my tent and crawl inside my cozy sleeping bag.

Next day after a breakfast of hot cereal and "true grit" coffee, I completed the Barrel Rapids portage during a heavy downpour of hailstones. Fortunately the storm didn't last, and I spent the afternoon floating down toward the expanse of Peterbell Marsh, dangling my socks over the gunwale to dry.

Make sure to slow your pace as you paddle through Peterbell Marsh. This complex wetland, home to a host of wildlife, and run through with numerous channels, is breaking away from the main waterway as a result of the current and the efforts of beaver. Floating down that smooth water, I startled black ducks and sandpipers as my canoe rounded the slower bends, watched a bald eagle soar majestically overhead and spied on a cow moose and her calf feeding in an isolated bog.

To me, the most awe-inspiring sight of the Peterbell Marsh is the clear transition from open wetland to dry, ridgetop habitat. In many places the flat horizon of swamp is broken by bluffs clad in pine and birch, providing excellent sites to pitch a tent.

Eventually, the current quickens its pace as it heads for Swamp Rapids. A 200-meter portage is located along the right bank, just past an old trapper's cabin. The next five sets of rapids can be run or lined, but be cautious at the fifth, called Deadwood Rapids. You should take the 135-meter portage to the right if you think the run is questionable.

Downriver from Deadwood Rapids the river splits into two channels, washing around Allan Island. The right channel is broken up by a logjam and a pile of jagged rocks. A 175-meter portage works its way around the

blockade of logs to the left, and a 75-meter portage may be necessary on the right to avoid the rock garden if water levels are low.

The left channel has only a single, 310-meter portage, located to the right of a stunted cascade (Allan Falls). A perfect campsite can also be found at the take-out, making it the better choice of the two channels if it is late in the day.

To a whitewater fanatic, the next section of the river would be the most challenging and exciting. Traveling solo, however, I opted to keep to the grueling portages. The first is a 180-meter path to the right of Wavy Rapids. The name is appropriate, as there are high-standing waves gushing down the gut of the rapid. If you chance the run, be prepared to take some water over the bow.

Greenhill Rapids is next. I bypassed this section of whitewater by using the 1,000-meter portage to the left. The carry through the bush is a lengthy and difficult one, but the rapid itself is encased by steep banks on either

side, making it impossible to turn tail once you begin the run.

The next portage is marked to the right of Calf Rapids. The previous year, hurricane winds had left the entire 550-meter trail cluttered with fallen trees. I was physically exhausted by the time I reached the next set—St. Peters Rapids—and opted to avoid using the 100-meter portages both on the right. I cautiously steered between half-submerged boulders, grinding the bottom of the canoe only once while trying to dodge the rocky shallows on one of the two swifts that follow shortly after the main drop.

After St. Peter's Rapids comes Split Rock Falls. A 200-meter portage with a scenic campsite near the put-in point is marked to the left of this stunted cascade. After a day of slogging along portages, I was eager to carry my gear over to the campsite and finish the day early. As I crested a hill midway along the portage, however, I startled a bear. The beast took off through the bush, but the sighting (number six if you're still counting) gave me second thoughts about camping at Split Rock, and I ended up paddling another 10 kilometers downriver to set up camp at Thunder Falls.

Just before the portage, marked on the right of Thunder Falls, there are two easy swifts that must be navigated through. Here, it's important to stay to the right bank until you reach the small bay where the 180-meter path, called St. Paul's Portage, begins. A small campsite is marked directly above the muddy embankment at the take-out. However, it's best to complete the portage and paddle to a nicer sandy tent site across the river.

Almost immediately following Thunder Falls, another portage (200 m) makes its way along the right of a second, less dramatic falls.

After the last drop in the river, the mood of the waterway changes, and it is seemingly still for a great distance. Only by peering down at the bent grasses rooted in the riverbed could one tell that the water was still alive.

Farther downriver, past where the Fire River joins up with the Missinaibi, a single strip of red ribbon marks the 1,600-meter portage to Brunswick Lake. From this point you must make the decision to either stay with the river or carry over to visit Brunswick Lake.

If you choose to portage into Brunswick Lake, be prepared to get your feet wet. The last 100 meters or so is cursed with knee-deep boot-sucking swamp ooze. But the lake itself, with its pine island campsites, can be the highlight of the trip.

To exit Brunswick Lake, paddle north, following the Brunswick River. All the rapids along the river are runnable, thanks to past voyageurs who dredged out a clear channel for their large trade canoes, all except for a thigh-high falls close to where the Brunswick River joins up with the Missinaibi. A 50-meter portage can be found to the right of the cascade.

I chose to avoid Brunswick Lake and stay with the river—not because of the muddy portage, but rather due to bear number seven, sighted at the take-out.

This stretch of the river is clogged with low-lying cedar rooted along the banks, and the odd swift en route to break up the relatively soft-flowing current. An island set in the middle of the waterway, approximately 10 kilometers downstream from the Brunswick portage, makes an excellent place to camp. To reach the site, take the 50-meter portage along the right bank from the put-in.

From the island campsite to the place where an unsightly iron bridge appears, the river seems somewhat monotonous. Only two fast swifts, halfway along, propel your canoe farther downstream.

Then, beyond the mouth of the Brunswick River, a 250-meter portage to the right works its way around Two Portage Falls. There is an adequate campsite along the portage, but I prefer the site at Pond Falls. Keep a watchful eye on the current here. The 200-meter portage along the right bank begins dangerously close to the brink of the falls.

The long stretch of whitewater below Pond Falls can be a graveyard for canoes. Aptly named, the first drop, Devil Cap Falls, can be portaged (125 m) to the right. A 590-meter portage, also along the right bank, follows. The path allows you to avoid running the rock-strewn Devil Shoepack Falls. Two short cascades remain; the first with a 185-meter portage to the right and the second, a 50-meter lift-over to the left.

Downstream the river's quickened pace remains constant, making its way around Wilson Bend, and then for 3 kilometers, through a boulder garden called Albany Rapids. Here, you must slowly maneuver your way like an Olympic skier on a slalom run. Only the last swift needs special attention, and you may wish to lift-over here. (More than one canoeist has drowned at the deadly sluice-hole at the base drop.)

The geology of the area begins to change after Albany Rapids. Big Beaver Rapids, Small Beaver Rapids, Sharprock Rapids and Glassy Falls all flow over fragmented bedrock. The sharp-edged souvenirs from the early Precambrian era make this one of the most scenic stretches en route, but can also make your canoe's hull seem fragile as an eggshell. Portages from the first three sets of rapids are along the left bank (300 m, 135 m and a steep 50 m). The Glassy Falls portage (100 m) is to the right and ends at a beautiful sandy beach.

A couple of shallow swifts and the navigable Crow Rapids (where yet another bear crossed my path as it swam downstream, only a stone's throw from my bow) bring the only interruptions in the slackened river current before you reach the riverside municipal park at Mattice. It is here that you will begin to notice small signs of the upcoming town.

The government dock at Mattice marked the end of my incredible adventure down the Missinaibi, and as I enjoyed a fresh coffee at the local restaurant, waiting for Owen from Missinaibi Outfitters to arrive with my truck, I glanced through the logbook the café has on hand for canoeists to sign after their trip down the river. I went through three cups of coffee and two slices of pie before I figured out what to jot down beside my signature. I wrote: "The spirits are still alive and well on the Missinaibi!"

LONGEST PORTAGE 1,600 m (Brunswick Lake) and 1,000 m (Greenhill Rapids)

FEE You must purchase a permit through Missinaibi Provincial Park before paddling the river. A campsite permit must also be purchased at the gatehouse if you decide to stay over at the Barclay Bay Campground on Missinaibi Lake. As well, a moderate fee is charged for the shuttle service.

ALTERNATIVE ACCESS Canoeists may access the route at either the Barclay Bay Campground on Missinaibi Lake or at the Peterbell train bridge. To reach Barclay Bay Campground, however, you must drive north of Chapleau on an 88-kilometer gravel road, and it is a pain to organize a shuttle from the campground. Accessing the river at Peterbell by train can also be a bother. The scheduled times of the train are sketchy, and in the future the train may not even stop at Peterbell.

ALTERNATIVE ROUTE If you drive north of Chapleau to the Barclay Bay Campground on Missinaibi Lake, you can spend an entire week exploring the surrounding area.

OUTFITTERS
Missinaibi Headwaters Outfitters
Box 1148
Chapleau, ON, P0M 1K0
855-226-6366
www.missinaibi.com

FOR MORE INFORMATION
Ministry of Natural Resources
705-864-1710
www.mnr.gov.on.ca

MAPS The Ministry of Natural Resources has produced a canoe route pamphlet: *Missinaibi River Canoe Route*. Hap Wilson's guidebook, *Missinaibi: Journey to the Northern Sky*, published by the Canadian Recreational Canoeing Association, is also an excellent reference.

TOPOGRAPHIC MAPS
42 C/8, 42 B/5, 42 B/6, 42 B/11, 42 B/14, 42 G/3, 42 G/6 & 42 G/11W

GPS COORDINATES
48.311748, -84.086999

Abitibi River

 2 days   None   ●----● 40 kilometers   **Some canoe-tripping skills would be an asset.**

THE ABITIBI IS a historic canoe route—but that doesn't mean you can't paddle it in a kayak. That was the boat I chose for my first trip down the river. Joining me was outfitter Rick Isaacson of Howling Wolf Expeditions, an expert kayaker who promised to teach me how to kayak ahead of a race I had casually signed up for. Rick is based in the town of Smooth Rock Falls, which is west of Cochrane, off Highway 11. From Smooth Rock we drove north on

Highway 634. It's about an hour's drive (74 km) to the access point near Abitibi Canyon Generating Station.

The dam at Abitibi Canyon, built in the early 1930s, is an engineering masterpiece. A village made up of 70 houses, a church and a school was erected beside it, but today nothing remains of the town—except the ghosts that are rumored to haunt the dam. It's said that over 200 workers became entombed in the concrete of the dam during its construction. A monument titled "The Sons of Martha" commemorates those lost workers. A second plaque honors 10 hydro employees who were killed in 1976 when their plane crashed into a nearby hydro tower.

The route's put-in is on the eastern side of the dam. Rick drove us over the colossal structure that holds back Trappers Creek and then turned left onto a secondary road to reach the access point downriver of the dam.

Day one saw us floating with the gentle current, stopping along the way to explore the old New Post trading station, which is marked by a clearing along the eastern shoreline, now taken over by raspberry bushes. This Hudson Bay Company trading post was established

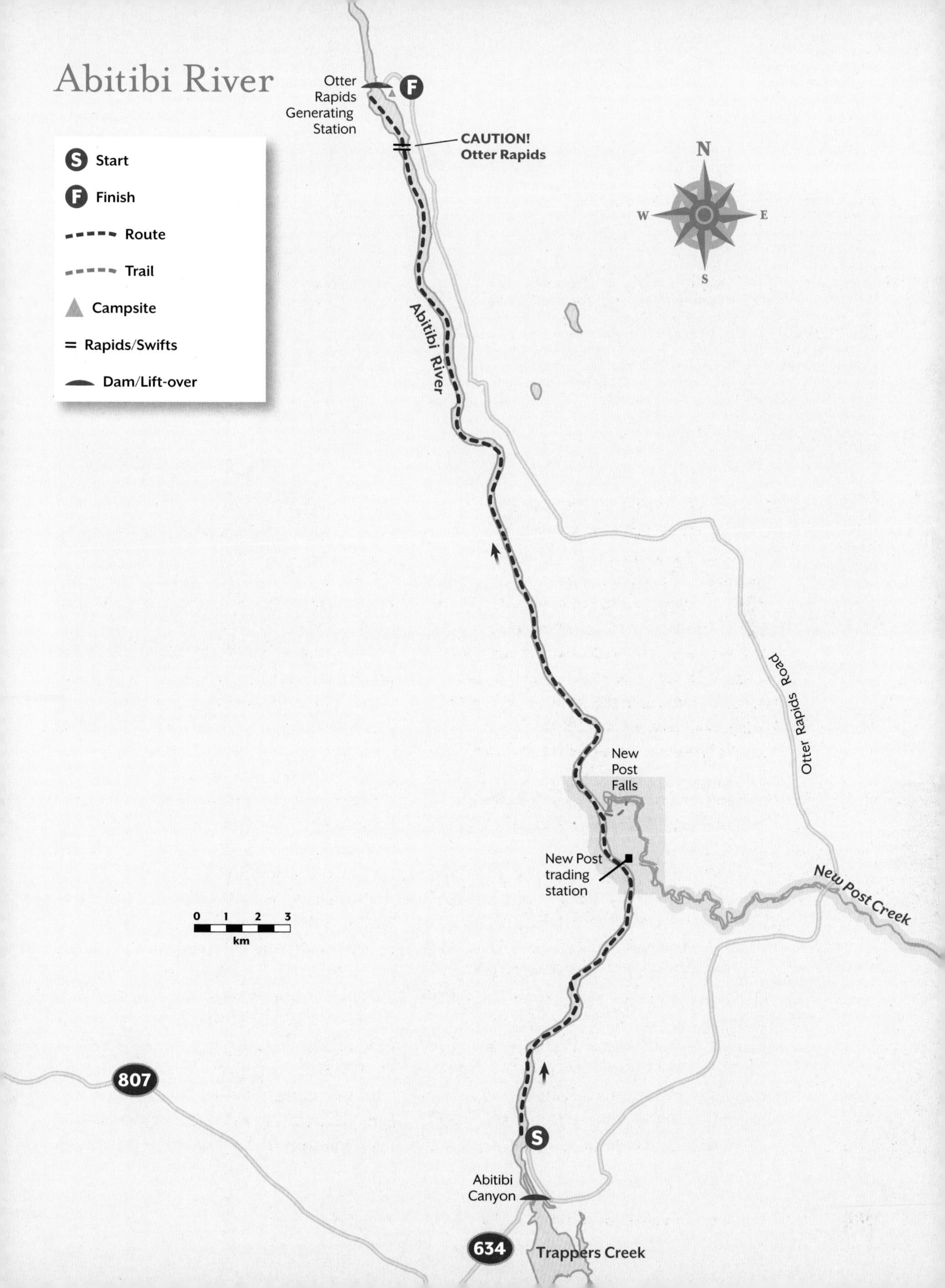

Abitibi River

Legend

S Start

F Finish

- - - - Route

- - - - Trail

▲ Campsite

= Rapids/Swifts

⏜ Dam/Lift-over

Otter Rapids Generating Station

F

**CAUTION!
Otter Rapids**

Abitibi River

N

W   E

S

Otter Rapids Road

New Post Falls

New Post trading station

New Post Creek

0 1 2 3
km

807

S

Abitibi Canyon

634   Trappers Creek

here in 1857 to provide a more suitable place for local First Nations to trade with European settlers than Temiscaming, which is farther to the south. A long set of rapids existed here prior to the construction of the dam, and the post was placed at the end of the portage used to avoid the fast water. When the railway was extended north in 1924, New Post was abandoned.

Not much remains of the Hudson Bay Company manager's house, the store and the two smaller buildings built to accommodate Cree who traded at the post. However, farther back in the bush, among a stand of poplar and spruce, is a cemetery. Stone markers and wrought-iron fences mark the European graves and cedar planks mark the Cree sites.

We made camp for the first evening near the base of New Post Falls—an incredibly scenic cascade and the highlight of the trip. Because the Abitibi rises and falls dramatically due to it being fully controlled by hydro dams, we strategically placed our tents higher up on a sand bar to avoid them being flushed downriver when the water rose in the morning.

We took time to check out New Post Falls early the next day before continuing our journey. A steep and muddy 250-meter trail on the right side of the falls allows you to get a good view of the 120-meter cascade. A slab of rock juts out from the initial drop and from there you can look down at where water from the Little Abitibi River, which has flowed along New Post Creek, tumbles into the silt-laden Abitibi.

Rick has some concerns over the potential damming of New Post Falls. It's on the list as a possible future power station. He's made his concerns known to the provincial government, and his passion for protecting this area has gained him allies with local Cree and Ojibway communities, politicians, hydro workers and Southern Ontario canoeists and kayakers. On past trips, as a representative of Lake Ontario Waterkeepers, he even guided Gord Downie and Robert F. Kennedy. His activism has also made him some enemies, but that comes with the territory, I guess.

After leaving the falls, we traveled downstream toward a second hydroelectric dam at Otter Rapids. This was our last stretch of river—a 25-kilometer run where the riverbank spreads out and the current gains momentum. A cluster of islands just before the Otter Rapids Generating Station breaks up the flow of the river and causes the current to boil up from beneath. Small swifts and large waves create an interesting but safe paddle the rest of the way downriver, and the landscape looks more like what you find along Georgian Bay.

The islands seem like a good place to camp; however, there's no tent site to be seen, and we ended up pitching our tents in a large clearing to the right of the dam. The take-out is to the left of the dam, so we had to haul our gear over to the opposite side. The road to the north ends here, but the railway that runs parallel to the Abitibi continues to Moosonee.

I've heard that some paddlers doing this route choose to flag down the train for a ride back to Fraserdale, near Abitibi Canyon. However, because we had shuttled a second vehicle to the take-out, the next morning we drove back south via Otter Rapids Road (a gravel road), which takes you past Abitibi Canyon and links to Highway 634. Rick and I had our kayak race in Timmins, called the Great Canadian Kayak Challenge, to get to. It was a long drive, and we arrived 20 minutes before the first heat of kayakers, called the Celebrity Challenge, paddled off the starting line. I was one of the chosen "celebrities," alongside the mayor, the police chief, the fire marshal, a couple of radio hosts and an assortment of city councilors. I quickly floated my kayak to the line, its hull still smeared with Abitibi mud. In the end I came in sixth, with the mayor just ahead of me. Not bad for a canoeist from Southern Ontario who had learned to kayak only two days before.

LONGEST PORTAGE This route has no portages, although I highly recommend you hike the 250-meter trail to view New Post Falls.

FEE The route travels through an unmanaged area and no fee structure is in place.

ALTERNATIVE ACCESS None

ALTERNATIVE ROUTE It is possible to paddle to New Post Falls and then back upriver to the access at Abitibi Canyon. Take note that the current is moderately strong and water levels do fluctuate.

OUTFITTERS
Howling Wolf Expeditions
705-338-2588 (ask for Rick)
www.howlingwolfexpeditions.com

FOR MORE INFORMATION
Ministry of Natural Resources
705-235-1300
www.mnr.gov.on.ca

TOPOGRAPHIC MAPS
42 I/11, 42 I/13 & 42 I/14

GPS COORDINATES
49.881381, -81.567869

Steel River Loop

🕐 8 to 10 days   🛶 16 portages   ●----● 157 km   **Moderate whitewater skills and advanced tripping skills needed for the portages and remoteness of route.**

I T WAS DIFFICULT to believe that the almost sheer slab of rock directly in front of us was actually the beginning of the Diablo Portage. It was not as if my wife and I thought that a wilderness trail named after Lucifer would be a walk in the park. In fact, everything Alana and I had heard and read before heading out on the Steel River, north of Lake Superior, had given us good reason to avoid this 1,000-meter portage, which immediately begins with an almost vertical cliff face.

In most cases, canoeists will choose to use a logging road north of Terrace Bay to access the main section of the river, reducing a 10-day trip to only five days and, at the same time, avoiding some of the most rugged topography en route. If you take the easy way out, however, you also have to organize a lengthy car shuttle—the plague of most river routes, one that I desperately try to avoid—instead of looping directly back to your vehicle. And besides, our pre-trip research also indicated that the first few days of the full 170-kilometer circuit allowed canoeists to travel through some of the most scenic landscape the province has to offer. Alana and I figured such a large chunk of wilderness was well worth portaging

through hell and back and decided to take on the infamous Diablo Portage despite the warnings of canoeists who had gone before us. After all, how bad could one portage really be?

The original access point for the Steel River Loop was the rail bridge close to the shore of Lake Superior. (Canadian Pacific Railway brochures of the 1890s advertised this route as a prime canoe destination.) But now canoeists use the government dock at the south end of Santoy Lake, located at the end of a gravel road leading in from Highway 17, 4.6 kilometers west of the highway bridge. The take-out for the Diablo Portage is actually 8 kilometers north on Santoy Lake, between two high mounds of rock and along the west shoreline. It's poorly marked by a strip of blue ribbon tied to an alder branch and the letter P spray-painted on the weathered trunk of an old cedar tree.

Our plan was to first haul our canoe and gear up the almost vertical section of the trail. Once we had everything up to the summit, Alana and I would then double-carry over what remained—a somewhat level but rugged path that worked through a steep-walled ravine for approximately 800 meters.

Steel River Loop

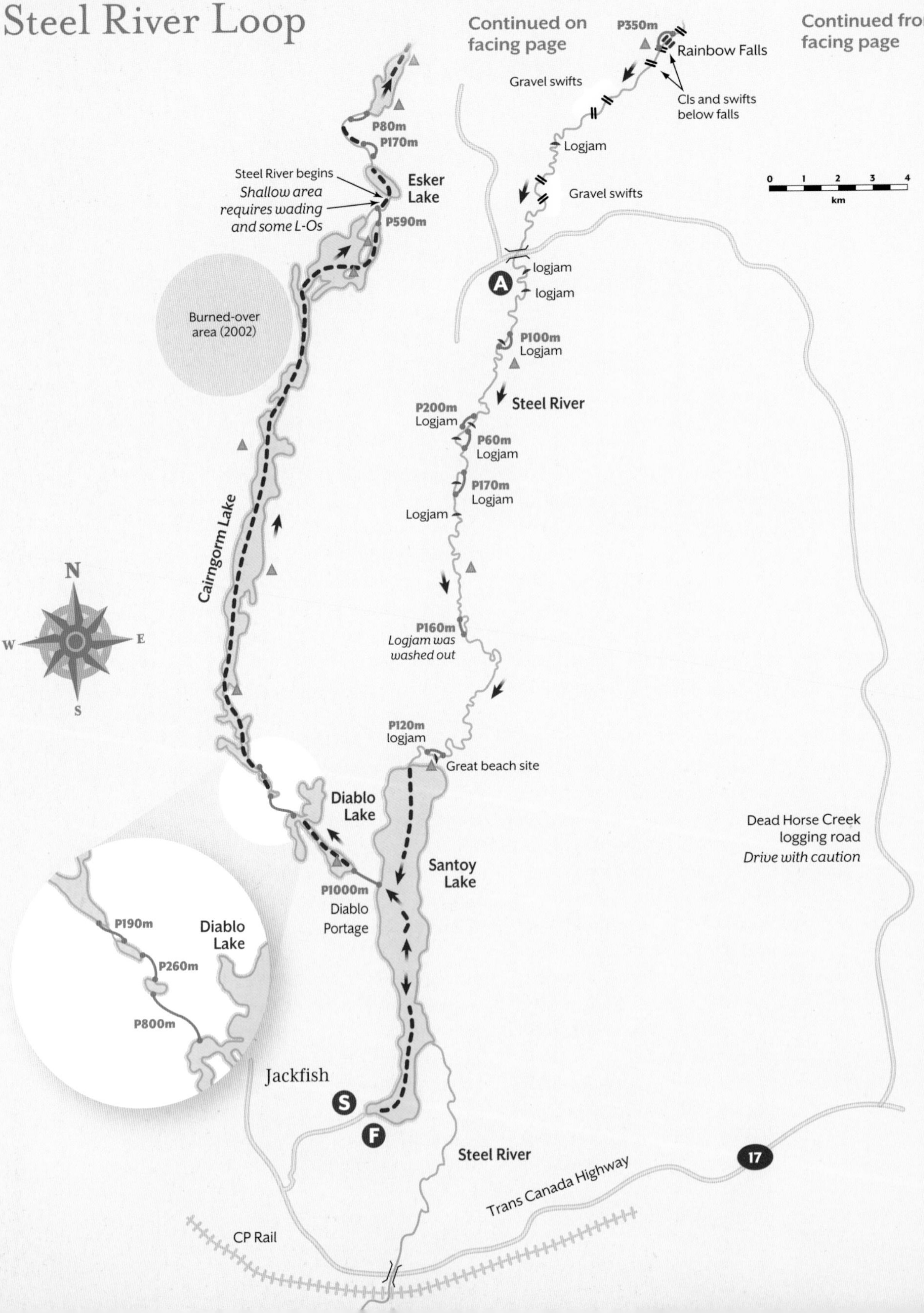

Continued on facing page

Continued from facing page

P350m

Rainbow Falls

Gravel swifts

CIs and swifts below falls

Logjam

Gravel swifts

P80m
P170m

Steel River begins
*Shallow area
requires wading
and some L-Os*

**Esker
Lake**

P590m

logjam

A

logjam

P100m
Logjam

Burned-over
area (2002)

P200m
Logjam

Steel River

P60m
Logjam

P170m
Logjam

Logjam

Cairngorm Lake

N
W   E
S

P160m
*Logjam was
washed out*

P120m
logjam

Great beach site

Dead Horse Creek
logging road
Drive with caution

Diablo
Lake

**Santoy
Lake**

P1000m
Diablo
Portage

Diablo Lake

P190m

P260m

Diablo
Lake

P800m

Jackfish

S

F

Steel River

Trans Canada Highway

17

CP Rail

0 1 2 3 4
km

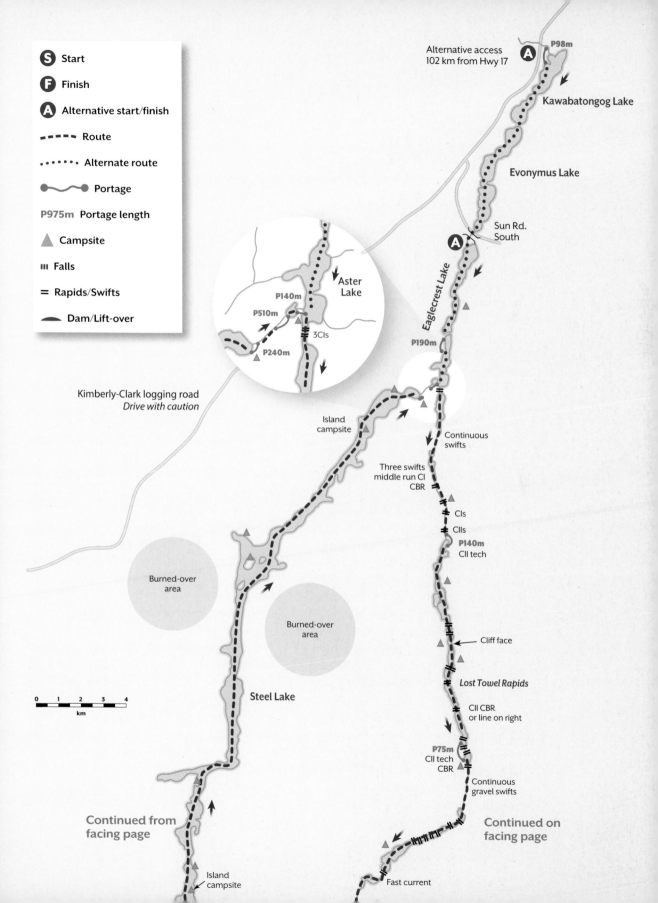

Legend

S Start

F Finish

A Alternative start/finish

- - - Route

· · · · · Alternate route

●━━━● Portage

P975m Portage length

▲ Campsite

ꠛ Falls

= Rapids/Swifts

⌒ Dam/Lift-over

P98m

Alternative access
102 km from Hwy 17

Kawabatongog Lake

Evonymus Lake

Sun Rd.
South

Eaglecrest Lake

Aster
Lake

P140m

P510m

P240m

3CIs

Kimberly-Clark logging road
Drive with caution

P190m

Island
campsite

Continuous
swifts

Three swifts
middle run CI
CBR

CIs

CIIs

P140m
CII tech

Burned-over
area

Burned-over
area

Cliff face

Lost Towel Rapids

CII CBR
or line on right

Steel Lake

P75m
CII tech
CBR

Continuous
gravel swifts

0 1 2 3 4
km

**Continued from
facing page**

**Continued on
facing page**

Island
campsite

Fast current

It sounded reasonable. But on any regular portage, walking with at least half your body weight strapped tight to your back is no easy task. Pulling yourself up a 30-degree slope, with loose rocks and fallen trees littering the path, is closer to suicide.

Somehow we managed to get the first two packs up. Even our hyper Springer spaniel, Bailey, coped with lugging her 10 days of dog kibble to the top. On the second trip, Alana had to deal with the largest of our packs, which she ended up dragging most of the way, and I had the darn canoe to carry. Although the weight of the boat was only 60 pounds (not bad for a plastic model), I felt uneasy blindly walking up a rock ledge with it balancing over my head.

I cursed a lot at first, hoping the profanity would give me some type of superhuman strength to help me along. But I finally had to give in about halfway. At this point the bow of the canoe was continuously ramming into the trail in front of me. Any forward motion became impossible and I had to resort to winching the canoe uphill by looping a rope around a solid tree at the top of the rise.

An hour later, Alana, Bailey and I had somehow successfully gathered everything to the top without serious injury. Thinking the worst was over, we immediately continued on to Diablo Lake. Little did we know the worst was yet to come.

It was apparent the trail had not been maintained for quite some time, as the correct path was extremely difficult to locate. Even when an obvious route was laid out in front of us, it was blocked either by a pile of jagged boulders or fallen trees. A network of well-hidden crevices also made walking with a full load of gear extremely hazardous.

Surprisingly, by the time the portage was completed we had had to deal with only three major mishaps: I fell into one of the trip holes and had the canoe come crashing down on me, leaving a large gash on my forehead; Alana took a tumble and managed to wedge her face between two sharp rocks (we renamed the trail Face-Plant Portage after the incident); and Bailey had a close encounter with a wild lynx while she rushed ahead of us on the portage (she's been afraid of our neighbor's cat ever since).

It took us half the day to complete the dreaded trip across Diablo, and once out on the lake we took the first campsite—a small island stuck out in the middle of the west bay. The three of us dragged our gear up to the site and, wherever we happened to collapse, Alana, Bailey and I took time out for a well-deserved snooze before cooking up dinner.

Obviously we were slow to start the next day. It wasn't until 10:00 a.m. that we began taking on the first of three consecutive portages leading into Cairngorm Lake. Fortunately the trail wasn't as steep as Diablo. But at times it seemed just as demanding. It measured a long 800 meters and, thanks again to poor maintenance over the years, the proper trail was extremely difficult to locate. The worst part, however, was getting to the put-in. For some reason the trail ended early, at least 200 meters away from the next lake, and Alana and I had to push our way through a bug-infested marsh to reach open water.

The second portage, found to the right of a small creek and measuring a seemingly long 260 meters, was easier to find but extremely wet in places. And once again a number of downed trees cluttered the path and turned what should have been a relatively easy carry-over into a frustrating and dangerous ordeal.

The take-out for the third portage (190 m)

was the most challenging to find. A beaver dam had covered the first section, and Alana and I searched both sides of the creek for half an hour before we discovered a faint path crossing over from right to left only 30 meters from the dam.

Eventually we reached Cairngorm Lake and were lucky enough to have a tailwind for the entire 16-kilometer crossing. Of course, with the south wind came rain. So rather than set up camp early on one of the islands clumped together at the far end of the lake, Alana and I decided to continue on to Steel Lake.

Cairngorm's far northern bay is where the Steel River begins, flushing itself over a moderate falls found at the northern tip of the lake. The portage, however, is nowhere near the falls. To reach the take-out for the

590-meter carry, you have to paddle to the far end of the northeast bay.

It's a surprisingly easy trail, at least when compared to what Alana and I had already endured. But the narrow stretch of river below the cascade was a different story. From here to Esker Lake we walked most of the way, wading over shallow riffles and lifting over several logjams blocking the stream.

Once on Esker Lake (an extremely scenic spot) we were forced to pull up on a beach along the north shore and spend some time orienting ourselves. The pamphlet supplied by the government made no sense here. It told of another portage (measuring 170 m and to the right of another cascade) at the far end of Esker Lake. The portage didn't exist, however, until at least another 15 to 20 minutes of paddling downriver, which made us second-guess everything the map told us from here on in.

It was quite late by the time we hauled all our gear over yet another rough carry-over. To make matters worse, it was still raining. And after consulting the map, we knew there was at least another hour of river paddling ahead, plus another portage to deal with (80 m and marked to the right of a small chute). By the looks of things, we would be setting up camp on the lower half of Steel Lake just before dark—cold, wet and very hungry.

Alana and I crawled out of the tent the next morning feeling a little anxious about the coming day's events. We had to cross the entire 30 kilometers of Steel Lake, which happens to be perfectly lined up with the prevailing winds. We also had to assume that the scenery wouldn't be all that exciting throughout the day, since most of Steel Lake's shoreline was burned to a crisp by a forest fire only two years earlier. Thinking back, though, paddling across this gigantic lake was actually a highlight of the trip. We were lucky enough to have a south wind help us down the lake and we made camp near the north end as early as 2:30 p.m. Seeing the effects of the fire was also a much more positive experience than we had expected. The new plant life growing thick beneath the blackened stumps was a true sign of how diverse this rugged landscape was. As well, only the tops of the ridges were severely scarred. Less exposed areas, where either stands of poplar and birch indicated deeper soil or where the fire had burned at night when the wind was down, proved how highly local a wildfire actually is.

The only negative part of the day was that it continued to rain down hard on us, especially when we stopped to make camp. Our site was on a small island that had little cover and the rain tarp had to be set up away from the fire pit. At first we would snuggle up under the tarp and then head over to the fire between bursts of rain to try and dry ourselves out. It wasn't long, however, before the constant drizzle put out our fire and the cold wind made sitting under the tarp unbearable. So we escaped to the tent and spent the night curled up in our sleeping bags, reading the books we'd packed along: Alana had chosen *A Walk in the Woods* by Bill Bryson and I had *The Tent Dwellers* by Albert Bigalow Paine. Reading about someone else's misadventures in the wilderness helped make our trip seem less of a disaster.

The storm continued through the night, and come morning it was difficult to leave the warmth of the sleeping bags to cook breakfast out in the rain. Actually, we had no need to get up early since the continuous south wind had left us at least two days ahead of schedule. But we were only three portages away from Aster Lake—the turnaround point of the trip—and were looking forward to beginning the river section.

It took us only an hour to pack up and paddle the remainder of Steel Lake. It was another two hours, however, before we'd finished the three portages leading to Aster Lake.

The first and third portages (240 and 140 m, marked on the right) were relatively easy. It was on the second portage (510 m and also marked on the right) that we spent most of our time. The trail worked its way alongside a steep ravine, where getting a good foothold was at times next to impossible. The ridge we were walking along had also been heavily burned over and, besides the normal problem of downed trees blocking the path, big patches of blueberry and raspberry bushes hid large sections of the trail.

It was beyond doubt that the entire area was a perfect feeding ground for black bears (we counted four piles of fresh bear scat directly at the take-out), and I actually considered lining the rapids instead. A quick look at the strength of the water being flushed through the chasm, however, confirmed that battling bear phobia along the portage would be far less stressful. We walked the trail making as much noise as possible.

Returning to the take-out for the second load, I spotted bear tracks beside our food barrel, tracks that weren't there before. I was amazed that nothing had been disturbed. His gait was straight, not irregular, and went directly toward a patch of ripe blueberries. The bear had obviously ignored whatever temptations our freeze-dried foods provided. (Having eaten the stuff for the previous four days, I couldn't blame him in the least).

Eventually we reached Aster Lake, turned south and almost immediately began running rapids. The whitewater was a welcome diversion. Only once did we have to portage, 140 meters to the left of a technical Class II rapid. The rest of the day was spent negotiating a combination of fast chutes, manageable Class Is, and easy swifts. In fact, the strong current remained consistent most of the way, squeezing itself through walls of granite or high gravel banks. Even when the river eventually broadened out, becoming more lake-like, the scenery still remained breathtaking. Jagged cliffs provided a backdrop to thick-forested banks, left untouched by the fire, and tiny islands of sand and gravel split the current in all directions. It was a place of awesome beauty, an absolute dreamscape.

We camped directly across from a spectacular cliff face and celebrated the day with an extra glass of wine. It continued to pour down rain while we set up camp, but at this point in the day nothing seemed to dampen our spirits. Even when Alana discovered we were missing two very important items from our pack—a bottle of biodegradable soap and our second roll of toilet paper—we calmly planned out a strategy. I replaced the soap with alcohol swabs from the first-aid kit and Alana began reading her paperback novel to provide surplus T.P.

Our second day on the river was just as exciting as the first. We spent a good part of the morning fishing between two swifts and caught a mess of walleye and pike. We also successfully ran two technical Class II rapids. Neither of them was marked on our map. But then again, none of the rapids were, and we were now used to checking out each and every bend in the river.

The first Class II was approximately 2 kilometers from the last swift. It looked possible to line along the right bank, but Alana and I chose to run straight through. The only disappointment was that we had forgotten to put away the towel Alana had left on top of the packs to dry and so had to name the set Lost Towel Rapids.

After already misplacing the soap and extra toilet paper during the trip, we thought losing the towel was quite a big deal—until we noticed a collection of someone else's camping gear washed up at the base of the rapid. One noticeable item was a T-shirt reading "I'm not as think as you drunk I am."

Not far downstream from Lost Towel Rapids were two more swifts and just beyond them was the second technical Class II rapid.

We checked the run from a rough 75-meter portage on the right and, after making the decision to attempt it, rushed back to the canoe and pushed off from shore. Just before

the drop I stood up to recheck our predetermined route while Alana gave Bailey the command to sit (the one thing our dog is good at is sitting still during rapids). It was all over quickly, and even though we took a totally different route than the one we had planned, only the stack of high waves at the end caused some concern. But we were able to slow the boat down just before smacking into the haystacks and kept most of the water out.

A quick current continued almost right up to the brink of Rainbow Falls. Here, the river opens up just ahead of the 20-meter drop, and Alana and I inched our canoe slowly toward the take-out for the 350-meter portage on the right.

It's a good trail around the falls, except for a steep section past the campsite marked three-quarters of the way along. The site is also well away from the water, and Alana and I chose to have our lunch break back near the take-out instead.

A good set of rapids begins immediately beyond the falls, with some sections that are even quite technical. But eventually the river leaves Shield country and its current tires out. The banks begin to meander uncontrollably, the water turns murky with silt, and any evidence of mountainous rock can be seen only in brief, distant glimpses.

A good number of logs were also beginning to block our path. Alana and I had to either walk around them, sinking up to our knees in the silty mud deposited along the shore, or lift directly over them, always being careful not to go broadside with the current.

Our map indicated where we had to actually portage around a total of five massive logjams later in the route. But soon after passing under a logging bridge, Alana and I came to a giant buildup of logs that had obviously been formed since the map was printed.

Neither side of the river showed any evidence of a portage, so, for no real reason, we chose to get out on the left bank. Then I volunteered to get out of the canoe, scramble up the 12-foot-high bank and search the shore for a way around the jam. Alana stayed behind to prevent our hyper dog, Bailey, from following me into the bush. Bailey is the greatest canoe-tripping dog and can actually find a portage better than I can. But she tries my patience at times, and this was not the moment for her to run into another lynx.

The second I entered the brush I hit a wall of deadfall. The best I could do was detour away from the eroded bank and head deeper and deeper into the woods. But there was still no apparent trail.

Just when I was about to call it quits and suggest to Alana that we paddle back to the logging road and thumb a ride, I looked down and spotted a Tootsie Roll wrapper. Usually when I see garbage left behind in the forest, I curse the thoughtless person who dropped it there. Now I thanked them. They had left a piece of encouragement, a bit of proof that someone else had actually made it around—and survived. I hurried back, and Alana and I began the ordeal of dragging our gear through an entanglement of fallen trees and dense vegetation.

The distance we covered was only 100 meters. The time it took us to haul everything up the incredibly steep bank, cut a trail with our flimsy camp-saw and follow it through like a couple of out-of-shape limbo contestants was an insane two hours and five minutes.

It was 7:00 p.m. by the time we stopped for the day, and the second we made camp a violent thunderstorm forced us into the confines of the tent. Our site was a small sand spit, as vulnerable as any place could possibly be, and at times we could actually feel the lightning strike the ground around us. But our weariness overpowered any fear we had of the chaos going on outside and we soon passed out with exhaustion.

Around midnight I crawled out of the tent to pee. The storm had moved on by then, leaving a clear evening sky and a welcome calm. I took a short walk barefoot along the beach, relieved myself and then sat down by the water to listen to two barred owls conversing with one another across the river. What a beautiful setting. This small, intimate river has so much to offer; it was just a matter of getting my mind set on the good points rather than the bad. So before crawling back into bed, I promised myself to have a more positive attitude toward whatever was waiting for us downstream.

Of course, come morning only a short 20-minute paddle brought us to the next logjam. It was bigger than the first, and the 200-meter portage that was supposed to be marked on the right bank had been completely washed out. It was raining again, and the moment we stepped out of the canoe, mosquitoes swarmed us by the thousands. Trying to remain positive, however, I allowed Bailey to go first this time to scout out a trial. And after considerable deliberation, she actually discovered a somewhat clear path around the worst of it. This time we were back on the river in less than an hour.

Another hour downstream was a third logjam, complete with a rough 60-meter path on the left, and not far beyond was a fourth.

This one was the largest yet, reaching at least 15 feet in height. The good news was that it actually had a marked portage (170 m) on the left. A new collection of logs had blocked the initial take-out, adding another 50 meters to the trail.

This was definitely a sign of better things to come, and we pushed on with more vigor than ever before. By noon we were paddling "through" the next pile of logs. Our map indicated a 160-meter portage on the right. Luckily, however, the entire blockage had been pushed aside by spring floodwaters.

Another two and a half hours of leisurely river paddling brought us to the last logjam (this one measured at least 21 feet high), complete with a clear 120-meter portage on the right, and eventually, the entrance to Santoy Lake.

Santoy is an enormous strip of blue reaching far off to the south and is bordered by huge mounds of granite. It's a place of incredible beauty but can also become extremely dangerous when the wind picks up. There was only a slight breeze when we arrived, and Alana and I even considered taking advantage of the calm to paddle the last 12 kilometers to the launch site that evening. One look at the gigantic beach stretching out across the entire north end of the lake, however, and we couldn't resist spending one more night out.

Our decision was, in hindsight, foolhardy. We began the crossing as early as 5:30 a.m. but by 6:00 a.m. we were bailing water out of the canoe about every fifth stroke.

To help beat the wind, Alana and I kept close to the west shore. It was the same rugged shoreline that held the dreadful Diablo Portage, and the high cliffs did little to protect us from the rough water. Rebounding waves slapped back from the rock and constantly tossed our canoe broadside to the wind.

I began shouting out, yelling obscenities at the wind, the rock, and the gulping waves. It was fatigue that was making me overreact. I guess we were destined to end the trip just as we had begun—in absolute fear. After all, isn't that what wilderness canoeing is all about? A painful, nerve-racking ordeal mixed together with the most peaceful, uplifting and self-satisfying thing you've ever done.

LONGEST PORTAGE 1,000 meters (Diablo Portage)

FEE No fee is required at this time.

ALTERNATIVE ACCESS Kawabatongog Lake, approximately 100 kilometers drive north of Terrace Bay on the Kimberly Clark Road, and at Deadhorse Creek Road bridge crossing, approximately 35 kilometers north of Highway 17.

ALTERNATIVE ROUTE To avoid the entire lake section of the trip as well as the difficult Diablo Portage, use the Kawabatongog Lake access for a five-day trip down the Steel River. Deadhorse Creek Road bridge crossing can also be used to eliminate all the logjams on the lower section of the river.

OUTFITTERS Jackfish Lake Motel & Efficiency Cottages Box 436 Terrace Bay, ON, P0T 2W0 807-825-9293

FOR MORE INFORMATION Steel River Provincial Park 807-887-5010 www.ontarioparks.com

TOPOGRAPHIC MAPS 42 D/15, 42 E/2 & 42 E/7

GPS COORDINATES 48.820535, -86.893917

Turtle River

5 to 7 days   27 portages   130 km   Novice whitewater experience needed, but the route is remote and moderate tripping skills are required.

IN JULY OF 1998, Alana and I spent a week paddling the Turtle River, a 160-kilometer provincial waterway park located north of Quetico Park and south of the town of Ignace. Apart from spotting 12 bald eagles and two golden eagles, spending an entire afternoon paddling through a bed of wild rice and leaving an offering of tobacco at half-a-dozen Native pictographs, the highlight of our travels down this remote river was making a special pilgrimage to Jimmy McOuat's White Otter Castle—one of the most mysterious hermitages of the north.

Alana and I were certainly not the first to visit White Otter Castle; this 28-by-38-foot log castle built entirely by a 60-year-old hermit eight decades earlier has been a local drawing card for years. One of the first visitors was canoeist C.L. Hodson, working on an article for *Rod and Gun* magazine in 1914.

Mile after mile of rugged shoreline drops behind and then about 2:30 p.m. "Old Jimmy's Place" quite suddenly slips into view. A hundred meters back from the lake it stands, on the edge of a small clearing. In the background are dark pine woods. No one speaks but with one accord the paddles pause here. Eyes strain. Heartbeats quicken. In the very air is mystery. Almost, we fear to approach this retreat of the wild man. We are intruders—trespassers. Then, slowly, the paddles dip. The bow grates on a strip of sandy beach. Gingerly we step ashore and approach the hermitage.

I felt a little gypped after reading about Hodson's visit. Sure, the castle itself is impressive—standing four stories high and made of 200 pine logs, averaging 37 feet long. But what made Hodson's arrival better than ours was that "Old Jimmy" (his name was pronounced McQuat) was home at the time and he was able to ask the hermit himself about why he built the bizarre monument. One of the most poetic stories he relayed involved a mail-order bride who canceled the marriage arrangement because Jimmy lacked a proper house.

It seems his construction rationale all had to do with being falsely accused of throwing a corncob at a bad-tempered schoolmaster (it was actually Jimmy's chum who threw the corn). For some reason, he was never able to

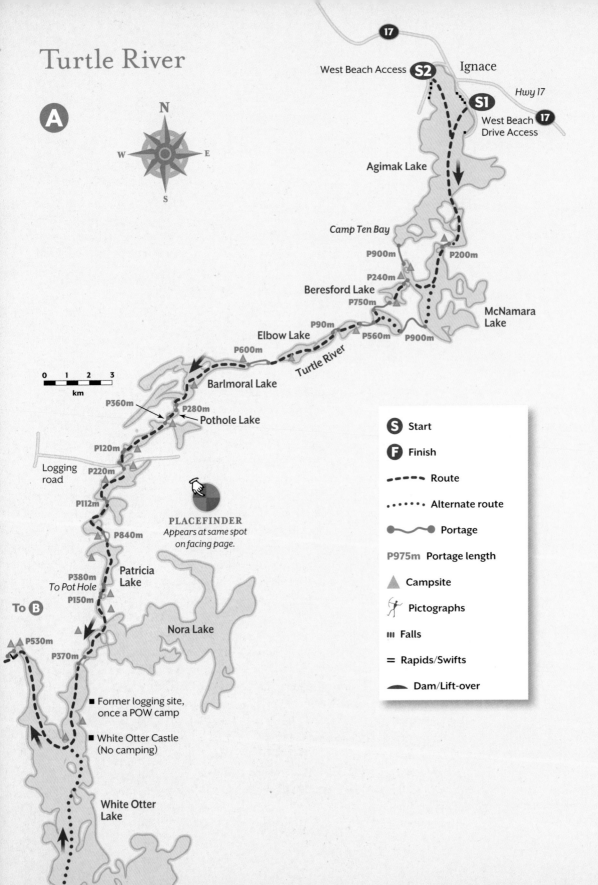

Turtle River

A

17

West Beach Access **S2** Ignace

Hwy 17

S1

17

West Beach
Drive Access

Agimak Lake

Camp Ten Bay

P900m   P200m

P240m

Beresford Lake

P750m

P90m   McNamara
Lake

Elbow Lake   P560m

P600m   P900m

Turtle River

Barlmoral Lake

P360m   P280m

Pothole Lake

P120m

Logging
road

P220m

P112m

P840m

PLACEFINDER
*Appears at same spot
on facing page.*

P380m
To Pot Hole   Patricia
Lake

P150m

To **B**   Nora Lake

P530m

P370m

■ Former logging site,
once a POW camp

■ White Otter Castle
(No camping)

White Otter
Lake

0 1 2 3
km

N
W E
S

Legend

S Start

F Finish

- - - - Route

⋯⋯⋯ Alternate route

●━━● Portage

P975m Portage length

▲ Campsite

Pictographs

ⅠⅠⅠ Falls

= Rapids/Swifts

Dam/Lift-over

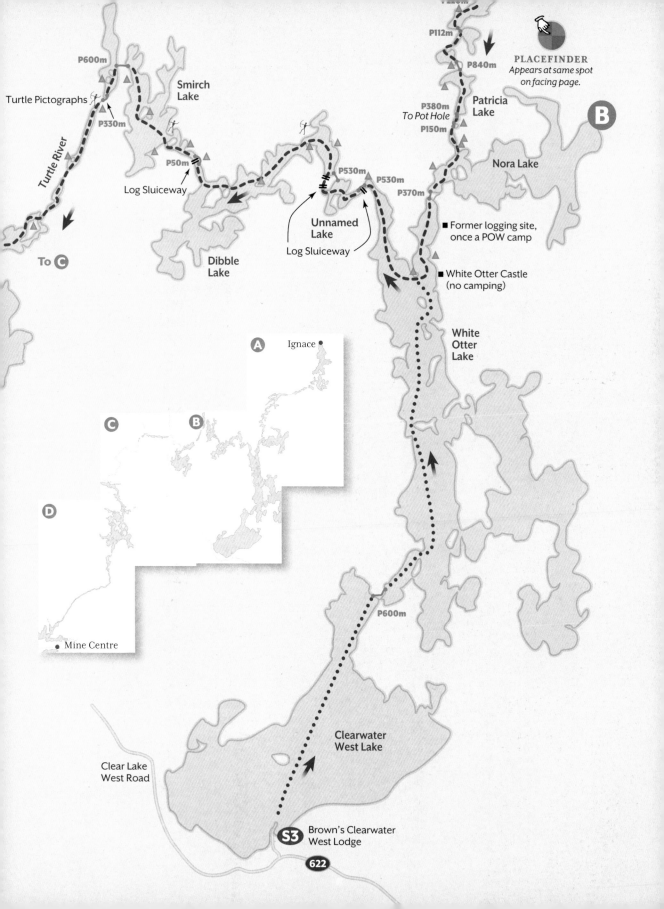

Turtle Pictographs

P600m

Smirch
Lake

P330m

Turtle River

P50m

Log Sluiceway

To C

Dibble
Lake

P530m

P530m

Unnamed
Lake

Log Sluiceway

P370m

P228m

P112m

P840m

P380m
To Pot Hole
P150m

Patricia
Lake

Nora Lake

■ Former logging site,
once a POW camp

■ White Otter Castle
(no camping)

PLACEFINDER
*Appears at same spot
on facing page.*

B

A   Ignace

C   B

D

Mine Centre

White
Otter
Lake

P600m

Clearwater
West Lake

Clear Lake
West Road

S3 Brown's Clearwater
West Lodge

622

Turtle River (continued)

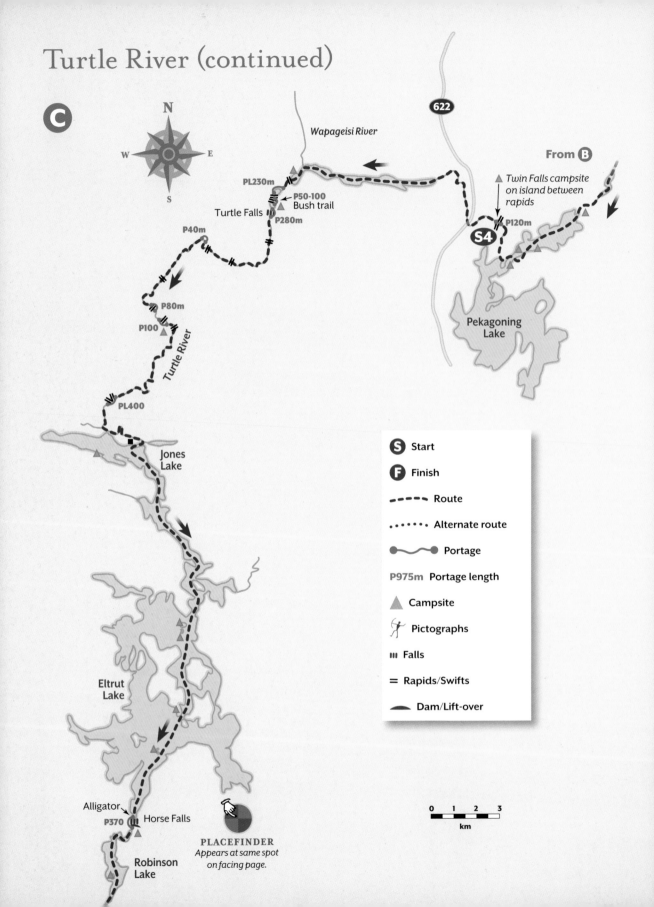

C

N
W   E
S

Wapageisi River

622

From B

PL230m

P50-100
Bush trail

Turtle Falls

P280m

Twin Falls campsite on island between rapids

S4

P120m

P40m

Pekagoning
Lake

P80m

P100

Turtle River

PL400

Jones
Lake

Eltrut
Lake

Legend

S	Start
F	Finish
●---●	Route
••••••	Alternate route
●~~~●	Portage
P975m	Portage length
▲	Campsite
🏹	Pictographs
⫼	Falls
=	Rapids/Swifts
▬	Dam/Lift-over

Alligator

P370   Horse Falls

PLACEFINDER
Appears at same spot on facing page.

0   1   2   3
km

Robinson
Lake

D

Eltrut
Lake

Alligator

P370 🏛 Horse Falls

🖐
PLACEFINDER
*Appears at same spot
on facing page.*

Robinson
Lake

◗ **PL400**
PR60

■ Old shack

Turtle River

P100 C2

P100
Bush trail

Heron River

Little Turtle
Lake

F Public launch

Mine Centre

11

Bad Vermillion
Lake

forget the curse given out by the angry man: "Jimmy McOuat—Ye'll never do any good! Ye'll die in a shack!" And, decades later, Jimmy found his accursed prophecy unfolding. After gambling his life savings away on a failed gold rush, he found himself on the shores of the remote White Otter Lake (known then as Big Clearwater Lake), living in a shack. "All the time I lived in a shack," Jimmy told Hodson, "I kept thinking—I must build me a house. And so I have. Ye couldn't call this a shack, could ye?"

After a day of exploring a few of White Otter Lake's 23 rock-painting sites, a logging camp that once served as a prisoner-of-war camp, the site of an old ranger station, and a guided walk through the castle, we paddled across to a nearby island to make camp for the first night.

Alana and I left the island campsite early the next day and arrived at our first portage well before 8:00 a.m. There is a choice of two trails to take you around to the right of an old logging sluice. From the rough campsite marked at the take-out, a 230-meter portage heads down a steep slope to the left and a 530-meter portage heads up a hill to the right. At first glance, the shorter trail seems easier. Don't bother, however. The longer 530-meter portage is much more direct and far less strenuous.

The portage leads you into Unnamed Lake, a scenic spot with round boulders sticking out everywhere. It looks as if a child's bag of marbles had been spilled out along the shoreline. Look for one rock in particular that holds a rusted logging pin that once supported a boom across the expanse of the lake.

An easy 530-meter portage—complete with an old trapper's shack halfway along—is marked well to the right of the next set of sluiceways. It takes you into the east bay of Dibble Lake. All across the lake are sandy beaches and rocky islands, each one of them an ideal lunch spot. Alana and I were fighting a strong northwest wind, however, and we chose to skip lunch and make the long haul along Dibble's north shore before the wind became unbearable.

By midday we had carried our gear over the 50-meter portage found to the right of yet another sluiceway and then stopped for our first break of the day at a pictograph site (an adult moose and a tally mark) located on the rock face to the left of the second bay, just before the entrance to Smirch Lake.

Smirch Lake is more bowl-shaped than Dibble, and with the northwest wind still building, it was becoming increasingly difficult for Alana and I to cross. The only thing that kept us going was that three-quarters of the way along, on the west shore, was a 600-meter portage that serves as a shortcut to where the waterway bends around and begins heading directly south. Once over the portage, Alana and I knew we could finally take advantage of the prevailing winds and make up the time we lost on the two large lakes.

Not far downstream from the put-in of the 600-meter portage is the first rapid that's not blocked by a logging sluiceway. A 330-meter portage is marked on the left bank, but Alana and I made a precision run just to the right of a large boulder set in midstream, and then eddied to the left to make use of the designated campsite marked on an outcrop of rock.

Two pictographs decorate the wall of rock lining the right bank; the first is above the rapid and is so faded that it's hard to distinguish. The second, situated a few meters below the rapid and almost directly across from the campsite, is a clear illustration of a

turtle with what appears to be a canoe emerging from its body and is most likely the reason for the river's name.

The next morning's paddle was almost dreamlike, with the mist hanging low over the river as we skirted the top end of Pekagoning Lake and right up until we carried over the 120-meter island portage at Twin Falls.

Not far from the falls is the Highway 622 bridge (an alternative access point), and beyond the paved road the change in environment couldn't become more dramatic. Hard granite is replaced almost completely by sand until just after the Wapageisi River flows in from the north and a long stretch of rapids mark the approach to Turtle Falls.

At first the river is simply squeezed between two rock points and the swift water that's formed can hardly be counted as a rapid. Almost immediately after, however, a

230-meter portage is marked to the right of some rougher water that can quickly become a mess during a dry spell.

Next up was a shallow section that twisted from right to left and then center, followed by a quick swift and then four major drops. A tight corner, with a souse hole bellowing up at the bottom, kept us from running the first of the four drops. We lifted over on the left before completing the run. (A bush trail on the left bank continues on if you wish to avoid all four drops.)

Then finally comes Turtle Falls, with a campsite up on a knoll to the left marking the take-out for the 280-meter portage. It's not a bad trail until the steep slope at the end, and it comes complete with a side trail leading to a scenic lookout three-quarters of the way along.

The river doesn't speed up again until an

hour past Turtle Falls, where it tumbles over a small cascade. A quick 40-meter portage is marked to the right. Then, another half-hour downstream, Alana and I came to a short rapid that wasn't marked on our government map. It was an easy run, but for the remainder of the trip I felt I couldn't totally trust the park's guide.

We came to another stretch of fast water just after the river turned to the southwest. Two sets run close together. The first rapid is a double run (Alana and I found the second drop questionable and used a poorly marked 80-m portage on the left). The next is a long set with an obvious route choice close to the left bank. A 100-meter portage is marked on the right, but Alana and I found enough courage to run the entire rapid this time. We finally called it a day at a nice campsite located at the end of the portage.

The morning of the fourth day was brisk, so we took time out to light our first breakfast fire of the trip, using one side to warm up our soggy boots and the other to fry up a 4-pound walleye Alana caught at the base of the rapids.

A couple of hours were spent paddling downriver to Jones Lake, where we encountered a small swift just beyond our campsite and, farther along, a good-sized ledge followed by some extremely technical rapids. After scouting from shore, we guessed the bottom rapids could only be run if the water was high, so we stayed to the left after the initial take-out and made full use of the 400-meter portage marked to the left.

Soon after, where alder flats take over thick stands of black spruce and a few patches of tamarack, a small creek empties into the Turtle River from the west and the waterway makes a dramatic turn to the left. Then, after

a good 20 minutes of monotonous paddling, the river twists again, this time to the southwest toward Jones Lake and then immediately to the southeast. The route out of Jones Lake, however, is almost totally obscured by swamp grass and wild rice. Alana and I, having missed the exit, paddled three-quarters of the way across the lake before realizing our mistake. Even when we did retrace our steps and eventually continue on down the river, however, the route looked nothing like the topo map, and it wasn't until we entered the top end of Eltrut Lake (Turtle spelled backward) that I was certain of our whereabouts.

The labyrinth, however, happened to be a haven for wildlife, and we managed to spot two golden eagles and half-a-dozen turkey vultures; the V-shape pattern of the vulture's wingspan was the only way Alana and I could distinguish between the two species while they soared high above us.

Eltrut Lake is full of sunken islands, dead-end inlets and huge beds of emergent water plants, so navigation remained a challenge as we made our way across. Luckily, there wasn't a strong wind to content with, which could have been a major hazard on the lower half of the lake. By mid-afternoon we were paddling down the southern outlet, taking time to check out an abandoned alligator beached on the west shore, just before to the take-out for the 370-meter portage to the right of Horse Falls.

The alligator, also known as a logger's warp tug, was one of the first labor-saving devices brought into the bush camps during the late 19th century. The steam-powered scow took over the job of oarsmen, who, with a pointer boat, would haul giant log-booms across a remote lake such as Eltrut. A powerful winch, equipped with a mile of steel cable and a

strong anchor, was also placed on the bow, allowing the boat to haul itself overland.

Horse Falls was a scenic spot, and a prime campsite was located near the base. But because the water was so low, a strong stench of rotten fish polluted the air below the cascade, and Alana and I decided to paddle farther downstream to make use of an island campsite on Robinson Lake. The moment we landed, however, all three of us were attacked by a swarm of angry wasps. Alana was stung twice on the hand, Bailey once on the eyelid and twice behind the ear, and I on my big toe.

We shoved off immediately and, after administering first aid to poor Bailey's eye, searched for an alternative site. The lake offered no other place to erect a tent, however, and we were actually forced back to the island to use a makeshift site on the far opposite end. I guess the upper section of the river

had bewitched us with its rocky islands, elongated beaches and campsites that couldn't be bettered until the next one came along. Now we found ourselves learning to enjoy a different environment, one of endless marsh, silt-colored water and the lack of any decent places to call it a night.

To leave Robinson Lake the next morning, Alana and I used a 400-meter portage that, at the take-out, climbed high up on the left bank and then continued along a bush road until it turned back down to the river. Then, once up and over a short 60-meter portage on the right, we were back on the river, where once again the vegetation growing along the banks takes on a dramatic change. Instead of the common boreal species—typified by jack pine, black spruce and balsam fir—rare occurrences of southern species such as oak, green ash and silver maple begin to appear.

As in the upper reaches of the river, loggers also attempted to gather logs from the lower portion during the 1940s (look for the remains of an old wooden bridge and an abandoned cabin hunkered back in the woods beside a side stream). Luckily, however, most of the trees along the bank were left untouched, and the ones that were cut have now been replaced by second growth, leaving this unique habitat to continue to dominate the landscape all the way down to the take-out.

You have to run three more sets of rapids, beginning about a three-hour paddle from Robinson Lake, before you enter Little Turtle Lake. The first is made up of four drops that quickly follow one after the other, increasing in volume as they go. The second is an extremely technical Class II that comes with a 100-meter portage on the left. And finally, there's a snakelike, rock-strewn rapid that rates as a moderate Class I with an optional 100-meter bush trail on the left.

Muddy banks continued to dominate the riverbank. Alana and I couldn't find a single spot where we could place a tent. So we paddled to Little Turtle Lake, only to find fishing lodges or family cottages taking over every possible site. By the time we had reached the far eastern inlet, leading toward the town of Mine Centre (turn right directly off Highway 11, and then stay right, keeping to the main road), we had to finally admit to ourselves that our life on the river was now over. Alana and I made our way down the inlet, looking for the public boat launch where Dennis had promised he would park our vehicle.

LONGEST PORTAGE 840 meters

FEE The Turtle River is an unmaintained provincial park and no camping permit is required for canoeing the river. A moderate fee is charged to shuttle your vehicle or access White Otter Lake by boat.

ALTERNATIVE ACCESS There are a couple of options to begin your trip: the town dock in Ignace on Agimak Lake and at the Highway 622 bridge.

ALTERNATIVE ROUTE The traditional route begins at Ignace but a good number of portages can be cut off by having an outfitter boat you up to White Otter Lake from Clearwater West Lake, or you can choose to begin at the Highway 622 bridge and reduce the trip to 4 days.

OUTFITTERS
Dream Catcher Tours
153 Balsam Street
Ignace, ON, P0T 1T0
807-934-6482

Browns' Clearwater West Lodge
Box 1766
Atikokan, ON, P0T 1C0
807-597-2884
www.brownsclearwaterlodge.com

Soft Wilderness Adventures
72 Spruce Road
Atikokan, ON, P0T 1C0
807-597-1377

Canoe Canada Outfitters
300 O'Brien Street
Atikokan, ON, P0T 1C0
807-597-6418
www.canoecanada.com

Agimak Lake Resort
Box 8, Highway 17
Ignace, ON, P0T 1T0
807-934-2891
www.agimaklake.com

FOR MORE INFORMATION
The Friends of White Otter Castle
807-934-6482

Ministry of Natural Resources
807-934-2233
www.mnr.gov.on.ca

MAPS The Ministry of Natural Resources has produced an excellent canoe route map for the Turtle River.

TOPOGRAPHIC MAPS
52 F/8, 52 G/5, 52 G/4 & 52 F/1
Provincial Series: Scale 1:100,000
Gulliver River 52 G/SW, Gold Rock 52 F/SE & Seine River 52 C/NE

GPS COORDINATES
49.405007, -91.667569

Kopka River

⏱ 6 to 8 days   🛶 23 portages   ●----● 146 km   **Advanced canoe-tripping skills needed due to the rugged terrain, and moderate whitewater skills.**

I GAVE MY CANOE mate, Andy Baxter, the job of choosing our route for this particular trip. On June 1, we headed north for the Kopka—northwestern Ontario's most doable unsung canoe route (according to Andy).

Joining us were Bill and Anne Ostrom. Bill had done the river twice before—a bonus, for sure—and his wife, Anne, is one top-notch paddler. Safety would be a key on this trip. The Kopka is remote, rugged and full of some nasty unmaintained portages; having a second canoe along would be a smart choice. It took two full days for Andy and I to drive north to the Ostroms' place near Thunder Bay, and another day to drive up the Armstrong Road to the CN railway which would take us to our access point at the south end of Wabakimi Provincial Park, where a few days of paddling a small, unnamed river and chain of elongated lakes would link us to Kopka. Taking the train is one option. Flying out of Armstrong to the headwaters (Uneven Lake is a popular put-in) or starting along the Graham Road are other options. But the train was far cheaper than the plane and a lot quicker than organizing a shuttle from the Graham Road, located

about 300 kilometers to the west. A mere $120 took all four of us to an unnamed lake west of Armstrong and just east of where the Lookout River flows under the railway tracks. The train left at 7:30 a.m., so arrangements were made through a local outfitter, Wilderness Connections, to stay at the renovated jailhouse in town. The outfitter also shuttled our vehicles to the designated take-out.

Everything went as planned. Well, almost everything. Our group almost missed the morning train because it was on time. The train in Armstrong is never on time. When it pulled in at 7:32 a.m. Andy was calling home, I was getting a second cup of coffee at the local diner. It was Bill and Anne, catching a nap at the station, who rounded us up before the train left.

What a Canadian experience it is to be dropped off in the middle of the northern bush by train; having all your gear and canoes tossed out of the baggage car; and then standing there on the tracks watching your only connection to the civilized world slowly disappear from sight. Take note: for some odd reason train service has since been changed, and the train goes through the area at night.

Kopka River

CN Mileage 33.3
CN Mileage 32.3
A
S
P30m
P300m
P350m
to Armstrong →

Beagle Lake

P450m

Laparde Lake

P200m
2xP30m *Line or wade*

P200m
Line or wade
P30m

Aldridge Lake

P250m

P50m
P900m
P1800m
CI–CII *check before running*
P70m
CI *check before running*

Kopka River

P200m

Fly-in **A**

Uneven Lake

P100m *Portage is left on island in middle channel*

CI *run or line*
P50m
P40m
Line or wade

4 CI

CI–CII
P300m

Sandison Lake

Small falls
P25m
P400m
P280m

Alt. portage
PR250m
PL150m

P60m
Small falls

Small falls
P60m

Kopka River

CII *check before running*
P80m

P440m

CI

Kenakskaniss Lake

Cliff portage
P150m

P700m

P300m
P50m
P175m
P250m
Boulder garden

Cliff portage
P150m

P700m

P300m
P50m

P250m
Boulder garden

P175m

0 1 2 3 4 5 6
km

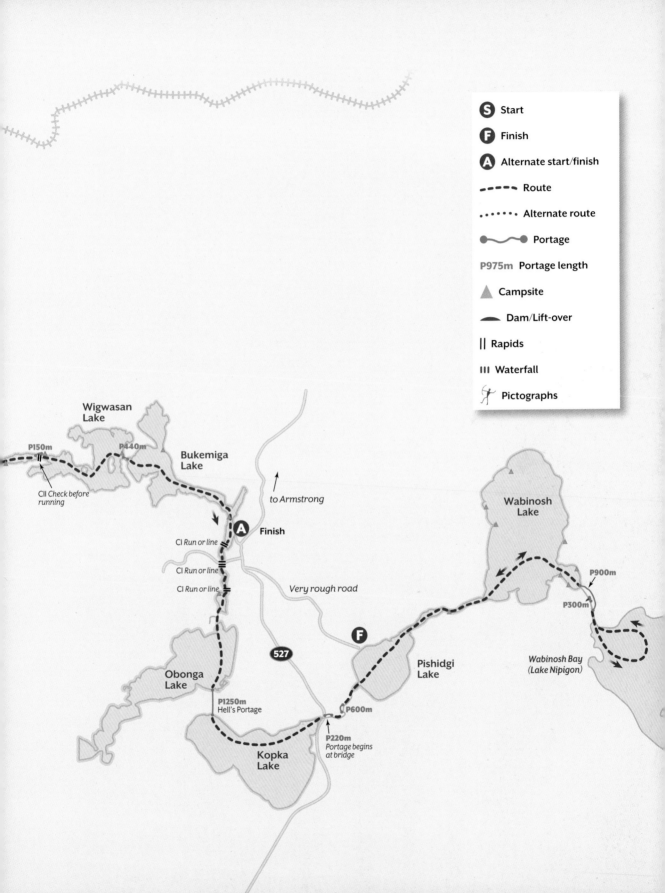

Start Ⓢ

Finish Ⓕ

Alternate start/finish Ⓐ

- - - - **Route**

· · · · · **Alternate route**

●∿● **Portage**

P975m **Portage length**

▲ **Campsite**

▬ **Dam/Lift-over**

‖ **Rapids**

‖‖ **Waterfall**

🯄 **Pictographs**

Wigwasan
Lake

P150m

P440m

Bukemiga
Lake

CII *Check before
running*

to Armstrong

Ⓐ **Finish**

CI *Run or line*

CI *Run or line*

CI *Run or line*

Very rough road

527

Ⓕ

Wabinosh
Lake

P900m

P300m

Pishidgi
Lake

*Wabinosh Bay
(Lake Nipigon)*

Obonga
Lake

P1250m
Hell's Portage

P600m

P220m
*Portage begins
at bridge*

Kopka
Lake

The drop-off is still doable, but expect to spend a few hours of waiting along a steep rail embankment before the sun comes up.

The first-day paddle from the put-in lake to Aldridge Lake was a long one. But like all first days of any trip, we were driven by enthusiasm; and thank goodness we were. That initial gusto, that eagerness we all get to be finally out paddling, was definitely a godsend that first day. The portages on our chosen route connecting the chain of lakes were all clogged with downed trees and the small river was flushing water in the opposite direction. The Kopka watershed was also in flood, and the portages around the rapids had to be extended at both the take-out and put-ins. All this mixed in with the fact that it was the first major trip of the season for all of us, and we were a tad out of shape, meant that only our keenness to be out would get us through the day.

The first portage of the trip (350 m marked to the left) was just a short paddle east on the unnamed lake and was followed soon after by a quick 30-meter lift-over on the right. It became obvious the moment we reached the put-in of the second portage that it would have been possible to have the train stop here rather than farther east on the unnamed lake, eliminating the first two portages and the bonus of having a nice campsite (located at the end of the second portage) if needed.

Not far past the second portage a third trail (300 m) takes the route southwest, to the north end of Beagle Lake and the home of a group of pictographs (search the cliffs along the upper east shoreline).

The portages didn't get really rough, though, until the fourth one—a 450-meter trail connecting Beagle Lake with Laparde Lake. A great number of jack pines blocked

the take-out and after it crossed an old logging road, the portage led straight through waist-deep muck and water where it became easier to float the canoe rather than carry it.

At the south end of Laparde was another portage measuring 200 meters, located away from the rapids and in the back bay to the left. The take-out led up a moderate slope, found to the extreme right. And immediately after were two short 30-meter portages, both on the left. We lined up the first and waded up the second, where I lost my footing and after floating back down, had to walk up against the hard current once again. Shortly after were two more portages; the first was a 200-meter trail on the right of a small rapid with a steep climb directly after the take-out, and the second was a 30-meter portage, also on the right, up a granite slope. Then, thankfully, we paddled halfway down Aldridge Lake to make camp on a small beach site.

Our second day en route, the portages were even worse. None were recently maintained, pesky deerflies were out in full force, and the temperature rose steadily all day (by midday it was 38 degrees in the shade).

Only two more portages were marked on our map, separating us from the Kopka. But this stretch was definitely not easy. First, the map showed a lengthy portage running from the south end of the unnamed pond to another unnamed pond, marked to the right of a creek connecting the two bodies of water. Problem was, we couldn't find it.

It took a good hour of searching before Andy and I happened upon it on the far southwestern bay—nowhere near the creek. The good news was that the portage ended up just being a short distance (50 m), leading us to the creek rather than avoiding it; and at this point the creek seemed navigable. Except for the bear blocking our route! He stood in midstream, munching on marsh grass, and only after some loud handclaps and boisterous yelling by all four of us did he manage to move on. We met up with him again though, around the next bend in the creek, motioned him to move on once again, only to have him block our path a third time around the next bend. A fourth encounter, the most unnerving of them all, was had directly on a 100-meter trail which we needed to carry over to avoid the remaining part of the now unnavigable creek. (I've never portaged so quickly in my life.)

A lengthy 1,800-meter portage, located almost directly across from the last portage, was all that remained before reaching the Kopka River. This one was brutal. The first section was a labyrinth of trails making their way through a large floating bog, and the remainder headed up and through an old burn area. What made it worse was the intense heat and bugs plaguing us the entire time. As I neared the end of the trail I've never been so happy to spot the hint of blue—that being the tranquil waters of the Kopka. Water levels had dropped somewhat by the time we were on the Kopka River but were high enough to have the fire ring on the lunch site we made use of just upstream still under water.

The take-out for the next portage was also tangibly close to the stretch of whitewater it was avoiding. Prior to that we ran three to four drops and after that there were half-a-dozen before the river emptied into Sandison Lake, where we camped for the night. The sets were rated no higher than Class II but all had to be scouted prior to running since more than once we discovered trees had fallen across the river after a blind bend in the river, the last one especially. It wasn't easy walking through the thick bush along the river bank where we had to cut down moderate-sized jack pine hanging low over boiling whitewater equipped only with a makeshift collapsible handsaw, but hitting a tree halfway through a run wasn't an option.

The Kopka at this point in the trip resembled an enlarged creek more than an actual river. It was a wonderful place to be, really. Apart from scouting and re-scouting sets of rapids, our day was spent spotting the abundant wildlife en route, including three more black bears and the backside of a woodland caribou as it ran off into the thick bush lining the bank. Birds were more abundant than anything else. Countless warblers fluttered across from bank to bank, bald eagle sightings became common fare, and a group of nighthawks we spotted on one of the portages revisited us by flying into camp that evening to help us diminish the bug population.

The Kopka began to stretch out its banks the next day, becoming more of a river than a constricted creek. At times it even resembled more of a lake than an actual river. But where it did squeeze together were plenty of rapids (most of which we ran) and an equal amount of moderate-sized cascades.

With the watershed still in flood, the take-out points for each portage were either tangibly close to the brink of a falls or had become hidden by the rapids themselves, making our progress slow at best.

The day started off simply enough. We rejoined the river where it flushes out of the northwest corner of Sandison Lake by making use of a 40-meter portage on the right, followed by three consecutive CI runs, a 50-meter portage left of a small falls and a long stretch of swift water. We even had a strong tailwind to help us across a large lake-like section.

After our morning sail, however, things

started to go downhill. On the northeast corner of the open stretch, where the river gets squeezed once again, we met up with the most complicated take-out spots of the day. Our map showed a take-out and trail to the left of some strong rapids. As we paddled into the inlet to the right, where the river begins to drop, we saw a shoreline thick with boulders and brush, but no portage.

We advanced a little farther, navigating a short swift that was uncomfortably close to the major drop, and searched the banks again for any sign of the portage; but still, nothing. Unwillingly we paddled back up against the current, thinking that we may have missed the take-out farther upstream somewhere. A half hour later we had retraced our steps back to the top of the rapids, still with no obvious place to begin portaging.

We ended up making our own trail and later discovered that the portage (100 m) was actually on the left of an island that sat in the mid-channel, not along the left shoreline. The high water, however, made it impossible to see or even think of using the trail. Cutting our own way through was the only option.

It was lunch time when we finally found our way around the moderate drop, and a group decision was made to take it easy for awhile and drift with the tailwind, munching away on our daily supply of P&J and bannock. We made our way across yet another unnamed lake until the Kopka flushed northward, where an old logging road crossed the river.

The portage here, which was mandatory for the great amount of water rushing through the drop at the time, began on the left bank and on the far side of the bridge. We took out on the other side, however. None of us wanted to get caught up in the strong current prior to the major drop.

This wasn't an easy portage. Our map only showed it to be 200 meters but we knew an extra 100 or more meters were added on by avoiding the top portion. The distance wasn't the issue. It was the amount of trees fallen across the trail as well as the steep slope near the put-in. Adding to all that, the temperature at the time was 38 degrees, the bugs were also out in full force, a major storm was approaching and the first campsite we checked out, in a bay to the left, was littered with toilet paper mounds and empty beer bottles.

We did, however, eventually find a good campsite farther along on a much larger island, and once the storm passed, Andy and I cooked up a mess of walleye we caught at the base of a small swift we ran though, below the rapid we had previously portaged around.

High water continued to make our trip interesting the next day, starting soon after we had left camp that morning. Our map indicated that the river took a dramatic turn to the right, at the end of an elongated eastern inlet. It did just that. But there was no way we were going to chance taking the two portages (250 m to the right of the first drop and 150 m to the left of the second). The water was way over the banks here and all of us were quite anxious about how strong the current would be between the two portages. So, we opted for an alternative way around the entire stretch of whitewater—a 400-meter portage located out of the way, on the left and in the far eastern bay. It was a safe choice but it was very obvious the trail saw little use. Again, our saws had to be unpacked to cut our way through. It was the worst portage yet.

What followed was a little simpler: a small falls with an obvious and quick 25-meter portage marked to the left, with the take-out immediately after a small swift. Then a 280-meter portage, also found on the left bank, which avoided a double cascade. It wasn't long before we had to get out of the canoes again to carry around another medium-sized falls, with a 60-meter portage on the right. And then another cascade, with another 60-meter carry on the left, which separated two unnamed lakes.

What awaited us next may not have been easily runnable, but at this point we were all somewhat desperate to paddle through some whitewater rather than carry around it. So we picked our way down the set of rapids found at the end of the second unnamed lake, which we rated as a Class II tech. (An 80-m portage was found on the left.) What awaited us directly after that, however, was definitely not navigable. It was a major drop that ended in a boulder garden and granite shelf. Thankfully, the 440-meter portage (marked on the left) had fewer blowdowns along it than the previous trails we had crawled over that morning.

Our camp that night was had on the west shoreline of Kenakskaniss Lake. But before that we enjoyed paddling through a long series of swifts and Class I rapids between where the river turns directly south to where it flushes into the north end of Kenakskaniss Lake. What a joy that last part of the day was, moving through fast water rather than carrying around it and then feasting on walleye fillets, battered, fried and served with a bed of red cabbage salad and a splash of white wine.

Day five of the trip was Father's Day and before breakfast Andy and I opened gifts packed away by our families. Andy received Tim Hortons gift certificates for us to use on our way home and I got some fishing lures, plus a lovely card signed by my daughter Kyla and wife Alana. Apart from the gifts, we were all looking forward to this day of the trip.

At the southeast end of Kenakskaniss, the river begins to drop dramatically. This area is where the true character of the Kopka River begins, an absolute paradise with one massive cascade after another—seven in total, hence the name Seven Sisters. Our map indicated a trail on the right of the first drop, titled Mink Portage. It's a historical route that avoided the entire stretch of falls and rapids and was used by the crew traveling with Edward Umfreville in 1784, who was working as a writer for the Hudson's Bay Company. At the time the crew was looking for an alternative route west due to the political problems associated with the Grand Portage.

We spent 20 or so minutes looking for any sign of a take-out but there wasn't anything. Not that we wanted to make use of the trail (other portages had later been cut around each specific drop, and the portage itself measured a good distance.) What we did find, however, was an obvious take-out to a portage on the left bank. It was a relatively flat trail, measuring about 700 meters, but it definitely wasn't easy. Midway along, we had to balance on top of a giant boulder garden. Thank goodness it wasn't raining at the time or one of us would have broken a leg or twisted an ankle for sure. We all hated carrying across but Bill cursed the portage more than the rest of us. He had paddled the river before so I thought for sure he had navigated this stretch of rapids. He didn't recall ever walking the boulder garden, so it's pretty likely he did run the rapids rather than portage. Problem was, however, the high water made the set unmanageable. And to prove the point, we found a Grumman canoe, from Cozy Corner rental, wrecked at the base of it.

Not far downstream was another drop, this one more significant than the previous one.

The take-out, found on the right, was uncomfortably close to the brink of the cascade, but at least the trail (300 m) was a clearer path. The ending was a little insane though. The trail made its way down an incredibly steep embankment resembling more of a mountain goat trail than an actual portage. The put-in was situated in a small bay and the next portage (a short 50 m) was easily located at the exit of the small inlet, to the right. Noticing the falls upstream, however, we couldn't resist wanting to get a closer look. A well-planned upstream ferry just above the rapids, and a few strong paddle strokes upstream got us to the base of the falls. There were a few anxious moments, but to float at the base of this giant waterfall, feeling the spray of the flood water

crashing into the pool below, was worth the trepidation of the event.

Almost immediately after the next portage, there was another drop, a falls larger than the previous one. And it was complete with another difficult portage, found to the right. The distance wasn't the issue. It only measured 175 meters, but the put-in spot was again insanely steep. We had two choices. The first, which happened to be the original, was straight down a moderate cliff face and to the very base of the falls. We opted out of that and took the second. The trail forked to the right, went through a mucky bog and then directly up a mound of granite, which we could only manage to scramble up after Andy made a makeshift ladder out of a fallen birch tree.

The good news was that a picture-perfect campsite was waiting for us at the end of the portage.

It was such a nice site, actually, that we ended up staying for two days. The first day was spent recuperating, and the second was had taking an excursion to an unnamed lake directly north of our site. No portage existed to it but we were used to making our own at this point. And the fishing wasn't what we thought it would be (we caught more off the campsite). But the cliffs that lined the top half of the lake were impressive enough to make the journey worth the effort.

It was raining the morning we left our site and, in retrospect, we should have hunkered down to stay one more night. The next portage, and the last around the falls section, was the steepest, rockiest, most insane portage I've ever done in my life. Having the rain greasing up the rocks for us made it even worse. The trail is to the left of the falls, and you only have to walk about 70 meters before you get to the "downward" section. It's down a sheer cliff. Seriously, a cliff! A cliff that you need climbing ropes and harnesses for, to get yourself and gear safely down to the bottom. Bill and Anne had warned us about this part, but both Andy and I thought they were exaggerating somewhat. They weren't. I haven't a clue how you could complete this carry, and not get injured, without at least a rope.

There is an alternative trail that Ontario Park's staff cut the previous year, found on the right shoreline. It doesn't have a cliff, but I personally think it's more dangerous. The entire route is clogged with giant boulders, and you'd definitely have a tougher time dragging yourself and your gear to the other side.

With Bill and Anne's climbing experience, we all managed to reach the bottom without major injury, and after a load of photos taken of the falls we had just climbed down beside, our crew took on the 440-meter portage to the left of the swift water existing at the base of the cascade.

Not far downriver of the last falls and remaining rapids was another section of whitewater, where the Kopka enters the far eastern end of Wigwasan Lake. A 150-meter portage was marked on the left bank, but we actually ran this one, rating it a technical CII. None of us were all that eager to be at this spot, exiting the rock chasm below the Seven Sisters. We were leaving some breathtaking scenery. But it wasn't just that. This portion of the route meant that Anne and Bill would be leaving us soon. They only had enough time off work to paddle to Highway 527 leading into Armstrong; for Andy and I, it meant our river portion of the trip was soon to be over. We had planned to continue on to Lake Nipigon — something we were quite excited about — but there's something to be said about keeping with a river rather than paddling across big water. The mood is more intimate and you feel more connected to the landscape around you. We had spent a good chunk of time on the Kopka at this point, immersing ourselves in so much of it, that it felt unnatural to leave it. The Kopka wasn't a mean river. Sure, it had some nasty portages. But it wasn't one of those fast and furious waterways with a killer current always trying to grab hold of you. It was an honest river, always letting you know what was coming up next. In retrospect, I think we were all somewhat grateful when we found ourselves windbound, right where a 440-meter portage links Wigwasan Lake with Bukemiga Lake. It meant we could spend more leisure time gawking at the scenery all around us, and it gave us a good excuse to snack on all the munchies Bill and Anne had left over in their food pack. Our unscheduled layover was made even better when our shuttle driver, Clement Quenville (working for Jim Pearson's Wilderness Connections), decided to boat over and give us an unannounced visit and treat us to the small bottle of rum we had left behind in his cabin prior to our trip departure. The only downfall was the campsite on the portage wasn't the best, forcing us to move to a better location farther down the lake after the winds had died, just after 10:00 p.m. Paddling that late wasn't an issue, however. This far north in June it really doesn't start getting dark until after 11:00 p.m. By mid-morning Andy and I were on our own. Clement had dropped off Bill and Anne's truck at the Bukemiga Lake access point (reached by a rough but drivable dirt road leading in from Highway 527) and we continued downstream.

Andy and I were traveling blind on this next section, where the Kopka River exits Bukemiga and enters Obonga Lake. Our map just indicated rapids, with no portages. But by taking it slow, and even getting out to wade, line and drag the canoe through the bush in some sections, it was all quite doable. On the opposite end of Obonga Lake it was a different story. There would be no question of running anything. We took the long (unmaintained) 1,250-meter "Hell's Portage," which avoids a steep drop into Kopka Lake. We knew just as little about this stretch as the one upriver.

Andy and I had no idea how famous we'd become during our time on the river and were quite shocked to find fan mail nailed to a tree on the next portage. Sure, we knew CBC Radio's *Fresh Air* show got a lot of listeners, and we knew we'd been interviewed by the host, Jeff Good, a number of times. But we also knew

the satellite phone rarely worked and half the interviews were cut off seconds after they started. Apparently, listeners couldn't wait to hear if we could get through to the radio station or not each time it aired. In less than a week we had reached celebrity status. The fan mail was found after Andy and I paddled the north shoreline of Kopka Lake to where the river flushes under the Highway 527 bridge. We took out on the left, walked over the road and there, at the beginning of the portage (a well-overgrown 220 m) was a note for us, sealed in a ziplock sandwich bag. It was from a group of paddlers from the United States who were on their way to Wabakimi to take part in a volunteer canoe route cleanup titled the Wabakimi Project. The group, who were obviously big admirers of the radio show, figured out our designated route and time of arrival and then left the note. Cool stuff if you think about it. Andy and I took pictures of us standing on the road with our fan mail and then humbled ourselves enough to continue on, lining a large swift directly after the first rapid and then portaging 600 meters on the left bank just around the next bend in the river. The last rapid flushed the Kopka into Pishidgi Lake, where we saw our vehicle parked at the public launch to the northwest. Our shuttle driver had driven it there for us to use on our return from Lake Nipigon (take note that the road in from the highway is definitely a rough one, and I wouldn't use it unless you have a truck or four-wheel vehicle). Our final week would be paddling to the north shore of Lake Nipigon by way of Pishidgi Lake, Wabinosh Lake and Wabinosh Bay. And the only thing standing in the way was one more set of rapids where the Kopka drains into Wabinosh Bay. The river section between Pishidgi and Wabinosh Lakes had a few swift sections but nothing to concern us, even for our paddle back upstream to our vehicle in a week's time.

Prior to taking on the portage from Wabinosh Lake to Nipigon's Wabinosh Bay we set up camp. The site resembled more of an urban backyard where the grass hadn't been cut; and the high water, which was still affecting our route, had the campfire ring completely under water. But we had a striking view of the incredible sheer cliffs surrounding the lake, and a single cast from shore provided us a decent-sized walleye for dinner.

The portage leading to Lake Nipigon hadn't got much use. Andy and I found the take-out a good distance upstream of where the Kopka drains out into the lake, and quite a few trees were down across the 900-meter trail. Of course, after we completed it, Andy and I discovered a second take-out farther downstream and closer to the actual rapids/falls where the river ends. It only measured just over 300 meters, but we would also have been paddling down the last stretch blind. Carrying 900 meters was fine by us. Over a dozen pelicans met us at the put-in and as we slid the canoe into the water, beside an old logging gator, another 20 or so birds flew upriver to fish at the base of the rapids. Spending a week paddling the north shore of Nipigon will remain in my memory forever. This is one magical place that I'm determined to paddle again.

LONGEST PORTAGE 1,800 meters

FEE The route travels through an unmanaged provincial park and a fee structure is not yet in place.

ALTERNATIVE ACCESS Flying out of Armstrong to the headwaters of Uneven Lake is a popular put-in. Or you could consider starting along Graham Road and following the river route from there.

ALTERNATIVE ROUTE By flying in and beginning in Uneven Lake you would have more time to spend on the Kopka River and avoid taking the train. Uneven Lake is about 2–3 days upstream from where our group began the river portion of the trip. You also might consider simply paddling upriver from the take-out at Bukemiga Lake access point (reached by a rough but drivable dirt road leading in from Highway 527) to the series of waterfalls and paddling the same way back.

OUTFITTERS
Wilderness Connections
Highway 527
Armstrong, ON, P0T 1A0
807-583-1888 (summer)
519-371-1416 (winter)
www.wildernessconnections.ca

Smoothrock Camps
Box 278
Armstrong, ON, P0T 1A0
807-583-2106
www.thunderhook.com

Wabakimi Wilderness Adventures
Frontier Trail, Hwy. 527
Armstrong, ON, P0T 1A0
807-583-2626
www.wabakimi.com

Mattice Lake Outfitters
Box 157
Armstrong, ON, P0T 1A0
807-583-2483
1-800-411-0334
www.walleye.ca

FOR MORE INFORMATION
Wabakimi Provincial Park
807-475-1634
www.ontarioparks.com

VIA Rail Canada
1-888-VIARAIL (1-888-842-7245)
www.viarail.ca

Ministry of Natural Resources
807-934-2233
www.mnr.gov.on.ca

MAPS The Ministry of Natural Resources has produced an excellent canoe route map for the Kopka River.

TOPOGRAPHIC MAPS
52 I/2, 52 I/3 & 52 I/4

GPS COORDINATES
50.252561, –89.685241

Wabakimi Provincial Park

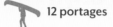

🕐 8 to 10 days   12 portages   ●▬▬▬● 86 km   The remoteness of the route requires advanced tripping skills.

IT WAS NANCY Scott, a park planner for Ontario, who first got me intrigued with the idea of paddling in Wabakimi Provincial Park, located 300 kilometers north of Thunder Bay. The fact that the park measures almost 2.5 million acres in size and contains over 2,000 kilometers of canoe trails was enough to catch my interest. But it was Nancy's story of eccentric inventor Wendell Beckwith, who lived alone for 20 years on Wabakimi's Whitewater Lake to devote his life to "pure" research, that finally convinced me to give this massive chunk of solitude a try.

Joining me on the pilgrimage was film producer Kip Spidell. It was our first trip together, but he was convinced that if he followed a bumbling canoehead like me through the wilderness for eight days, he'd get enough good film footage to make the trip worth his while.

Mercifully, Nancy also agreed to tag along as guide. Not only did she know the exact where-abouts of Wendell's hermitage on Whitewater Lake, but she also knew the locations of all the unmarked portages and campsites along the way—a bonus for any group traveling in such

a remote park, where woodland caribou far outnumber the canoeists.

The three possible ways to access the park are road, rail and floatplane. The road is obviously the cheapest, but not necessarily the best overall. It's a relatively easy drive to the launch on Caribou Lake, 12 kilometers north of Armstrong via the Armstrong Road (Highway 527) and then Caribou Lake Road. But the full day's paddle across the expanse of Caribou Lake to the actual park boundary can be a real bore, not to mention extremely hazardous should the wind pick up.

However, keeping to the train schedule can be a pain at times, and the flights in and out can be very costly. So after looking over all the options, our group finally decided on a combination plan. We would access the south section by train (check VIA Rail Canada for updated schedules and fees), fly out of Mattice Lake Outfitters on Whitewater Lake by way of Don Elliot's Wabakimi Air Service and then have Don shuttle us back to the train station in Armstrong.

Since Kip and I live in the Toronto area, we planned to take the VIA Rail service directly out of Union Station. Then, if all went well,

Wabakimi Provincial Park

Legend:

- **S** Start
- **F** Finish
- **A** Alternative start/finish
- – – – Route
- · · · · Alternate route
- ●—● Portage
- P975m Portage length
- ▲ Campsite
- ‖‖ Falls
- = Rapids/Swifts
- ▬ Dam/Lift-over

N W E S (compass)

0 1 2 3 4 km

Map labels:

- Whitewater Lake
- Outpost cabin
- Wendell Beckwith's cabin
- Ogoki Outpost Lodge
- P20m L-O
- Whitewater Lake Native community
- Best Island
- Don Elliot's Outpost Lodge (Mattice Lake Outfitters / Wabakimi Air)
- **F**
- Six runs of CI–CII CBR or line
- Outpost lodge
- P650m
- Large swift CBR or line
- Ogoki River
- Ogoki River
- P30m
- P200m
- P400m
- CI–CII CBR
- Berg River
- P900m
- P440m
- McKinley Lake
- P480m
- P50m
- Laurant Lake
- P50m
- P125m Can paddle through in high water
- Lonebreast Bay
- P80m
- P70m CI CBR
- Island Rapids
- Berg River
- P500m
- Outlet Bay
- Caribou Bay
- Caribou River
- Line or run south channel
- P80m
- P100m
- P80m
- Caribou River
- P80m
- P100m
- Outlet Bay
- Smoothrock Lake
- Caribou Lake
- P250m
- Little Caribou Lake
- P900m Fantasia Portage
- Spring Lake
- P150m CI CBR
- P100m
- P40m
- P100m
- Caribou Lake
- **A** **A** Use this route if winds are high
- Caribou Lake Road 12 km to public launch
- Armstrong
- P50m
- Lookout River
- P100m CI CBR
- Shultz's Trail
- **S**
- CN Rail
- Onamakawash River
- 527
- *Flew back here to Mattice Lake Outfitters*

we would meet up with Nancy 24 hours later at the Armstrong station and continue east for another 39 kilometers where we'd be dropped off at the designated access point — Shultz's Trail — at the south end of Onamakawash Lake.

Under the watchful eyes of the tourists we had befriended in the Budd car along the way, the three of us waved our good-byes, dragged our gear down a steep gravel embankment and then paddled off into the Wabakimi wilderness.

We paddled first to the northeast bay of Onamakawash Lake and flushed ourselves down the first rapid of the Lookout River (a 100-m portage is marked to the left), all the time being pursued by a massive black cloud.

Nancy had warned us about the severity of the storms in Wabakimi. But Kip and I thought we could get in at least the first day of paddling before we had to deal with one. Suddenly, the black squall caught up to us. There was no buildup, no prelude, just a smack of hard rain, strong wind and a lather of whitecaps. We pushed for the second stretch of rapids, hastily made camp at the take-out for the 50-meter portage marked along the left bank and then watched from under a sagging rain tarp as the storm moved across the sky.

For our second day out, we pushed off from camp early, attempting to film our own version of the Bob Izumi fishing show at the base of the rapids, with no luck, of course. And by 8:00 a.m. we were heading off downriver.

The Lookout River was the first of three rivers we had planned to travel to reach Whitewater Lake. And thinking back, it also happened to be my favorite. Of the series of five rapids between our first night's camp

and Spring Lake, only the fourth could be safely run. But all the portages were extremely short (100 m on the left, 100 m and 40 m on the right, a possible lift-over on the left, and 150 m on the left), and the scenery along the intimate little stream was absolutely breathtaking. Even the last portage of the day — a 900-meter trail connecting Spring Lake with Smoothrock Lake — was a pleasure to walk. Aptly named Fantasia Portage for its fairyland appearance and rumored to be the most scenic portage in the north, the trail led us through a stand of pine, spruce and birch, all rooted in a thick carpet of caribou moss, bunchberries and knuckle-sized blueberries.

Smoothrock Lake (named for its cluster of islands, scoured smooth by passing glaciers) was a different story, however. Almost the entire 30 kilometers of shoreline had been affected by fire that went through the area in the early 1980s. We finally found a suitable spot on a tiny knob of rock situated in the center of the lake around 6:00 p.m., just minutes before the nightly storm moved in.

It was amazingly calm the next day when we began our six-hour crossing of Smoothrock Lake. On such a large lake, we were grateful for the lack of wind. But the payback was an intense heat, reaching 32 degrees by 8:00 a.m. We kept close to the shoreline most of the day, searching for a bit of shade. The previous fire had scarred most of the trees along the shore, however, and escaping the direct sun soon became a lost cause. To make matters worse, we could smell smoke from a distant fire, probably lit by a lightning strike from the previous night's storm. Soon, a thin veil of haze hung low over the lake, and breathing became more difficult throughout the day.

By late afternoon, as we entered Smooth-rock's Outlet Bay (the second of three channels that lead northward out of the lake), a soft breeze was helping cleanse the air and we were finally free of the smoke. The quick shift in the wind, however, also indicated to us that another evening storm was brewing. In the distance, we spotted anvil-shaped clouds moving our way. This time they had a green hue to them, something Nancy seemed quite concerned about, so we immediately headed for shore.

The second we pulled up on shore, the storm hit. And what a storm it was! The temperature dropped to freezing in a matter of minutes; hail the size of marbles smacked down hard, leaving dimple marks on the overturned canoes; and a gale-force wind brought trees down all around us.

It was a horrifying experience. But it lasted a mere five minutes. And as we crept out to the water's edge to check the damage done to our two canoes, we realized how lucky we were to make it through the storm without serious injury. The original point we had intended on pulling up on was now a jumbled mess, littered with uprooted trees. It was obvious that if we had stayed there, all three of us might have been crushed to death. It was a humbling experience, to say the least.

The next morning we had only an hour's paddling left on Smoothrock Lake before we reached the portage leading to the Berg River. The trail was only 500 meters long, but this section of forest had been recently burned over and it took us another hour to haul our gear and canoes through the charred debris. Once on the Berg, however, we made quick progress. We easily ran the first set of rapids, even though a short 70-meter portage was marked on the left. The second set, Island Rapids, had to be portaged. But the 80-meter trail along the left bank was an easy carry. Once we reached the third set, we decided to call it an early day and camped along the 400-meter portage, also marked to the left.

The morning of day five saw us finishing the remainder of the Berg River, and before noon we had entered the Ogoki River. This was the last of the three rivers en route and also happened to be the largest and least exciting to paddle. It's slow and meandering in this section, with only one section of quick water, and that can be easily run or lined down. We also began seeing fishermen from the neighboring lodges. (Wabakimi Provincial Park has seven main lodges and 40 fly-in outpost camps.) So, rather than taking the regular 650-meter portage marked to the right of where the main section of the Ogoki empties into Whitewater Lake, we made a sharp left turn just over 1 kilometer up from the take-out and navigated a small side stream instead.

There were no portages, and we had to wade, line and blindly run down a series of rock-strewn rapids. But in a way, the narrow outlet was a far better introduction to Whitewater Lake. And there to greet us at the entranceway to Wendell's "Center of the Universe" was our first woodland caribou. The encounter lasted only a couple of seconds, but even the brief glimpse we had was well worth it. Throughout Wabakimi, the second-largest park in the province, only 300 of these elusive creatures remain.

However, the park superintendent is continuing to promote its high number of hunting and fishing lodges developed throughout its expansion area. Most canoeists traveling in the park feel ambivalent about the camps. In one way they seem intrusive—they don't

seem to fit the "wilderness experience." On the other hand, they can be extremely handy as a link to the outside world. Occasionally, trippers use them as a meeting place for floatplanes or to pick up extra supplies. Others have had to use them in severe emergency situations.

Our group was no different. Before our trip to Wabakimi, the park superintendent offered to have Walter, the interior park warden, meet us at the lodge situated at the mouth of the Ogoki River. From here he would give us a tow across to the Wendell Beckwith site on Best Island, situated on the far southeast bay of Whitewater Lake—a distance of approximately 20 kilometers.

In a way, it was a bit of a cop-out to accept the free ride. But Walter was also a member of the small group of aboriginal people who lived on Whitewater Lake during Wendell Beckwith's time here, and Kip thought that an interview with him would help his film a great deal. So early the next morning, our group gathered on the lodge's dock and waited for Walter to show. The following day we were still waiting. At 3:00 a.m. of the second day, the same day we had scheduled a plane to pick us up at another lodge just south of Best Island, we were forced to find our own way across. When we reached the other side, Walter was there to great us.

Excited to be within reach of the Beckwith site, we went off to explore. Walter gave us a tour of the three cabins and a couple of storage sheds that still remain on the island, all connected by a flagstone walkway and surrounded by a decorative cedar-rail fence. Each structure was perfectly designed, with every roof shingle and floorboard precisely cut to the same size and shape. Elaborate carving adorned all three entranceways, and pieces of the inventor's scientific contraptions and scores of Ojibwa artifacts were scattered about. Walter even pointed out parts of a homemade telescope he had found down by the beach, and sections of Wendell's "lunar gun" (a device constructed to compute and predict lunar cycles and eclipses) resting beside one of the storage sheds.

The cabins didn't actually belong to Wendell. Harry Wirth, a San Francisco architect and developer, used the island site as a retreat and hired Wendell as a caretaker. In 1955, after producing at least 14 patents—most of them for the Parker Pen Company—Wendell left behind a wife and five children in Wisconsin and began his solitary life on Whitewater Lake.

Wendell wasn't the only one to choose Wabakimi as a wilderness retreat. From 1977 to 1982, Joel and Mary Crookham trapped and homesteaded on the nearby Wabakimi Lake and raised their two young children, Sarah and Jason. And in the spring of 1994, Les Stroud and Sue Jamison lived "on what the bush provided" on Goldsborough Lake to work on their film *Snowshoes and Solitude*. Even Zabe, a graduate of Lakehead University's Outdoor Recreation program, attempted to overwinter at Wendell's place. After a close encounter with a pack of wolves, however, she decided to walk back out to Armstrong in February, just five months after she began her sojourn.

But Wendell Beckwith was surely the most unique. During his time here the eccentric inventor worked on various theories, ranging from the idea that the mathematical term "Pi" was constantly reoccurring in nature to the idea that Whitewater Lake was in complete triangulation with the Great Pyramids and Stonehenge (hence the "Center of the Universe" premise).

Obviously, this was no simple hermitage built by a man trying to escape the civilized world; it was a laboratory, observation post and research station.

The main cabin, the only structure not completely designed by Beckwith, came with its own icebox that was lowered underground to keep food from spoiling, and a sizable homemade birchbark canoe lashed to the south wall. This was where Wendell stayed at first, but he soon found it far too showy and impractical. The massive stone fireplace was especially ineffective at heating the cabin during the long winter months, and he became concerned about his reduced hours of research.

By 1978, he had completed construction on the "Snail," a circular cabin built directly into the side of a hill. The structure was far more heat-efficient, especially with a skylight centered above a sunken stove, equipped with rotating conical shield to direct the heat and a pivoting chimney to allow for maximum draft. It was an environmental masterpiece, and touring through the unconventional earth-cabin was the highlight of the trip for me.

To end our visit to Best Island, Walter walked us down to the small beach near the Snail and showed us where Wendell died of a heart attack back in 1980, alone but content. It was then that we noticed yet another storm brewing overhead. Since the lodge where we had planned for Don Elliot's air service to pick us up was another 4 kilometers south of Best Island, we made the call to leave immediately.

On cue, good old Walter took off, never offering us a tow, and we hastily went in all directions to complete our different tasks. Nancy prepared the boats, Kip finished filming the interior of the cabins, and I went off to sign our names in the registry book resting on the table inside the Snail. It was here that I saw an entry from Wendell's daughter, Laura, dated August 6, 1997: "Very proud to be the daughter of such a man. Wish everyone could have seen his 'domain' as it was while he was alive. By all accounts he was an exceptional and extraordinary man whose ideas and theories we may never comprehend—but we can all admire what he built here and the life he fashioned for himself. I last hugged him on the beach here—and I feel his presence still. Good bye again, Dad."

Nothing could better have described this charismatic person. Beckwith's "vision"—to have a community of researchers living on the island in their own Snails, "cleansing their minds of the mental paraphernalia in the outside world"—may not have been a bad idea. Truly, he was not some mad scientist, something that Kip and I constantly joked about before our trip here, but a pure Renaissance man who designed a perfect life for himself in this wild place called Wabakimi.

LONGEST PORTAGE 900 meters (Fantasia Portage)

FEE An interior camping permit must be purchased for Wabakimi Provincial Park.

ALTERNATIVE ACCESS Rather than access the park by rail or floatplane, you can drive directly to a public launch on Caribou Lake, 12 kilometers north of Armstrong, by way of Armstrong Road (Highway 527) and then Caribou Lake Road. A small parking area, located to the right approximately halfway along Caribou Lake Road, can also be used to access Little Caribou Lake—an alternative route to avoid the more exposed southern half of Caribou Lake.

ALTERNATIVE ROUTE Smoothrock Lake can be reached by paddling across Caribou Lake (use Little Caribou Lake if winds are too high) to Outlet Bay and then down the Caribou River to Caribou Bay.

Then, once you've followed the regular route to Whitewater Lake's Best Island, you can loop back to Smoothrock Lake by heading south through McKinley Lake, Laurent Lake and Smoothrock's Lonebreast Bay. From here you then backtrack on the Caribou River and Caribou Lake.

OUTFITTERS
Mattice Lake Outfitters
Box 157
Armstrong, ON, P0T 1A0
807-583-2483
www.walleye.ca

Wabakimi Wilderness Adventures
Frontier Trail, Highway 527
Armstrong, ON, P0T 1A0
807-583-2626
www.wabakimi.com

Smoothrock Camps
Box 278
Armstrong, ON, P0T 1A0
807-583-2106
www.smoothrock.com

Wilderness Connections
Highway 527
Armstrong, ON, P0T 1A0
807-583-1888 (summer)
519-371-1416 (winter)
www.wildernessconnections.ca

FOR MORE INFORMATION
Wabakimi Provincial Park
807-475-1634
www.wabakimi.on.ca

VIA Rail Canada
1-888-VIARAIL (1-888-842-7245)
www.viarail.ca

MAPS Wabakimi Project has produced a series of interior maps for Wabakimi Provincial Park (www.wabakimi.org/project).

TOPOGRAPHIC MAPS
52 I/6, 52 I/11, 52 I/12, 52 I/14 & 53 I/5

GPS COORDINATES
50.286502, -89.525003

Hunter Island Loop

🕐 12 to 14 days   🚶 42 portages   ●----● 320 km   **Moderate to advanced due to its length and the amount of large lakes to paddle across.**

ACCORDING TO PARK regulars, the ultimate Quetico canoe trip is the Island Loop. Glancing at the map, however, it's hard to grasp why: for the most part, the route is made up of large, windy lakes; it passes through some of the busiest access points; the trip itself measures over 320 kilometers and takes at least 12 days to complete; and it's not even a real island, just a land mass that splits the two historically significant fur-trade waterway routes, Kaministiquia and Grand Portage. The only real reason I gave it a try was that one of my frequent canoemates, Andy Baxter, is one of those "park regulars," and he had repeatedly praised Hunter Island as a definitive Quetico canoe trip and wouldn't allow me to ignore it as a contender for a place in the top 50.

We chose a couple of weeks in June to paddle the loop, and after completing the route I had to admit that Andy was right, the Hunter Island trip is an essential Quetico canoe trip. Mind you, our trip did have a few shortcomings: an early June timeline made for one of the buggiest trips of my life; wind was a huge issue on some of the larger lakes; we met up with vast crowds of canoeists along the border lakes; and even at the end of the trip, I still couldn't grasp the "island" idea. What I did find, however, was that we paddled and portaged past so many natural and historical treasures, which typify what Quetico is really all about.

We started at the French Lake access. This is definitely not the norm, as it adds two or three extra days of paddling to the trip. Most paddlers link up with the central loop from the west, south or southeast end of the park, but that's due to the fact that over 80 percent of the paddlers in Quetico are from the United States. Andy and I chose French Lake for two main reasons. We were both Canadians, so logistically it was much easier to begin at a common access point in Canada. The second reason was that the northern portion of the park is less busy, and there's nothing worse than beginning Quetico's "ultimate canoe route" battling through crowds of other canoeists.

Our plan worked perfectly. In the two days of paddling French Lake to Pickerel Lake to Doré Lake to Twin Lakes to Sturgeon Lake, we encountered only four other groups. The previous season I had started a trip from Ely's

Moose Lake and counted 226 canoes in the first hour and a half of the trip. Andy and I had definitely made the right decision.

Day three was spent paddling almost the entire length of Sturgeon Lake. The wind direction was against us, but it only amounted to a slight breeze most of the time, pleasant enough to keep the blackflies and mosquitoes down a bit while we crept along the northern shore.

Camp was made just prior to the large bay where Jean Creek empties into the lake. Rarely am I up and out of the tent before Andy, but what awaited us on day four had me outside brewing morning coffee a half hour before sunrise. The plan that day was to paddle down the Maligne River to Tanner Lake, then camp near Tanner Rapids.

The Maligne River (*maligne* is French for "bad") is a beautiful waterway to paddle. Our morning began with an hour's paddle across what remained of Sturgeon Lake. Then we took on Portage de Gros Rocher ("big boulder"), the first portage, a flat 260-meter trail to the right of some rapids. The take-out is a safe distance from the drop and has an old boiler from a tug used by the first settlers heading west across Sturgeon Lake. It's an easy carry, and the only worry is a giant patch of poison ivy midway across the trail. Another portage (307 m) also on the right quickly followed, making use of an old logging road of the Shelvin Clark Lumber Company, who logged here extensively in 1937 and 1938.

Hunter Island Loop

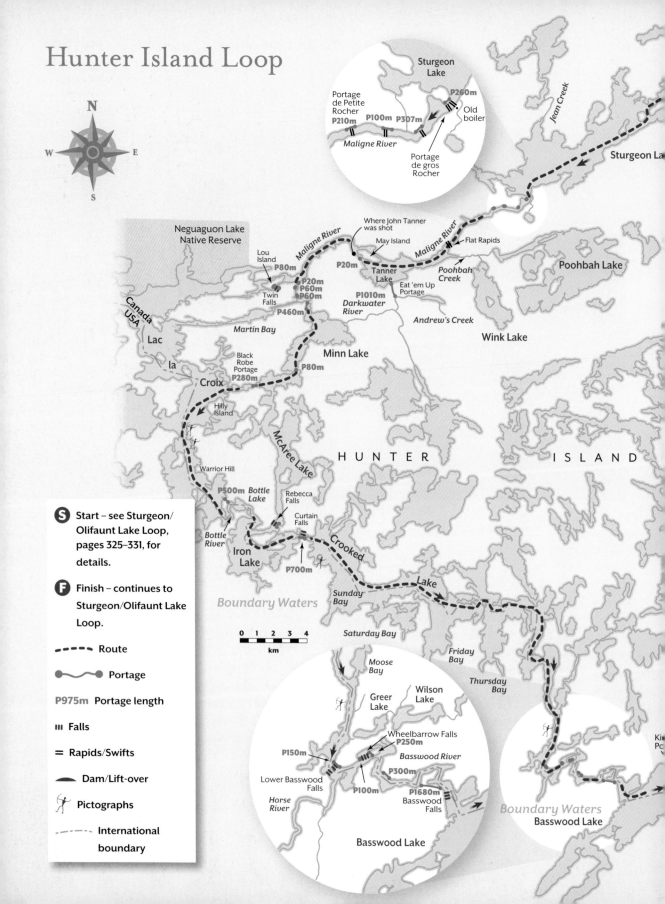

N / W / S / E (compass rose)

Sturgeon Lake

Portage de Petite Rocher
P210m   P100m   P307m   P260m   Old boiler

Maligne River

Portage de gros Rocher

Jean Creek

Sturgeon La

Neguaguon Lake Native Reserve

Where John Tanner was shot

May Island

Maligne River

Flat Rapids

Poohbah Lake

Lou Island
P80m

Maligne River

P20m

Tanner Lake

Poohbah Creek

P20m
P60m
P60m

Twin Falls

P460m

P1010m
Darkwater River

Eat 'em Up Portage

Andrew's Creek

Wink Lake

Martin Bay

Minn Lake

Canada
USA

Lac

la

Croix

Black Robe Portage
P280m

P80m

Hilly Island

McAree Lake

H U N T E R   I S L A N D

Warrior Hill

P500m   *Bottle Lake*

Rebecca Falls

Curtain Falls

Crooked

Bottle River

Iron Lake

P700m

Sunday Bay

Lake

Boundary Waters

Saturday Bay

Friday Bay

Thursday Bay

Legend

S Start – see Sturgeon/Olifaunt Lake Loop, pages 325–331, for details.

F Finish – continues to Sturgeon/Olifaunt Lake Loop.

- - - - Route

●—● Portage

P975m Portage length

||| Falls

= Rapids/Swifts

⌒ Dam/Lift-over

Pictographs

–·–· International boundary

Scale: 0 1 2 3 4 km

Moose Bay

Greer Lake

Wilson Lake

Wheelbarrow Falls
P250m

Basswood River

P150m

P300m

Lower Basswood Falls

P100m

P1680m
Basswood Falls

Horse River

Boundary Waters

Basswood Lake

Basswood Lake

Ki
Po

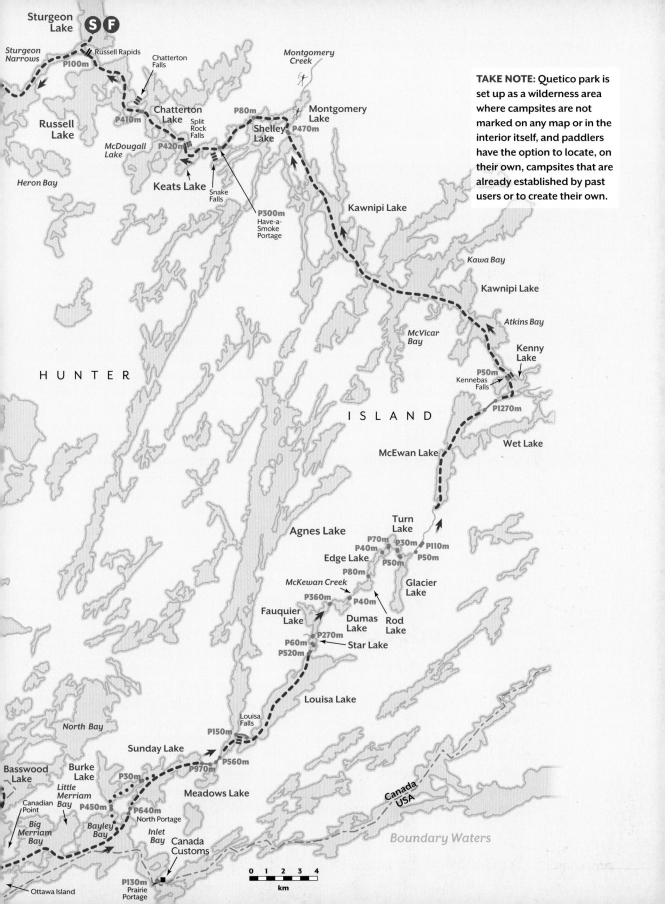

Sturgeon Lake
S **F**

Sturgeon Narrows

Russell Rapids
P100m

Chatterton Falls

P410m

Russell Lake

McDougall Lake

Heron Bay

Chatterton Lake

P420m
Split Rock Falls

Keats Lake

Snake Falls

P80m
Shelley Lake

Montgomery Creek

Montgomery Lake
P470m

P300m
Have-a-Smoke Portage

Kawnipi Lake

H U N T E R

Kawa Bay

Kawnipi Lake

Atkins Bay

McVicar Bay

Kenny Lake

P50m
Kennebas Falls

I S L A N D

P1270m

Wet Lake

McEwan Lake

Turn Lake

Agnes Lake

P70m P30m P110m
P40m
Edge Lake   P50m
P80m   P50m
Glacier Lake

McKewan Creek

P360m   P40m

Fauquier Lake   Dumas Lake   Rod Lake

P60m   P270m
P520m   Star Lake

Louisa Lake

Louisa Falls

P150m

North Bay

Sunday Lake   P560m

Burke Lake   P970m

Basswood Lake   P30m   Meadows Lake

Little Merriam Bay
P450m   P640m
North Portage

Canadian Point
Bayley Bay
Big Merriam Bay   *Inlet Bay*   Canada Customs

Canada
USA

Boundary Waters

Ottawa Island

P130m
Prairie Portage

0 1 2 3 4
km

An easy double swift allowed us to drift by some impressive pine, rooted along the banks, some of which still have cable scars from when boats were hauled around the fast water during the logging era. Soon after is another swift, with a 100-meter bush portage on the right used mostly by paddlers heading upstream. It's a clear run to the far right, but you might want to get out and check it out from the portage first. The take-out for the third and final portage of the day, Portage de Petite Rocher ("small boulder"), was just around the bend and again to the right, a 210-meter trail. Three or four more swift sections continued, all easily navigable, with the biggest being the last, Flat Rapids. Soon we were flushed into Tanner Lake.

On day five of our trip I definitely didn't have the same urgency to get up and out on the water that I had the previous day. Our Tanner Lake campsite was only half-a-day's travel from Lac la Croix, and I felt incredibly anxious about paddling this huge chunk of water. Lac la Croix is notorious for heavy winds and waves. It's named after Sieur de la Croix, who drowned during Jacques de Noyon's 1688 trip from Fort Frances. His birchbark canoe overturned while he and his companions were crossing the lake during a storm. All the occupants managed to hold onto the craft except for poor Sieur de la Croix. The lake is even in the shape of a graveyard cross—how spooky is that?

I suggested to Andy that we at least use a "shortcut," the extensive 1,010-meter "Eat 'em Up Portage" from the south shore of Tanner Lake. From there we would wind our way through Andrew's Creek to the Darkwater River, then link up with Minn and McAree lakes. This would eliminate a large portion of paddling on Lac la Croix. Andy would have

nothing to do with my plan, however. He had traveled on Lac la Croix a number of times before and promised me it was a wonderful place to paddle, claiming it was one of the most scenic lakes in all of Quetico.

We compromised and cut out the lake's most northeastern section by using Minn Lake. After portaging 20 meters to the left of Tanner Rapids, on the south side of May Island, we paddled down the Maligne River once again to just before Lou Island. The river forks here and a series of portages would take us to Minn Lake. Before we headed to Minn Lake, however, Andy insisted we have a look at Twin Falls, located on the south side of Lou Island, before heading south.

We walked Island Portage, an 80-meter trail found on the far right of the twin cascades, took a couple of snapshots of this incredible spot, then backtracked to where the river splits toward Minn Lake. Not long after we began navigating the side route, however, I started second-guessing myself. Of the four portages that were supposed to take us to Minn Lake, the first two, a 20-meter trail to the left and a 60-meter trail to the right, were nonexistent. We lifted over two gigantic beaver dams instead, then we bushwhacked through where a third portage, a 60-meter trail to the left of a set of rapids, was supposed to lead us to Lac la Croix's Martin Bay. The fourth portage had to be the worst, however. We found it by turning left on Martin Bay, paddling to the far end of the inlet, then going south. The 460-meter trail was to the left of a set of rapids and falls flushing into Minn Lake. At least this portage existed, but as it was so overgrown and had muddy sections, in hindsight paddling the full length of Lac la Croix after Twin Falls might have been a better option. The only plus was Minn Lake itself. It was full of pine-clad islands, and we caught some amazing bass by trolling along the far west shore.

The 80-meter portage connecting the south end of Minn to the top end of McAree Lake was more of a lift-over than an actual portage, and the trail connecting McAree with Lac la Croix—measuring 280 meters and called Black Robe Portage—was a straightforward carry.

Our campsite that night was on an island southeast of Hilly Island on Lac la Croix. We took advantage of an early morning calm on Lac la Croix and pushed off from our island site before 6:00 a.m. We kept close to the eastern shoreline, not only to stay in Canada (the United States boundary runs straight down the middle of the lake) but also because we wanted to check out two historically significant sites: Lac la Croix's Native pictographs and Warrior Hill.

The rock paintings are spread out along two massive cliff faces just 5 kilometers from our previous campsite, south of Coleman Island's southwestern end. The most striking paintings in the first cluster of pictographs are of moose. There's also a series of animal tracks leading away from a man with braided hair, sitting and smoking a pipe. Then, on a second slab of granite, separated from the first pictograph by a crack in the rock, is another smoker, sitting with exposed genitals. And to the left of the male figure, "L R 1781" has been chipped away in the rock.

Farther south is another piece of flat granite with two more panels. The first is a man carrying a spear, below him is a caribou or elk, above that is a stick figure under a dome-shaped structure, and scattered throughout are a number of handprints. The second, just to the south, is made up of a small wolf surrounded by more handprints.

Some historians have labeled this grouping of pictographs as the "warrior" panel because of their close proximity to Warrior Hill. This steep chunk of rock is located just over a kilometer to the south, along the east shore, and is thought to have been either a lookout where the Ojibwa watched for their enemies the Sioux, or a hill where young Ojibwa braves raced to the top to test their strength and stamina as warriors.

We spent a good part of the morning gawking at all the Lac la Croix pictographs, and even spent some time attempting to sprint up to the top of Warrior Hill—with limited success, I might add. It was noon before we paddled the full length of Lac la Croix and crossed over the extremely mud-filled 500-meter portage to Bottle Lake.

A short stretch along the Bottle River linked us up with Iron Lake. Before we moved on to Crooked Lake we took a side trip to view Rebecca Falls on the north shore. This magnificent cascade plunges 8 meters into McAree Lake. To check out the falls we approached the central island just above the drop and made use of a bush trail leading to the base of the falls.

At the base of the falls we boiled up a pot of tea and munched on cinnamon bannock that I had cooked that morning, then started our portage to Crooked Lake. The 700-meter trail is marked to the right of the Curtain Falls and has a steep climb shortly after the take-out. The put-in was also a little too close to the brink of the falls, and we decided to walk farther upstream before pushing off. There are a number of side trails along the portage, and the 30-foot Curtain Falls is even more impressive than Rebecca.

Campsites were abundant along the right-hand shoreline, but we hadn't purchased a

Boundary Waters camping permit prior to our trip, so we had to resort to a poor tent site on the Canadian side, directly across from Sunday Bay.

The southern bays of Crooked Lake are named after the days of the week that a group of canoeists found themselves lost here (Sunday to Wednesday). Believe me, it's easy to find yourself lost here. Several such accounts have been documented, one being that of a group of paddlers from Nebraska who ventured here in 1915: "We started across Crooked Lake at 7 a.m. and were lost three times before noon and as many times after,

and camped at night on a river branch of Crooked Lake as totally ignorant of where we were as anyone could be."

Andy and I were confused more than I care to admit while traveling across Crooked Lake the next day. We only became aware of our exact location on the map when we approached Table Rock, a historic campsite used by the early fur-traders and marked by a giant slab of granite resting flat along the southern shoreline. Table Rock is also located a short distance from another cluster of Native pictographs, reported to be one of the best in the park.

The rock-painting site also marks the famed "Rock of Arrows" spot first recorded by Alexander Mackenzie in 1793.

It was past 4:00 p.m. by the time we reached the first of a series of portages leading to Basswood Lake. However, it stays light well past 10:00 p.m. in June, so we made a silly decision to try and keep going all the way to Basswood. The portages weren't altogether difficult.

The first, to the left of Lower Basswood Falls, measured only 150 meters and had a slight incline right after the take-out. The second had two choices: a 250-meter trail to the left of the main cascade, titled Wheelbarrow Falls, or a 100-meter portage to the extreme left, beside a side chute along the north shore. We took the shorter of the two trails. The third had a portage on both sides of the falls, each measuring 300 meters. We stayed to the Canadian side of the river. And the last carry, titled Horse Portage, was a long but flat 1,680-meter trail to the right of Upper Basswood Falls. By the time we began carrying across Horse Portage, however, we were completely exhausted. We changed our minds about making it all the way to Basswood by the end of the first portage. The problem was, every time we went to make camp we found the site already occupied. This is one busy part of Quetico and as a rule if you don't stop around 3:00 in the afternoon to look for a spot to camp, then you'll never find one. It was 9:30 p.m. when we found ourselves stopping three-quarters of the way across Horse Portage and simply pitching the tent right on the trail.

That night, while camped out in the middle of Horse Portage, we celebrated the accomplishments of "The Voyageurs" by doing exactly what they did each night at camp: we read aloud a quote that dealt directly with wilderness values. I chose the group's favorite. It was from group member Omond Solandt's mother: "I often feel the need to go camping in the woods. It irons the wrinkles out of my soul."

Most of day seven of our trip was spent battling wind on Basswood Lake. The lake has such a volume and breadth of scale to it that once a strong wind begins to ruffle its surface, the immense body of water takes forever to calm itself. With our attention more on inching our way forward, and at times even just keeping the canoe upright, we had to ignore any plans of visiting the many historical sites along Basswood, including searching for a French fur-trading post reported in David Thompson's journals and the remains of two of the first ranger cabins for Quetico, constructed on King Point and Cabin 16 Island.

Progress seemed slow at first, but eventually we checked the map and realized the mileage was adding up. We spent our time on the water talking sporadically, retelling stories of past trips and sharing dreams of places we've yet to paddle. Most of the time, however, was spent gawking at the scenery as we floated along. Halfway across, our ability to paddle in heavy winds required little thought: paddle two strokes forward, brace for an oncoming big wave, then paddle two strokes forward and brace again. Our shoulders were less sore from the strain of each stroke, and we developed a rhythm that was actually relaxing.

By late afternoon we had made it to the entrance to Basswood's Inlet Bay. Not far ahead was Prairie Portage, a 130-meter trail marking Quetico's most southern access point. From there a series of lakes running straight along the border of the United States and Canada would link us to Saganaga Lake, where the two waterways split to form Hunter Island. And once at Saganaga, the route turned northwest toward Kawnipi Lake and back toward Pickerel Lake. The problem was, however, we noticed a lineup of canoeists waiting to use Prairie Portage, and we weren't too thrilled about dealing with crowds again. We were also worried that if we continued east along the major route without an overnight camping permit for the Boundary Waters Country Area Wilderness, we would get stuck again looking for a spot to set up the tent. Andy recommended we backtrack a little ways, portage into Sunday Lake and then head northeast to McEwen Lake and Kawnipi Lake. That would definitely take us away from one of the most crowded areas of the park, but it would also eliminate some of the most scenic and historically significant places en route. For example, Knife Lake is a gorgeous spot and comes complete with a hiking trail to the top of Thunder Point and a visit to Dorothy Molter's Isles of Pines. Until her death in 1986, Dorothy was a legendary figure for thousands of canoeists who knew her as the "Root Beer Lady" and who stopped by her island home for a bottle of homemade root beer.

We saw another large group of canoeists heading toward Prairie Portage, making a total of 12 canoes and 17 kayaks gathered at the take-out. We decided on the shortcut.

There are two ways to reach Sunday Lake from Basswood's Bayley Bay. The first is to take an easy 450-meter portage from the top end of Bayley Bay into Burke Lake and then turn east to a quick lift-over beside a small creek. The second is a 640-meter trail called the North Portage that begins from Bayley

Bay's northeastern Sunday Bay. Andy and I took the North Portage, thinking it would save time, which it did, but we had an uphill battle most of the way across, so the moment we paddled out into Sunday Lake we called it a day and made camp on the first island to our right.

Fortunately the wind had changed direction by morning, and we were able to race the full length of Sunday Lake. It was a mixed blessing, since we weren't too keen on what was waiting for us at the other end. A 970-meter portage took us into Meadows Lake, and a 560-meter portage took us out. The first trail was relatively flat but cursed with lots and lots of mud. The second was shorter but had a much steeper incline with a few ankle-twisting rocks to balance on. The payoff, however, was brunch and a swim at Louisa Falls. There was an insanely steep 150-meter portage to the right of the falls, but once we carried the canoe and gear up to the top, we were able to return to the halfway point and relax in the natural Jacuzzi formed in a glacial bowl below the first drop of the 100-foot falls.

The route between Bayley Bay and Agnes Lake can be busy at times, and the Louisa Falls pool is an extremely popular destination for paddlers, but once we began paddling northeast across Louisa Lake we knew that crowds wouldn't be an issue. Louisa is a very large, scenic destination lake, but the route that follows is barely used by canoeists.

The first portage, measuring 520 meters and leading out of the far northeast end, was overgrown and had seen little traffic. It also happens to be all uphill. We missed the 60-meter portage to Star Lake completely. It was supposed to be somewhere in a bay to the left. Instead we found a rarely used 60-meter trail to the left of the creek flowing out of Star

Lake. We paddled a twisting channel through the center of a marshy area and then lifted 20 meters over and through a giant patch of poison ivy to Star Lake. The third (270 meters into Fauquier) could only be reached by getting out and pulling the canoe up a small creek surrounded by muskeg. A few blow-downs blocked the path, but at least it was downhill all the way.

From Fauquier to Dumas Lake, a spot where the flow of water changes direction, the going got worse. The 360-meter portage was rocky, narrow and wet, with an abrupt crevasse and patches of poison ivy. The small brook, however, was gorgeous. Crystal clear water flushed over medium-sized boulders covered in vibrant-colored moss; the entire section had a fairyland appearance to it and was a highlight of the day. Then, from the eastern inlet of Dumas, there was more creek paddling; the lakes themselves were mere ponds, but each with a character of its own. The center of the creek bed swayed with lime-green angel hair, and the edges were lined with thick patches of white and yellow lilies, pitcher plants and the occasional calypso orchid.

As we rounded the first bend in the creek after Dumas Lake, we witnessed a wolf prey-ing on a raven. We heard the commotion first, two ravens screaming, and slowed the canoe. We drifted around the corner in time to see a large timber wolf latch onto one raven's wing while the other bird repeatedly dive-bombed the attacker. The wind wasn't in our favor, but the wolf was so preoccupied with both ravens that we were able to float close to the action. It was like watching a nature documentary unfolding right in front of us.

We took on a 40-meter portage along the right bank of McEwen Creek soon after leaving the wolf/raven incident. Between Rod and Edge lakes there was another short portage to the left, complete with an awkward take-out spot. To get from Edge to Turn Lake, we first considered walking the section of shal-low rapids rather than taking the 40-meter portage to the left. The take-out was covered in poison ivy. But fallen trees on the far side made the idea impossible, so we tiptoed our way through the poison ivy, walked alongside the creek, then climbed over a slab of granite, trudging on until the waterway deepened enough to be navigable again. The next portage is 70 meters and found to the right of the creek. It leads directly into Turn Lake and was one of the easiest en route.

The creek became even more weed-choked from here, but we managed to find a way to Glacier Lake by keeping to the center and making use of two more portages to take us around two sections of swift water, the first being an easy 30-meter trail to the right and the second being a 50-meter trail also to the right, with the take-out hidden by a large boulder.

Our plan was to reach McEwen Lake by the end of the day, which we could have done by taking two more portages—a 50-meter trail to the left, which splits after the take-out and either takes you over a steep mound of rock or keeps you close to the creek, and a 110-meter trail to the right of a shallow, rock-bound rapid (you could actually line down this one rather than portage)—followed by a couple more kilometers of twisting McEwen Creek. Glacier Lake, however, was too perfect to pass up. It was a clear, deep lake surrounded by cliffs and loaded with feisty smallmouth bass. And best of all, no one was there. The lake was so perfect that we made our campsite east of the island, directly in front of a granite bluff.

This would be our home for two solid days.

Having a rest day during an extensive trip is a must for canoe trippers. The midway point is the best time for it. You're in too much of a hurry at the beginning, and way too much of a hurry at the end of your trip, but by the midway point, your body and mind are in need of a rest. Our time off was spent brewing an extra pot of coffee in the morning, cooking up extra bannock for lunch and exploring an unnamed lake to the northeast of Turn Lake, a lake that is off the regular canoe route and that turned out to be full of bass.

There was a slight drizzle on day 10, but it meant there were no winds pushing hard against us as we paddled the expanse of McEwen Lake and then Kawnipi Lake. And we only had two portages to deal with. The first, measuring a lengthy 1,270 meters and connecting the northeastern inlet of McEwen Lake to Kenny Lake, wasn't too bad of a walk. It took us under two hours to complete both carries, and most of the steep parts were downhill. The second portage connected Kenny to Kawnipi Lake. It measures less than 50 meters but was more problematic than the much longer trail. This portage is on the left-hand side of Kennebas Falls, the last drop in what's called the "Falls Chain." The water was high, and the take-out is unnervingly close to the brink of the falls.

The rest of the day was spent paddling effortlessly along the shoreline of Kawnipi Lake, finally moving over to the western shore to check out the two pictograph sites at the entrance to Kawa Bay. The first painting is near the southern entrance to the bay, and the second is near the northern entrance. Of the two sites, only the first is easily recognizable. The second, believed to be of Misshepeshu (the Great Lynx), is far too faded. We located the first panel directly below an obvious crack in the rock face. The pictograph portrayed two (possibly three) Maymaygwayshi sitting in a canoe. The figures had what seemed to be horns on their heads and were sitting in the canoe with their arms bent at their waists. To me, they looked like spirits standing on guard, almost daring you to enter a sacred place, which may make sense since Kawa Bay and the river at the far eastern end (Wawiag River) were part of a well-known Ojibwa travel route.

We camped that night on an island in the center of Kawa Bay, with enough time to catch and clean a few walleye for supper. At this point in the trip, we were down to freeze-dried meals and just a few fingers of rum to wash it down with. Fresh fish was always a welcome change, and mixing the rum with clear tea helped our supply of spirits last a little longer.

We left our Kawnipi Lake campsite just before 9:00 a.m., waiting patiently for the wind to shift and clear the morning rain clouds. We chose to continue north into Montgomery Lake rather than twist around to the southwest to Kahshahpiwi Creek. Either way would have allowed us to continue down the Maligne River, but the Kahshahpiwi route required a 40-meter portage to either the left or the right of some rapids that Andy remembered from a previous trip as having a take-out uncomfortably close to the main drop. The Montgomery route had an overgrown 470-meter portage, with the first section of the trail skirting close to the right of a large, muddy swamp. But Montgomery was by far the better route choice. We had the lake all to ourselves and even took half a day off to explore the out-of-the-way Montgomery Creek pictographs. Sadly, our attempt to locate the paintings failed. Andy and I managed to drag ourselves, and the canoe, up to a small pond, where we searched in vain. When we later talked to the park staff about the route to the Montgomery Creek paintings, they informed us that the pictograph site was quite a ways north of the pond.

The paintings were discovered by local trapper Phil Sawdo, who came upon them while snowshoeing through the area in the winter of 1983. They're isolated, far away from any known navigable route. Two of the three animal symbols depict caribou, and the third, reported to be a moose, could quite possibly be a caribou as well. One of the human figures is armed with a bow and arrow—a rare symbol to find in Quetico. Sawdo believed the paintings marked a spot where hunters ambushed herds of caribou. Woodland caribou were present in the Quetico area up to the 1930s, but if the symbols represent barrenland caribou, it would date the paintings at over a thousand years old.

Andy and I weren't too upset about not getting to see the remote Montgomery Creek paintings, especially because we spotted a rarely viewed pictograph directly below our campsite on Montgomery Lake (the painting, which is of a male stick-figure with an erect penis, was discovered in 1984 by David Ingebrigtsen). We were camped high atop a ridge, on the easternmost section of a small island, north of a large central island and separated by a long section of rock. Both the tent site and the painting were exceptional.

Leaving Montgomery, we headed west. We portaged a quick 80 meters into the top end of Shelley Lake, then followed the right-hand shoreline all the way to the 300-meter Have-a-Smoke Portage. The map showed another route to the south, where a couple of shorter

but much steeper portages are marked to the right of what's labeled Snake Falls. Andy and I, however, chose to take the simpler trail and thankfully discovered Have-a-Smoke to be uneventful.

Split Rock Portage was next. It's marked to the right and measures a total 420 meters if you use the high-water take-out, which you definitely want to do. From there we paddled across Chatterton Lake and carried across the 410-meter portage to the south of Chatterton Falls. This trail is about a kilometer south of the falls, and even though it was the most rugged of the day, it definitely doesn't compare to the nasty trail that's directly beside the falls on the left bank. I've walked that trail before, and it's a great way to view the cascade, but

I wouldn't even dream of carrying a canoe across it. Instead, we carried across the portage to the south, then paddled up to the base of Chatterton Falls to have a look.

The remainder of the afternoon was spent paddling across scenic Russell Lake, then flushing down the set of rapids linking Russell with the upper end of Sturgeon Lake (a 100-m portage is also located to the left). We decided to camp that night on the very same site we had occupied our second night out. We'd finally come full circle, and from here we only had to retrace our familiar route back to French Lake over the next couple of days. To celebrate, we finished off the remainder of our rum supply.

At dawn I walked down to the shoreline to fill up the coffee pot and noticed bear tracks, prints in the sand that I'm sure weren't there the night before. Nothing on the site had been disturbed. The tracks were in a straight line away from the direction of our food cache. The bear had obviously ignored what our camp had to offer, which wasn't much by this point in the trip.

The interesting part about the event was my reaction. It was the complete opposite of what it would have been if the bear had walked through our camp at the beginning of the trip. I would have definitely felt anxious—terrified, actually. Now I was more upset that we hadn't managed to spot the bruin wandering by. A close encounter with a bear would have been an exciting addition to our trip, not a reason for panic. I liked that feeling, a feeling that by completing the Hunter Island Loop, I had become comfortable with these surroundings, a "Quetico regular."

LONGEST PORTAGE 1,680 meters

FEE An interior camping permit must be purchased for Quetico Provincial Park.

ALTERNATIVE ACCESS This route can be accessed by any entry point in the park. The one we chose is best only if you are a Canadian who doesn't want to cross the border to the United States The best overall entry point, especially if you are entering from the United States, is at Saganaga Lake. To reach the public launch on the most southerly inlet of Saganaga Lake, take the 90-kilometer Cook County Lake Road (Gunflint Trail Road) to its most northwestern end. The road begins in the town of Grand Marais, Minnesota.

ALTERNATIVE ROUTE None

OUTFITTERS
Canoe Canada Outfitters
300 O'Brien Street
Atikokan, ON, P0T 1C0
807-597-6418
www.canoecanada.com

QuetiQuest Outfitters
Box 1060
Atikokan, ON, P0T 1C0
807-929-2266
www.quetiquest.com

FOR MORE INFORMATION
Quetico Provincial Park
807-597-2735
1-888-668-7275 or 519-826-5290 outside of North America (reservations)
www.ontarioparks.com

Friends of Quetico
807-929-2571
www.friendsofquetico.com

Quetico Foundation
416-941-9388
www.queticofoundation.org

MAPS Chrismar and the Friends of Quetico have produced an excellent map for Quetico Provincial Park.

TOPOGRAPHIC MAPS
52 B/3, 52 B/4, 52 B/5, 52 B/6 & 52 B/11

GPS COORDINATES
48.657438, -91.338510

Leopold's North Country Loop

I'LL ADMIT THAT it may have seemed a little odd: two Canadian canoeists wanting to enter the United States so that they can re-enter Canada's Quetico Park from the U.S. side and thereby retrace the historic route taken by American conservationist Aldo Leopold. The U.S. border guard found the whole idea a bit too quirky, but I wasn't about to let one man in uniform deter us from our quest, so I broke all border-crossing etiquette, and rather than politely agreeing with him and retreating back to Canada, I launched into a spiel about how important the trip was to us. My speech was short. I only got to the part about my long-time desire to visit the same lakes and rivers that Aldo Leopold, a wilderness visionary and author of the quintessential environmental book *Sand County Almanac*, had, when the guard simply waved us through. I'm not sure if he suddenly agreed with the reasoning behind our trip or just couldn't bear to listen to my detailed explanation, but he let us pass. In a couple of hours my wife, Alana, and I along with our dog, Bailey, arrived at Ely, Minnesota, to begin our pilgrimage.

We accessed Quetico Provincial Park just as Leopold did in 1924, by way of the remote ranger station situated on Basswood Lake's Prairie Portage. Once we arrived, and portaged the 130 meters across to Canada, we still had to wait in line for over an hour before being able to register.

Eventually we were on our way, paddling full tilt down the middle of Basswood Lake, with the United States to the left of us and Canada to the right. To mark the occasion, we fastened an American flag to one gunwale and a Canadian flag to the other.

Alana and I made it all the way down Basswood Lake and set up camp at 4:00 p.m.

By 9:00 a.m. the next morning, Alana, Bailey and I found ourselves carrying around Horse Portage, to the left, the first of four portages on the Basswood River. The waterway connects Basswood Lake with Crooked Lake via a series of falls and turbulent rapids. It's rated as one of the most captivating places in all of Quetico. Horse Portage is also an easy carry, which is great, since it's 1,680 meters long. The only problem was the crowds. By the time we reached the end, we had seen a grand total of 112 canoeists and kayakers. I'm not kidding!

Leopold's North Country Loop

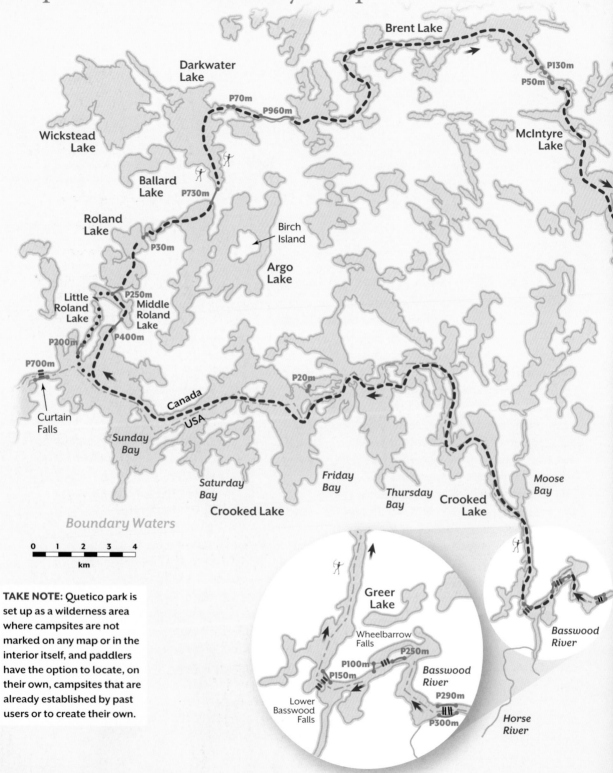

Brent Lake

Darkwater Lake

P70m

P960m

P130m

P50m

Wickstead Lake

McIntyre Lake

Ballard Lake

P730m

Roland Lake

P30m

Birch Island

Argo Lake

Little Roland Lake

P250m

Middle Roland Lake

P200m

P400m

P700m

Canada

P20m

Curtain Falls

USA

Sunday Bay

Saturday Bay

Friday Bay

Thursday Bay

Crooked Lake

Moose Bay

Crooked Lake

Boundary Waters

0	1	2	3	4

km

TAKE NOTE: Quetico park is set up as a wilderness area where campsites are not marked on any map or in the interior itself, and paddlers have the option to locate, on their own, campsites that are already established by past users or to create their own.

Greer Lake

Wheelbarrow Falls

P250m

P100m

P150m

Basswood River

Lower Basswood Falls

Basswood River

P290m

P300m

Horse River

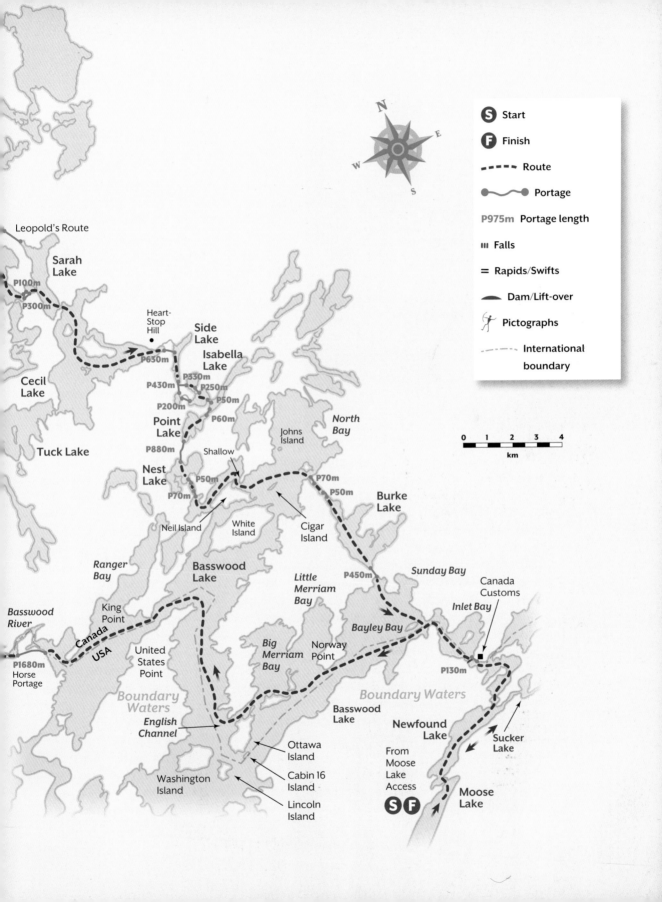

Leopold's Route

Sarah Lake

P100m

P300m

Cecil Lake

Tuck Lake

Heart-Stop Hill

Side Lake

Isabella Lake

P630m

P330m

P430m   P250m

P200m   P50m

P60m

Point Lake

P880m

Nest Lake

Shallow

P50m

P70m

Neil Island

White Island

Johns Island

North Bay

Cigar Island

P70m

P50m

Burke Lake

P450m

Sunday Bay

Canada Customs

Inlet Bay

Bayley Bay

Ranger Bay

Basswood Lake

Little Merriam Bay

King Point

Canada

USA

Basswood River

P1680m
Horse Portage

United States Point

Big Merriam Bay

Norway Point

Boundary Waters

English Channel

Ottawa Island

Cabin 16 Island

Lincoln Island

Washington Island

Boundary Waters

Basswood Lake

Newfound Lake

From Moose Lake Access

S **F**

P130m

Sucker Lake

Moose Lake

S Start

F Finish

- - - Route

●━━● Portage

P975m Portage length

ɪɪɪ Falls

= Rapids/Swifts

━ Dam/Lift-over

⚑ Pictographs

–·– International boundary

0 1 2 3 4
km

The second portage, not far downstream, is also an easy carry. It has two portages, one on the American side and the other on the Canadian shore. Both measure approximately 300 meters, and the only difference is that the American trail has a better put-in.

The river twists to the right, and it's another 10 minutes of paddling before you have to get out and portage again, this time around Wheelbarrow Falls. You have two options here. You can take a 250-meter trail to the right of the main cascade or paddle around a channel to the far right and then take a shorter 100-meter portage to the right of a side chute. Alana and I took the smaller trail, but I was told later by other canoeists that the first option is the preferred choice. Either way, it's an easy carry.

Only one more portage remained for us before we could paddle out into the expanse of Crooked Lake and finally escape the crowds.

It measured only 150 meters and had a huge take-out well back from the brink of Lower Basswood Falls.

After making camp close to Curtain Falls our third night, we portaged north into Roland Lake using a grown-over 400-meter bush trail to Middle Roland and a 250-meter portage that begins a short way up a creek coming out of Roland, on the left-hand side. The regular route is up the Siobhan River (Little Roland Lake), using an easy 200-meter portage to the left of where the river flows into Crooked Lake, a short lift-over to the left of where a small cascade flushes out of Middle Roland, and then the 250-meter portage into Roland. The bush trail was obviously more difficult, but it was also the way Alana and I believed Leopold's group had gone.

From Roland to Sarah Lake, a distance that took us four leisurely days, we saw no other canoeists. It was absolute bliss. Leopold also found solace here. His first evening, camping on Roland Lake, he wrote in his journal: "The number of adventures awaiting us in the blessed country seems without end. Watching the gray twilight settling upon our lake we could truly say that 'all our ways are pleasantness and all our paths are peace.'"

Surprisingly, the landscape has changed little since Leopold's time. Alana and I had similar wildlife sightings: moose, deer, beaver, bald eagles, grouse, loons and an assortment of other waterfowl. And the lakes themselves still had "the green water of the real north country, rather than the brown water of Crooked and Basswood Lakes."

There were a few differences, the most notable being regeneration of the stands of fire-destroyed pine that Leopold's group had witnessed on the 730-meter portage between Argo and Darky Lake (recently reassigned its original name, Darkwater Lake). Another variance between the two trips was that Alana and I found the Native paintings Leopold had failed to locate on Darkwater Lake. It's a shame Leopold never saw the pictographs. They were the highlight of our trip. We had already seen paintings on Crooked Lake, located about a kilometer below Lower Basswood Falls, just to the north of an imposing overhang, but the Crooked Lake site is quite extraordinary and includes a pelican with horns and a moose smoking a pipe. We found the Darkwater Lake paintings to be the best we've ever witnessed. The first site, on the west shore of the south bay, depicts Maymaygwayshi (mischievous, hairy-faced little men who dwell in the cracks of the cliff). The second site, on the east shore of the south bay, depicts two small moose (one of which is missing its heart), a man firing a projectile and a horned serpent known as Misshepeshu overturning a group of canoes.

We paddled the Darkwater River connecting us to Brent Lake. Twenty minutes into it, we performed a quick carry over a 70-meter portage along the left bank, and then soon after, a much lengthier 960-meter portage, also to the left. The longer portage worked its way around a series of ponds, the last of which you have to actually paddle across to finish the remaining 50 meters of trail.

The remainder of our day was spent paddling across the expanse of Brent and McIntyre lakes. Brent Lake, made up of a series of narrow, twisting channels, is more like a river than a lake at times. It was tough to catch enough wind here to sail the canoe. It blew steadily out of the northwest, but because the lake zigzagged all over the place, we couldn't seem to keep the tarp up long enough to snag a breeze.

It was late afternoon by the time we reached the other side of Brent. Alana and I should have stopped here, but it was such a pleasant day, and the only thing between us and McIntyre were two short but rugged portages, one 130 meters and the other 50 meters, linking an unnamed lake between the southeast bay of Brent and the far northern end of McIntyre. We went for it, and ended the day with a late peanut-butter-and-jelly-sandwich dinner on a gorgeous island campsite.

Our extra time on the water on day four allowed us a much more leisurely pace on day five. We spent a good deal of the morning doing laundry (something Alana insists on doing halfway through any trip) and then explored a narrow inlet in the northwest corner of McIntyre Lake. Apparently Leopold took a portage here to connect with Sarah Lake. Our map showed no evidence of a trail and none existed. We did manage to walk

through the thick brush to Sarah, but decided it would be foolish to carry our canoe and gear through. Our dog, Bailey, even refused to shoulder her pack. Alana and I managed to spook a moose before returning to the canoe and paddling south of McIntyre to take the present-day portage.

There's a choice of two trails. I only knew of the 100-meter portage, known as "the hill." It's an incredibly steep downhill ramble through ankle-breaking boulders to a poor put-in spot. The other portage, a rarely used 300-meter trail, is just to the south. It's obviously longer, but is supposed to be much easier.

We camped on Sarah Lake for two full days. The extended stay wasn't scheduled, and it meant we would have to push hard over the next couple of days to end the trip on time, but our campsite was just too perfect to leave. It was situated in the remote northeast corner of the lake, with a steep mound of rock to sit on and watch the sun set and a ridiculous amount of blueberries to munch on for breakfast. Besides, Alana and I suspected that it wouldn't be long after leaving Sarah Lake that we would start seeing the crowds again. We were right. The moment we reached the portage leading out of Sarah Lake's southeast corner, we encountered a dozen paddlers lining up to use the trail.

You have two choices for getting from Sarah to Side Lake, either a steep 630-meter portage labeled "Heart-stop Hill" or a creek with three separate trails. And once again, I only knew about the steep one. The creek has some elevation on the first and second carry (135 m and 110 m), and there's mud to contend with on the remaining 35 meters, but it's no "heart-stopper." Just make sure to paddle to the right when creek splits after the first carry.

We also had more than one option heading out of Side Lake. The initial portage, located at the southern corner of the lake, splits close to the take-out. Here, an alternative route goes right, in and out of an unnamed pond. But Alana and I kept to the regular route, a 330-meter goat trail with a much steeper grade than the previous portage. We weren't sure if going right would have been easier, but everyone we saw heading in and out of Side Lake seemed to be using the trail to the left.

Thankfully, things got easier after we carried out of Side Lake. From there we paddled across another unnamed lake and up a shallow creek clogged with deadheads, and then we began a 250-meter portage to the left of an old beaver dam. We sprinted across two relatively flat portages, the first being a 50-meter trail to the right of a creek entering the lower end of Isabella Lake, and the second a 60-meter trail going from the south end of Isabella to Point Lake.

Alana and I were surprised to see how unused the portage to Point Lake was. I guess most paddlers (except for Aldo Leopold) head up to the top end of Isabella to connect with Basswood Lake's North Bay. But Point Lake is extremely scenic, with turquoise waters and three incredible campsites. We stopped at the first site and rested from the previous uphill slog and even caught a few decent-sized bass.

With Point Lake's seeming lack of use, we worried about the 880-meter portage that would take us out to Nest Lake, but again it was surprisingly easy, only a bit of mud to be dealt with. Fifteen minutes later we were paddling across Nest Lake and taking on two rocky but short 50- and 70-meter portages in and out of a shallow, mucky pond. That's when we realized why people don't generally travel this way. If the water level had been any lower, I doubt we could have got through.

Water level also became an issue while we traveled along the north channel of North Bay's Neil Island. It was a quicker route than having to paddle all the way around the south side, but a number of large boulders and blown-down pine trees kept us guessing as to the best route through.

The downed pines were remnants of the giant windstorm that hit the park back in 1999. It swept through the Boundary Waters and Quetico Provincial Park on July 4, downing 12 million trees and endangering hundreds of canoeists. Surprisingly, there were no deaths. But many were injured, and search-and-rescue teams worked for days to extract people from the interior. Countless stories have been told by the survivors, all of whom have called it one of the worst sudden storms they've ever witnessed.

Relieved to be out in open water, Alana and I decided to sail across, first to Cigar Island and then to where our map showed a portage heading into Burke Lake. And, once again, we had two options. We took the first one we came to, just after a small island campsite and before the elongated point along the south shore. The portage was less than 50 meters, but we had to wade up a small gravel swift before completing it. The put-in and take-out were full of huge rocks that marked up our canoe and frustrated the hell out of poor Bailey. Only after we completed our trip across did we become aware of the second route that began a little farther past the point. It measured 70 meters but was a much easier trail.

To end our day, a very long one at that, Alana and I took on one more obstacle before making camp. We waded up a shallow creek, luckily with sand at the bottom and not boot-sucking muck, and then portaged over an easy 50-meter trail to Burke Lake.

All that remained for us the last two days out was a well-worn 450-meter portage from Burke to Basswood Lake's Bayley Bay and the familiar Prairie Portage.

LONGEST PORTAGE 1,680 meters

FEE An interior camping permit must be purchased for Quetico Provincial Park.

ALTERNATIVE ACCESS None

ALTERNATIVE ROUTE None

OUTFITTERS
La Tourell's Moose Lake Outfitters
Box 239
Ely, MN, 55731
1-800-365-4531
www.latourells.com

Piragis Northwoods Company
105 N Central Avenue
Ely, MN, 55731
1-800-223-6565
www.piragis.com

FOR MORE INFORMATION
Quetico Provincial Park
807-597-2735
1-888-668-7275 or 519-826-5290
outside of North America
(reservations)
www.ontarioparks.com

Friends of Quetico
807-929-2571
www.friendsofquetico.com

Quetico Foundation
416-941-9388
www.queticofoundation.org

MAPS Chrismar and the Friends of Quetico have produced an excellent map for Quetico Provincial Park.

TOPOGRAPHIC MAPS
52 B/3, 52 B/4 & 52 B/5

GPS COORDINATES
47.987054, −91.500431

The Pines Loop

 5 to 7 days

 38 portages

 112 km

Some portages are steep or muddy and knowledge of wilderness navigation is a must.

IT'S INTERESTING HOW canoeists are attracted to the familiar, a landscape they like to call their own. Algonquin is where I do most of my paddling, not only because it's near my home in Peterborough, Ontario, but also because it has what I like on a trip: deep, turquoise-colored lakes filled with trout and surrounded by large white pine. So it's no surprise that for one of my initial trips in Quetico I chose a route with much the same character. Located west of Agnes Lake is a circular trip made up of a series of seemingly bottomless, blue-tinted lakes that yield good-sized lake trout and have some of the oldest white pine in North America rooted along the shoreline.

The trip started at Prairie Portage, the most southern access point in Quetico, reached by paddling up Moose, Newfound and Sucker lakes. I booked a boat shuttle with La Tourell's Moose Lake Outfitters, made it to the access point in 20 minutes and then portaged 130 meters over to Basswood Lake. It was a quick way to get there. But then it took until noon to go through the lineup to register at the ranger cabin, leaving me only enough daylight to paddle across to Basswood's Bayley

Bay and carry over the trouble-free 450-meter portage into Burke Lake.

I had a quick breakfast of porridge and coffee the next morning so I could head out across Basswood Lake's North Bay before the winds picked up, and I was rewarded by spotting a black bear wading through the shallow parts of the creek connecting Burke Lake and North Bay. Two portages, measuring 50 and 70 meters, are located at each end of the creek and were quick and easy to carry across. There was even enough water in the weed-choked creek leading up the northeast corner of North Bay that I only had to get out and drag the canoe twice before reaching the 50-meter portage leading into South Lake.

Another straightforward 50-meter carry, to the northeast and beside a small cascade tumbling into South Lake, took me into West Lake. And keeping to the right-hand shore of West Lake, I found two more portages leading into Shade Lake. The first was approximately 100 meters, going up a short incline and alongside another small waterfall, and the other was an uncomplicated 50-meter portage on the left-hand side of the creek.

Before continuing on, I drifted down the

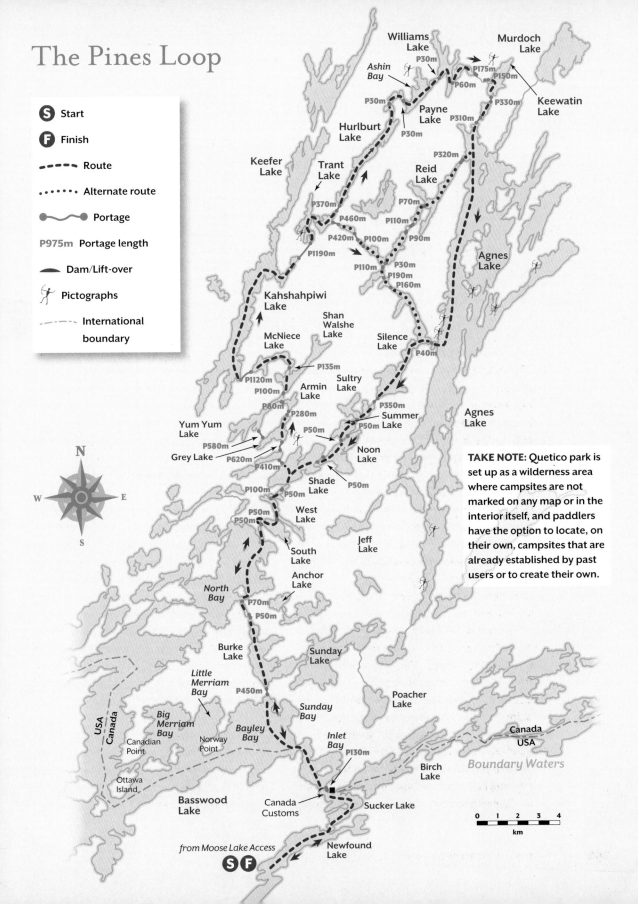

The Pines Loop

Legend:
- **S** Start
- **F** Finish
- - - - Route
- ······ Alternate route
- ●∼● Portage
- **P975m** Portage length
- ▬ Dam/Lift-over
- 🏹 Pictographs
- –·–·– International boundary

TAKE NOTE: Quetico park is set up as a wilderness area where campsites are not marked on any map or in the interior itself, and paddlers have the option to locate, on their own, campsites that are already established by past users or to create their own.

Williams Lake
Murdoch Lake
Ashin Bay
P30m
P175m
P150m
P60m
Keewatin Lake
P30m
Payne Lake
P330m
Hurlburt Lake
P310m
P30m
Keefer Lake
Trant Lake
Reid Lake
P320m
P370m
P70m
P460m
P110m
P420m
P100m
P90m
P1190m
P110m
P30m
P190m
P160m
Agnes Lake
Kahshahpiwi Lake
Shan Walshe Lake
Silence Lake
P40m
McNiece Lake
Agnes Lake
P135m
Sultry Lake
P1120m
P100m
Armin Lake
P350m
P80m
Summer Lake
P280m
P50m
Yum Yum Lake
P50m
Noon Lake
P580m
Grey Lake
P620m
P410m
Shade Lake
P50m
P100m
P50m
West Lake
Jeff Lake
P50m
P50m
South Lake
Anchor Lake
North Bay
P70m
P50m
Burke Lake
Sunday Lake
Little Merriam Bay
Poacher Lake
P450m
Big Merriam Bay
Sunday Bay
USA Canada
Canada USA
Norway Point
Bayley Bay
Inlet Bay
P130m
Birch Lake
Canadian Point
Boundary Waters
Ottawa Island
Basswood Lake
Canada Customs
Sucker Lake
from Moose Lake Access
Newfound Lake
S **F**

N W E S

0 1 2 3 4 km

far northeastern bay of Shade Lake to check out the faded Native pictographs (two abstract thunderbirds) and then backtracked to carry over two additional portages: a 410-meter portage to an unnamed lake and, almost to the immediate right, a 620-meter portage to Grey Lake. The first carry wasn't a problem, but the longer one, into Grey, began and ended with a steep slope and a beaver meadow filled with boot-sucking mud. It's also a confusing trail to follow, with two take-outs and a very puzzling intersection just before the halfway point (when in doubt, go right).

Yum Yum Lake was next. It can be reached by either a 580-meter portage just to the left of the previous portage or two shorter portages in and out of Armin Lake, measuring 280 and 80 meters. I took the easier route, of course, but it only took me to the far north-eastern tip of Yum Yum and didn't allow me to check out the large pine growing along the lakeshore. Grey and Armin Lakes have their fair share of old-growth pine, and the next lake, connected to Yum Yum by a 100-meter portage, had some enormous trees.

I considered staying on Shan Walshe Lake for my second night out, but I still had enough time and energy to do one more carry, a 135-meter portage linking the lower north-west corner of Shan Walshe to McNiece Lake. It was an easy walk, and the trail went straight through some of the most impressive old-growth pine of the entire trip. Some were over 3 feet in diameter and had to be at least 250 to 300 years old. Campsites were limited on McNiece, however, and I ended up brushing out a spot on an outcrop of rock overlooking the western bay.

After dinner I paddled around the lake to check out the trees. White pine dominated, but there were also a few scattered old-growth red pine and cedar trees, some of which had to be close to 400 years old. The largest patch was along the northwest corner. I pulled the canoe ashore here and walked through the stand.

Red and white pine were never the main species in the park, and past logging practices made them even more scarce. The pine on McNiece Lake were scheduled to be cut in the 1960s until the government put a stop to the logging plan after receiving over 2,000 letters from concerned citizens. It was fire suppression, however, that did the most damage to this delicate environment. Wildfires open up areas of the forest and enrich the soil to allow for new growth. With thick bark and its main branches positioned higher up, an old-growth pine usually survives a fire and helps regenerate the forest, but when the fires were suppressed in Quetico, spruce and balsam took over instead. While walking among the McNiece Lake stand, I noticed a few pine seedlings rooted below the larger trees, but I also noticed significant patches of young spruce and balsam taking hold. This ancient forest is changing, and not for the better.

The next day I carried southwest into Kahshahpiwi Lake by way of a 1,120-meter portage. This trail definitely gave me a work-out. Near the end I descended into a swampy bog, then hauled myself out again by clambering up an almost sheer slab of rock. It was exhausting but not impossible; besides, it was this rugged landscape that initially protected the pine from the logger's axe. To me, that's worth a bit of suffering.

I had a couple hours of paddling north on scenic Kahshahpiwi Lake before taking on another portage, this one leading to Trant Lake. It's a lengthy one as well, measuring 1,190 meters. But the trail wasn't as bad as the one coming out of McNiece. Getting there, however, was a little tough, since it was tucked away on the far end of Kahshahpiwi's northeast bay, and I had to pull the canoe up a shallow, muddy creek to reach the take-out along the right bank. The footing was difficult in sections where, close to the put-in, ankle-twisting roots and rocks blocked the way.

I spent a good hour at the bottom end of Trant Lake looking for the Native pictographs reported to be here. I finally spotted them near the base of a high cliff along the western shore, directly beside the bay where the portage comes into Trant Lake, a totally different location than suggested in my park booklet. The booklet also noted that a canoe with two paddlers and three moose could be discerned in the pictograph. But, to me, one of the moose resembled a snowshoe hare and another had straight antlers, which made it look more like a young elk.

From here I could head north through a chain of lakes leading to the top end of Agnes Lake or choose a shortcut east through a series of small unnamed lakes to Silence Lake, where I had planned on heading southwest back to the North Arm. I had traveled the shortcut before as a day trip from Agnes and remembered it to be a gorgeous area with clear blue lakes and magnificent white pine. It was also hardly used and the portages weren't all that difficult either. The first, measuring 460 meters, was rocky at first, with a moderate hill midway (but with a nice view of the grassy creek below) and a muddy section near the end. The second (420 m) was about the same, except it pointed downhill most of the way. And the third (100 m and marked to the left of a creek) was littered with boulders but had an incredible number of massive white pine growing near the put-in. What remained was

quite easy, three somewhat rocky but short portages (110 m, 190 m and 160 m), all marked to the left. The route was perfect, really, one of the best areas in the park in my opinion, but I had lots of time left in my trip and had no need for a shortcut, so I opted to head farther north to Agnes before turning back.

I ended day three by carrying over one more portage, a very rocky but short uphill (370 m) from Trant to Hurlburt Lake. Even though Trant Lake had a number of spots to pitch a tent, Hurlburt had a few more options. It also had better fishing. That evening I dined on a 2-pound smallmouth bass, smothered in butter and fresh lemon, then wrapped in tinfoil and baked in the hot coals of the campfire.

Day four was the longest and the toughest of the trip. I managed to reach the top of

Hurlburt Lake before 10:00 a.m. and made good time reaching Payne and William lakes. The map showed two portages linking an unnamed lake between Hurlburt and Payne. The first obstacle was just a lift-over across a couple of logs midway up a shallow creek, and the second was a quick 30-meter trail on the left. The portage from Payne to Williams wasn't even necessary; I was able to squeeze through the narrow channel connecting the two lakes. As a bonus, Payne Lake's Ahsin Bay held some incredible pictographs. The vibrant paintings—a thunderbird, cow moose and an odd-looking fish—were located on the west side of the bay, just before the narrow inlet to the north. Surrounded by hills of pine and hemlock, Williams Lake was what I was searching for on my trip.

The difficult portion of my journey really didn't begin until I left Williams Lake by way of the 60-meter portage tucked away in the southeast corner. It began to drizzle during my carry-over and then poured rain as I made my way over the 175-meter portage down to Hurlburt Creek. The trail hadn't been used for quite some time and thick brush closed in from all directions. But at least I found this portage. The next wasn't so easy. My map indicated that the trail was just to the left of where Hurlburt Creek flushes into the Keewatin Lake. It's not! During a trip a few years later, I discovered that the portage actually exits the creek well before this and climbs down 150 meters toward a small bay, north of where the creek comes in. On this trip, however, I never found it. Instead I spent a good hour dragging my gear and canoe straight through a large patch of spruce trees rooted along the left side of the waterway.

Keewatin Lake features a group of pictographs not far up from the creek, along the west shoreline. It consists of scattered individual paintings (an overweight moose, a thunderbird, a faded zigzag line) and a main cluster (canoe with two paddlers, two thunderbirds, and what seems to be a moose and cross). The zigzag line is probably the most interesting, since it's supposed to be a record of the artist's lifeline, one that changed direction many times.

Keewatin is Ojibwa for "northwest wind," a word that didn't match the character of the lake when I was on it. The wind was directly from the south, a big problem since I was planning on paddling over half the length of Agnes Lake before calling it a day. I tried to convince myself the wind wouldn't be that big an issue once I reached Agnes Lake. But after carrying in and out of an unnamed lake prior to Agnes, connected by an uphill 330-meter portage with a few ankle-twisting rocks and a 310-meter portage with a slightly sloped take-out, I quickly realized my anxiety was well justified. The wind was whipping up the water something fierce, and I found it difficult enough to push off from the put-in, let alone paddle down the lake. I started my way across Agnes at 2:30 p.m. and found myself lifting over the 40-meter trail of rock and mud leading to Silence Lake just after 8:00 p.m.

In hindsight I should have seriously considered taking a side route off the top end of Agnes and down Reid Lake and a series of unnamed lakes to Silence. But I knew nothing about the difficulty of the portages en route (eight in total, the shortest being 30 m and the longest being 320 m), and I just couldn't pass up the chance to explore Agnes Lake. The lake has always been a popular destination for canoeists because of its natural beauty, but more importantly, it was a gathering place

for Native people as well, and six known pictograph sites are found here, and one very unique petroglyph.

Due to the heavy winds blowing across Agnes, I had to keep to the western shoreline and could only check out two of the Native sites. Too bad; the southern end of the lake has two newly discovered sites, a Maymaygwayshi (mischievous spirit people living among the cracks in the cliff, who act as a go-between with the spirit world) and two figures in a canoe. The elongated bay to the east has a faded "X" on a tan rock and a moose or caribou, and the westernmost of two central islands holds the largest collection, whose images consist of a small bear, a cross, another canoe with two occupants and a number of hand smears and other indistinguishable red wash marks.

The sites I did check out were noteworthy. Both were located just north of the portage into Silence Lake. The first pictograph was of two snowshoe hares. These symbols are rare in the park but are extremely important in the spiritual culture of the Ojibwa. The hare was one of the few species that didn't abandon Spirit Woman, who gave birth to all animals during the creation of the earth. The hare was also the animal that was always plentiful when others were not, and thus it saved the people from starvation.

Only about 50 meters south of the pictograph site are the Native petroglyphs. They are images chiseled into the rock rather than painted on them, and they are the only known petroglyphs in the Quetico and Boundary Waters region. They depict four caribou, indicating a herd, which has led some experts to speculate that barrenland caribou once existed here before the solitary woodland caribou. If this is true, it would make the petroglyphs hundreds of years older than any known Native paintings.

My stay on Silence Lake was fitting. I camped just south of the portage, along the eastern shoreline, and had the lake to myself. It was one of the most peaceful sleeps I've ever had.

From Silence Lake my route headed southwest, back to familiar Shade Lake. The first portage was the longest of the day, measuring 350 meters. It was a bit confusing to follow; going right of a creek, over bare rock, through a strip of meadow grass, over the creek, then forking off in all directions toward the put-in at Sultry Lake. It was one of those trails where you weren't exactly lost, just confused as to your exact whereabouts most of the time.

Then a 50-meter trail located in the far left corner of Sultry Lake took me up a moderate slope and into Summer Lake. From here it was a choice of two portages to Noon Lake. Both were located along the left shoreline and both were approximately 50 meters in length. The only difference was that the first one was up a steeper hill than the second, but not so much steeper that I elected not to use it. A choice of two 50-meter trails also exited from the northwest corner of Noon Lake to Shade Lake. And again, there wasn't much difference between the two. So, to be different, I chose the second rather than the first this time.

From Shade Lake I backtracked to Basswood Lake's North Bay through West and South lakes, spending my last night on an island on the northeast corner. It was an early finish, especially when compared to the previous 12-hour day, and I only had to head back to Prairie Portage by way of Burke Lake and Bayley Bay on my final day out. Besides, the campsite I chose had a tent spot situated under an old pine and overlooking the tranquil blue waters familiar in a place that I wasn't familiar with in the beginning. And it was a route, I later discovered, that would become my favorite in all of Quetico.

LONGEST PORTAGE 1,190 meters

FEE An interior camping permit must be purchased for Quetico Provincial Park.

ALTERNATIVE ACCESS None

ALTERNATIVE ROUTE An extension can be placed on the route by way of Hurlburt, Payne, Williams, Keewatin, Agnes and Silence lakes.

OUTFITTERS
La Tourell's Moose Lake Outfitters
Box 239
Ely, MN, 55731
1-800-365-4531
www.latourells.com

Piragis Northwoods Company
105 N Central Avenue
Ely, MN, 55731
1-800-223-6565
www.piragis.com

FOR MORE INFORMATION
Quetico Provincial Park
807-597-2735
1-888-668-7275 or 519-826-5290
outside of North America
(reservations)
www.ontarioparks.com

Friends of Quetico
807-929-2571
www.friendsofquetico.com

Quetico Foundation
416-941-9388
www.queticofoundation.org

MAPS Chrismar and the Friends of Quetico have produced an excellent map for Quetico Provincial Park.

TOPOGRAPHIC MAPS
52 B/3, 52 B/4, 52 B/5 & 52 B/6

GPS COORDINATES
47.987054, -91.500431

Bentpine Creek Loop

🕐 5 to 6 days    18 portages   ●----● 64 km   **Knowledge of wilderness navigation is a must.**

I DOUBT THERE'S A single paddler who's not thankful that logging in Quetico was stopped back in 1971. At the same time, many of us feel some sense of admiration for the loggers themselves. Timbermen have always had a culture all their own, especially in the era prior to mechanization. There was a romance to the logger's life, an appreciation for the hardships of living and working in the bush. Loggers had their own customs, songs, tall tales, even their own dialect. Eventually the ring of the axe fell silent beneath the din of motorized saws and cutters, horse-drawn sleighs were replaced by diesel trucks, and lumber barons, often with shortsighted economics, political sponsorship and motivated by just plain gluttony, took all the romance away.

For canoeists who wish to visit this lost era and see remnants of old lumber camps where the songs were sung and the tall tales told, and also to witness where the resilient forests have regrown, there's no better place than the Bentpine Creek watershed in Quetico's northwest corner.

The route begins at Beaverhouse Lake, which is reached by driving west for 39 kilometers

from Atikokan on Highway 11, then south on the dirt road opposite Flanders Road (look for the park sign). It is 22 kilometers to the parking area. The road is gravel but well maintained until where it forks at the 15-kilometer mark. Take the left fork here. The remaining way is a rough, much smaller roadway. Make sure you contact the park prior to your trip and ask about conditions. To reach the lake, you have to portage straight south from the parking area for 600 meters.

All of the large lakes in Quetico can become problematic in high winds, but Beaverhouse has to be the worst. It's not the size of the lake that's an issue, really. It's where you have to travel on it. The route between the access point and the ranger station follows the eastern portion of the lake, heading from north to south. The wind generally blows from the west, and this can make for dangerous paddling conditions.

Andy Baxter and I chose this route for our trip in 2006. We had just finished a 14-day trip in the east end of the park and had no issues with wind the entire time we were out. The moment we began our way across Beaverhouse, however, the winds rose, and we found

Bentpine Creek Loop

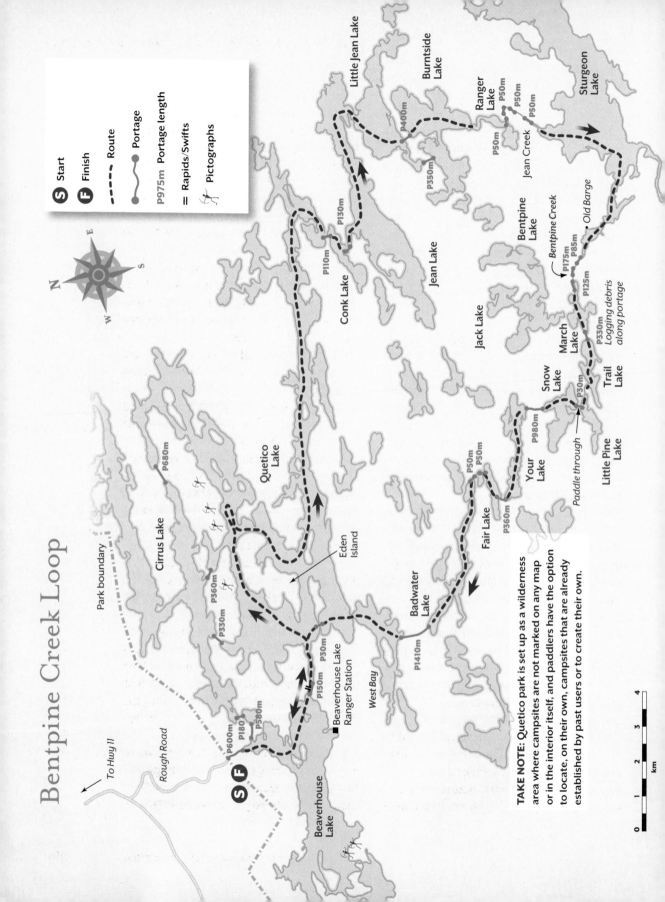

To Hwy 11

Rough Road

Park boundary

N E S W

Start Ⓢ
Finish Ⓕ
Route ------
Portage ●——●
P975m Portage length
Rapids/Swifts =
Pictographs 🜨

Beaverhouse Lake

Cirrus Lake

P680m

P360m

P330m

P600m
P180
P580m

Ⓢ Ⓕ

P150m
P30m
Beaverhouse Lake Ranger Station ■

West Bay

Quetico Lake

Eden Island

P1410m

Badwater Lake

Fair Lake

P360m

P50m
P50m

Your Lake

P980m

Snow Lake

P30m

Little Pine Lake

Paddle through

Trail Lake

P330m
Logging debris along portage

March Lake

P125m

P85m

P175m

Bentpine Creek

Old Barge ●

Jean Creek

P50m
P50m
P50m
P50m

Bentpine Lake

Jack Lake

Jean Lake

P110m

P130m

Conk Lake

P350m

P400m

Little Jean Lake

Burntside Lake

Ranger Lake

Sturgeon Lake

TAKE NOTE: Quetico park is set up as a wilderness area where campsites are not marked on any map or in the interior itself, and paddlers have the option to locate, on their own, campsites that are already established by past users or to create their own.

0 1 2 3 4 km

ourselves stuck on a large island halfway to the ranger station.

There's a real danger of becoming wind-bound early in your trip. You're usually so excited about finally being able to go paddling that there's a tendency to ignore logic and attempt to make it through the heavy chop. It happened to Andy and me. The entire time we waited for the wind to die down, we fought the urge to paddle. And we weren't alone. Two other parties joined us on the island. A third group passed us and headed blindly out across the center of the bay, and soon paid the consequences. Almost immediately they were broadsided by a large swell and flipped over. None of us could help them from where we were. We could only watch as they drifted with the wind, desperately holding onto their overturned canoe. Ten minutes into the ordeal, a rescue was attempted by the ranger from the nearby station. We watched as he tried to maneuver his motorboat toward them, but even he couldn't manage the waves.

Thankfully they reached the opposite shoreline about half an hour later. We watched through binoculars as they dragged their sodden bodies up on the beach site like a pair of drowned rats.

By 6:00 p.m. the wind had calmed enough for us to safely cross over to the ranger station and check in, then paddle over to camp where the Quetico River flushes into Beaverhouse Lake. Along the way, we took time to visit the canoeists who had flipped over earlier on. Other then their pride, the only injuries were a few bruises to their legs and arms, caused by holding onto the canoe and being tossed about in the waves. Their gear had got the worst of it. Everything except for a few necessities, a tent and sleeping bags, had been lost. They were

forced to call it quits. How ironic that a trip they had planned for months was over simply because they were in a rush to begin it.

In the morning we only had to paddle 10 minutes up the Quetico River from our camp-site to reach the first portage. The 150-meter trail is to the right of a moderate cascade and offers a good display of logging relics. There's a short swift prior to the take-out, which we decided to paddle up. It might have been a better idea to wade or line the canoe. Halfway up we noticed bits and pieces of camping gear resting on the bottom, an obvious sign that some canoes hadn't made it.

There are two possible take-outs after the swift. Both lead you up the steep riverbank and through a large field cluttered with the remains of a lumber camp. Taking the second allows you a closer look at an old logging chute rotting close to the shoreline.

A lot of wood went through here. In 1918 four million board feet of pine were cut out of Quetico and Beaverhouse Lakes, 26 million the following year—and the logging camp was just one of five established by the Shelvin-Clark company in the area.

After the put-in Andy and I continued up the Quetico River for a half hour or so, with the waterway becoming wider the closer it came to Quetico Lake. From here our route was directly to the east, keeping close to the south shore. The north shore, however, holds a major display of pictographs, and we couldn't pass up the chance to check them out. We took the long way around Quetico Lake, hoping the morning calm would continue long enough for us to visit the Native paintings.

What an incredible place! The north shore holds four amazing clusters of paintings. The first group is located directly north of Eden Island, above a large pile of boulders. The site consists mainly of a circular disk surrounded by handprints. The symbols themselves aren't as clear as those at other sites, but what they represent is really quite unique. The disk is thought to be a shield, and the handprints encircling it signify the coming of war. Alternatively, the disk is the door to the spirit world, with the handprints having been left behind as a taunting gesture by the mischievous Maymaygwayshi.

The next three pictograph sites are found farther to the east along the northern arm of Quetico Lake. The first is made up of a line of dots, representing the path taken by the artist on his journey of becoming a shaman; the second is a series of zigzag lines and what appears to be, to me anyway, the head of a cow moose. The last site, which I'd consider to be one of the most striking in all of Quetico Park, features a large group of images: a moose, a caribou, a large vertical line, two crosses, two Maymaygwayshi (one with an erect penis) and two canoes (a small one with two occupants and a larger one with six paddlers, one standing up with his arms reaching toward the sky).

We spent a good two hours checking out the pictographs and then paddled back south to Quetico's eastern inlet. From there, we still had another 12 kilometers to go to reach the end of the lake. With only a slight breeze blowing from the west, conditions were perfect to sail our canoe. By mid-afternoon we had reached the far end of Quetico Lake, where we had intended on camping. With extra time on our hands, however, we decided to continue south and take on the two portages, 110 m and 130 m, into Jean Lake before calling it a day.

The first carry was a short but relatively steep portage located in the corner of the southern bay. The take-out is to the extreme right of a 30-foot cascade gushing out of Conk Lake. And the second is an even easier trail located almost directly across Conk Lake. Both portages have logging artifacts to check out, and it was at the put-in on Jean Lake that the first timber cruiser, L.W. Ayer, who was sent out in 1903 to what is now Quetico, wrote in his journal: "The timber is at this point the best I have seen in Canada. It is 25 percent white pine, 46 percent Norway [red pine]." After that statement, the race was on. By 1904 the Rainy River Lumber Company had begun operations, and in less than six years it split into several competitors, the largest being Shelvin-Clark. By 1954 that company alone had processed 800 million board feet of lumber.

The decision to camp on Jean Lake made for a long day. Andy and I had paddled 39 kilometers in total.

Our second day out was a great success. Our third day was even better. The 400-meter portage over from the south end of Jean to Burntside Lake was an easy walk, except for a slightly muddy section near the end, and we got to check out the remains of the ranger's cabin close to the put-in. After Rouge Lake, the next four portages, all found to the left along Jean Creek, measured no more than 50 meters, and due to high water the last one wasn't even necessary. Sturgeon Lake was also surprisingly calm, and it took us only until noon to paddle near the entrance to the northwestern inlet, which leads up to Bentpine Creek.

Once again we altered our camping plans. The islands on the west end of Sturgeon were to have been our original stopover sites for day three. However, we noticed that over half the campsites were already taken, so we opted to continue up Bentpine. Crowds would definitely not be an issue here. And besides,

the trip really didn't get started for us until we reached Bentpine Creek. This was new territory for both of us, and we were looking forward to finding more logging-era relics. Bentpine Creek houses some of the best in the park.

Not far from the first portage was an old barge pushed up along the eastern shoreline, and to the left of the take-out were the ruins of a third logging chute. Both date back to the late 1930s.

The trail, found to the right of the creek, measures only 85 meters and leads up a slight incline. Due to its lack of use, however, it has a few drawbacks. The take-out was in a mud hole, and the whereabouts of the put-in was questionable at best (we ended up finding it to the right of a rock ledge). Giant patches of poison ivy also grew thick along its edges. And worst of all were the dozen or so ticks that grabbed onto our pant legs as we walked through.

The next portage was better. It measured 175 meters. And a third, almost directly after the second, measured 125 meters. Both had more logging artifacts to check out. But they were cursed with muddy take-outs—and more ticks! We had performed a tick check at the end of each previous portage and found none seriously attached to our clothes. Just as we were about to push off from the third carry, however, I felt a tickle on my left thigh. Lifting my pant leg I discovered four had embedded themselves in my skin. Andy then checked himself and found three.

We tried not to panic. If you yank them out, you're liable to pull them in half, leaving the head inside your skin and increasing the chance of infection. Staying relatively calm, Andy sprayed a good dose of bug repellent on the exposed tick to make it relax its grip (it actually breathes out of its back end while its head is lodged in your skin). Then, after allowing some time for the repellent to kick

in, he took hold of each of the parasites in turn with a pair of tweezers, and, without squeezing, gently pulled each one out. It was my turn. I reached over to grab the tweezers from Andy and suddenly felt another tickle, this time under my private parts. Complete hysteria set in! I pulled my trousers down, reached under my apparatus and yanked the tick away.

The pain wasn't immediate, but eventually there was uncontrollable burning and itching at the spot where the tick had plunged its sharp mouthpart deep inside me and secreted its cement-like saliva to glue itself in place. My first-aid manual said to have someone check the bitten area (ticks are known vectors of Lyme disease), but Andy would have nothing to do with it, so I resorted to using my compass mirror. I gingerly applied some ointment to the growing rash and used my life jacket as a seat cushion for the remainder of the trip.

Before calling it a day on Trail Lake, we first had to paddle across a widening in the creek and then portage 330 meters up and over a moderate slope. To the left side of the last portage, leading into Trail Lake, we found a run of steel rollers that had been used to haul logs overland. The system was built from Trail Lake to March Lake by J.A. Mathieu of Shelvin-Clarke Company in 1936 and was the longest ever used. It's impressive, to say the least, but technology such as this also marked the beginning of the end for the lumbermen. Close to 50 million board feet were cut and hauled out of here by Shelvin-Clarke.

The story of Shelvin-Clarke and the Quetico forest is so similar to Dr. Seuss's book *The Lorax*, it's frightening. As early as 1917 the company was known for its over-the-top logging practices. A deal with the Minister of Lands and Forests to pay half the market value for 13,340 acres of Quetico forest created one of the greatest scandals in Ontario provincial politics. By 1936 even the company's workers questioned their employer's motives and went on strike. Mathieu and other northern timber barons were quickly losing face.

Conservationists then had to move quickly to save what was left of the forest. In 1941 a new park superintendent was appointed, Frank MacDougall, the first ever to make logging second to tourism as a park priority. Three decades later, in 1970, the Quetico Park Advisory Committee held public meetings regarding the future of logging in the park and came up with this definition of how Quetico should be managed: "...it's preservation, in perpetuity, for the people of Ontario as an area of wilderness not adversely affected by human activities and containing a natural environment of aesthetic, historical and recreational significance." A year later, logging was banned from the park.

Day four of our trip was the shortest distance we paddled overall, and again we made camp that night at a spot other than the one in our original plan. We figured we'd push all the way to Quetico Lake, but we only made it to Badwater Lake. We hadn't even considered camping on this lake prior to the trip, first because of the name (the early loggers reported it to have bad-tasting water) and second because other canoeists told us that it had no campsites. In fact, we were told by the same canoeists that the portages between Trail and Badwater Lakes were unmanageable and that the lakes in between weren't even worth visiting. These accounts were completely inaccurate, of course.

First off, the portages from Trail to Badwater were much easier then we thought. The first, a 30-meter portage from Little Pine Lake to Snow Lake (found to the left of a small swift shortly after the navigable stream takes you out of Trail Lake), wasn't even necessary. We just paddled through. The 980-meter portage from the northeast corner of Snow Lake to Your Lake wasn't what we thought either. It was certainly a long haul, with two small hills and one medium-sized mud hole in between. Overall, though, it wasn't a bad carry, and there were some impressive old cedar trees to gawk at along the way. The third portage, linking the far northwest end of Your Lake to Fair Lake, was also a couple hundred meters shorter than what our map indicated. Mind you, its exact whereabouts was confusing at first. Andy and I attempted to paddle up the creek and were forced to turn back after spotting three massive beaver dams blocking the way. We then found a false trail on the left side of the creek that led to nowhere in particular. Finally, to the far left of the creek, we discovered an actual 150-meter portage linking us to a small pond that connects to the south end of Fair Lake. And the two remaining portages, taking us in and out of another pond before reaching Badwater Lake, measured less than 100 meters. The first, located at the far eastern end of Fair, went up and over a small knoll, and the second crossed a creek near the take-out and over a boggy area near the put-in.

The claims that Badwater Lake had no campsites were completely untrue. There are at least eight prime spots to pitch a tent. Andy and I took the first one we spotted, located on an island just past the portage, because we thought it would be the only campsite on the lake. By doing so, we had ended our day early. But that was okay; Badwater was an excellent spot to hang out. We caught walleye, pike and lake trout not far from the island. A bald eagle gave us a visit just before super. Three otters walked past our beached canoe, with one stopping to give it a sniff. Behind our tent, Andy was chased by a mother grouse protecting her nest (I'd never heard a grouse hiss at someone before). And a painted turtle surprised us by walking straight out of the water and over to the fire pit where we were sitting. I guess it's true—beauty is in the eye of the beholder. This was the best stopover we had during the entire trip.

Badwater Lake stretches out to almost 8 kilometers in length. It took us most of the morning to reach the portage at the far end, then most of the afternoon to carry over the 1,410 meters to Quetico Lake's west bay. The same group of canoeists who alleged that the previous portages were tough and that Badwater Lake had no campsites also reported that the portage out of Badwater was absolutely horrible. They were right this time. But that was only because the maintenance crew hadn't been in yet that year to clear out some fallen trees. The hills they told us about didn't exist, and the two swamps along the way had logs placed to make walking across the muddy spots more manageable. Still, we were pretty tired by the end of it, and to make matters worse a strong northwest wind was blowing across Quetico Lake when we arrived.

Andy and I were able to paddle across the west bay, but when we carried over the 30-meter portage linking the bay with the rest of Quetico Lake, the conditions were far too rough for us to continue on. The wind was so severe at this point (we later found out that the area had received tornado warnings) that a row of whitecaps had formed all the way across to the mouth of the Quetico River. This was to have been our route for the rest of the day, back to familiar Beaverhouse Lake (by way of the 150-m portage) to make camp on the same site we had stayed on the first night. One look at the brutal waves out on the lake, however, and we knew that reaching Beaverhouse was definitely not going to happen. So, once again we altered our plans and set up our tent directly on the put-in of the 30-meter portage.

It was an ideal spot to camp our last evening out really. There was a gorgeous sandy beach and a fire pit tucked away in the backwoods, well protected from the heavy gusts of wind. But that wasn't the main reason. Quetico Lake was much more fitting than Beaverhouse because of its name. Three reasons are given as to how as it got labeled in the first place, and all three have some significance to our journey. The first is that the word "Quetico" is a short term for the Quebec Timber Company; the second is that Quetico is an Ojibwa word for "bad," "dangerous," "a place where it's better to paddle along the shore because of high winds"; and the third is that it comes from an older Ojibwa word, one with mythological connotations, a label given to a place holding some type of "benevolent spirit."

Of the three definitions, the third is the least likely to be true. However, it was the one we chose to believe in. This area we had just paddled, as with the rest of Quetico Park, undeniably deserves such a strong and beautiful description.

LONGEST PORTAGE 1,410 meters

FEE An interior camping permit must be purchased for Quetico Provincial Park.

ALTERNATIVE ACCESS It's possible for outfitters from Crane Lake or Ely to fly you in to Beaverhouse Lake.

ALTERNATIVE ROUTE None

OUTFITTERS
Canoe Canada Outfitters
300 O'Brien Street
Atikokan, ON, P0T 1C0
807-597-6418
www.canoecanada.com

QuetiQuest Outfitters
Box 1060
Atikokan, ON, P0T 1C0
807-929-2266
www.quetiquest.com

FOR MORE INFORMATION
Quetico Provincial Park
807-597-2735
1-888-668-7275 or 519-826-5290
outside of North America
(reservations)
www.ontarioparks.com

Friends of Quetico
807-929-2571
www.friendsofquetico.com

Quetico Foundation
416-941-9388
www.queticofoundation.org

MAPS Chrismar and the Friends of Quetico have produced an excellent map for Quetico Provincial Park.

TOPOGRAPHIC MAPS
52 B/5, 52 B/12 & 52 C/12

GPS COORDINATES
48.574459, -92.060115

Sturgeon/Olifaunt Lake Loop

 5 to 6 days   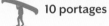 10 portages   ●- - - -● 102 km   **Possible wind and waves on some large lakes and knowledge of wilderness navigation is a must.**

I**T SEEMED LIKE** a great idea at the time: rather than drive the two full days to reach the park, our group—a film crew working on a project for the Friends of Quetico—decided it would be less of a hassle to fly from Toronto to Thunder Bay. But after hauling all our gear through the airport, our flight was canceled; after being airborne only 10 minutes, the next flight was forced to return to Toronto due to a mechanical failure (the front wheel was broken); then there was a three-hour delay before boarding the third flight. Even the rental car to shuttle us from the Thunder Bay airport to the desired access point in the park turned out to be a mix up, a convertible rather then the minivan we had ordered. The rental company thought we wouldn't mind; that is, until we showed them the pile of camping and filming gear we had to transport. Andy, Kip and I had never begun a canoe trip so badly in our lives.

Thankfully our bad luck ended, and we were even able to have an outfitter from Atikokan (Canoe Canada) pick us up and drive us directly to the put-in on Pickerel Lake's Stanton Bay, which meant we had a full hour of daylight left to soak in our much-appreciated new surroundings (and locate a campsite before dark).

After such a long travel day, none of us were too keen on an early start the next day, but we couldn't afford to become windbound, something easily done on Pickerel Lake, so by 7:00 a.m. we left our comfortable campsite on the south end of Lookout Island, Kip and Andy in one canoe and me paddling solo, and headed southwest to locate the first portage in Pine Portage Bay.

By mid-morning it was rain that slowed our progress rather than wind, and as luck would have it, all three of us had stored our rain gear at the bottom of our packs. We were completely soaked by the time we reached the far side of the lake, where we stopped for brunch on Wetasi Island. The name Wetasi (yes, "wet ass"-i) was given to the island when a group of park rangers found shelter there after being drenched in a storm.

We definitely didn't welcome the poor weather, but the gray skies made for perfect light conditions for our first film project—capturing footage of the old boiler and other rusted machine parts from a sunken tugboat left behind in the 1870s. The old junk

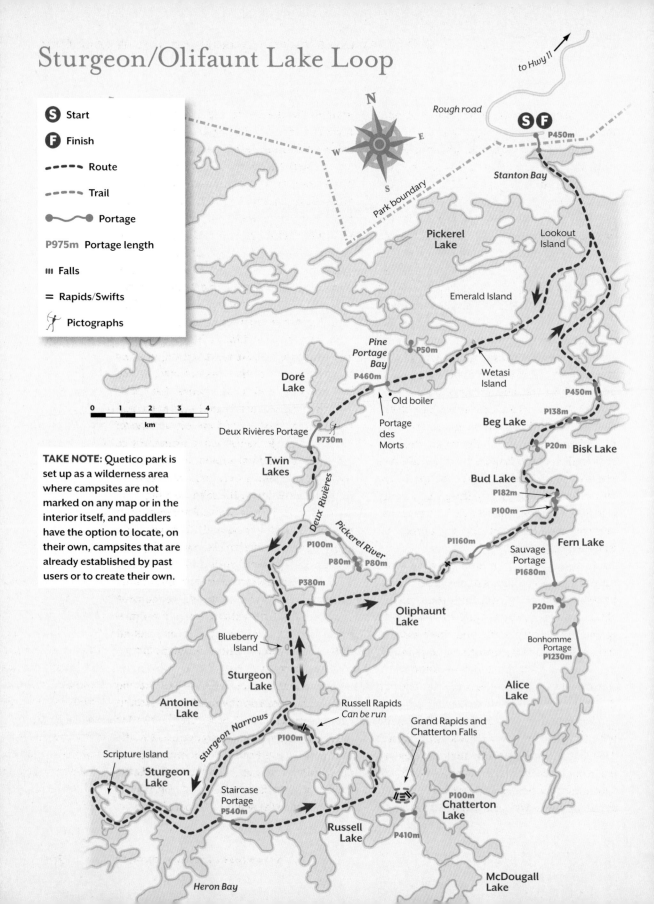

Sturgeon/Olifaunt Lake Loop

S Start
F Finish
- - - Route
- - - Trail
•~~~• Portage
P975m Portage length
⫶ Falls
= Rapids/Swifts
🏃 Pictographs

TAKE NOTE: Quetico park is set up as a wilderness area where campsites are not marked on any map or in the interior itself, and paddlers have the option to locate, on their own, campsites that are already established by past users or to create their own.

to Hwy 11

Rough road

S F P450m

Stanton Bay

Lookout Island

Pickerel Lake

Emerald Island

Pine Portage Bay P50m

Doré Lake

P460m

• Old boiler

Portage des Morts

Wetasi Island

Beg Lake

P450m

P138m

P20m Bisk Lake

Deux Rivières Portage P730m

Twin Lakes

Bud Lake

P182m

P100m

Fern Lake

Deux Rivières

Pickerel River

P100m

P80m P80m

P1160m

Sauvage Portage P1680m

P380m

Oliphaunt Lake

P20m

Bonhomme Portage P1230m

Blueberry Island

Sturgeon Lake

Alice Lake

Antoine Lake

Sturgeon Narrows

Russell Rapids *Can be run*

Grand Rapids and Chatterton Falls

Scripture Island

Sturgeon Lake

P100m

P100m

Chatterton Lake

Staircase Portage P540m

Russell Lake

P410m

Heron Bay

McDougall Lake

N W E S

0 1 2 3 4 km

Park boundary

is just offshore and to the left of the take-out for the 460-meter portage—labeled Portage des Morts after a voyageur was crushed to death by the weight of his own canoe and then buried nearby.

The next portage, Deux Rivières, is even more noteworthy in Canadian history. It's the original Dawson Trail—the first all-Canadian route built for the Red River settlers.

Our group carried across Deux Rivières Portage, measuring 730 meters and located at the southwest end of Doré Lake, to the right of a small creek.

A shallow stream located at the southeast corner of the lake takes you out of Twin Lakes. It's been called Deux Rivières because it parallels the old extension of the Deux Rivières Portage, but its original name is more fitting: Grass River. The waterway is clogged with swamp grass, broken only by a couple of beaver dams that require a quick lift-over. The stream widens the closer you get to the entrance to the top end of Sturgeon Lake but remains blocked by patches of sedge, reeds and wild rice almost all the way to the first island on the lake.

To the east the Pickerel River empties out into Sturgeon, and it was our original plan to loop back to Pickerel Lake, but the best part about canoe tripping in Quetico is that once you've entered the park, you don't have to stick to your predetermined route plan. We had covered more ground than anticipated, so we decided to continue south for an extra day or two.

Our second night's camp was set up to the left of where the lake narrows, on a perfect rock outcrop overlooking the large island north of Blueberry Island. It was an incredible spot, one of the best campsites I've ever stayed at in the park. We picked blueberries right

around the fire circle and made blueberry turnovers for dessert. Andy even caught a few walleye for dinner by just casting a lure to the left of where Kip and I went in for a swim. Of course, we later found out that the site was one of the worst for nuisance bear encounters. Fortunately we never had a visit—and thankfully the news that it was a problem site was told to us after we had slept there.

The next day we lingered around camp until brunch, filming some scenes for the film. Kip had wanted to capture footage of me drudging through a nasty portage.

We finished our filming just before noon and headed across Sturgeon but stopped just short of Sturgeon Narrows, drained by the extreme heat and a brisk wind that made forward progress nearly impossible. We had an extended rest, lying beneath a stand of stout pine and jumping in for a swim every 20 minutes. And then at 10:00 p.m. we headed out again, paddling over half the length of Sturgeon Lake during the calm, cool night air.

It was like a dreamscape. A three-quarter moon lighted the way, and we hugged the shoreline, listening to the water lapping against the rocks and letting it guide us. Kip filmed this experience, of course, but I didn't want him to. I wanted to stay in the moment, to soak in and mentally preserve these precious few hours of my life. It may sound selfish, but I didn't want it recorded on tape for others to view.

We backtracked on day four after having a half-day snooze on the third-largest island west of Sturgeon Lake's Scripture Island. Our camp that night was in Heron Bay, just southwest of Sturgeon Narrows. The campsite was Andy's idea. He was desperate to revisit a cluster of egg-shaped rocks that pop up out of the water to the south of the bay. Of course,

Kip and I teased him all day about having to paddle out of our way just so he could view a bunch of white rocks that he once saw sticking out of the water. But when we witnessed the geological phenomena for ourselves, the mocking stopped immediately. This is one really cool-looking place in Quetico, rock deposits left over from the time when glaciers scoured the continental landmass and left massive erratic formations like the one in Heron Bay along its path.

We were slow to start up again the next morning. The high temperatures were now gone. In fact it became quite cold (my thermometer now read 17 degrees Celsius. The wind had also changed, but to our advantage. We were able to lash the two canoes together,

sail all the way across Russell Lake and reach the base of Chatterton Falls by noon.

We set up camp at the bottom of the falls and spent the remainder of the day filming along a rough trail that makes its way along the south shore. The entire cascade is gorgeous, and the walk along this path is well worth the effort. I definitely wouldn't use this trail as a portage, however, or even the old portage found on the other side of the falls. The proper portage to Chatterton is found about a kilometer south of the falls, beginning on a sandy beach. There's a steep grade near the start and quite a few boulders blocking the 410-meter path, but it's far easier, and safer, than using the hiking trail around Chatterton Falls.

At the base of Chatterton you'll see the left-over debris from when 8,000 red and white pine logs were flushed downriver all at once, causing a massive jam. The incident happened in 1936, around the same time lumber baron J.A. Mathieu made a formal complaint about the lack of cutting available in the park. His grievances were quickly ignored after his company did nothing to remove the logjam at the falls. It was one of the biggest wastes of timber in northern Ontario's history. It also led to further protection of Quetico's forests. In 1941 Frank MacDougall became superintendent of Quetico and made major changes to protect timber in the park.

Our sixth day was the best yet. We headed out from our camp below Chatterton Falls just as the sun began burning off the morning mist. There wasn't even a slight breeze to hold us back while crossing Russell and Sturgeon lakes, and we were able to flush easily down Russell Rapids, swift water that separates the two lakes, rather than use the 100-meter portage along the west bank (take note that the portage is plagued by poison ivy).

Before noon we found ourselves slogging across a flat but very muddy 380-meter portage to Olifaunt Lake. We raced across the bowl-shaped Olifaunt Lake, then paddled up the Pickerel River to have a late lunch at a short lift-over to the left of a small drop.

From there the day got a little more difficult. The remaining portage of the day, a 1,160-meter trail along the left bank of the Pickerel River, is a long, rugged carry. A few side trails lead off to sections of the river between rapids but only tease you into thinking you're getting close to the end. None of them are worth the hassle of loading and unloading gear. Just keep going. The view three-quarters of the way along is wonderful, though, and makes the entire ordeal worthwhile.

As we entered Fern Lake, we met a group of volunteers who were on their way back from doing maintenance on the portage that leads to a chain of lakes to the south. Seconds into the conversation Kip asked them for an interview, too. It was getting late, so we decided to do it in the morning, back on the portage. The volunteers chose the center island to camp on, and we picked a rock point to the southwest. I think they got the better site. Ours had seen little use, and with a wasp nest directly beside the fire ring, we were forced to cook our dinner on a camp stove and pitch our tents well back in the bush.

I guess our tents were a little too far back in the bush. The morning sun, which usually wakes us up bright and early, didn't hit the sides of our tents until after 8:00 a.m., and all three of us were still snug in our bags when a couple of the volunteers paddled over to offer us freshly brewed coffee and toasted cinnamon bannock.

By 9:30 a.m. Kip had the camera set up at the section of trail where the volunteers were cutting and placing logs across a giant swamp. It was an excellent backdrop for deliberating the reasons for being here, working for free. Russ James, a councilor who had been with Camp Kooch-i-ching since he was 10, started it off: "It was just time to pay back all the others who worked on the portages before me. Back at camp we have a saying above our mantel: 'Chop your own wood and it will warm you twice.'"

All their statements reflected the idea of how precious and unique Quetico is, but the statement made by councilor Matt Brown from Kentucky just blew me away: "Preserving a place like this really allows us all that experience, that contact with nature that's slipping away from our modern society. These kids could be at home playing Nintendo or doing whatever, and they all say after the trip, 'You know, that's what I wanted to be doing—and my friends, they're getting cheated by not having it.' I hope my own kids enjoy Quetico, and I hope they remember what Henry David Thoreau said: 'I went to the woods because I wished to live deliberately, to front only the essential facts of life, and to see if I could not learn what it had to teach, and not, when I came to die, discover that I had not lived.'"

We helped the volunteers with the trail for a couple more hours before heading off. It felt good to lend a hand, but we also had to reach Pickerel Lake by the end of the day since our plane was scheduled to leave Thunder Bay at 2:00 p.m. the following day.

It was a quick paddle across to the north shore, where the Pickerel River emptied into Fern Lake, and we simply waded up the rapids rather than take the grown-over 100-meter portage found to the right. Then, as the river twists right toward a stunted cascade, we pulled up to the 182-meter portage on the left. It was a gorgeous carry alongside tumbling waterfalls decorated with giant pine and old gnarly white cedar trees.

From there we paddled west and then north on Bud Lake, which is simply a widening of the Pickerel River. The banks narrowed at times, bringing us close to the remnants of an old burn and forcing us to push against a strong current at times. Only once did we actually have to get out of the canoes and carry, that was over a slab of rock, for 20 meters, just to the far right of where a small chute links Bud Lake with Beg Lake.

The route went east now, heading into Bisk Lake by way of a 138-meter portage to the right of another scenic falls. It's an easy carry, with only a slight rise along the first quarter of the trail.

The last portage of the day was only a short paddle up the northern inlet of Bisk Lake. Here a 450-meter trail runs along the left side of where the Pickerel River flushes out of Pickerel Lake. We were able to shorten the carry a bit by paddling a few extra strokes upstream.

The portage ends at a giant concrete dam built in 1872 by Simon Dawson and the Dominion Government to raise the water levels between the French and Pickerel lakes to allow passage of steamboats carrying soldiers and settlers out to the Red River Settlements. The dam was rebuilt in 1927 by timber barons Shevlin-Clarke to raise the water again and run logs down the Quetico River. It was washed out during a spring flood in 1941, and the concrete structure wasn't built until 1956. Then, after years of debate over the use of dams in the park, it was decided in the late 1970s to gradually remove the stop logs to allow the French and Pickerel lakes to return to their natural levels.

It was late in the afternoon and we considered camping next to the dam. There were places to put the tents, but the site itself wasn't attractive. Besides, it was the last night of our trip and we wanted to end it somewhere more charming than alongside a big slab of cement. So we continued on, pushing hard against a steady wind out of the northwest. And it wasn't long before we started to regret our decision—especially me. I was already exhausted from paddling solo all day and now I had to battle a heavy chop.

To escape the more open part of Pickerel Lake we headed directly across from the dam, then took a weedy channel to the northeast. Our map showed the small inlet as unnavigable—which is probably true most of the time—but we managed to push our way through to the next bay.

This was the first time on the trip that we had trouble finding an unoccupied site. It was also the worst time for this to happen to us. I would have even settled for any flat piece of land to curl up on for the night, but there was nowhere to stop.

We continued on for another hour or so before we were forced to settle for a miniature island near where we had stopped our first night out. There was a small site, but a recent windstorm had blown several trees down, leaving limited space. We managed. Kip placed his tent between two fallen jack pine, and we squeezed ours uncomfortably close to the lakeshore.

Being surrounded by downed timber, we decided against having a campfire that night. Instead we lit a couple of candles, poured a double shot of rum into our camp mugs, then used up the remainder of the camera battery to view all the footage Kip had filmed throughout the trip.

LONGEST PORTAGE 1,160 meters

FEE An interior camping permit must be purchased for Quetico Provincial Park.

ALTERNATIVE ACCESS Dawson Trail Ranger Station, located at the main campground in the northeast corner of the park, just south off Highway 11. It's a 210-kilometer drive west of Thunder Bay and 39 kilometers east of Atikokan.

ALTERNATIVE ROUTE An extension can be placed on the route by using Chatterton, Alice and Fern lakes.

OUTFITTERS
Canoe Canada Outfitters
300 O'Brien Street
Atikokan, ON, P0T 1C0
807-597-6418
www.canoecanada.com

QuetiQuest Outfitters
Box 1060
Atikokan, ON, P0T 1C0
807-929-2266
www.quetiquest.com

FOR MORE INFORMATION
Quetico Provincial Park
807-597-2735
1-888-668-7275 or 519-826-5290
outside of North America
(reservations)
www.ontarioparks.com

Friends of Quetico
807-929-2571
www.friendsofquetico.com

Quetico Foundation
416-941-9388
www.queticofoundation.org

MAPS Chrismar and the Friends of Quetico have produced an excellent map for Quetico Provincial Park.

TOPOGRAPHIC MAPS
52 B/5, 52 B/6, 52 B/11 & 52 B/12

GPS COORDINATES
48.657438, -91.338510

Woodland Caribou Provincial Park

 10 days    53 portages    138 km

This is a medium-to-hard trip due to the remoteness of the area. Good canoe-tripping skills are essential.

HURRY UP AND wait—that's how it always is when you're about to take a bush plane on a northwestern Ontario canoe trip. My canoe companions, Andy Baxter and Bill and Anne Ostrom, and I were waiting for the weather to lift before we could be flown into Woodland Caribou Provincial Park, and it seemed like it wasn't going to happen anytime soon. The forecast had called for torrential rain and hail and even warned of a tornado, so the pilot asked us to relax but stay close to the hangar just in case things changed for the better. Two days later we finally lifted off from Red Lake. The flight was a go and our trip of a lifetime was about to begin.

Minutes into the flight I started searching the thick boreal forest below, hoping to spot the elusive animal that gives the park its name. I knew full well I had little chance of spotting a woodland caribou amongst the endless patchwork of bog and black spruce, but looking down on the landscape was a little easier to stomach than glancing ahead at the dark, menacing clouds the pilot still had to fly through to get us to our starting point.

What I saw below quickly bewitched me.

I expected it to resemble a shag carpet that decorated some bungalow from the '70s. Instead it was an ecological masterpiece: a rich tapestry of old-growth conifer forest, interspersed with birch and poplar, and elongated bands of exposed bedrock jutting out between labyrinths of lakes, creeks and rivers. I couldn't wait for the plane to land so we could start our canoe journey—whether that meant spotting a caribou or not.

Our 10 days in Woodland Caribou—an expansive 450,000-hectare wilderness area—would have us traveling across the provincial park, from Artery Lake in the northwest to Leano Lake in the southeast. Along the way we paddled past the best Native pictographs I've ever seen, portaged through dream-like black spruce forests, slept under starlit skies and cooked up fish fillets for almost every meal.

The landscape here is prairie-boreal—a much hotter and drier environment than most of the boreal forests that stretch across the top of Ontario. It's not at all like the neighboring Wabakimi or Quetico provincial parks. Even the fish populations are different. Woodland Caribou has the typical walleye and pike lakes, but it also has plenty of lake trout waters to choose from. Each day of paddling brings you such a mixture of fishing possibilities that it's truly an angler's paradise.

We reached Woodland Caribou Provincial Park by driving a solid five hours from Thunder Bay north to the town of Red Lake. From there you have some options on how to enter the park's interior. You can drive in: a series of bush roads link up with a handful of access points. Flying in by bush plane is also an option, especially for the more northern sections of the park. Our group chose to have Harlan Schwartz of Red Lake Outfitters organize a flight with Viking Outpost Airways to Lower Artery Lake as well as a shuttle to pick us up at Leano Lake. Taking a bush plane can be an expensive way to access the park, but it's also an experience all paddlers should have at least once in their lives. There's nothing more uplifting (and terrifying) than watching the plane you just disembarked fly off and leave you alone to the northern elements.

After one last wave to the bush pilot as he banked over our drop-off point, we started paddling up the Bloodvein River system, a Canadian Heritage River that flows though Woodland Caribou and the neighboring Atikaki Provincial Park in Manitoba.

We soon had our first portage—an easy 100-meter carry found to the left of a small cascade, connecting Lower Artery Lake to Artery Lake. We shared the trail with a group of anglers who had booked a nearby outfitters cabin for the week. The park allows a handful of outpost camps in the interior, but they're kept to the larger lakes and don't really take away from the park's feeling of isolation. These were the only anglers we spotted on our entire trip. The park sees an average of 700 paddlers per season, and we didn't spot another soul until our last day.

Artery Lake's pictograph sites should not be missed. I've seen countless Native paintings in my travels but none compare to the ones on Artery. The biggest cluster of red ochre images can be found along the southern shoreline where the lake channels into the Bloodvein River. Dozens of images can be seen here but the most noteworthy are the rock people with stone canoes (called *memegwaysiwuk*), a shaman with lightning bolts overhead, a mystic water lynx, a bison and a caribou. These are symbols used by different First Nations from hundreds of kilometers away—a sure sign that this was a major travel corridor for centuries.

As you continue up the Bloodvein River another small chute has to be portaged around (175 m to the left), taking you into Mary's Lake. Farther up the Bloodvein is Barclay Lake. This section of the park is more like lowlands, with black spruce and swamp dominating the area. It's not until you paddle south on Barclay, where we made our first camp, that the landscape becomes characterized by rock

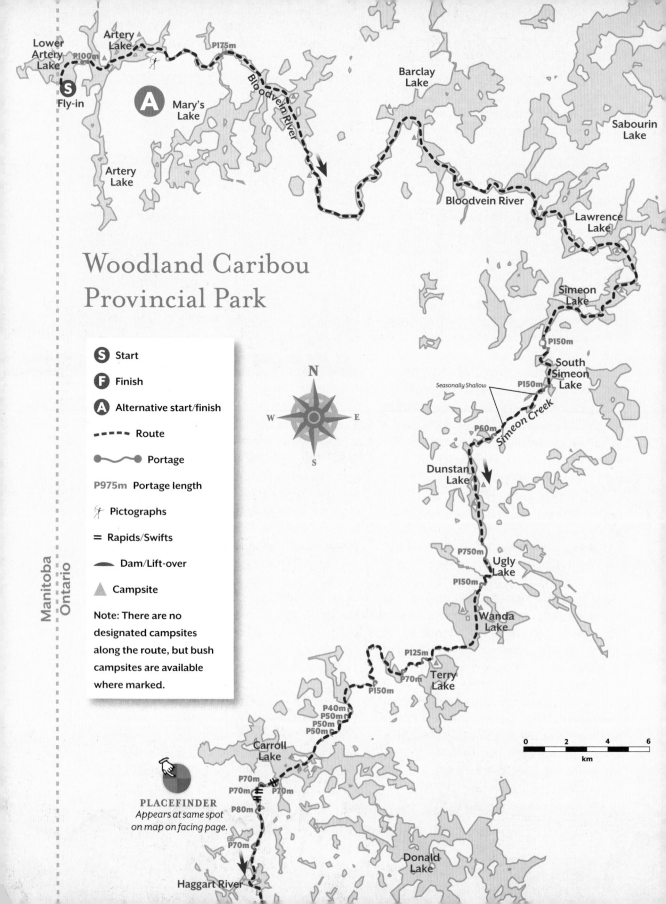

Lower Artery Lake
P100m
Artery Lake
S
Fly-in
A
Mary's Lake
Artery Lake
P175m
Bloodvein River
Barclay Lake
Sabourin Lake
Bloodvein River
Lawrence Lake
Simeon Lake
P150m
South Simeon Lake
Seasonally Shallow
P150m
P60m
Simeon Creek
Dunstan Lake
P750m
Ugly Lake
P150m
Wanda Lake
P125m
P70m
Terry Lake
P150m
P40m
P50m
P50m
P50m
Carroll Lake
P70m
P70m   P70m
P80m
P70m
Donald Lake
Haggart River

Woodland Caribou Provincial Park

S Start

F Finish

A Alternative start/finish

- - - Route

●∿● Portage

P975m Portage length

⚐ Pictographs

= Rapids/Swifts

⌒ Dam/Lift-over

▲ Campsite

Note: There are no designated campsites along the route, but bush campsites are available where marked.

N
W   E
S

Manitoba
Ontario

0   2   4   6
km

☞ PLACEFINDER
Appears at same spot on map on facing page.

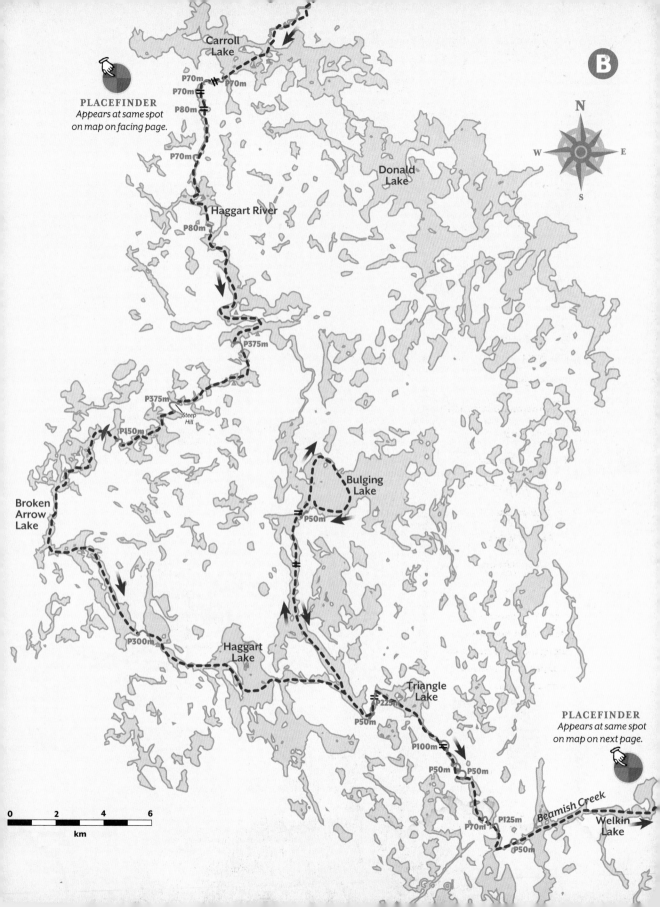

Carroll
Lake

P70m P70m
P70m
P80m

PLACEFINDER
*Appears at same spot
on map on facing page.*

P70m

Haggart River

P80m

P375m

P375m

*Steep
Hill*

P150m

Broken
Arrow
Lake

Bulging
Lake

P50m

P300m

Haggart
Lake

Triangle
Lake

P225m

P50m

P100m

PLACEFINDER
*Appears at same spot
on map on next page.*

P50m   P50m

Beamish Creek

Welkin
Lake

P70m   P125m

P50m

Donald
Lake

N
W   E
S

B

0   2   4   6

km

Woodland Caribou Provincial Park (continued)

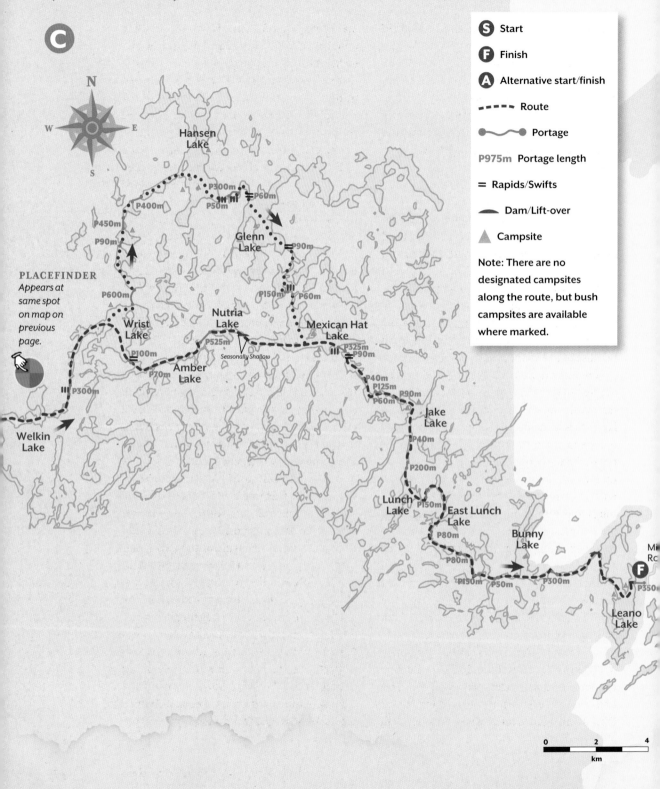

C

N
W E
S

Legend

S Start

F Finish

A Alternative start/finish

- - - - Route

●~~~~● Portage

P975m Portage length

= Rapids/Swifts

⬭ Dam/Lift-over

▲ Campsite

Note: There are no designated campsites along the route, but bush campsites are available where marked.

PLACEFINDER
Appears at same spot on map on previous page.

Hansen Lake

P300m
P50m
P60m

P400m

P450m

P90m

Glenn Lake
P90m

P600m

P150m
P60m

Nutria Lake

Mexican Hat Lake

Wrist Lake
P100m

P525m
Seasonally Shallow

P325m
P90m

P70m

Amber Lake

P40m
P125m
P60m
P90m

P300m

Welkin Lake

Jake Lake

P40m

P200m

Lunch Lake
P150m

East Lunch Lake

P80m

Bunny Lake

P80m

P150m
P50m
P300m

F

P350m

Leano Lake

0   2   4
km

mounds, patches of jack pine and the scars of old forest fires.

Day two turned into a bit of a challenge. It only rained on us once in the 10 days we were out, but the park received 15 consecutive days of rain before we arrived. The water levels were maximized. Navigating across the park meant we would be going downstream and upstream depending on what creek or river we chose to paddle on. We headed east to Lawrence Lake and then south to Simeon Lake. We took a 150-meter portage and ran a medium swift into South Simeon Lake. Another 150-meter portage, well hidden and marked only with an axe blade lodged in a stunted jack pine, led us into Simeon Creek, which, due to the unusually high water levels, was swollen and an easy paddle. Most of the time this stretch can be difficult to navigate because of low water levels.

A moose and her calf feeding in the reeds marked the entrance to the last portage of the day—a 60-meter carry leading to Dunstan Lake. This is the lake we planned on camping on; we just had to wait for the moose to get out of the way first. An hour later we were set up on a island in the central part of the lake, enjoying whiskey out of stainless steel camp mugs and dining on walleye we caught just after our last portage.

The morning of day three was spent taking a 750-meter portage into Ugly Lake—which is more of a weedy pond—and then another portage (150 m) into Wanda Lake. We were glad to be traveling with the current from Wanda Lake to Carroll Lake. It's still possible to paddle against the current but the abnormally high water levels would have made it a challenge. The fast flow sped us downstream and we were even able to float directly over then-submerged islands of weeds rather than

maneuver around them. However, the high water did float out some of the portages and make the put-ins dangerously close to the cascades we were trying to avoid. Between Wanda Lake and Carroll Lake the creek normally has seven short portages (125 m, 70 m, 150 m, 40 m, 50 m, 50 m and 50 m).

On night three we camped on Carroll Lake, a massive body of water with countless islands. We ate more walleye fillets for dinner, washed down with wild spruce tea.

High water remained a problem the next day while we continued upstream from Carroll Lake to the Haggart River. Seven short portages (all measuring between 70 and 80 m) took us more than half the day to complete. We were forced to extend each trail at the beginning and the end to avoid fast water, and twice we had to cut our own trails on the opposite side of the river, to the right of the falls, rather than use the trails on the left. We just couldn't reach the designated take-outs. We were fine with the challenge but it reminded us that canoe tripping in Woodland Caribou is not fit for novice paddlers.

Exhausted, we pitched our tents on a burned-over point just before another short 80-meter portage that leads into the widened section of the Haggart River. Burned-over areas are common across Woodland Caribou. They make up a huge part of the park's delicate ecology. Without the burns there would be no caribou since fires force regeneration of the old-growth jack pine that dominate the landscape here, and the regenerated trees provide food for the caribou. Without forest fires the caribou would likely die of starvation.

By the end of the fifth day we had reached the top end of Broken Arrow Lake by following a series of channels and small, unnamed ponds. We portaged three times (375 m, 375 m and 150 m) and completed a lift-over not far from Broken Arrow. The second portage was a struggle. The initial section of the trail just after the take-out is quite steep, but the trail gives you a good view of the surrounding landscape. That night we made camp just after the last portage on a knob of granite carpeted with 100-year-old jack pine.

On day six we paddled through my favorite series of lakes in Woodland Caribou: Haggart and Bulging lakes. The water is clearer, the forest is lusher, the shoreline is steeper. It's also trout water rather than the typical walleye and pike waters throughout the park. Lunch consisted of battered lake trout fillets fried in oil. Yum!

A 300-meter portage leads out of the southern end of Broken Arrow into Haggart Lake, and a quick 50-meter carry to the left of a small cascade leads from the top end of Haggart Lake into Bulging Lake. It was an easy day, and we ended it on an incredible sandy beach on Bulging Lake. Entertainment for the evening was a cool swim and watching a bald eagle feed its young in a nest adjacent to our site.

Day seven found us a bit behind schedule, so we altered our route to reach our shuttle from Leano Lake on time. That's the beauty of canoe tripping in Woodland Caribou—there are just so many options. The lakes are so close to one another, a mere bushwhack can create any number of short cuts.

We backtracked to Haggart Lake in the morning and went down the eastern inlet to Triangle Lake, portaging a short 50 meters and then another 225 meters to the right of some rapids. From there we made an upstream paddle on Beamish Creek to Welkin Lake. Six portages block the way (100 m, 50 m, 50 m, 70 m, 125 m and 50 m) but all are quick and very scenic.

The island campsite we set up on Welkin Lake had a cluster of green trees untouched by a recent forest fire. Surrounding us were the charred, skeletal remains of jack pine, silhouetted against the setting sun. It was the summer solstice—the longest day of the year—and the group stayed up later than usual. We sat by the evening fire, sipping our various spirits from our camp mugs, gazing into the flames. We only had a few more days left on our trip and none of us wanted it to end.

Mexican Hat Lake was our destination for day eight. During a calm morning, with the lake shrouded in mist, we continued up Beamish Creek, which looks more like an eastern extension of Welkin Lake. The route eventually narrows and bends to the north to Wrist Lake. You'll find a 300-meter portage to the right of a falls about quarter of the way.

There are a couple ways to get to Mexican Hat Lake from Wrist Lake. You can continue north and paddle a series of large lakes (Hansen and Glenn lakes). The portages are long, however. Hansen has two pictograph sites, one at the north end near the outlet and one to the southwest after the portage coming in from Wrist Lake. Or you can continue east through two small lakes (Amber and Nutria lakes). It's a much shorter route and only has three portages (100 m, 70 m and 525 m) and one or two lift-overs. The problem with this route is that if the water levels are low it could be a bit of a grind to get through. The levels were still up for us, however, and we made it with no issues.

We arrived at Mexican Hat Lake early and took some time out to fish. It was amazing! We caught walleye after walleye and even a few pike to change it up now and then. Prior to our trip, the outfitter told us that where the falls enter Mexican Hat's southeast corner is a great spot to try our luck. However, we caught so many fish on the way there, we ended up skipping the falls to make camp and prepare our dinner.

We continued more upstream paddling the next day. We portaged 325 meters to the right of the falls flushing into Mexican Hat. The rest of the day was spent jumping in and out of our canoes to take on a series of short portages. After five portages (90 m, 40 m, 125 m, 60 m and 90 m) we landed in Jake Lake, and another two (40 m and 200 m) got us to Lunch Lake.

It was another early day. We had one more night and we didn't want to camp too close to the take-out. A small island on Lunch Lake seemed the perfect spot to take in what remained of our route through Woodland Caribou.

This place is truly bewitching. It represents a pure piece of wilderness where one can paddle for days and have a better chance of spotting an elusive woodland caribou than another canoeist. I've paddled in many places but I've never taken such a keen interest in a region than I have in Woodland Caribou. Maybe because it was new to me, or it wasn't at all what I anticipated, or I had only gotten a taste of this wild place—whatever the reason, I'm going back for sure.

A strong headwind plagued us on our final day of paddling, but the route was short, giving us lots of time to meet our outfitter and have him drive us back to our vehicles in Red Lake. A 150-meter portage took us into East Lunch Lake. Then we headed southeast, portaging four times (80 m, 80 m, 150 m and 50 m) before Bunny Lake. A 300-meter portage and a quick lift-over led us to the final lake—Leano—and we pushed against the wind all the way to the east side where the access point is. A 350-meter portage got us to the parking area.

We could have driven our vehicles down to the launch ourselves rather than hire Red Lake Outfitters to pick us up. However, Iriam Road (which is a gravel road) and the turn off to Leano Lake's access point (Mile 51 Road) can be a rough go. It was far worth the money to have the outfitters come and get us, and they were waiting to greet us with six cold beers stored in a cooler. Now that's service.

LONGEST PORTAGE 750 meters

FEE A camping permit for the interior must be purchased from the park either by phoning Woodland Caribou Provincial Park or at the Ontario Parks office in Red Lake.

ALTERNATIVE ACCESS You can skip the fly-in portion and access the park from Leano Lake.

ALTERNATIVE ROUTE By putting in at Leano Lake access you can create countless routes. Both Haggart and Bulging lakes are very scenic.

OUTFITTERS
Red Lake Outfitters
P.O. Box 1484
Red Lake, ON, P0V 2M0
1-888-352-4870 or 807-728-0803
www.redlakeoutfitters.com

Goldseekers Outfitting
75 Forestry Road, Box 1152
Red Lake, ON, P0V 2M0
807-727-2353
www.goldseekers.net

FOR MORE INFORMATION
Woodland Caribou Provincial Park
227 Howey Street
Red Lake, ON, P0V 2M0
807-727-1329

MAPS Chrismar has produced an excellent canoe route map for all of Woodland Caribou Provincial Park.

TOPOGRAPHIC MAPS
63 M/6, 63 M/7, 63 M/2, 63 M/3, 63 M/14 & 63 M/15

GPS COORDINATES
51.339919, -95.118284

Bibliography

Beymer, Robert. *A Paddler's Guide to Quetico Provincial Park*. Minnesota: W.A. Fisher Company, 1985.

Campbell, William A. *Northeastern Georgian Bay and its People*. Sudbury, Ontario: Central Printers, 2000.

Friends of the Mattawa River Heritage Park. Mattawa River Heritage Map, 1997.

Friends of White Otter Castle. *Souvenir Booklet of the White Otter Castle*, 1992, 1994, 1996.

Harting, Toni. *French River: Canoeing the River of the Stick-Wavers*. Erin: Boston Mills Press, 1996.

Harting, Toni. "Steel River." *Nastawgan: The Quarterly Journal of the Wilderness Canoe Association*. Toronto: Wilderness Canoe Association, autumn 1992.

Kates, Joanne. *Exploring Algonquin Park*. Vancouver/Toronto: Douglas & McIntyre, 1983.

Ministry of Natural Resources, Chapleau District. *Missinaibi Provincial Park* (pamphlet), 1990.

Ministry of Natural Resources, Ignace District. *Turtle River Provincial Park Background Information*, 1990.

Ministry of Natural Resources, Minden District. *Poker Lake System Canoe Route* (pamphlet).

Ministry of Natural Resources, Parks and Recreational Areas Branch, in cooperation with McClelland & Stewart. *Canoe Routes of Ontario*. Toronto: 1981.

Ministry of Natural Resources. *Charleston Lake Provincial Park Management Plan*, 1991.

Ministry of Natural Resources, Recreation Resource Inventory. *Kopka River Provincial Park: Waterway Class*, 2003.

Reid, Ron, and Janet Grand. *Canoeing Ontario's Rivers*. Vancouver/Toronto: Douglas & McIntyre.

Reid, Ron. "The Trappers of Wabakimi Lake." *Seasons*. Toronto: Federation of Ontario Naturalists, summer 1981.

The Upper Thames Conservation Authority. *The Upper Thames Canoe Route: St Marys to Delaware* (pamphlet).

Wilson, Hap. *Missinaibi: Journey to the Northern Sky — From Lake Superior to James Bay by Canoe*. Erin: Boston Mills Press, 2004.

Wilson, Hap. *Rivers of the Upper Ottawa Valley: Myth, Magic and Adventure*. Erin: Boston Mills Press, 2004.

Wilson, Hap. *Temagami Canoe Routes*. Northern Concepts, 1999.

WEB RESOURCES

www.algonquinadventures.com
www.myccr.com
www.ottertooth.com
www.wabakimi.com
www.yip.org/~erhard/mozhabongL-route.htm

Index